The Cowboys' Turtle Association
The Birth of Professional Rodeo

Gail Hughbanks Woerner
Illustration Drawn by and Courtesy of Gail Gandolfi

*In Cooperation With
The Prorodeo Hall of Fame
& Museum of The American Cowboy*
www.prorodeohalloffame.com

Wild Horse Press

ISBN-10 - 0-9814903-6-0   ISBN-13 - 978-0-9814903-6-6

Copyright © 2011
Gail Hughbanks Woerner

All Rights Reserved
No part of this book may be reproduced in any form
or by any means without permission in writing from
Wild Horse Press.

Printed in the United States

All inquiries regarding this book should be addressed to
Wild Horse Press
PO Box 3 • Walnut Springs, TX 76690
Telephone - 254-797-2629
E-mail - wildhorsepress@att.net
www.WildHorsePress.com

Wild Horse Press

Table Of Contents

Preface 7
Introduction 11
Chapter One: Twenty Years Of Complainin' 13
Chapter Two: Earlier Attempts At Organizing 23
Chapter Three: The Strike 31
Chapter Four: Let's Get Organized! 37
Chapter Five: Over Anxious Turtles Cause Misunderstandings ... 51
Chapter Six: Rodeos Threaten To Go Non-Professional 65
Chapter Seven: Turtles Still Getting Opposition 77
Chapter Eight: Who Is Jimmie Minotto? 89
Chapter Nine: First C.T.A. Convention 93
Chapter Ten: Cowgirls Join In 99
Chapter Eleven: 1938 – CTA's Second Year 113
Chapter Twelve: C.T.A. Starts To Hear 'Good News' 123
Chapter Thirteen: New Year, New Rules 137
Chapter Fourteen: 1941 – A Spirit Of Cooperation 153
Chapter Fifteen: World War II Affects Everyone 163
Chapter Sixteen: Hoofs & Horns Goes Abroad 173
Chapter Seventeen: Meanwhile Back in the States 183
Chapter Eighteen: Farewell Cowboys' Turtle Association ... 195

Appendix 213
First Articles Of Association By Maxwell McNutt 215
1938 C.T.A. Book, Articles, By-Laws, Rules & Membership .. 221
1940 C.T.A. Book, Articles, By-Laws, Rules & Membership .. 237
1944 C.T.A. Book, Articles, By-Laws, Rules & Membership .. 263
R.A.A. Rules Of Rodeo 295
Cowboys' Turtle Association Members In WW II Service .. 307
Footnotes 311
Index 317

Preface

Everyone who knows and loves rodeo is aware that when the Cowboys' Turtle Association, finally organized in 1936, rodeos became more professional. It came about because the top competing cowboys were not able to make enough money competing, even when they won, to get ahead. Most of the rodeo producers were not offering enough prize money even though cowboys had to pay entry fees in order to be able to compete; and, if they had to travel away from home there was always the additional expense of meals and lodging.

The complaints of the cowboys had been the same for quite some time. They wanted rodeos to increase the prize money. They also wanted the purse to include their entry fees which was not being added at most rodeos. They also knew many of the judges weren't as qualified as they should be to make good judging decisions. They wanted competing cowboy judges that could honestly judge a good performance from one that did not measure up.

The newly formed Cowboys' Turtle Association [CTA] worked with the Rodeo Association of America [RAA] (which was formed in 1929), whose members were rodeo committees and producers, for the purpose of standardizing rodeo across the country. The rodeos that joined the RAA followed RAA rules for rodeo, paying a percentage of their purse to the organization, for their promotion and prestige. The RAA counted points for monies won, not including entry fees, to determine World Champions in each event. When the cowboys organized the CTA, now both the rodeo and the contestants were represented. But CTA did not find a smooth transition with their demands of existing rodeos. Rodeo committees were not accustomed to being told by the contestants how they had to operate their rodeos.

The men who joined the Turtles were willing to step up and become the ramrods of this fledgling group. They were experienced competing rodeo cowboys, who had years of experience in the arena. Their efforts, as well as their failures, and the criticism they received for the things they did, were many. They made numerous mistakes in handling situations that offended existing rodeo management teams, and the directors of the RAA. But the Turtles were relentless and knew that their demands were necessary in order for rodeo to improve and become a respected professional sport. The Turtles knew as cowboys that they were professional competitors by their years of experience. Many had competed from New York to California, and all points between, and had won many competitions, with little to show for it. It was time to 'raise the bar' of rodeo for the cowboy.

Although the story of the Petition which was presented at Boston Garden on October 31, 1936 has been told and re-told, there is much more to tell. What happened before that day, which led up to those demands of Colonel W. T. Johnson, producer of the Boston rodeo, not only in the weeks before, but for several years, has seldom been mentioned. If it was, it was buried in a newspaper article here and there, or mentioned briefly in a book.

The intricate details of the first meetings of the Cowboys' Turtle Association are covered in this book, along with meetings and dealings with the Rodeo Association of America. RAA officials knew the advent of the Turtles was a good thing for rodeo, even if they didn't always see 'eye to eye' on how it was to be implemented.

Those early day Turtles truly 'stuck their necks out' and were determined to improve the sport. They were hated by some. They often left rodeos refusing to compete, which was very costly to them personally. It took men with conviction, determination and perseverance, — and above all, patience. But they believed in their cause and knew they were right. They had a job to do and they succeeded. Professional rodeo cowboys of today should tip their hats to these early day Turtles for all they endured. If it weren't for these first 'professional' cowboys and their determination to succeed, rodeo would not be the prestigious sport we honor today.

This book would not have been possible if it weren't for many people who have helped in numerous ways to gather this information. Thanks go to Walter Dennis, who sent me copies of CTA letters, minutes of the first meetings and photos he had gotten from Hugh Bennett, the first Secretary-Treasurer. Bennett was also one of the original organizers of this fledgling association. Walter and his mother, Millie Dennis, were neighbors of the Bennett's on the outskirts of Colorado Springs, but Millie was also Bennett's nurse and caretaker in the last years of his life. Gail Gandolfi also has my thanks and appreciation for her illustration of the 'Cowboy Turtle' which graces each chapter heading. She never disappoints me. I also appreciate Trevor Brazile for taking the time to write the Introduction since I know how very little time he has to spare with his full-time rodeo schedule. Thanks also go to the following friends and people whose unending assistance in my research is so well appreciated: Imogene Veach Beals, Donna Clark, Gerrianne Schaad, Melissa Gonzales, Tom Decker, Roy Durfey, Sharon Shoulders, Liz Kesler, Paul Bond, Cecil Jones, Bill Fedderson, D'Lynn McGinty Terry, D'Lyla Kerscher Longo, Peggy & Robert Robinson, Bob Chambers, Bern Gregory, Louis Quirk, Frank Quirk, Tater Decker, Don 'Jug' Reynolds, Mitzi Lucas Riley, Buff Douthitt, Bart Clennon, Faye Blackstone, G. K. Lewallen, Ray Wharton, Richard Eaton, Nancy Bragg Witmer, Shoat Webster, Gene McLaughlin, Derek Clark, Kevin Fitzpatrick, Marie Geibel, Emma 'PeeWee' Burge Ott, Bucky Echols, Sandy Brazile and Billy Huckaby, just to mention a few. If I have forgotten anyone who helped it was not intentional. And last, but never least, my husband, Cliff Woerner, who not only supports all my projects, but edits them time and time again. To him I am forever grateful.

Introduction

By
Trevor Brazile
Fourteen-time PRCA World Champion

Trevor Brazile 14 Time World Champion, doing what he does best. *PRCA ProRodeo Photo by Tom Donoghue.*

"If it weren't for the determination of the founding fathers of the Cowboys' Turtle Association the competing cowboys of today wouldn't have the outstanding opportunities we are given. I'm sure in 1936 those cowboys that gave up so much and fought so hard to make professional rodeo better wouldn't have imagined, in their wildest dreams, what we have today. I'm grateful for the cowboys of seventy-five years ago that worked so hard and had the foresight in organizing what has evolved in to the Professional Rodeo Cowboys Association, and the levels of competition all members should be proud of."

CHAPTER ONE

Twenty Years of Complainin'

Early day rodeo was a plethora of problems. Many ranch cowboys introduced to rodeo competition were excited to have the opportunity to use their ranch skills against other cowboys. They were also happy to leave the ranch from time to time. Some even enjoyed the challenge of competing in front of a crowd that would cheer them on. But as time passed and more and more rodeos began to crop up around the country there was much variation in the events held and the rules from one rodeo to the next. This often caused the cowboy a lot of frustration.

The major complaints of the cowboys were that the prizes for winning were too small. Advertisements for a rodeo often promised larger prizes than were handed out when it was time to pay the winners. Judges often were not qualified. Some judges would favor a local cowboy, whom they personally knew, over more qualified contestants. There were even a few promoters that had a tendency to run off with the prize money and the gate money, and then no one got paid.

But in spite of the problems, the cowboys continued to compete in rodeos. They might get together with a half dozen or so contestants, while at a rodeo, and complain to one another about the problems but they seldom did anything about it. Once in a while they might approach a rodeo committee, or the rodeo promoter, but it seldom made a difference. Whenever a rodeo was over, cowboys scattered to the north, south, east or west, either heading home, or to another rodeo. Cowboys never traveled in a pack and often they wouldn't see the fellows they had contested against at one rodeo for months. Consequently, the cowboys had much to criticize, but nothing changed.

Much has been written as to how the sport evolved in early days. Community picnics, such as the 4th of July celebrations would attract cowboys from nearby ranches who tried to outdo each other in bronc riding and roping; it became a popular occurrence, following on the heels of the infamous Wild West shows. Many spectators who just didn't realize the difference, considered rodeo to be similar to a Wild West show. The differences in the two, however, were vast. In a Wild West show, performers got paid to ride broncs and rope, whereas in a rodeo the competitor paid to compete and went home empty-handed if he didn't score well enough to win. Many of the earliest rodeo promoters were more interested in providing entertainment for spectators, with little regard as to how much money the cowboys could earn in the arena.

Eventually rodeo became recognized and appreciated as an American sport with rules that were standardized governing each event. Cowboys enjoyed the competition and the opportunity to travel, and to test their skills against others. But the small size of most of the purses, and object lack of qualified judges, began to affect the competitors. The evolution of rodeo from its very beginnings to present day has been 'a work in progress.' It has been 75 years of continual development and effort to improve the sport. Some ideas and changes worked and made it better, but some didn't. Those early cowboys who were committed to becoming professional rodeo competitors, and who were making rodeo a better sport for everyone involved, should be applauded and commended. They stuck their necks out (like the *turtle*) and took on a challenge that had never been tackled before as they met odds at every corner, but they didn't quit until they succeeded.

Turtle? Why Turtle?

The first successful organization by the rodeo cowboys was called the Cowboys' Turtle Association. Many people have seemed to wonder why the name 'Turtle' was chosen. Some say it was because the cowboys had been complaining about the rodeos, in which they competed, for over twenty years before they got around to organizing.

Turtles are known to be slow creatures, as well, just as the cowboy had been. Once the cowboys did strike, however, at Boston, and followed up by forming the organization, the men who struck were bound and determined to make sure their demands were met. The turtle is known to grab hold of something and won't let go, and like the turtle the cowboys wouldn't let go until they succeeded. The cowboy was there to enforce their rules, no matter what. Regardless of the reason the striking cowboys chose the name 'Cowboys' Turtle Association' (CTA), it got everyone's attention. Those cowboys had a specific focus – to keep the CTA alive and well for the betterment of professional rodeo.

The cowboys finally took control and organized in 1936 at Boston Garden, where Colonel W. T. Johnson, the premier rodeo producer of the day, was holding his Sixth Annual World's Championship Rodeo. Boston was his second annual eastern rodeo, starting a few days after ending an 18 day run of 26 performances at Madison Square Garden in New York City. The Colonel, who had been a successful Texas banker and rancher (owning five ranches in Texas, New Mexico and Mexico), decided in 1928 to hold and promote rodeos for the public. His previous financial successes enabled him to buy the best bucking stock, the best roping stock, matching parade horses, handsome silver laden saddles and tack. His shows were spectacularly promoted and he brought to the sport creative ways of enticing spectators who had never witnessed rodeos, to come to the shows. The Colonel, with his contacts and unique publicity, held the biggest and the best rodeos in the country during the early 1930s.

The Colonel even put together a Rodeo Train which held only cowboys, cowgirls and rodeo stock. It began in San Antonio, Texas, and stopped in Fort Worth to pick up cowboys and cowgirls, and their horses, and then traveled to New York City and Boston. It had a stopover in Fort Madison, Iowa, for a few days, to rest the stock. Eventually, they even started holding a rodeo in Fort Madison, during the stopover which continued annually for many years afterwards.

The criticisms of the competitors had been voiced from time to time to Colonel Johnson. He just ignored them. The cowboys knew they were right in their demands, especially when they would win money and still had to struggle financially to get from one rodeo to the next. They considered it too unjust.

The Petition

Once they arrived in New York City, in October, 1936, a large group of the competing cowboys, unknown to Colonel Johnson, spent their spare time when not in competition, plotting and making plans to submit a petition that essentially said, they were refusing to compete at the Boston rodeo unless the Colonel increased the prize monies by including the cowboys' entry fees. The one page petition was eventually signed by 61 cowboys stating:

"For the Boston Show, we the undersigned demand that the Purses be doubled and the Entrance Fees added in each and every event. Any Contestant failing to sign this Petition will not be permitted to contest, for order of the undersigned, October 30, 1936".

Those who signed were:

Everett Shaw	Carl Shepard	Dick Truitt
Roy Matthews	Joe Welch	Dick Griffith
Red Thompson	Jonas DeArman	Joel Fleming
Hub Whiteman	Melvin Harper	Bob Matthews
Hugh Bennett	Paul Carney	Joe Wolf
Herman Linder	Howard Westfall	Dick Anderton
Eddie Curtis	Leo Murray	Canada Kid
Burel Mulkey	Ralph Bennett	Dick Slappert
Hoytt Hefner	Everett Bowman	E. Pardee
George Conwell	Jake McClure	Dogtown Slim
Cleve Kelley	Clinton Booth	Jim Whiteman
John Beasley	Frank Finley	Jimmie McGee
Walter Cravens	Manerd Gaylor	Ralph Stanton
Hughie Long	Rusty McGinty	John Bowman
Hub Meyers	Howard McCrory	Tom Breeden
Whitey Koed	Carl Hybik	Melvin Tivis
David Longricker	Hipe Wolrich	Buel Johnson
Roy Burns	Speedy Densmore	Buttons Yonnick
Rusty Vaughn	Pete Knight	Tommy Horner

    Bart Clennon   Bob Lerosh   Johnie Williams
John McIntire" [#1]

    Hugh Bennett was one of the cowboys who was heavily involved in all of the secret meetings and discussions at New York of just how they were going to demand that the entry fees were to be added to the purse when they got to Boston. Hugh said that he and his wife, Josie, had discussed organizing a cowboy group for over a year, long before they arrived in New York. The cowboys made all kinds of arrangements and plans so that the strike would go smoothly. Bennett started trying to talk the Colonel into adding the money before they arrived in Boston, but to no avail. The Colonel kept trying to get him to work for him so Bennett could make some money. Bennett refused, and said he would just go back to Arizona and work on his own place. [#2]

    When the petition was presented to the Colonel, he ignored their demands again. He contacted cowboys competing at a Chicago rodeo, and entreated them to come to Boston. He even offered to pay them to come. Unknown to the Colonel, the cowboys at the Chicago rodeo knew of the plans to protest as planned by the cowboys in New York. At the last minute, when none of the cowboys arrived prior to the first performance at Boston, Johnson had to improvise. He rounded up stable hands, grooms, 'scabs' and any other men available who would be a competitor at that first evening performance.

    Gene & Don McLaughlin, ages 7 and 9, were juvenile trick ropers that were very popular performers at rodeos. Their dad was their manager and he made sure they worked every performance because the money they made was important to the family. The boys had competed at Madison Square Garden just prior to Boston. However, the night of the 'strike,' dad insisted that the boys not trick rope. Although he was not a competing cowboy, he had heard enough that he knew how important the impending strike meant to the cowboys, and he was behind them 100%. Gene said, "The following night we performed as usual."[#127]

    Meanwhile, the protesting cowboys bought tickets to the first night's performance and sat in the stands and boo-ed and catcalled every time

October 30, 1936.

For the Boston Show, we the undersigned <u>demand</u> that the Purses be doubled and the Entrance Fees added in each and every event. Any Contestant failing to sign this Petition will not be permitted to contest, by order of the undersigned.

[Signatures of contestants]

The Petition presented to Colonel W. T. Johnson at Boston Garden, on October 30, 1936 which caused the strike.
Courtesy of the ProRodeo Hall of Fame and Museum of the American Cowboy.

the pseudo-cowboys tried to ride or rope. Halfway through the performance, the manager of the Garden, Walter Brown, called a halt to the rodeo. He saw that the spectators were refunded the price of admission. He also insisted that Colonel Johnson meet the demands of the cowboys or he threatened the Colonel by saying, "If you don't, you'll never have another rodeo in Boston." Reluctantly, Johnson agreed.

Bart Clennon who was in the audience and had signed the petition laughingly said, "I didn't yell much because I was sitting next to Howard McCrory who yelled loud enough for both of us." Plus, he said, "the cowboys each received $20, ten times more than we paid for the price of admission."[#3]

The next night, the rodeo went on as usual with all the cowboys competing. The purse had been raised and more than doubled to $14,000. [#4] The cowboys had won their battle and now it was time to organize.

Colonel Johnson wasn't the only rodeo producer, in those days, who was criticized for paying small purses and who refused to include the entry fees. In fact, his purses were as good, and generally better, than any other rodeo being held at that time; and the top cowboys chose his rodeos to compete in because he had the best stock, put on the best rodeos, and had the biggest crowds. Colonel Johnson definitely raised the bar of rodeo from what it had been before he began producing rodeos in 1928.

His previous experiences as a banker and as a successful rancher had given him the know-how to market and entice the public to his rodeos, especially the prominent 'movers and shakers' of the eastern cities. The reason the cowboys decided to strike against the Colonel was because he *was* the best. They knew if they could get him to meet their demands other rodeo producers around the country would follow his lead and hopefully do the same. Hugh Bennett had this to say about the Colonel, "He was one of the greatest producers of rodeo who had more class than any man before or since." [#2]

After the opening night fiasco in Boston the striking cowboys immediately got busy and formed The United Cowboy's Turtle

Association within a few days of the Boston strike. And, as they say, *The Rest Is History.*

Leap forward 75 years, and what that little band of competing cowboys, who picked that ridiculous name, Cowboys' Turtle Association, into which has evolved the Professional Rodeo Cowboys' Association. In 2010, the PRCA had 5,323 members and 1,881 permit holders and 570 sanctioned rodeos. All of that was the result of those early day determined history-makers. In the 75 years since the CTA formed, it is possible that a professional rodeo cowboy can now win more than half a million dollars in a single year; as evidenced by all-around world champion, tie-down champion, and team roping

Presenting a plaque to Verne Elliott, rodeo producer, during the "Cavalcade of Texas" at the 1936 Texas Centennial. Back row, left to right: Ward Watkins, Don Nesbitt, Rube Roberts, Dick Griffith, Joe Welch & Dick Shelton. Middle Row, left to right: Lucyle Richards, Reine Shelton, Vaughan Krieg, Verne Elliott, Bea Kirnan, Bob Calen & Paul Carney. Front row, left to right: Louis Kubitz, Lynn Huskey, Tommy Kirnan, and Mrs. Homer Holcomb. *Photographer unknown. Courtesy of the Jack Long Collection.*

champion, Trevor Brazile, who in 2010 had $507,921 in total monies earned. [#5]

But, there is so much more to be told of the events that led up to the well known historic presentation of the Petition, both before, and after the Boston strike. Read on. . . .

CHAPTER TWO
Earlier Attempts at Organizing

The plotting of the cowboys while contesting at Madison Square Garden in 1936 was nothing new. It has been reported that as early as 1915, Homer S. Wilson and Fay Ward formed The Wild Bunch Contest Fair and Roundup Association, an organization of competing cowboys. It disbanded before the year in which it began was over. It has been determined that they tried 'too early,' and were 'ahead of their time'. [#4]

Bits of information about disgruntled cowboys over the small purses at rodeos, and poorly qualified judges throughout the west were mentioned in the media, from time to time, but nothing ever came of their complaints. Purses, by rodeo producers and committees, were held to a minimum. The promoters used such excuses as; they seldom knew how much they would make on ticket sales, or they did not know how many cowboys might show up to compete. Often the amount of a purse advertised in advance was severely lessened by rodeo time. Some shyster rodeo promoters would even leave town before anyone got paid. This put a bad taste in the competitors' mouth about rodeo.

The First Successful Rodeo Organization

The first organization to be established successfully in rodeo was formed by rodeo managers or rodeo committees across the country as the Rodeo Association of America (RAA). It was the Association's goal to standardize rodeos, regardless of their location and to deter unscrupulous producers who did not hesitate to attempt to dupe the competitors. The RAA made rules and regulations in which rodeos in any area could follow, which would allow competitors to know what to expect when they arrived at a RAA designated rodeo. The rodeos which joined RAA paid a small percentage of their profits to the organization. Not every rodeo in the country joined the RAA, but some who did were: Cheyenne, Wyo.; Salinas, Calif.; Monte Vista, Colo.; Tucson, Ariz.; Sidney, Iowa; Calgary, Alberta; Reno, Nevada and others. The organization's success didn't happen overnight but in time, rodeo definitely became a lot more standardized and reliable. There was, however, still room for improvement, particularly from the competing cowboys' points of view.

Heated discussions and arguments by cowboys about the meager prize monies and poorly-qualified judges had been hashed and rehashed since the 1915 attempt to organize had ended. The cowboys often presented their gripes to the rodeo producers with no real results.

Homer Holcomb, one of the first bullfighters, using a cape. *Photographer unknown. Courtesy of Stan Searle from the Hoofs & Horns Collection.*

Earlier Attempts at Organizing

Colonel Johnson's World Champion Cowgirls, Madison Square Garden, 1935. Back row, left to right: Peggy Long, Pauline Nesbitt, Mary Keen Wilson, Fannie Nielson, Vaughn Krieg, Vivian White, Brida Gafford, Velda Tindall, Tad Lucas, Alice Greenough, Myrtle Compton Goodrich & Iva Del Jacobs Draeksler. Front row, left to right: Grace White, Alice Adams, Mary Parks, Mildred Mix Horner, Colonel Johnson, Unknown, Florence Randolph, Reine Shelton, Betty Meyer and Unknown. *Photo by E. J. Kelty, Courtesy of Jack Long Collection.*

    M. D. Fanning, a cattleman from Fort Worth, Texas, was responsible for gathering a group of cowboys together at the National Western Stock Show, Rodeo and Horse Show in Denver, in early 1932, where he was hired as a rodeo timer. They formed a group whom he called 'a protective association' and named it the Cowboy Contestants Association. The original purpose was to provide help to cowboys injured while competing and to raise the standards of the sport. [#6]

    It was reported in a Denver newspaper with the headline, "First 'Cowboys' Union' Ever Organized Will Be Formed in Denver". The article went on to say there was no criticism by the cowboys about the Denver rodeo. Fanning was quoted as saying, "I've been talking it over with the boys, and we've agreed that in our kind of business there ought to be some sort of standards. We intend to lay down a 'set of rules' that will keep every member from participating in a show where there isn't a chance of making any money". Ninety-five cowboys attended the meeting and the hat was passed collecting over $300 to initiate the fund. Abe Lefton was chairman of forming eight committees representing each event in rodeo. [7, 8] The Fort Worth Star Telegram, March 12, 1932, printed a photograph of Fanning calling him the secretary-treasurer of the newly formed group. Unfortunately, the organization did not endure. [9]

How many times the cowboys confronted a promoter or a rodeo producer concerning the small purses, will never be known. Paul Bond, CTA #395, remembered a rodeo in Fort Worth, produced by a man named Robinson, using Beutler stock, who was asked to up the purse and when he refused, the cowboys quit midway through the rodeo. He couldn't remember the year. [10] The cowboys confronted rodeo management, from time to time, but seldom reacted with any strength. Those cowboys that were 'bit by the rodeo bug' had to compete and try to win, no matter what size the purse, even if the producers refused to increase the monies.

Earlier 'Strike' Won

A "strike" at the Fort Worth rodeo, on March 15, 1935, was another attempt by the cowboys to show their dissatisfaction that the entry fees were not being included in the purse. In *Billboard* (primarily a vaudeville magazine) was a column called, 'The Corral,' written by Rowdy Waddy, which covered information about Wild West performers and rodeo cowboys and cowgirls. The following account was written about that strike:

"Capacity crowds attended practically every performance the first four days of the rodeo in connection with the Southwestern Exposition and Fat Stock Show, which runs through March 24. The rodeo has 17 events. Contracts include Hardy Murphy's trained horse, Silver Cloud; Homer Holcomb and his mule and dummy used during the steer riding; Ted Elder, Roman riding over an automobile. Judges: Ranger Captain Tom Hickman, Carl Arnold and Harry Knight. Ed McCarty and Verne Elliott, who furnish the livestock, arena directors. Louis Kubitz, superintendent of stock; Rube Roberts and Donald Nesbit, pick-up men; Bob Calen, general announcer; John Jordan announced trick and fancy roping. George McIntosh had both legs crushed when two horses collided during wild-horse racing. Is in Baptist Hospital here.

"There was a 'strike' of contestants on March 15, which almost stopped the parade that annually opens the stock show and rodeo. However, the contestants won their point, the addition of entry fee money, $4,030, in all to the winnings. The contestants' first demand for the extra money was made on the preceding night, when a petition signed by 93 of the 138 contestants was presented to Manager John B. Davis, who refused the demands, explaining the show was a civic enterprise and was not making money. The performers then refused to compete, and a managerial notice was posted that every contestant who failed to appear at 1 p.m. for the participation in the parade would be disqualified from the show. As they did not mount at 1 p.m. for the parade, show officials acceded to the demands for all the entry fees at 1:45, in time for the show to go on." [11]

Colonel Johnson and a few of his World Champion Cowgirls meet with Kansas City ladies during the American Royal, 1934. Cowgirls left to right are: Reine Shelton, Tad Lucas, Vivian White, Mary Keen Wilson, Myrtle Goodrich Compton, and Grace White. *Photo by Anderson*[5]. *Courtesy of the Jack Long Collection.*

The same article also included the names of winners of the various events. Some of those signing the Fort Worth petition were the same cowboys who signed the petition the following year that was presented to Colonel Johnson at Boston; Hugh Bennett, Roy Matthews, Joe Welch, Red Thompson, Everett Bowman, Rusty McGinty, E. Pardee, Jake McClure and others. [11]

This Fort Worth petition and successful strike was very possibly the catalyst that spurred on the cowboys, who had complained for so long about the low prize money, to plot and plan their Boston strike a year later. Although the Fort Worth strike had won the demands which the cowboys were seeking (the addition of $4,030 [the entry fees] to the purse), when the rodeo was over they merely went off in different directions. This meant that each and every time they were unhappy about the entry fees not being included in the purse; they would have to strike again and again. The only rational solution was to form an organization which would continue to fight for these demands until every rodeo in the country was willing to comply with their requests. [135]

Jimmie Nesbitt, CTA #1, rodeo clown who scratched his name out on the Boston Petition. *Photo by R. R. Doubleday. From the Hoofs & Horns Collection. Courtesy of the Dickinson Research Center, National Cowboy & Western Heritage Museum.*

Tom Bride, from Ismay, Mont., was a roughstock rider, who felt if the cowboys got together and formed an 'association' maybe they could do some good. On a trip to compete in Arizona, Bride talked with Everett Bowman about his idea, and Bowman brought Hugh Bennett into the discussion. Whether or not this is where the idea started, we'll never know for sure, but at least it 'planted a seed.' [12]

CHAPTER THREE
The Strike

The first person to have had the brilliant idea that the cowboys needed to organize, is lost to time, but those cowboys who went to New York to compete at Madison Square Garden and then on to Boston, in 1936, had a plan. They had more to think about than just competing to win at riding and roping. The preparation for the strike at Boston, was accomplished behind closed doors of the Belvedere Hotel in New York City, and only the cowboys that could be trusted to keep their plans a secret, were involved. They did not want Colonel Johnson, to get wind of their plans. Over the course of several days in which their plans and strategies were being developed, they tried to think of every possible alternative that could happen to squelch their attempt.

Many of the cowboys and cowgirls, who had traveled to New York and on to Boston, did so on the Rodeo Train. This was Colonel Johnson's train and if he got mad enough to refuse to let them return home on the train, what could they do? The travelers paid a small amount of money to travel on the train, and they also were allowed to haul their horses in a boxcar. Richard Merchant was assigned the responsibility to find alternative transportation for the cowboys and their mounts, if everything went sour. Merchant had the background in rodeo management and he knew how to get these things done.

Mitzi Lucas Riley, CTA #479, said her mother, Tad Lucas, and all the lady bronc riders and trick riders were very fond of Colonel Johnson. "He liked having the girls in his shows and they were definitely favored at a Johnson rodeo. The Johnson string of horses for the gals was the best ever and that is why he was well respected."

Although the cowboys criticized the Colonel, and it was common knowledge he was tough on them, they still chose his rodeos over the rest as they knew he had the best stock, the most colorful rodeo, the best money, and the biggest crowds. Colonel Johnson had been a cowboy very briefly in his youth. He never fraternized with the cowboys and was definitely never considered 'one of the boys,' but they knew he ran a rodeo that was considered the best. [#143]

The decision was made as to when to present the petition and signatures were collected. Most of those signing had time to consider the consequences of putting their signature on the demand. Only one signer decided he should remove his name. Jimmy Nesbitt, a rodeo clown hired by Colonel Johnson, thought he'd better remove his name or he might be fired, not paid, and be stranded in New York with no money. His name was blacked out. Although it was obvious Nesbitt believed in what the cowboys were doing because when the organization formed, Nesbitt was the first person to pay dues and sign up. He carried Cowboy Turtle Association membership No. 1 for the rest of his life. #1, [#13]

Second Petition

Meanwhile in Chicago, the Chicago Stadium Corporation was presenting 'World's Greatest Rodeo', produced and managed by Barnes–Carruthers, from October 16 to November 1. Many of the cowboys who had been competing in the northwest and were unable to reach New York in time to compete at Madison Square Garden, had signed on for the mid-west show. They had been informed of the upcoming strike, by cowboy friends in-on-the-plot, and by a second petition on Chicago Stadium letterhead stationary, which was circulated in Chicago depicting those cowboys who supported their Boston 'brothers.'

It stated:

"We, the undersigned Cowboys showing at the Chicago Stadium do hereby agree not to go to the Boston Show, unless the demands of the Cowboys now at Boston are met. The boys at Boston now, must be allowed to work and not barred from that show."

Those cowboys signing the Chicago petition were:

Tom Hogan	Bill Buschbom	Vic Rogers
J. D. West	Druward Ryon	Tom Shipman
Bill Parks	Joe Cody	Herschell Ross
Ole Rice	Mickey McCrory	Kenn Roberts
Chuck Williams	(illegible)	Earl Blevins
Guy Cash	Red McCormick	Hugh Ridley
Elmer Martin	Jim Massey	Joe Thompson
Heavy Henson	Bob Hess	Curly Kelly
Bob Askin	Homer Pettigrew	Bud Mefford
Bill Truck	Lynn Huskey	Glenn Soward
Shorty McCrory	Tex Slocum	Allan Hotcher
R. L. Nelson	Len Jacobs	Joe McMackin
Maurice Reilly	Bill Truan	Grady Wilson
Ed Davis	Tom Taylor	King Merritt
Billy Wilkinson	Jack Jackson	Amye Gamblin
Frank Marion	Barton Carter	Jim Wilkinson
Ted (illegible)	Earl Wort	Roy Mayeo
Jack Bolton	Buck Stuart	Lonnie Rooney
Ted Buschbom	Blacky Rucker	Jay Snively
Oral Zumwalt	Thelma Warner	Pete Adams
Pete Shipman	Buck Standifer	Del Hinton
Virgil Earp	Holloway Grace	Bud McDaniel
Arvil Gilliam	Shorty Creed	A. J. Pettigrew
Toots Ayres	John Evans	Eddie Collins
Harold Johnson	Curly Bill	Harold Piper
Jerry Littrell	Jack (illegible)	Earl Moore
Trail City Kid	Fred Beeson	George Pitman
Bill McMackin	Joe Farrell	Gene Creed
Mary Parks	Margie Greenough	Buck Sorrells
Snooks Jones	Ed Herman	Dave Campbell
Vaughn Krieg	Bob Spratt	Milt Moe
Sonny Hancock	Frank Martz	Shorty Ricker

Les Karstad	Curly McCall	Ben Bender
Clay Carr	Jim Snively	Jack Quait
Buster Brown		

(Three names were marked out; the only one legible was Alice Adams) [14]

It can only be assumed that the reason this petition was not presented with the one signed at Boston, is that it did not arrive in time. This petition (four pages) was part of Hugh Bennett's CTA papers given to the ProRodeo Hall of Fame.

Cowboys at the Boston strike, October 30, 1936. Back Row, left to right: Everett Bowman, Bugs Yale, E. Pardee, Jake McClure, Everett Shaw. Front Row, left to Right: Dick Truitt, Rusty McGinty, Eddie Curtis, Hub Whiteman and Hugh Bennett. *Photographer Unknown. Courtesy of the Jack Long Collection.*

The Strike

CHICAGO STADIUM CORPORATION
Presents
WORLD'S GREATEST RODEO
Every Event a Contest
October 16th to November 1st

We, the undersigned Cowboys showing at the Chicago Stadium do hereby agree not to go to the Boston Show, unless the demands of the Cowboys now at Boston are met. The boys at Boston now, must be allowed to work and not barred from that show.

[signatures]

Address all Communications to Chicago Stadium Corporation 1800 W. Madison St. Chicago, Ill.

First page of the four page Chicago Petition. *Courtesy of the ProRodeo Hall of Fame and Museum of the American Cowboy, from the Hugh Bennett Collection.*

CHAPTER FOUR

Let's Get Organized!

The first official meeting of the 'Turtles' was held on November 6, 1936, less than a week after the Boston 'strike.' This gathering was held while everyone was still in Boston. At first, the organization was named United Cowboys Turtle Association. The president was Rusty McGinty; vice president, Eddie Woods; secretary-treasurer, Hugh Bennett, and speaker, Everett Bowman. Representatives of five events were named: bareback riders, by Dick Griffin (this is an error and should have read <u>Griffith</u>); calf ropers, Bob Crosby; bronc riders, Eddie Curtis; bulldoggers, Hub Whiteman; and steer riders, Paul Carney.

A one page list of Rules and Regulations was written and members were to abide by them as stipulated:

Rule No. 1. Any cowboy or cowgirl will be assessed and required to pay $500 to the Association to re-enter the Union if he or she performs or competes in that particular rodeo where a strike is called. The re-entry of said strike-breakers must be voted upon by silent vote by all members of the Turtle Association.

Rule No. 2. The $500.00 paid to the United Cowboys Turtle Association by the strike-breakers or violators of the association will go to a trust fund, to be used for lawyer fees, telephone calls, telegrams, or for a representative to be sent to any rodeo committee, which the Cowboys Association agrees is offering insufficient and unfair purses. It is further understood and agreed that a fine of $100.00 must be paid to the Association by any cowgirl or cowboy for disgraceful conduct, which must be proven before the Board of Directors.

It is to be the ruling of this organization that each member shall be assessed a yearly fee of $5.00, which will go into a trust fund, to be put into a bank that is agreeable to all members of the Association. It is further understood that no member of this organization may check upon this fund. All checks must be signed by at least four members of the Board of Directors or officials. No representative, speaker or member of the Board of Directors is to be paid a salary for his services. This is to be given free of charge to the organization.

It is also understood that a representative must be present at that certain rodeo on which a strike is called, and be able to prove that any member of this association has competed at that certain rodeo.

Rule No. 3. Strikes are not to be called by any one member of this association, because he or she may be dissatisfied by the decision of the judges, rules and regulations, or by finding fault with the committee or prize list, but must be passed upon by all members of the association, and if it is passed upon, a representative is to go to the committee with a list signed by all of the members. After a member has once signed his or her name to this list, the association has the right to use his name on any list that is to be sent to a rodeo committee where the purses are considered unsatisfactory and unfair. No one person has the right to send in a list that is not approved by all the members of this organization, and should anyone do this, he or she will be expelled from this association, and will be assessed the $500.00 as stipulated in Rule No. 1 to re-enter the Union.

Rule No. 4. It is not the rule of this organization to interfere with personal disagreements among members, nor with personal demands of a cowboy for his rights. For instance: Should a show have a judge who is thought unfair in his decisions, a cowboy has the right to demand a fair deal, without the interference of the Association. The Union has a right to demand capable and fair judges, and should there be judges who do not come up to this standard, the Union reserves the right to

Let's Get Organized

send a representative to the rodeo committee to ask for a change of judges. #15

Rodeo Association of America, Before the Turtles

The Rodeo Association of America (RAA) had been organized in 1929 and membership was made up of rodeo committees and producers from across the country. The RAA was formed in Salinas, Calif., after successfully defeating a measure to put rodeos out of business in California. #16 The purpose of the organization was to share ideas with rodeos which joined RAA so that each individual rodeo did not have to 're-invent the wheel.' To gain continuity in the performances, competing cowboys traveling from one locale to the next, could now find similar rules and regulations, as put forth by RAA. It also was formed to discourage dishonest rodeo promoters who would 'skip town' after a performance, or would pay off winners with a lot less monies than had been advertised. Those actions always 'soured' cowboys that competed well enough to get in the money and expected a reasonable purse and then only to receive much less or nothing at all. Not all rodeos joined the RAA, but enough did such that the RAA made a very significant

Hugh Bennett, CTA's first secretary-treasurer, bulldogging at Brockton rodeo. *Photo by R. R. Doubleday. Courtesy of the Dickinson Research Center, National Cowboy & Western Heritage Museum.*

COWBOYS TURTLE ASSOCIATION

OFFICERS
PRESIDENT
EVERETT BOWMAN
HILLSIDE, ARIZONA
FIRST VICE-PRESIDENT
HERMAN LINDER
CARDSTON, ALBERTA CANADA
SECOND VICE-PRESIDENT
RUSTY McGINTY
PLAINS, TEXAS
SECRETARY-TREASURER
HUGH BENNETT
FORT THOMAS, ARIZONA

REPRESENTATIVES
BARE-BACK BRONC RIDING
HUGHIE LONG
FORT WORTH, TEXAS
CALF ROPING
EVERETT SHAW
STONEWALL, OKLAHOMA
BRONC RIDING
HARRY KNIGHT
FLORENCE, ARIZONA
BULL DOGGING
DICK TRUITT
STONEWALL, OKLAHOMA
STEER RIDING
EDDIE CURTIS
EL RENO, OKLAHOMA

Cowboys Turtle Association letterhead, listing Officers and Representatives. *Courtesy of the ProRodeo Hall of Fame & Museum of the American Cowboy, Hugh Bennett Collection.*

impact on the sport of rodeo. Rodeo was on its way to becoming more unified. However, competing cowboys still had no voice in rodeo.

When the strike occurred in Boston and the CTA was formed, the RAA was wholly supportive of the new cowboy competitor organization. Although RAA represented rodeo committees and management, it realized the need for competitor representation. In fact, RAA President Maxwell McNutt, wrote the first Articles of the Association for CTA.

The Media Ready to Publicize Rodeo Happenings

It didn't take long for reporters of newspapers and magazines to want to be the first to report the news. It is the American way – "free speech." Hugh Bennett received the following letter from Tex Sherman on December 14th, 1936, just a month after the Turtles were formed. The letter was written on *Ranch Romances* stationary with his personal logo, "Out of the Chutes with Tex Sherman", across the top.

It read:

"Dear Hugh: I received a letter from Colonel Johnson, telling me his side of the Boston strike, but would like to have the cowboys side of the story, as you must know that the above magazine and myself is strictly neutral, as I am dealing with the public, and believe that I have the largest following of rodeo fans than any other writer in the game.

I want you to know that I AM for the cowboys organization, and there is nothing in the world that I want to see succeed than your organization, and rest assured that if you will send me news from time to time, you will get publicity, and NO promoter or manager can get to me, as I am just as interested in seeing the new association succeed than anyone in the world.

If you wish, rest assure that I will be glad to be placed on the publicity committee, and handle the publicity for the organization, and DO NOT look for any money, but just the good will of all concerned.

May I expect to hear from you stating the true facts, and wish you would have it typewritten and double spaced so I can send it to my editor without any changes, but just as you write it.

If you see Merchant tell him that I am interested in handling the publicity for the Phoenix show, also the announcing, and then you and the committee and myself can get together on news to be released through news syndicates.

Please remember me to Mrs. Bennett, and let me hear from you, pronto.

Sincerely your friend,
Tex Sherman" [17]

The letter Sherman obviously received from Hugh Bennett is unknown and not available, however, a second letter from Sherman was sent to Bennett dated December 19, 1936.

It read:

"Dear Hugh: Thanks for your swell letter and will say that you need have no fear that the letter will be published I received from Colonel Johnson, and rest sure that you will have the complete backing of my rodeo column, and it would be a good idea to have the above magazine as your official publication, as we have a paid circulation of 228,000 copies per month and issued every two weeks.

That organization of yours should have a publication that will hit the public, and with public support behind you, your organization cannot but help succeed, and it will cost you nothing and I DO NOT want any advertising from anyone, not even the promoters, all we want is rodeo news that is legitimate, and not done from wild west shows, but exclusively rodeos.

Hoofs and Horns is a swell paper but it only has a circulation of only 3,300 copies a month, but my column hits the public, and that's what you want.

At the present time I cannot send you a copy of Johnson's letter, as I sent it to my editor with strict instructions, to publishing NOTHING, unless it comes from me, and you know I have been known to rodeo contestants and the public for over 30 years, and never have I broken a promise I made.

I am trying to get Merchant, to give me that job (publicity) and then if I get it, I will get together with you and take the matter up with your executive board and see if they want me to handle the publicity for the organization, but it must be understood that only myself will release news to any paper, because if there is more than one, it eventually will get news mixed and that won't do anyone any good.

The above address will reach me here till March 1st and if you come to Hollywood, be sure and get in touch with me.

My best wishes for happy holidays to you and Mrs. Bennett.

Sincerely,
Tex Sherman" [18]

Apparently, all of Mr. Sherman's efforts were in vain because it was *Hoofs & Horns* that printed the first Cowboys' Turtle Association brochure entitled: "Cowboys' Turtle Association Articles of Association, By-Laws, Rules and List of Members to April 1, 1938" (See Appendix).[13] *Hoofs & Horns* also contained a page of CTA news and information which began in the December, 1937 issue with a list of the Turtles who totaled 439 at publication time. From then on, there was generally a page for CTA news in *Hoofs & Horns*, which had the by-line of being the 'official publication' for CTA. [19]

The Bennetts

It is evident in reading about the new CTA organization, that Hugh (CTA #8), and his wife, Josie, were extremely committed and worked diligently toward the success of the group. It is common knowledge that they actually worked 'out of their car' and accepted dues from cowboys and kept records as they traveled from rodeo to rodeo. In fact, Hugh was very proud of Josie for her commitment to the cause.

He told of a time they were staying in a tent at a rodeo and an unknown person robbed Hugh of several hundred dollars by coming into their tent and finding Hugh's billfold lying on the cot. Josie had the Turtle money hidden in a trunk; it was not touched, thanks to her diligence.

The Bennett's were quick to give credit to others, and said that Mrs. Alvie Gordon often did the typing for them at meetings. Richard Merchant was also complimented, as he had the expertise to organize and coordinate travel plans for the group. Bennett also said Everett Bowman didn't do much in the plotting stages of forming the Turtles, (he was working for Colonel Johnson during the New York rodeo), but once CTA was formed, and he was elected president, which was at Hugh's suggestion, he said the Turtles couldn't have had a better president. Bowman worked day and night at representing the group and making the demands of the Turtles known. [#2]

Bob Reagan (son of Rocky Reagan, who produced rodeos in South Texas during this era), in a conversation with the author, recalled that Rusty McGinty, first CTA president, phoned his dad from Boston and told him that they had formed the Cowboys' Turtle Association and that Rocky needed to pay at least $100 per event at his rodeos. The Beeville, Texas rodeo was held in November shortly after the first CTA meeting, which always had lots of cowboy competitors since it was the first rodeo in the area after the Rodeo Train had arrived back in San Antonio coming from the eastern rodeos. Rocky informed his friend, McGinty, that he already was paying $100 per event. Rocky Reagan & Sons produced CTA approved rodeos in Beeville, Corpus Christi, and Kingsville throughout the 1940s. [#141]

At the end of 1936 the following cowboys were World Champions in the following events, according to RAA points:

All-Around – John Bowman, Oakdale, Calif., CTA #10
Bareback Riding – Smoky Snyder, Bellflower, Calif. CTA #40
Steer Wrestling – Jack Kerscher, Miles City, Mont., CTA #218
Team Roping – John Rhodes, Sombrero Butte, Ariz., CTA #56
Saddle Bronc Riding – Pete Knight, Crossfield, Alberta, CTA #78
Calf Roping – Clyde Burk, Comanche, Okla., CTA #144

Bull Riding – Smoky Snyder, Bellflower, Calif., CTA #40
Steer Roping – John Bowman, Oakdale, Calif., CTA #10. [#20]

RAA points were gathered from monies earned by competitors at RAA approved rodeos, excluding entry fees.

First RAA Meeting
After CTA Was Formed

The first RAA convention, after the Boston strike, was held in Reno, Nev., on January 29 and 30, 1937, at the Riverside Hotel. The newly organized CTA directors were invited to attend. A tentative schedule of the program was circulated in advance. A variety of issues and information was planned, including; "The Future of RAA," by Maxwell McNutt, president of RAA; "The Working of the RAA Office" by E. J. Leach, vice president of the Salinas, Calif., rodeo. "The Rodeo Situation in the Eastern District" by Howard Harris, manager of the Salem County Fair-Rodeo at Woodstown, N.J. and RAA director for the entire eastern U. S., east of the west line of Iowa, South Dakota, North Dakota, Missouri, Arkansas and Louisiana. Also on the list was to be an address — "The Turtle Cowboy Association" by Hugh Bennett, or some other person delegated to speak for this group. [#21]

Herman Linder, a bronc rider, from Cardston, Alberta, CTA #22, who had been extremely active before

Smokey Snyder, World Champion Bull Rider, 1931, 1932 tied with Johnie Schneider, 1935, '36 & '37 and World Champion Bareback Rider 1932 & 1936. *Photographer Unknown. Courtesy of the Jack Long Collection.*

Let's Get Organized

and during the Boston strike, had planned to attend the RAA convention. A postal telegram arrived at the Reno Rodeo Convention for Hugh Bennett, on January 30th saying:

"Jack received your letter today am sorry that we couldn't get to the convention we are snowed in and it is impossible to get out at present please give the boys my regards and sincerely hope the convention is a success and that the turtles gain a few points. Herman Linder" [22]

What actually transpired at the RAA convention regarding the newly organized Turtle Association was described in *The Bulletin*, the RAA monthly report, which was printed in *Hoofs & Horns*. Secretary McCargar reported that contestant representatives (Turtles) present complained that:

1. Entry fees seldom put in the prize money. They requested that entry fees always be put in the prize money. They explained that often they paid out more to compete than they won.

2. They asked for assistance from RAA to get at least $100 in each event for prize money.

3. Sometimes the payoff was less than a rodeo had advertised before the rodeo, but once they got there would be forced to compete just to get enough money to get home.

McCargar wrote that the following was agreed to by RAA directors, members and CTA:

1. RAA would request member rodeos to have their prize list in circulation and printed in *The Bulletin* at least 30 days in advance of their rodeo, plus a guarantee that the prize money would be paid. Contestants (including Turtles) could then decide if they wanted to compete in that rodeo or not.

2. There would be no strikes by contestants, if these two requirements were complied with.

3. If there were complaints they should be filed with RAA, not taken up with the rodeo.

4. RAA officials agreed to encourage member rodeos to increase prize money with the aim of reaching $100 or more, in each event, as soon as possible. [23]

Hugh Bennett received the following telegram on February 13th, 1937, from president Maxwell McNutt of the RAA which might shed some light on what transpired after the January Convention of RAA and what went on in the following 30 days.

The telegram said:

"Tucson officials notify me you have served notice demanding increase their prize list STOP You agreed at Reno that if shows would file prize list and would file guarantee that contestants would not go to shows not offering fair money in contestants opinion STOP This I understand Tucson has done STOP as agreed at Reno it is none of either contestants or RAA associations business as to amounts offered by a show but only your business and our business to protect contestants from going long distances under wrong impression as to amounts offered and then assurance that winnings will be paid but for your information Tucson was one of the very largest rodeos in the United States in money paid contestants last year STOP such action as yours will unquestionably make many shows change to nonprofessional as there is already a demand see local cattlemen that local boys be given a chance to win money offered and not just a few top professionals STOP you know from spectators standpoint a local contestant being bucked off brings a bigger gate than seeing the worlds champion ride the worst bucking horse and that many shows are being urged by spectators to eliminate the roping altogether STOP as records show many top cowboys make from five to ten thousand a year while local contestants who help build the shows and pay the entrée fees seldom win anything STOP the RAA has taken the side of the professional cowboy many times we have saved your winnings for you and by publishing amounts paid by shows have automatically caused increases in prize money STOP your cooperation as promised at Reno will help build the rodeo and help the professional cowboy otherwise not advise. Maxwell McNutt, President of the Rodeo Association of America." [24]

Turtles Get Interest from Up-And Coming Rodeos

A letter on stationary with the letterhead 'Forty-first Annual SOUTHWESTERN EXPOSITION AND FAT STOCK SHOW, March 12th to 21st, 1937, (Fort Worth) written by secretary-manager, John B. Davis to Hugh Bennett, secretary-treasurer of United Cowboys' Turtle Association, Ft. Thomas, Ariz., dated February 22, 1937 said:

"Dear Hugh: I have your letter of February 19 and would like to have a copy of the rules and regulations of your Association. It seems to me that an organization of this kind, if properly officered and administered, working in cooperation with the rodeo managers, should be of value to both contestants and managements.

I am, of course, not familiar with the details of the rules of your organization or the complaint which prompts your request that we withhold the acceptance of entries of the three contestants mentioned in your letter. However, we will be glad to comply with your request and hope that whatever disagreement exists between these gentlemen and your organization can be satisfactorily worked out between you before our Show opens.

I would suggest that the officers of your Association be there two or three days before the opening of the Show in order that these matters, as you say, might be straightened out without any embarrassment to anyone.

We are planning on a great Show and all indications are quite encouraging for a large attendance. I extend kindest personal regards and best wishes.

Yours very truly,

J. B. Davis, Secretary-Manager"[25]

A second letter from Maxwell McNutt to Hugh, dated February 24, 1937, said in part:

"... I have been obliged to prepare the Articles and By-Laws with some haste; but they are, in the main, modeled upon those of the R.A.A. and I feel that they will serve your purpose..."

The second paragraph said;

"It was a great pleasure to be with you all and I hope some good may come of it for all concerned. We should all bear in mind that we must keep rodeos on the plane of sports, and in the event they should become or participation therein should be regarded as mere business, success would be questionable. I realize that in everything in life there is room for different opinions but have no doubt that all difficulties may be avoided by cool deliberation rather than by precipitate action. Your aims and our aims have much in common. Neither organization can hope for complete success at the expense of the other. Cooperation is necessary. If at any time you think I can serve you I want you to feel free to call upon me.

With best regards to all the boys,
Maxwell McNutt

P.S. Under separate cover the documents referred to have been mailed to you."[26]

(See the Articles in the Appendix)

Second Turtle Meeting Addresses Judging

Minutes for the second meeting of the Cowboys' Turtle Association, held in Fort Worth, Texas, on March 11, 1937, at the Butcher's Union Hall was circulated as:

Herman Linder, chairman of the election committee, called the meeting to order.

He read the Articles and By-Laws of the Association.

Officers elected for 1937 were:
Everett Bowman, President
Herman Linder, First Vice President
Rusty McGinty, Second Vice President
Hugh Bennett, Secretary-Treasurer

"Representatives of competitive events were:
Bareback Bronc Riding..........Hughie Long, Ft Worth, Texas
Calf Roping.................Everett Shaw, Stonewall, Okla.
Saddle Bronc Riding............Harry Knight, Florence, Ariz.

Let's Get Organized

> Bull dogging .... Dick Truitt, Stonewall, Okla.
> Steer Riding .... Eddie Curtis, El Reno, Okla.

"It had been decided that a carbon copy be furnished to each judge and one to the Secretary for the Timed Events, to eliminate changing the markings.

"It was decided each show print on their prize list any contestant turning down stock, failing to make an honest effort in roping events, or failing to jump at steers in dogging, would be disqualified at next years show.

"Any shows not belonging to R. A. A. were laying themselves liable to boys not entering their show because the purses have not been approved by the CTA.

A list selected by the Bronc Riders who are qualified to judge rodeos:

Harry Knight	Bob Crosby	Breezy Cox
Leo Murray	Andy Jauregui	Floyd Gale
Lloyd Saunders	Everett Chetham	Everett Bowman
Bob Askins	Carl Arnold	Richard Merchant
Jack Kerscher	Floyd Stillings	King Merritt
Earl Thode	Hugh Bennett	Don Nesbitt
Andy Curtis	Dick Truitt	Barton Carter
Jay Snively		

These names were added to the following qualified list:

Chock Dyer	Dave Campbell	Perry Ivory
Shorty Williamson	Ki Silacci	Frank Sharp
Herman Linder	Pat Burton	Milt Moe" [27]

Note: On the heading of the Minutes the official name of the organization had dropped **"United"**, and before this meeting had also dropped **"The"** from the official name of the **Cowboys' Turtle Association**

CTA Articles of Association, By-Laws and Rules

The first Articles of the Association, By-Laws & Rules were prepared by Maxwell McNutt, (Judge of the Superior Court of San Mateo County, Calif.) and president of the Rodeo Association of

America, as mentioned in his letter to Bennett dated February 24, 1937. *(See Appendix)* [28]

In a telephone conversation with D'Lynn Terry, daughter of Rusty McGinty, CTA # 2, and first CTA president, she reported, "that her dad had resigned his presidency in the Turtles, because he 'had to make a living' for his family and felt he could not devote the time necessary as the leader of the group. However, he did hold a lesser office and was quite active. He was very humbled by the fact that the guys had thought he would be a good president." [128]

Much interest about rodeo and the significant efforts put forth by rodeo associations to have more consistency in all rodeos throughout the country was circulating and it was not surprising that Bennett received a letter dated April 27, 1937, from Harry Montgomery, Chief of the Bureau of the Associated Press asking that he understood the Cowboys' Turtle Association was a "union that would seek to improve the standards of the profession of rodeo performers" and would Bennett write and tell him all about the organization. He also stated there was much interest throughout the country regarding this issue. [29]

CHAPTER FIVE

Over-Anxious Turtles Cause Misunderstandings

The year 1937, was one of 'trial and error,' and often resulted in major criticism of the CTA. There were well-meaning members of CTA who made demands on various rodeo committees on the eve of their first rodeo performance which caused major last minute frustrations to the committees and often did not get resolved to the satisfaction of everyone involved. It had been agreed at the January RAA meeting attended by CTA representatives, that their requests to rodeo committees be given 30 days in advance of their earliest performance, which would give the committees plenty of time to correct a problem and would not impose on them at the last minute.

Another problem which had to be addressed in the first organizing year was that some cowboys, who were members of the CTA, continued to compete at rodeos not sanctioned by CTA. Cowboys were independent by nature, taken with the fact that those who considered rodeo their livelihood, and had to make a living by winning monies at rodeo competitions, spurned the problem. Some tried to 'slide by' the CTA rules at some of the smaller rodeos which weren't approved by CTA. These smaller rodeos often were not able to increase their purses to meet CTA requirements, or hire judges that were sanctioned by CTA.

Hoofs & Horns published letters to and from the RAA officers and the President, and 'voice' of the CTA, Everett Bowman, in numerous issues of the 1937 periodical. It was evident that both organizations (CTA & RAA) were working very hard to do 'the right thing,' but often

CTA was criticized for their unprofessional or 'last minute' ways of handling matters with certain rodeo committees.

A RAA column in *Hoofs & Horns* written by the Secretary, Fred S. McCargar, said the following in the 'Secretary's Message':

"– Apparently there has been some misunderstanding as to what took place at the Reno Convention (of RAA in January 1937) and therefore, I am going to outline it again briefly. The Reno Argument; several representatives of the Cowboy Turtle Association, the new organization of cowboys, appeared and discussed various things. They were represented on all committees and a very fair settlement was made in regard to a number of very controversial questions. The contestants believed that they have not received their fair share of the gate receipts of some shows and actually brought facts to show that in some instances the contestants paid in more money in entrance fees than was paid in prize money; that in many instances they were unable to get the prize lists in advance of the show and when they got to the show they were out of money and had to compete, even though the prize money offered was not sufficient in their opinion; also oftentimes in the past even though they won the prize money, some of the shows failed to pay off; that many of the prize lists didn't show whether the entrance fees were added or not.

Everett Bowman, President of the Cowboys' Turtle Association, and World Champion All-Around Cowboy, Calf Roper, Steer Roper and Steer Wrestler. *Photographer Unknown. Courtesy of the Jack Long Collection.*

The agreement made was that the members of the RAA must have their prize lists in circulation and printed in the RAA bulletin at least thirty days before their show and at that time there must be on file in the RAA office a guarantee that the prize money would be paid and then the contestants could determine whether they cared to go to the show or not and they would not go if they did not feel that sufficient money was being offered and that there would be no strikes by the contestants if these two requirements were complied with.

The contestants asked for the assistance of the RAA to secure at least an average of $100 per day in all events with the entrance fees added or, if the show retained the entrance fees, for an equivalent amount offered by the show, and the RAA officials personally agreed to encourage the increasing of the prize money with the aim of reaching this as soon as possible.

File Complaints with RAA. Complaints against any show must be filed with the RAA and not taken up with the show, if it failed to comply with any of the agreements that were made. It appears that some of the contestants have somewhat of a misunderstanding of what the agreement at Reno was and on the other hand some of the shows that were represented at Reno haven't complied themselves with their agreement.

This rodeo business is a business. The rodeo management must, if they expect to get the cooperation of the contestants, comply with their part of the agreement. By looking at the chart in this bulletin you will see that a large number of shows have not filed their prize lists and a great many have not filed their guarantees. It is true that a number have had difficulty in getting guarantees. Several shows lately have complied by placing in escrow the amount of prize money, with the escrow papers being sent to the RAA office. Judge McNutt has ruled that this is perfectly satisfactory. Also, if the institution is a public institution, such as county fairs, district fairs, and the board will send a certified copy of a resolution stating that they guarantee the prize money, Judge McNutt ruled that is satisfactory." [23]

Rules Made, Rules Broken

In the June, 1937 issue of *Hoofs & Horns* the RAA President Maxwell McNutt wrote a 'President's Message' and this is what it said:

"Dear Sir:

Under date of April 22nd you forwarded to me a letter dated April 20th, addressed to you as Secretary of Rodeo Association of America from Cowboy Turtle Association, Everett Bowman, President, copy of which follows:

Fred S. McCargar, Sec.
Rodeo Association of America
Salinas, California

Dear Mr. McCargar:

We, the Turtle Association, want cowboy judges and flagmen.

We want all shows to have their day monies divided 40-30-20-10 as well as final money. If the show does not belong to the RAA we do not guarantee the boys to enter after they get there as we want all shows to belong to the RAA as this is an insurance to the cowboys that the money will be paid.

We know there are probably several little shows which can't afford to put up large purses, but there are several that can. However, if the cowboys work for small purses at one show, they are oftentimes expected to work for similar purses at shows which can easily afford larger ones. So we feel that the Cowboys' Turtle Association should not protect a show which is smaller than one hundred dollars ($100.00) day money in each major event.

If the cowboys go to a show that pays less than one hundred dollars day money in each major event and fail to enter, it should not be held against the Turtle Association as there are too many shows that expect the cowboys to work for less.

We classify major events as bronc riding, calf roping, bull dogging, single steer roping and team roping. Bull riding is classified in the RAA as a major event and we feel that it should be, therefore it should be paid as a major event.

In our meeting at Fort Worth the bronc riders and bull riders selected approximately twenty-five (25) names of cowboys who are qualified judges; this list you should be in receipt of now. Evidently you have not received same as it has not been published in the RAA Bulletin to date. Perry Ivory should also be added to the list of judges.

We agreed to give a show thirty (30) days notice if its prize list was satisfactory, but we have had difficulty in getting the prize lists in time to give said notice.

We have passed on Cheyenne and Sheridan, Wyoming, prize lists and to date have experienced no difficulty. However, they agreed to let us split the money after the entrance fees were all in as we saw fit.

We want all shows to put up what they can afford and add all entrance fees without exception.

We would like for you to send every member of the RAA a letter telling them what the Cowboys' Turtle Association expects of each show. Then if the shows fail to comply with the Turtle Association rules and have trouble with the cowboys, it is their own fault as we want to do what is right.

>Very truly yours,
>(signed)
>Everett Bowman, Pres.
>Cowboys' Turtle Association"

"You ask my views thereon for the benefit of the directors of RAA and of its members; some years ago RAA was organized with the view of raising the quality of rodeos, protecting the interests and welfare of all involved, namely: the contestant, the animal, the organization holding individual shows and the public, or , as expressed in its constitution: 'The purpose for which this association is formed is: To insure harmony among the rodeo association in America and to perpetuate traditions connected with the livestock industry and cowboy sports incident thereto; to standardize rules looking towards the holding of contests upon uniform bases; to minimize so far as practicable conflict in dates of contests; and to place such sports so nearly as may be possible on a par with amateur athletic events.'

As a result of untiring and unselfish effort upon the part of our members, directors, and officers, much has been achieved, and the chief beneficiary of this endeavor, from a material standpoint, is the contestant. Not only has the organization brought better results from the individual show's standpoint, but it has increased the purses and prizes because of increased attendance. It has compelled every one of our members to lodge with the president of RAA a bank guarantee of the payment of every prize offered to a contestant in RAA events, and has harmonized the relationship between rodeos generally, and various protective societies, many of which have adopted our rules for their own guidance. It is a fact, unfortunately perhaps, that there are many human beings who can not balance success and power. No doubt persons of this quality fail to recognize that in the arbitrary exercise of this power are the seeds of destruction. The Cowboy Turtle Association had representatives at our last convention in Reno, held in January of this year, and there declared exactly what they wanted, with the result that between them and us, as representatives of our members, an agreement was reached. Almost immediately on the heels of that convention the Fiesta de los Vaqueros was to be held in Tucson. In violation of the agreement reached at Reno the Turtle Association, on the night before the show and when the entries were in progress, demanded under threat of strike, that the show accept from it a blacklist. It seems that one who had joined the Association had violated a rule thereof and had entered at Tucson. By request of the Turtle Association and of the Tucson management I arrived at Tucson the night before the show. It was evident to me that, if this man's entry fee were not returned, the show would not take place. The city was full of visitors who had come to witness the performance. On my suggestion, and over the protest of some of the individual directors of that show, the entrance fee of the undesired cowboy was returned and he was given expense money. The Turtle Association, through its representative, squarely promised that if this were done, all of its members would proceed to enter and the show would go on. Immediately thereafter, however, they demanded, as a condition of the participation of their members, that they name the three bronc riding judges. Thereupon Jack Kinney, President of the

Over-Anxious Turtles Cause Misunderstandings Page 57

Hoofs & Horns Magazine cover, edited by 'Ma' Hopkins from 1932. It became The official publication of the Cowboys' Turtle Association.

Tucson Rodeo and I left the meeting. A few minutes thereafter I was called upon in the hotel by a committee of the Turtle Association, asking me if I would come back to the meeting. I did so and endeavored to explain to them that no business could be conducted in that manner, that they were virtually in the position of one asserting a claim who demanded the right to name the three arbitrators. Of course, the show occupied no adversary relation to the contestants. We arrived at the expedient of having the Turtle Association name one, the show one, and two to name the third. The show went on and was successful.

Some weeks ago I received a letter from Mr. Roy W. Ritner, Business Manager of the Round-up at Pendleton, informing me that the cowboys (meaning CTA) had advised them that for the 1937 shows they demanded the right to choose judges and flagmen from their own ranks. Mr. Ritner sought my views upon that subject, and asked what stand the Association (RAA) would take. I deferred answering because I believed that in a short time the matter would be crystallized by a written demand from the Turtle Association upon some other show, and such has come about. The members of this Association have been led to believe, contrary to the fact, that our individual members conduct shows for mere personal profit and are making fortunes. They overlook the fact that this is true, namely: that the merchants of different communities underwrite shows, bear all the losses during the bad years, and when they make a profit put the same in to capital investment in the way of improvements. One cannot read the concluding paragraph of the Bowman letter without appreciating the menace of its tenor. Not only do I, as President of the RAA and a director thereof, disapprove of the policy laid down therein, but the same meets with my unqualified condemnation, and for the following reasons: first, it is diametrically opposed to the avowed purpose of that Association, as declared by its article of Association and bylaws; Second, it involves a breach of an agreement solemnly made by it, through its constituted officers; third, it is contrary to justice, decency and horse sense; fourth, it is utterly destructive of the constructive purposes of Rodeo Association of America; fifth, it is equally destructive of the possibility for success of individual shows; last, and perhaps more important than all, if Rodeo Association of America and its members are to be ousted of the reasonable control of a class of sports which requires harmonizing with the viewpoint of protective societies, it will become nothing but a business racket and very soon cease to exist. I do not know what the views of the other directors and our individual members may be, but consideration of self-respect would cause me to desist from having aught to do with an organization which will put up with arbitrary, unreasonable, and wholly selfish dominance by any one of the many elements or factors which go to make up the rodeos as an exhibition and a means of public enjoyment and recreation. It is perhaps true that in two or three of the large cities where our members give performances that they are, more or less dependent upon the Turtle Association. Such I believe is not the fact in those centers where shows are held in the cattle country. All of necessity started as amateurs and they will wind up that way. The rodeo is not a necessary institution. It exists for public edification and enjoyment, and when it ceases to have any aspect of sport it will not exist at all.

If the Turtle Association can point out that some individual flagman or timer is not competent, or that some individual judge is in the same category, that matter can be adjusted. Apparently, this Association desires to be given the means of making champions. I suggest that, if there are to be three judges of riding, that Turtle Association name one, the individual member name one, and RAA name one. Something in the nature of the same adjustment could be made with regard to the other field officials. It's members should bear in mind that no sport has endured after it has become a business to be exploited for the benefit of one class of participants therein. No more perfect analogy could exist than that between the instant situation and that of racing prior to 1910. The bookmaker had become the dominating factor. The riders and the men in charge of the stables had become to such an extent subservient to his will that the public became disgusted and racing, for almost a generation, was outlawed. It was brought back in this and in some other states through the adoption of laws creating racing, a position comparable to that of RAA in the rodeo field. While RAA exists and is governed by those whose only object is to protect the interest of all concerned, as above set forth, no legislation upon the subject is necessary. If its guidance is to be supplanted, law is the next step, and it will be a simple matter to draw a uniform rodeo bill which will, probably, result in the ultimate banning of bull-dogging and the use of tied ropes for contest purposes everywhere.

It may well be that our members are not greatly concerned as to how day monies are to be divided or allotted, but the idea that Turtle

Association shall have the right to dictate the amounts that are to be paid in my opinion has no basis in reason, and is intolerable. No one connected with Rodeos has been more concerned than have I to see contestants fairly treated, well paid and fairly judged, and no one will be, provided however that they act within the bounds of reason. I appeal to the sense of fairness of the individual contestant, as well as to that of the individual show, and trust that they may not be misled by fomenters of strife among them who are evidently averse to reason and sportsmanship. I suggest that you have mimeographed copies of this letter sent to the directors and members of RAA and to Cowboy Turtle Association.

You have asked that I go to the meeting at Saugus to discuss with Everett Bowman the matter involved. I cannot see that it will serve any good purpose for me to have further discussion with an organization which has up to date broken every agreement that it has made.

                 Very truly yours,
                 (Signed)
                 Maxwell McNutt"[30]

First, You Have To Get Their Attention

The July, 1937 issue of Hoofs & Horns had a follow-up President's Message from Mr. McNutt:

"Office of Maxwell McNutt, President, Rodeo Ass'n of America to Fred S. McCargar, Secretary RAA, Salinas, California

My Dear Sir:

The RAA Bulletin for May carried a letter to RAA from Everett Bowman, President of the Cowboy Turtle Association, and my reply thereto. On Friday May 14, pursuant to Mr. Bowman's request, a meeting was had with him, Elton Hebbron, Third Vice President of RAA, Fred S. McCargar, Secretary thereof, and myself. The spirit of this meeting, while to some extent informal, was most friendly in character. Mr. Bowman told us that perhaps his letter had contained things which he did not intend or were capable of misinterpretation, and that all he and his organization wished was harmony and cooperation with the managements of our members. In substance, the complaints of the contestants, as expressed by him, are that the amounts paid by managements are in, in some instances, insufficient, and that the judging, flagging and timing at some of the shows are unsatisfactory. So far as concerns amounts paid I agreed that I would do all in my power to so increase the purses offered by our various members that a minimum of $100 per day net to contestants in each of the major events would be established; that the matter would receive consideration at our next convention at Ogden. I am mindful, however, that there was no precise definition given by Mr. Bowman as to what comprised 'major events'.

In the matter of judging, we agreed with Mr. Bowman that from time to time there had been errors of judgment and that flagging and timing had on occasions not been up to standard, and that in consequence everything should be done to obtain the services of the best officials possible; I explained, however, or at least endeavored to, that contestants should not be allowed to be judges in shows in which they were participants, as such course would not be in keeping with that pursued in any line of sport or contests. On the other hand, we agreed that judges who were not satisfactory to contestants should either give way or be replaced by those as to whose qualifications no question could arise. Mr. Bowman agreed that the contestants would write the managements of our various members, giving the names of men who, as judges, had not in the past proved satisfactory to the contestants. I agreed to present this matter to the members of the RAA and ask them to accept the condition that, if they received timely notice in advance of objections to named or proposed judges, that the management should select others. Should a majority of the contestants at any show express dissatisfaction with those selected to serve as judges, I suggest that a new judge be secured in the place of the one who is not desired, we made it clear that the managements must remain free to select the judges, and that they be not compelled to pick them from particular lists. Mr. Bowman read a list of those who had been selected by his association as proper material to judge shows, and I must say that on that list I observed that there were many men for whom I have, as the result of personal contact and friendship, both in point of ability and honor, the very highest regard. I feel that it is fair that one who assumes to act as the judge of bronc riding (or bull riding) should be a person who, at some time or another, has been a contestant.

In consideration of the offer on my part to make these recommendations and to endeavor to take such steps as will bring about a satisfactory understanding at our next meeting at Ogden, Mr. Bowman informs us that he was authorized by the Turtle Association to agree, and hence did agree, that for the remainder of the rodeo year, the contestants would make no direct demands on any members of RAA for further increase in purses, and would not threaten strikes on the eve of shows.

I believe that the above views fairly reflect the result of the conference referred to.

> Yours sincerely,
> Maxwell McNutt" [31]

It was extremely important that the two organizations work together for the good of professional rodeo. Since the RAA had been formed seven years earlier, they were much more in command as to how and what could be accomplished. The respect for RAA, and their directors, had been established with member rodeo committees across the country. RAA could do much to assist the novice Turtle Association as they made efforts with various rodeos to improve and comply with Turtle rules. There were 102 RAA member rodeos across the United States in 1937 including some of the oldest and biggest in the country – Prescott, Pendleton, Calgary, Cheyenne, Madison Square Garden, Sidney, etc.

Over-Anxious Turtles Cause Misunderstandings

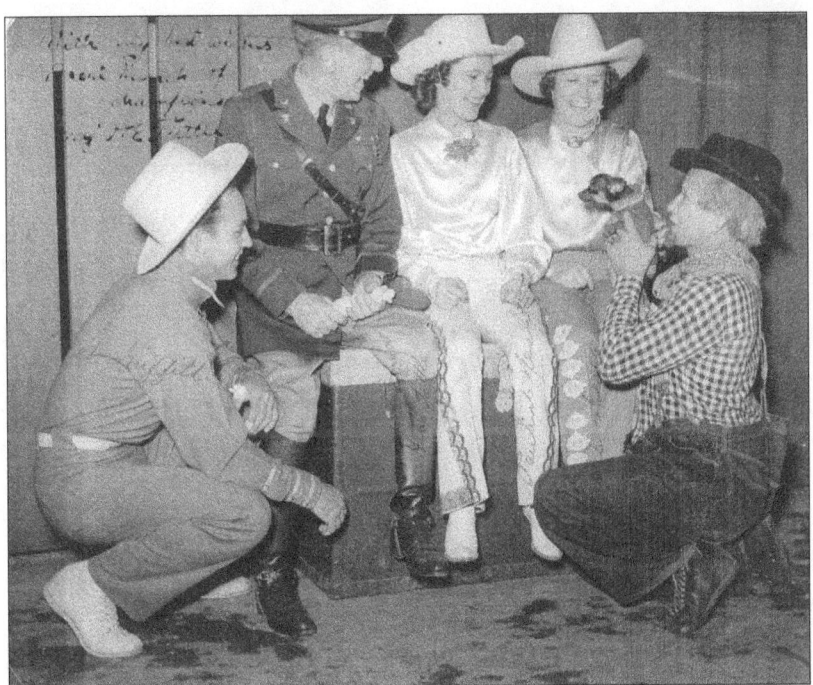

Homer Holcomb, rodeo clown kneeling on right, entertaining (left to right) Dick Griffith, Major Hiram E. Tuttle, dressage artist. Pauline Nesbitt, and Gene Creed at Denver Stock Show & Rodeo, 1939. *Photographer Unknown. Courtesy of Jack Long Collection.*

CHAPTER SIX

Rodeos Threaten To Go Non-Professional

The Cowboys' Turtle Association's problems were still not solved. The RAA Secretary's Message in the October, 1937 issue of *Hoofs & Horns* reported:

"COWBOYS' TURTLE ASSOCIATION- There is a general feeling of dissatisfaction over the activities of the Cowboy Turtle Association and some of its members, by a number of member shows of the RAA. Commencing with the strike at Tucson, the beginning of the year, down to the present time, there has been trouble at a number of shows. At least a half dozen of them have signified their intention to go non-professional next year.

It is the opinion of many, that the cowboys have violated their promise they made at Reno and the one made by Everett Bowman, on their behalf, with Judge McNutt, later in the summer.

According to the latter agreement, the cowboys were going on and finish this year out, without causing trouble to any member show which definitely puts up its guarantee at least thirty days prior to the show.

In spite of this, Ellensburg, Washington, received certain demands, but we have not heard what decision was reached there. Hinton, Oklahoma, had some trouble and immediately put their show on a non-professional basis. According to reports, their show was a success.

They stated the strike hurt their show on the first day but after that the amateur cowboys came in and both the public and the local cowboys were more than satisfied. Monte Vista, Colorado, writes that the Cowboy Turtle Association made certain demands on them, all of which were granted.

At the time we are going to press with this bulletin, Pendleton is having a controversy with the cowboys, who are demanding that they name the judges. Pendleton is insisting on their right to name the judges and are being definitely backed by Judge McNutt in their position.

There have been many letters written as to what took place in Salinas. This is the first year that Salinas used cowboy judges. In Calf Roping, the flag judge gave John Bowman time, but sometime later changed his decision and gave him no time, claiming that Bowman did not let his calf up before he threw him down and tied him. The money was paid according to the judge's decision, but the California Rodeo has decided to give Bowman the amount he would have won, or $450.00.

The question of points, however, is a rather serious one. At the Reno convention it was voted that no show would be allowed to give more money than advertised in its prize lists, the obvious reason being to protect the early RAA shows against "upping' during the last part of the season, in order to win the RAA championships.

The matter has been submitted to the Directors of the RAA for decision. Cheyenne is in somewhat the same position. They have paid double in three different cases and the question is, should both winners be given points." [32]

Busy Third Turtle Board Meeting

The third meeting of the Cowboys Turtle Association was held at Cheyenne, Wyo., July 27, 1937, the minutes were as follows:

"Everett Bowman, President in the chair.

Officers present were:
   Everett Bowman, Pres.   Rusty McGinty, Vice-Pres.
   Hugh Bennett, Sec.-Treas.

Representatives:
- Harry Knight, Bronc Riding
- Hughie Long, Bare-back bronc riding
- Eddie Curtis, Steer Riding
- Dick Truitt, Bull dogging
- Everett Shaw, Calf Roping

"A motion was made by Everett Bowman, President, that the money at Cheyenne, Wyo. be divided 60% day money, 40% average. 40-30-20-10 percents. It passed unanimously.

A motion was made by Eddie Curtis that steer money all divided into day money, no finals. It passed unanimously.

Hughie Long motioned bare back money all divided into day money, no finals. Passed.

Motion was made by Everett Bowman and seconded by Dick Truitt that no members of the Cowboys' Turtle Association to contest at rodeos holding entrance fees, instead of adding and to advise of same in ample time before dates to open.

Objection by Eddie Curtis that if entry fee added before show starts should be good enough. Motion as made by Everett Bowman passed.

Eddie Curtis appointed to notify Hinton, Oklahoma, regards entry fee to be added.

Everett Bowman motioned to have a bona fide set of rules to present to R.A.A. meeting at Ogden, Utah for 1938. Passed.

Everett Bowman motioned that membership fee be $25.00 after end of 1937. All that are not charter members must pay $25.00. Passed.

Motion made by Everett Shaw that all members abide by Committee and Representatives decisions and that all shows live up to and abide by Rules set down by Cowboys' Turtle Association. Passed. Motion by Floyd Stillings that all shows use active contestant judges, as Turtle rules call for but have not been lived up to. Passed.

Motion by Hugh Bennett that a set of Turtle Rules be gotten up on or before the next R.A.A. meeting and be gotten up in a printed form so as all members can have set of Rules and by-laws. A copy to be mailed to all shows for 1938. Passed.

Motion by Everett Shaw that any one during a meeting be required to raise their hand and get approval of whoever is occupying the chair before speaking during Cowboys' Turtle Association meeting. Failure to raise hand before talking and getting approval from chair subjects member to a 25 cent fine. Passed.

Motion by Red Thompson that cowboys be allowed to work but not to contest at shows that are not in line with Cowboys Turtle Association. Passed.

Motion by Irby Mundy to stick and stay with your Representatives decision. Passed.

Motion by Hughie Long for bare back riders to draw stock and have regulation rigging. Judges to draw chutes. Passed.

Motion by Everett Bowman that a vote be taken by all Turtles that were at Boston, Mass., whether or not the $500.00 fine assessed stands. 18 for. 1 against.

Motion by Rusty McGinty that any and all disputes be settled by a two-thirds majority vote of various representatives. In case representatives not present, one man from each event to be selected. In the event a tie vote among representatives the matter to be decided by the President. Motion seconded by Eddie Woods.

Motion by Burel Mulkey for Hamley Saddles with a 15 inch tree to be used at all 1938 shows. Passed.

Harry Knight resigns as Representative of Bronc Riding. Resignation accepted.

Nominations:
  Burel Mulkey   Floyd Stillings   Hub Whiteman

Secret vote by Bronc Riders present. Result of vote:
Burel Mulkey – 14
Floyd Stillings – 6
Hub Whiteman – 4

Mulkey elected and made a talk to boys. Mulkey will try to get all R.A.A. shows to post markings of all judges, markings totaled together of each contestant.

Slogan adopted by all Turtles present 'UNITED WE STAND. DIVIDED WE FALL'

Meeting called to order and dismissed by Everett Bowman." [33]

It was evident, that the CTA and Board of Directors, Representatives, and members still had much work to do. Although the rules were made and circulated which stated that RAA rodeos were suppose to inform RAA and CTA, in a significant amount of time so that a response could be made 30 days in advance of the rodeo, it didn't always happen. Reports stated that RAA member rodeos didn't always get their prize list in within the time required as intended. Maybe the criticism of last-minute actions by certain Turtles happened because rodeos were late in posting their information. It appeared that the blame should not be directed to the Turtles but to those rodeos that refused to send information in time, as requested.

A Follow-Up Meeting Held Three Days Later

July 30, 1937 a Cowboys' Turtle Association meeting was held. The minutes read:

"The meeting was opened at 8:30 PM. There were twelve members present. Everett Bowman was President of the meeting. Minutes of the meeting that was held July 27th at Cheyenne, Wyoming, were read and amended. All of the motions were accepted by the members except number 12, but it was decided that it would be left as is at the present in the steer riding event. (*This is confusing, as there was no mention of steer riding in the minutes of the July 27th meeting*)

Motion was made by Everett Bowman that any member of our Association found guilty of beating his room or board bill must pay this debt before being allowed to work or contest at any rodeo. Second offense would be fined according to the amount of the debt. Seconded by Eddie Curtis.

Motion was made by Everett Bowman and seconded by Dick Truitt that at present we use the magazine "Hoofs & Horns" for our official publication.

Motion was made by Herman Linder that the Association send to the Editor of the Hoofs & Horns the sum of $50.00 for our appreciation for what they have done for the Cowboys' Turtle Association. This was seconded by all members present.

Motion was made by Everett Shaw and seconded by Rusty McGinty that a list of judges be sent to the Hoofs & Horns magazine to be published.

Letter from Pueblo, Colorado Fair Committee was read and discussed. Also letter was read by Herman Linder from Livingston, Montana, Rodeo Committee in regards to the rodeo held there, also about the judges that were being used from the Dude Ranch country.

Telegram was sent to Mr. Means, Head of the Fair Committee at Pueblo, Colo.. A clipping from one of the Calgary newspapers was read by Herman Linder in regards to our Cowboys' Turtle Association.

A letter was written to Hamley Saddle Shop of Pendleton, Oregon, in regards to the saddles to be used in the Bronc riding. Must be 15 inch Hamley regulation Association saddle, made for all rodeo promoters. No orders to be made in the future like the ones made for Johnson for the spring of 1935. We insist that Hamley saddles be the only rodeo saddle to be used in the Bronc riding." [34]

Bart Clennon, age 100 as of this writing, said Colonel Johnson had new association saddles made every year by Hamley's for the bronc riding. Every one knows that saddle bronc riders don't like 'new' saddles and do all sorts of things to 'break them in'. Casey Tibbs even soaked his in the bath tub and ran over it with a pickup truck. Johnson's new saddles were always used for the first time at the Madison Square Garden rodeo, and when they arrived they were packed in oil cloth and sewed inside a gunny sack.

Bart recalled, "There were ten chutes at Madison Square Garden and Johnson had one saddle made for each chute. We'd have to cut 'em out of the gunny sacks and set our stirrups. In 1935, the saddles were not made right and we found them damn hard to ride. The three-quarter riggin' that was usually placed half-way between the swell and the centerfire, was cock-eyed."

Bart Clennon celebrating at his 100th birthday celebration in Marana, Arizona, at the Cattleman's Café, November 5, 2010. *Photograph taken by and courtesy of Donna Clark & Imogene Veach Beals.*

Derek Clark, former National Finals saddle bronc rider and former member of the PRCA board, explained that if the riggings on each side aren't parallel it makes the saddle pull crooked and would definitely be tough to ride. [#144]

Bart went on to add, "Stub Bartlemay went to Hamley's and found the two saddle makers who made those saddles for Johnson, and they admitted they'd placed the riggings cock-eyed on Johnson's request. The next year at Madison Square Garden, Stub turned his stock out he was so disgusted!" [#142]

October 8, 1937 CTA Meeting

"The meeting was called to order by Everett Bowman, in the chair at 11 o'clock A. M. October 8, 1937. Ten members were present. The minutes of the last meeting were read by the secretary, Hugh Bennett. Motion made by Hughie Long and seconded by Rusty McGinty that the minutes of the last meeting be accepted as correct.

Discussion was made on Tom Breedon's fine. Everett Shaw made a motion to let Tom Breedon compete at Madison Square Garden upon a receipt of an order from Tom Breedon for his wages at the Garden to make good his back fine.

A motion was made by Jack Kerscher, seconded by Rusty McGinty that all active rodeo contestants that follow the rodeo business and make their living that way, must pay $25.00 to become a member after 1937, if not a member, young boys showing class coming up, may become members for the regular fee of $5.00. Dues must be paid at first show he attends before allowed to work in 1938.

It was decided not to have a hearing of the boys who worked at the rodeo at Pueblo, Colo., Ellensburg, Wash., Hinton, Okla., and Pendleton, Ore., until the Fort Worth, Texas meeting. All of those contestants that worked at the above rodeos are to be barred from Turtle shows until after their hearing at Fort Worth." [35]

A Special CTA Meeting Held in New York City

The minutes read:

"A special meeting was held by the members of the Cowboys' Turtle Association, October 22, 1937 at 1:30 O'clock at New York City.

The meeting was called to order by Everett Bowman, President of the Cowboys' Turtle Association.

> Officers present were:
> Everett Bowman, President
> Rusty McGinty, 2nd Vice President
> Herman Linder, 1st Vice President
> Hugh Bennett, Secretary-Treasurer

Representatives present were:
 Everett Shaw, Calf-roper
 Dick Truitt, Bull-Dogger
 Burel Mulkey, Bronc Rider
 Eddie Curtis, Steer Rider
 Hughie Long, Bare-back Rider

Visitors:
Floyd Gale   Herb Myers   Floyd Stillings
Smokey Snyder   Doff Aber   Tom Breedon

The special meeting was held for the purpose of making some new rules for 1938.

Rule I. At all shows or rodeos for the year of 1938 all entrance fees must be added in each event to prize money

Rule II. Each rodeo must have as their judges for their rodeo, two active cowboy contestants (*scratched out was 'who are members of the Cowboys' Turtle Association'*).

Rule III. All members of the Cowboys' Turtle Association are not allowed to compete at any amateur rodeo or work in any way connected with the rodeo.

Rule IV. Any cowboy who makes as many as four (4) rodeos in one (1) year shall be classed as a professional, and must have a Cowboys' Turtle Association card before entering at any rodeo contest in 1938.

Rule V. Any member of the Cowboys' Turtle Association who leaves a room or board bill, the Cowboys Turtle Association will pay them, or any other bill they see fit to pay. Cowboys that owe bills of this kind will not be permitted to contest or work at any rodeo until the CTA is paid in full. They will be subject to a fine also.

Rule VI. Instead of the Cowboys' Turtle Association giving a thirty (30) day notice to a rodeo that the members of the Cowboys' Turtle Association will work after they get to a rodeo or show, let each show write to the CTA if they want a guarantee that the members will work after they get there and have it printed on their prize list "OK by the CTA Officials". No member will be allowed to go to any show or rodeo after the CTA Officials have passed on their prize list and Judges, and raise a "fuss". If the contestants are not satisfied with what the Officials have done, they should stay away. The Officials of the CTA should have plenty of time to see all the Representatives of the CTA and each Representative and president sign his name to the OK.

Rule VII. Any contestant that has contested at any place where the CTA has refused to work, then he shall be fined before he can work again with the members of the CTA. Any time any member of the CTA finds a boy contesting, or working on the chutes or with stock, who has not lived up to the rules of the CTA, should report this boy to the Management of this rodeo, and his entrance fees should be refunded and not be allowed to contest, or work in the arena or with the stock, until he has squared himself with the CTA.

Rule VIII. Any cowboy who is paying on a fine, should pay not less than $50.00 down and ¼ of what he wins until his fine has been paid. The first time he refuses or neglects to send in ¼ of what he wins, then he is laying himself liable, to be put out again and forfeits all he has paid on his fine.

Rules presented by Hughie Long, representative of Bare-back Riders, for 1938.

Rule I. That bare-back riders be allowed to use their own riggings, if rigging is not over ten (10) inches in width at hand hold, and not over a six inch in D ring, or not a freak. Judges to decide on freak rigging.

Rule II. Horses to be numbered and drawn for by the Judges at all shows.

Rule III. Rider who is knocked off or horse falls out of chute, to be entitled to a re-ride on the same horse.

Rule IV. All shows having bare-back riding will have it as a contest event, not mount money or exhibition.

Rodeos Threaten to Go Non-Professional

Rule V. (Submitted by Hughie Long) Any rider "suckin" around judges be fined not less than ten (10) points

Meeting adjourned by Everett Bowman, President, of Cowboys Turtle Association." [36]

(The above Rules I through VIII (excluding the bareback rules that followed) were printed on an 8"x 14" legal size sheet of paper titled 'COWBOYS' TURTLE ASSOCIATION RULES FOR 1938. (Subject to change at R.A.A. Convention)' written under the title. [37]

Paul Bond, CTA #395, remembered the Turtle days fondly. He joined in 1937 at the Tucson rodeo, with his friend, Bobby Wilkinson, CTA #463. Paul was a bronc rider, a trick rider, and today is known for his expertise in making custom boots at the Paul Bond Boot Company, Nogales, Ariz. Paul said, "The Turtles did a lot more than get the prize money raised. Some of the cowboys were bandits, and the promoters, too. They got rid of the guys writing hot checks and running off with the money. They improved the conduct of the cowboy." [10]

Frank Quirk, CTA #441, a bull rider, had heard all about the Turtles before he joined. He was told by other cowboys that they would not mark a cowboy who was not a Turtle. He gave $5.00 to Everett Bowman at the end of the 1937 season and told him he wanted to join the Turtles. Everett responded, "Frank, the season is over. It won't do you any good now." And with that, Bowman tried to hand back to him his five dollar bill. Frank said, "You had better take it now, because next spring I might not have it." The following spring, at the Fort Worth rodeo, Bowman brought Frank his Turtle card and pin. [138]

Meanwhile, in the world of competition the cowboys listed below had the following RAA points at the end of the 1937 and were declared World Champions. *(Note: no entry fees were included in points toward championships by RAA).*

All Around World Champion in 1937 was Everett Bowman with 7021 points. Those next in points for All-Around were:

Burel Mulkey	5518
Eddie Woods	5389
Paul Carney	5149
Smoky Snyder	4952

RAA World Champions in their events were:
- Bareback Riding – Paul Carney, Galeton, Colo.
- Steer Wrestling – Gene Ross, Sayre, Okla.
- Team Roping – Asbury Schell, Camp Verde, Ariz.
- Saddle Bronc Riding – Burel Mulkey, Salmon, Idaho
- Calf Roping – Everett Bowman, Hillside, Ariz.
- Steer Roping – Everett Bowman, Hillside, Ariz. [20]

World Champion Rodeo Cowboy & Cowgirl Contestants, taken at City Hall, New York City, 1937. *Photo by Edward J. Kelty of Century Photography. Courtesy of the Dickinson Research Center, National Cowboy & Western Heritage Museum.*

CHAPTER SEVEN

Turtles Still Getting Opposition

The first year was a tough one for the Turtles. It was also a learning curve for those cowboys who were so dedicated to the improvement of the sport. They got their hands slapped from time to time for their efforts to get more qualified judges, amongst other demands but they didn't waiver. A well known example is Pendleton RoundUp refusing the requests by Turtle representatives, as expressed in the following letter which was sent to RAA, and published in the November *Hoofs & Horns* under the title 'R.A.A. Shows and Turtle Assn. Disagree.' A letter from H. L. Anderson, President of the Ellensburg Rodeo, Ellensburg, Wash., said, in part:

"In regards to the Ellensburg Rodeo – We went Non-Professional, and put on one of our best shows. The crowd was larger and more enthusiastic than ever before. Pendleton also went Non-Professional, and had the same results. From Oregon, Washington, and Idaho we have truly Western Cowboys that will give those Turtles a run for their money. Our show was started as a community proposition and we intend to keep it as such." [41]

A second letter from Pendleton RoundUp to RAA read, in part:

"The Turtle Association has notified us that they will not compete at Pendleton unless they can name their own judges. Our Board of Directors is unanimous in the opinion that we should run our own show and we have appointed three very competent judges who have served several times in the past; William Switzler of Umatilla, Ben Boone of Seattle and Allen Drumheller of Walla Walla. They have all been cowboys in their younger days and Drumheller has contested many times in relay races at the RoundUp. We feel that we would sooner give up holding the RoundUp than to permit a bunch of outsiders to run it for their own benefit." [42]

CTA Pin made in to a ring, by Pete Kerscher. *Photographer unknown. Courtesy of D'Lyla Kerscher Longo.*

Pendleton RoundUp held off from allowing the Turtles to compete for their rodeo in 1937 and 1938, but by 1939 they and the Turtles had resolved their differences. Ellensburg eventually accepted the Turtles demands as well.

But not all feelings from rodeo committees were so negative. The following letter to Mr. Everett Bowman from Herbert S. Maddy of the JE (Eskew) Ranch Rodeo read:

"Please accept my sincere thanks for the $45.00 check covering the indebtedness to us incurred by one of your members. The action was prompt and decisive and more was accomplished in a week through the Turtles than I was able to accomplish in months.

I trust that we will never again have to bother you all with any other bills of a like nature but, if any turn up I sure know where to go for action.

It is a pleasure to know that you and your officials are striving to make your personnel clean. That was a fine gesture, Mr. Bowman, and one the officials deserve credit for.

And your purse to the mother of that unfortunate Oklahoma cowboy (Walter Cravens, age 29, was killed from injuries sustained in a Brahma bull ride Oct. 9) who met his death at the Garden show (Madison Square Garden), was another gesture of kindness and sympathy that the Great Arena Director of the Universe will surely reward the boys for.

So, Mr. Bowman, count me as a true friend of the Turtles. Any time I can be of any help to the Association, call on me and I will respond to the best of my ability." #42

Another letter printed in the December issue of *Hoofs & Horns* to Hugh Bennett from J. C. Howe, a committee member of the Sidney, Iowa, rodeo read:

"Dear Hugh, This will acknowledge receipt of your letter containing Everett Bowman's check in the amount of $18.25, said check being for payment of a member's unpaid check for 1936 entry fees at the Sidney rodeo. Thanks very much for straightening out this matter, Hugh, as the boys appreciate the courtesy. It also puts in another good lick in favor of the Turtle association insofar as the Sidney gang is concerned.

With best regards to the gang, Mrs. Bennett and yourself, I remain – J.C. Howe." #42

In the December, 1937, issue of *Hoofs & Horns* a full page was allotted for the Turtle Association. In that issue, in addition to the two letters listed above, it consisted of a list of 439 CTA members, their Turtle number and their hometown.

In the same issue, the RAA column had a report from Secretary McCargar on the up-coming RAA convention in Ogden, Utah, January 7 and 8, 1938. It stated, "that the Turtle Association representatives did not feel they had adequate time at the RAA 1937 convention to present their requests. This year they will have 15 minutes to outline their requests and the reasons for same, provided that the paper to be presented be in the RAA office, in Salinas, Calif., by December 20th."
There were more letters from some of the same rodeos that had written letters previously in retaliation of the Turtles demands. In fact, a letter from Roy Ritner of Pendleton RoundUp reviewed all of the differences between the Turtles and RoundUp and finished his letter by stating:

"If Calgary, Cheyenne, Salinas and Fort Worth would stand together we could eliminate this organization (CTA) from dominating our shows."

Phil M. Tobin, President of the Nevada Rodeo wrote:

"The night preceding the Winnemucca show on September 4th, 5th and 6th, a number of bucking contestants came to me and advised me that unless the judges and flagmen for the show were members of the Turtle Association that they would not ride. Inasmuch as I had selected one Turtle Association member for a judge from the two that we put on, and also employed a Turtle Association member as a flagman, I felt that I should be entitled to the selection of one judge.

I so advised them, and further advised them that until such time as the cowboys were signing the checks I would continue to run the show. They finally decided to appear, but intimated to me that next year they would not show unless field judges and flagmen were men of their own selection.

I appreciate very much the fact that the transient cowboys who are members of the Turtle Association contribute considerably toward the show, and it is my desire to cooperate with them in every way. However, it is not my intention to permit them to run the show, as long as I am responsible for its successful operation, and I feel that I am within my rights in reserving the privilege of selecting men as judges and at the same time to cooperate with the desires of the contestants.

For the information of your Association, if it is to be a regular practice of the professional contestants to stage a strike on the night preceding the show, I propose to next year put on my rodeo with local men and local horses." #42

Another Voice Heard

Under the RAA column, December 13, 1937, printed in the January issue of *Hoofs & Horns* a letter from Doff Aber, a well-known rodeo cowboy, from Wolf, Wyo., who would become World Champion Saddle Bronc Rider in 1941 and '42. He wrote to the RAA Secretary, Fred S. McCargar:

"Dear Fred: After reading reports from several Rodeo Managers and committees, that the Turtles are trying to run their shows I decided to say a word to all concerned, that we are trying to make a living from these shows, just as they are from their various chosen businesses.

They don't want men to run their business that aren't qualified to do so; why should we – I am very sorry to say, that very few ranchmen or old-time contestants, are capable of judging modern contests, as the rules change year by year and as in any other business, one has to be in constant touch with it to be capable of judging.

I played football ten or twelve years ago – but could I, with the constant changing rules – go see a game once a year – and still be a capable referee? I think not. And yet we are asked to perform under just such conditions.

Doff Aber, World Champion Saddle Bronc Rider, 1941 and 1942. *Photographer Unknown. Courtesy of Stan Searle from the Hoofs & Horns Collection.*

Naturally the directors of some of the shows think that we are trying to run their business, but on the other hand if they would just try to see our side of the argument, we can perhaps come to a better understanding.

Mr. Ritner, of Pendleton, has made a rather broad statement about several shows standing together to discredit the 'Turtles,' perhaps Mr. Ritner, at least two of the shows you mentioned would rather have 'Turtles'. They aren't situated in a part of the country, where non-professionals are prevalent enough to support their type of show.

Perhaps you don't realize, Mr. Ritner, that your winners every one were professional cowboys, following Rodeos for a living. None of them good enough to win their events where the going was tough, one exception, Bill McMackin, in the riding event.

Fred, I've seen all the association letters printed and would certainly like to see one of the cowboys' letters in your Bulletins. Respectfully, Doff Aber." #43

1938 Rodeo Association of America Convention

The January RAA Convention was extremely important to the Cowboys' Turtle Association members. The past year had been one of turmoil and opposition, yet the new cowboy group was determined to get better results at rodeos for cowboys that spent their life as a professional cowboy trying to make a living in rodeo. It was admittedly an awkward time for the fledgling association. Although everyone had similar goals for improvement of the sport, it often was handled in ways that caused dissention, frustration and made some rodeo representatives 'downright mad!' Many committees were threatening to hold non-professional rodeos to keep the 'Turtles' from interfering with their rodeos. "Who do they think they are?" was a catch-phrase often used during this time in reference to the Turtle organization. The up-coming RAA convention, where the CTA was to present their demands, rule changes and the reasons for them, was tremendously important toward the future success of the CTA. Everyone would be listening and expecting them to fail. Some RAA members just knew the CTA would continue to cause trouble. Would it end up that way?

The Cowboys' Turtle Association pulled off their presentation at the convention without a hitch, much to everyone's surprise. Jimmie Minotto, of Arizona, was asked to be the spokesman for the Turtles. The report of the RAA Convention, and the part the Cowboys' Turtle Association played in it, was written by Jimmie Minotto in the February issue of *Hoofs & Horns*.

He wrote:

"Dear 'Ma' Hopkins: As you know I went to the Rodeo Association of America convention at Ogden, Utah, last week at the request of the officers and directors of the Cowboys' Turtle Association and was asked to act as spokesman for the Turtles.

After the convention adjourned Everett Bowman, Dick Truitt, Burel Mulkey, Hughie Long, Everett Shaw, and Eddie Curtis asked me to

Directors of RAA, 1938 RAA Convention, Ogden, Utah. Top row, left to right: Laurenson of Idaho; Richardson of Alberta Canada; Kinney of Arizona; Kressmann of Illinois; Frank of Montana and Ritner of Oregon. Middle row, left to right: Hebbron, 3rd VP of California; Sadlier 1st VP of Nevada; McNutt, President of California; Sylvester 2nd VP of Colorado; McCarger, Secretary of California. Bottom row, left to right: Jim Howe of Iowa; Mayor Perry of Ogden, UT; Frank Moore of New York, and Unknown. *Photographer Link-Tiffan. Courtesy of Stan Searle from the Hoofs & Horns Collection.*

give you a brief report of what happened at Ogden, so that all of us Turtles who read *Hoofs and Horns* would get some information from our side. This is particularly important, since some of the newspapers have not given an accurate account of what took place.

We submitted to the Board of Directors of the RAA our various requests, such as, that all entrance fees must be added to the purses, that judges should be elected from a list submitted by the Turtles, and that all professional contestants should be members of the Cowboys' Turtle Association. We also wanted to have changes made in the rules governing various contests.

On the other hand the RAA wanted to give up the rule that all shows must put up a guarantee for the purses that they advertise for the various events. We had a number of long drawn out meetings at which all this was discussed back and forth.

Finally we presented our requests before the convention at the morning meeting, January 7th. During the noon recess we came to the conclusion, that we would not be able to have the RAA delegates accept our requests regarding our appointment of judges and also were advised by nearly all the delegates that while they considered the Turtles the most important part of the contest, they would not stand for all professionals being obliged to be Turtles. Maxwell McNutt, the RAA President brought this out very forcefully and convincingly, that the cowboy was the greatest sportsman of all, and that his whole standing in the eyes of the American public would suffer untold damage if it appeared that contests were no longer open to the world and championships could only be won with a union card. Also that it was unheard of that champions and contestants can select their own judges.

All of us felt that there was a great deal of merit in what was said by the other side and, after all, the success of rodeos and the success of the Turtles depend entirely on how the public feels about cowboy contests. We therefore settled down and made a compromise, that we feel was fair to all concerned and that certainly placed the Turtles in a very advantageous position, not only as far as the American public is concerned, but also in the eyes of the RAA and all rodeo managements.

AT NO TIME was there any fight or any refusal of our demands in open session. Everything went off as smoothly as possible. Here is what we all agreed on:

1. All entrance fees must be added to the purses.

2. All RAA contests must put up a guarantee for the money prizes they advertise, so that the contestants are sure to get their money after the contests are over.

3. Only qualified judges will be selected by the various rodeo managements, these judges can be members of the Cowboys' Turtle Association and the list of judges for all RAA shows must be submitted to the RAA Secretary, Fred S. McCargar at Salinas, Calif. The Turtles have the right to object, through their Officers and Directors to any judge that they don't consider qualified. At the time of such objection

Turtle members attending the 1938 RAA Convention in Ogden, Utah. Left to right: Herman Linder, Huey Long, Eddie Curtis, Everett Bowman, Jimmie Minotto, Dick Truitt, Everett Shaw and Burel Mulkey. *Photographer unknown. Courtesy of Imogene Veach Beals.*

cause must be stated in writing and if cause for objection is justified such judge will be removed by the RAA.

All changes of rules in various contests that were submitted by us were granted.

Another important matter that was settled is, that there will be no trouble at either the Pendleton Roundup or at the Ellensburg, Washington, rodeo this year. The Turtles will be welcome and the incidents of last year will not occur in 1938. I believe that many Turtles will be pleased to know that they are not barred from contesting at local shows, which means a great deal to all concerned.

As you know the meeting was one of the best and most harmonious that has ever taken place between two organizations and gave the Turtles a wonderful opportunity to become a great organization in 1938.

The Turtles know that the cowboys are true sportsmen, whom have always been the idols of American children and they deserve to continue to be.

I feel that a bit of history was made at the Ogden meeting. In this day of strikes and lockouts, sit-downs, and threats of retaliation, and the general use of force, the Turtles settled their problems with the RAA as true sportsmen. They wanted the assurance of fair and impartial judges and they got it and now the machinery is set up by the RAA to provide the Turtles the protection from exploitation and biased judges which their skill and sportsmanship deserve.

Great credit for this accomplishment goes to Everett Bowman, Dick Truitt, Eddie Curtis, Burel Mulkey, Everett Shaw, Hughie Long, Herman Linder, Andy Jauregui, Jimmie Nesbitt, Leonard Ward, Smoky Snyder, Richard Merchant, Harry Knight, Pete and Jack Kerscher, Perry Ivory, and other Turtles that were present. Also credit should be given to Maxwell McNutt and Fred S. McCargar for the fine way in which they did their part to make this such a splendid and successful meeting.

I plan to be at the annual Turtle Convention at Fort Worth, Texas, in March and hope to meet everybody and tell them in person all about what happened. I also want to suggest that we have a speaker of national prominence talk to us Turtles at that time, so that the people and the newspapers, in particular, know that the Turtles are not only a fine organization, but that they have the respect and good will of every one that admires a real and true sportsman. Sincerely, Jimmie Minotto" [44]

The *RAA Bulletin* published in the same issue of *Hoofs & Horns* also had a report on the Ogden Convention by RAA Secretary Fred S. McCargar, and he reported, in part:

"The 1938 convention of the RAA at Ogden is now one of history and it was the unanimous opinion of everyone that it was the most outstanding and the most worthwhile meeting of contest managers and contestants ever held anywhere, anytime."

Later in his report he said:

"The outstanding accomplishments of the convention were made possible not only by the spirit of give and take and the 100% true sportsmanship of everyone, but by the fact that the Cowboys' Turtle Association had as their spokesman their own member, James Minotto, of Phoenix, Ariz. The thoroughness, the sincerity, clearness, forcefulness, coolness, and fairness of the way he presented the Turtle Association side of the case – the generosity not only toward contests and contest managers, but also toward other contestants, not members of the Turtle Association, was to me one of the finest demonstration of leadership that I have ever seen and it is a wonder he was given the title of 'Minotto the Miracle-man.'"

McCargar's report was quite lengthy and included all the changes made in the rules of each event, but it was also noted to member rodeos that "if any variation from the standard rules of the RAA are to be enforced it needs to be printed with the prize list.' The prize list is required to be sent to RAA and CTA 30 days prior to their event." [44]

CHAPTER EIGHT
Who Is Jimmie Minotto?

The spokesman for the CTA at the January RAA meeting, Jimmie Minotto, who received so many compliments for having such an eloquent manner of presenting rule changes, addition of entry fees and competent cowboy judges, was not well known in the rodeo world, if you weren't from Arizona. However, he had been involved in the Prescott rodeo for years, and even had rodeos on his ranch, the Z Triangle, but never gave out cash prizes. Minotto had tried his hand at calf roping and team tying, but never went down 'the rodeo road.' Everett Bowman and he were neighbors and lived close enough to each other that they became good friends. Bowman's nephew, Louis Bowman, remembered that his uncle Everett had a close relationship with Minotto.

Bowman was very aware that the person who would represent the Turtles at the RAA convention must have an ability to present the Turtle demands and rule changes in such a way that it would be acceptable to all involved. Bowman realized he personally had not been as successful as he would have hoped in this regard, and the Turtles needed someone who had an ability to speak with authority and a certain degree of eloquent charm. Bowman and the directors choice of Jimmie Minotto as CTA spokesman was an excellent one, and he certainly had the ability to handle the situation with finesse. He did exactly what was necessary for the Turtles at the Ogden meeting. But, who was Jimmie Minotto?

Jimmie Minotto roping a calf at the Remuda Ranch Rodeo, Wickenburg, AZ, 1935. *Photo by R. R. Doubleday. Courtesy of Dickinson Research Center, National Cowboy & Western Heritage Museum.*

James Minotto was born to a retired German actress, Agnes Zaremba, who went by the name of Agnes Sorma, and Italian Count, DeMetrio Minotto. Zaremba and the Count were married in 1890. James was born February 17, 1891 in Berlin, Germany. He lived most of his young life in Italy. Because of his heritage James, too, was considered a Count. After completing his education in all the finest schools, James became a representative of Deutche Bank, a German bank, and spent his time with the Bank in Berlin and London. In 1914 he immigrated to the United States and worked for several banking institutions. Because he spoke six languages he was assigned to spend time in South America studying the banking business there.

Minotto married Ida Mae Swift in 1916. She was from Chicago, and the daughter of the Swift meat packing family. Minotto became a citizen of the United States in 1922 and renounced his title of 'Count.' He had several professions other than banking, such as dairyman in Illinois, but eventually he moved to Arizona and became a rancher.

The Phoenix rodeo needed financial help in 1931 and Minotto gave them $16,000 to help finance it and he also gave them a plan to make their rodeo a success. They netted $22,000. When the rodeo committee, which was the Junior Chamber of Commerce in Phoenix, tried to give Minotto the profit he refused and gave the $6,000 profit back to the Jaycees, who continued to run the rodeo under his advised pattern. Because of this success he was asked to put on a rodeo to be held at the Chicago World's Fair in 1933.

He became an Arizona senator in 1932 and held the office for three different legislative sessions. An unsuccessful run for governor of Arizona in 1934 did not discourage his interest in politics or his personal business life. He was appointed as Ambassador to Bolivia that year. Minotto was most interested in rodeos, in spite of his other activities, and competed in rodeos as a calf and steer roper.

Combining this expertise with his past experience of representing banks, the State of Arizona, and the United States as an Ambassador, his ability to speak publicly and handle difficult situations was well known. He was at home wherever he was in the world and could handle any difficult situation. [#45, #46, #12]

The Cowboys' Turtle Association leaders needed someone like Minotto to represent them. Someone who had the ability to express themselves in a professional and diplomatic manner, but yet in such a congenial way that it would be acceptable to those who would be affected. One of the biggest criticisms of the CTA was the fact rodeo committees felt as if the Turtles wanted to 'take over' their hometown rodeos, which, of course, offended them, but was not true. Although the CTA demands were important to improve the sport, and would only make rodeo more professional, it was a 'bitter pill' for some committees to accept.

The act of appearing on the eve of a rodeo and demanding changes or the threat that Turtles would not compete made committees quite hostile toward them. The men who made up the Turtle membership were the best cowboys in the rodeo business and committees knew they would attract more spectators if they were competing at their rodeos. But was their participation worth the 'insults' the committees received through Turtles' requests? Of course, making a threat the night before a rodeo was not what the Turtle representatives had previously promised they would do, either. It was apparent that some of the Turtle representatives were too aggressive and thought they had a power that would make rodeos agree to their demands. Wrong! The former Italian banker-senator-ambassador-diplomat Minotto had the experience of dealing with a variety of peoples and had the perfect way of expressing himself. Plus he was a strong supporter of the sport of rodeo. He was just the person the Turtles needed to represent them. What a coup!

CHAPTER NINE

First CTA Convention

On March 10, 1938, in Fort Worth, Texas the first CTA convention was held. Minutes reported:

"First item of business was report of Secretary and Treasurer, Hugh Bennett, as follows:

The Association now has 516 paid members totaling		$2,580.00
Monies paid in for fines		<u>1,849.75</u>
	Total	$4,429.75
Expense since start of Association		$1,021.00
Expense from Nov. 1, 1936 to Jan 1, 1938		
	Total	$3,407.94
Membership fees		$ 985.00
153 Members in 1937 - 44 members in 1938		
	Total:	$4,392.94
Fines since Jan 1, 1938		$ 230.40
Bank Balance:		$4,623.34

Eighteen boys now paying fines and only one person has given a bad check in the amount of $5.00

The next item of business was the reading by Mr. J. Minotto of the Articles of Incorporation and By-Laws for the approval of the meeting.

Motion was made by John Jordan, Phoenix, Arizona, that the By-Laws be adopted as read and this motion was duly seconded by Howard McCrory, Deadwood, S.D.

Mr. Minotto then asked the question: It has been duly motioned and seconded that the Articles of Incorporation and By-Laws of the Cowboys Turtle Association be adopted as read. Those in favor say "Aye" – all opposed say "No". Motion carried unanimously.

Then there followed a general discussion with reference to horses being put into parades. It was stated by Red Thompson that he would rather pay money than to put his horses in parades and he felt an amendment should be prepared to this effect. This is to be taken up by the Board of Directors at a later date.

Gene Ross then brought up the subject of whether or not a contestant should be allowed to leave one show to go to another if he felt he had a better opportunity to win more prizes. Opinions were given by several and it was expressed by Mr. Everett Bowman, president, that if a contender does something to violate the rules of the show, the Association could not uphold them as it could not afford to take issue with the show in regard to its rules. It was therefore decided to strike from the Rules paragraph two of Section VI.

Motion was then duly made by Gene Ross and seconded by Hub Whiteman that the rules be adopted as read. The question was put before the meeting and the motion was unanimously carried.

(The following Representatives were nominated and voted on for their respective events):

Bulldoggers nominated the following:

	Final Vote
Gene Ross	11
Rusty McGinty	14
Tom Hogan	3
Dave Campbell	8
Dick Truitt	8
Jim Whiteman	2

Rusty McGinty was elected

Calf Ropers nominated:

Everett Shaw	23
Buck Sorrels	5
Hub Myers	10

Everett Shaw was elected

Bronc Riders nominated:

Pete Grubb	4
Eddie Curtis	17
Burel Mulkey	15

Eddie Curtis was elected

Bull Riders nominated:

Paul Carney	13
Canada Kid	5
Hughie Long	16

Hughie Long was elected

Bareback Riders nominated:

Paul Carney	20
Smokey Snyder	6
Jim Whiteman	10

Paul Carney was elected

Team Ropers nominated:
Motion was made on this election by Dick Truitt that Jimmie Minotto be elected unanimously and was duly carried by Burel Mulkey. Carried

While the newly elected representatives held a meeting, a talk was made by Mr. Pete Kerscher on the importance of each member having a Social Security number and card. A request was made that each member see to this detail.

The Representatives then reported the election of officers for the Cowboy Turtle Association as follows:

President	Everett Bowman	Hillside, Ariz.
1st Vice President	Herman Linder	Cardston, Alberta
2nd Vice President	Rusty McGinty	Plains, Texas
Secretary/Treasurer	Hugh Bennett	Ft Thomas, Ariz.

Telegrams of greetings and good wishes for the success of the Convention were read from the following:

Ma Hopkins, *Hoofs & Horns* Editor
Twin Falls County Fair
Midland Fair, Inc.
Kiwanis Club, Hinton, Okla.
Shrine National Convention Rodeo, Los Angeles, Calif.

A standing vote of thanks was given to the following:
Levi Strauss and Company, San Francisco, Calif.
Plymouth Cordage Company, North Plymouth, Mass.
Porter Saddle and Harness Co., Phoenix, Ariz.
and to Representatives of the Fort Worth Press;
Miss Stephenson and Mr. Richhart

Red Thompson then brought to the attention of the meeting the fact that the Southwestern Exposition and Fat Stock Show (Fort Worth) have a printed sign at the Coliseum to the effect that an ambulance will be on hand to take the injured to the hospital but the performers will have to pay for this service themselves. Thompson said that most every place, even little towns, took care of this matter for performers.

In this regard Eddie Curtis suggested that a committee call on Mr. Davis of the Show and go into the matter with him and he believed arrangements could be made whereby the show would furnish this transportation for anyone injured during the run of the show.

Mr. Minotto expressed the belief that he doubted this would be necessary as the discussion had been heard by the Press and this would probably be all that would be required to have the condition corrected.

There being no further business to bring before the meeting, upon motion duly made and seconded, it was adjourned." [38]

The first full year of the Cowboys Turtle Association had ended and they held their first convention. They were making great strides. It was evident that each member was making every effort to correct mistakes which had been made in the past, and seriously addressing some very embarrassing problems that some member cowboys had caused, such as running out without paying room and/or board. It was evident the new organization had many things to consider and correct. It would take time to resolve all the problems facing professional cowboys. But the grit and determination of those men who 'stepped up to the plate' and became directors and representatives in those formidable times must be applauded and admired. They encountered great odds and there is no doubt they sacrificed a great deal to help improve the world of the competing cowboy. The next few years weren't going to be easy.

One of the biggest problems the organization had to face was the 'majority rule' which had to be enforced. Cowboys are known for their independent ways and it was not unusual for each one to have a different idea as to how things should be handled. The resulting votes, and the majority rule, didn't always set well with some members. Agreeing and complying with the rules set forth were sometimes hard to accept and even harder to carry out.

CHAPTER TEN

Cowgirls Join In

Shortly after their Fort Worth convention, a committee of the CTA met with some of the cowgirl bronc riders, and the following statement was made and signed by Peggy Long, representative of the Cow Girl Bronk Riders:

"After having attended a meeting with the committee of Turtle Association March 16, 1938, in Fort Worth, Texas, the Cow Girl Bronk Riders joined 100%. The purposes for which we joined the Association are:

1st: To ride for a set price at all contract rodeos.

$2^{nd:}$ To reach an agreement with managers of contests as to rules and purses.

At all rodeos where Cow Girl Bronk Riding is contracted we have agreed to:

Rule #1. Ride a Bronk for not less than $15.00 at the small shows and for not less than $25.00 a mount at the larger shows.

Rule #2. To fine any Cow Girl Bronk Rider riding for less than the amount stated above. Fine set is $200.00 payable to Secretary, Turtle Association. $50.00 down and one fourth of all contract or contest money received until fine is paid. Any Cow Girl fined will be required to make down payment of $50.00 before any Turtle Cow Girl Bronk Rider will ride, either contract or contest at any rodeo with said Cow Girl.

Rule #3. Any Cow Girl Bronk Rider, whether member or non-member, breaking rule #1 is liable to above fine.

Rule #4. That all Bronk Riding and Trick Riding contracts be drawn up separately. At any contest we request that any Cow Girl drawing a horse that absolutely refuses to buck be given a re-ride. Horse to be drawn for." [39]

Mitzi Lucas Riley, CTA #479, said she was just a kid when her mother, Tad Lucas, CTA #601, paid Mitzi's dues to join the Turtles. She thought it was probably in 1938, when she was nine years old. Tad was a trick rider, as well as a lady bronc rider, and Mitzi grew up trick riding also. They definitely wanted to work Turtle sanctioned rodeos, which required membership, even though the women were not eligible to vote. She also remembered that by the time the Turtles had formed, her dad, Buck Lucas, a competitive bulldogger, had injured his arm and was unable to continue to compete. She said he did a lot of judging after he quit competing, but that she did not think that he ever joined the CTA. She knew he had not gone to Boston when the cowboys struck, as he had a judging job elsewhere. [143]

Tad Lucas, CTA # 601, with her Metro-Goldwyn Mayer trophy. *Photographer Unknown. Courtesy of the Jack Long Collection.*

CTA's First Book of Rules and Members Printed

The first CTA booklet, printed by Ma Hopkins and the *Hoofs & Horns* magazine staff, for the Cowboys' Turtle Association was dated April 1, 1938. It was titled "Articles of Association, By-Laws, Rules, *plus* List of Members To April 1, 1938". The last paragraph reads:

"The above amended rules of the C.T.A. were unanimously adopted at a special meeting held by the Board of Directors of the C.T.A. in Phoenix, Arizona, January 3, 1938."

It is signed Cowboy Turtle Association, Everett Bowman, President, Hugh Bennett, Secretary, Dick Truitt, Director, Hughie Long, Director, Eddie Curtis, Director and Burel Mulkey, Director." *(See Appendix)*

The booklet also includes a roster of members by Turtle number. Number one was Jimmie Nesbitt of Fort Worth, Texas, who was the only Boston Petition signer that marked his name out before it was presented to Colonel Johnson. He was a rodeo clown that had been hired by the Colonel for Madison Square Garden and Boston rodeos in 1936. He was very concerned that the Colonel might see his name on the Petition and fire him. Although he scratched his name off the petition, he obviously believed strongly in the CTA since he was the first cowboy to pay his dues. Rusty McGinty of Plains, Texas held Number Two. In total, there were 621 names listed as members by the time this sixteen page booklet went to press. [#13]

CTA Say Cowgirls, You're On Your Own!

Cowgirl Bronk Riders filed a demand on the Cleveland (Ohio) Rodeo for mount money. They were asking for $15 a day for small rodeos and $25 a day for large rodeos. When Maxwell McNutt, was contacted by the Cleveland committee he advised them not to pay mount money in any event "for reasons explained in 'Legal Liabilities of Rodeos;' that lady bronc riding was a dangerous feature."

When Minotto was contacted he conveyed that Everett Bowman had told him the lady bronc riders had been asked to be 'honorary members' in the CTA, but they had no vote or say in the CTA as far as business was concerned. In finality, he said the CTA would not help the lady bronc riders in their difficulties and as Everett put it, "They will have to stand on their own feet and sit in their own saddles."[48]

1938 In Full Swing, & Still Controversial

Although the Ogden RAA convention was to have cleared up all the differences between the demands of the Turtles, the rodeo committees, and the RAA organization, but it didn't. As the year progressed it was evident that not everyone was on 'the same page' as to what was agreed on, and then new problems began to arise.

Many problems and differences had to be resolved within the sport of rodeo, but before this could be accomplished, there were numerous differences within the Turtle organization from member to member that needed to be resolved before they could approach any other organization or rodeo committee with their requests.

In the June issue of *Hoofs & Horns*, a copy of a letter from Jimmie Minotto to Roy Ritner, of Pendleton RoundUp, was printed, indicating he was going to Pendleton and they would sit down and discuss the problems and resolve any differences. In part he wrote:

"I believe you and I had a very satisfactory and gentlemanly talk at Ogden and I do believe that I understand your situation as well as possible. I agree with you that if there is to be harmony there must be no retributions or retaliations on either side for the unhappy incidents of last year. This I have made very clear to Everett Bowman and to the other boys and they understand perfectly well that I mean what I say ——"

Later in his letter he went on to write:

"You and I both realize that we have a difficult problem, we are dealing with people who are easily misled and who easily misunderstand. For the good of all the rodeos and for the preservation of a fine clean sport, I hope that you will join hands with me and work this matter out to the satisfaction of all concerned ——"[49]

Minotto, as spokesperson for the CTA had agreed with the RAA representatives and the rodeo committees that no retaliation would be taken toward the rodeos or the contestants that were involved in the 1937 problems at Ellensburg and Pendleton rodeos. However, some

Steve Heacock CTA #71, Shorty Ricker CTA# 131 and Shorty Creed CTA# 127, contesting cowboys all sporting identical watch fobs, often given in those days when paying entry fees to rodeo. *Photographer unknown. Courtesy of the Flaxie Fletcher Collection*

of the Turtles, led by Everett Bowman, claimed they didn't understand the meaning of the word 'retaliation,' and had prepared a blacklist of 56 cowboys, and twelve of those blacklisted had entered those two rodeos. The Turtles said they were not going to work or compete at rodeos that would allow any of these 56 cowboys to enter.

Minotto, in spite of his efforts, had no control over what Bowman or other Turtles wanted to enforce. Regardless of what rules had been agreed upon at the last meeting with the RAA certain Turtles seemed to continue to make demands that were in conflict with what everyone else expected, including Minotto.

1938 CTA Meeting, Ogden, Utah, July 24th

The minutes read:

"Meeting was called to order by President, Everett Bowman of the Cowboys' Turtle Association.

A talk given by C. O. Leuschner, *(a steer wresting competitor, also known as Dogtown Slim, married to stock contractor Harry Rowell's daughter, who also acted as a stock contractor).*

'Mr. President and fellow men. I am speaking on behalf of myself and Harry Rowell, who was unable to meet with you today as he had to meet with the Filer Rodeo Committee. I wish to say that whatever you do or whatever you agree on, I, myself am for you, 100%, as a Promoter.'

Mayor Perry of Ogden said, 'I appreciate you Turtles holding your convention here at Ogden this year and wish that you would make it an annual affair. The Ogden Rodeo started with a Horse Show and the crowds were small but when the rodeo started we had large crowds. The Turtles have all been very cooperative and we have had no disagreement with them. I want all of the Salt Lake boys to be guests at the Ogden Rodeo tonight; I will make arrangements with Everett Bowman.'

Reese Lockett (Honorary CTA member), said, 'As a member of the Cowboys' Turtle Association, I do not have a vote but I wish to say a few things. Organizations are fine things. I belong to many. Always work for the betterment of what you are in, and when you vote always stick by what you voted for. Rodeos are growing fast. There are so many new boys I believe they must grow on prune trees. Here are two shows within 50 miles of each other and over a hundred boys at each. Always live up to what you vote for, and let the majority win and stick by them for 'A House Divided Will Soon Fail.' Whatever you vote for stick by it so that the President and the Directors can enforce all Laws. This is a game of give and take. The Producers can not get along without the Cowboys and the Cowboys can not get along without the Producers.'

The business meeting was called to order by Pete Kerscher.

Letters and telegrams were read by E. Bowman from Jimmie Minotto. The trouble we are having is the 'Closed Shop,' County Rodeo and Restricted Shows. The agreement at Ogden, Utah in January, 1938, was not to have 'Closed Shops.' Telegram read in regards to the King

City and Gilroy Rodeos. Next year they are to be open to all. At Reno, Nevada, two Turtles worked in the Nevada events. No R.A.A. points were given but a state event that is closed, only protect the boys from talent coming in. Anyone working in a closed event is subject to a fine. A bill was posted in the Reno Rodeo Office in regards to this Nevada event.

Pete Kerscher announced: Get your Social Security cards and keep them with you at all times. It will soon be a fine of $10,000 for anyone hiring a man who does not have his Social Security card. The Sun Valley Rodeo does not start until the 12th of August but get your entries in before or by August 10th.

Floyd Stillings: About the bucking horse riders' judges. At Red Lodge Rodeo the Judges did not know how to judge the riding events. The list that is in the *Hoofs & Horns* is large and not half of them are known to the riders. The boys riding at the Cody Rodeo did not know the judges. Let the boys pick their own judges.

Everett Bowman: If a boy sees that a judge isn't right, let the Office know about it.

Eddie Curtis: Let the boys who are riding vote in the judges.

Reese Lockett: The boys who are riding are the ones who are interested. Let the boys select the judges. Our idea is to put on the entrance blank a place for the boys to write in the name of the boys they would like to have as a judge and the one getting the most vote is the one to be judge, but elect experienced boys.

Eddie Curtis: They have cut the judges from 3 to 2. I suggest that 3 judges be voted in, let 2 judge and the third one do the flagging.

Dick Truitt: Suggested to have the men selected for judges, ride the horses (*broncs*) before they judge.

Slats Jacobs: Crippled men can not ride bucking horses but the riders know when a man is qualified.

Everett Bowman: You boys can help to save trouble by picking capable judges. You will solve the problem when the boys quit cheating on one another.

Eddie Curtis: Stand by the judges. If they make a mistake stand behind them.

Jack Kerscher: I should like to ask a few of the boys some questions. I have heard that I have been paid off while I have been a judge. As a judge at places where you have been, have I or have I not been fair in judging?

Harry Hart: You have been fair.

Hughie Long: I guess I am the man you can put your finger on but since the organization of the Turtles you have been a good judge.

Breezy Cox: You have never been off more than two points in judging when I have judged with you.

Andy Jauregui: No complaint.

Slats Jacobs: I should like to know, Everett Bowman, as I have heard it that you have been paid your entrance fees to bring your trophies to different rodeos?

Everett Bowman: About my trophies. I value my trophies very high and I have a large number of them. The first time that I was asked about displaying them, Porters Store in Phoenix asked me. They said that they would pay my entrance fees of $130 if I would let them put them in their window. No one would turn down an offer like that. A picture was taken of that window display and I have sent it to different rodeos to advertise their rodeo.

Dave Campbell: I have been told that it has been said out in public that I bought the cattle that I dogged at the Chicago rodeo. The man who said this is a LIAR.

Everett Bowman: If all men are as good as Dave Campbell, we would be good men.

Shorty Ricker: The boys did not see the drawing of the stock at the Chicago rodeo. Judges didn't see what was drawn. Fred Beeson did the drawing and it was given to the bookkeeper.

Red Allen: I was told before the Chicago rodeo that in order to win a person had to belong to (blank) outfit, or be one of them.

Pete Kerscher: I have been Secretary of many rodeos and the best way to draw the stock is to have enough of the boys present at the drawing that there will not be a complaint. Let the boys do the drawing themselves. Let the judges' books be open for inspection.

Cliff Helm: At Chicago I split with Lonnie Rooney. I know there was no fixing the judges. Since the organization of the Turtles I have won more money than before and I know that I am not as good a man as I was several years ago. At Chicago Lonnie Rooney and I were the best bronc riders there.

Trophies, plaques, buckles and such Everett Bowman had won. He allowed various sponsors to display them during a rodeo and in turn they paid entry fees to the local rodeo. This may have been the first rodeo sponsors for cowboys. *Photograph by McCulloch Brothers. Courtesy of Stan Searle from the Hoofs & Horns Collection.*

Frank Van Meter: I did not come here to fight. I think that if a judge is proven crooked, he should be fined. At Chicago Cliff Helm and Lonnie Rooney drew or got the best stock. Instead of being the best riders, I would say they were lucky in drawing.

John Bowman: I suggest that the judges be bonded.

Hughie Long: Before the organization of the Turtles, some of the judges could be fixed.

Breezy Cox: No one ever tried to fix me when I was a judge.

Dick Griffith: How about the trick riders riding bulls at closed shops?

Buff Brady: When you vote in a President stay behind him 100% right or wrong. What the Turtles need is power and with proper power we can press these shows like Ellensburg and Pendleton. If all the Turtles stay together we will succeed. If the amateur shows can not get the talent at the closed shows they will have to close their shows. If the boys work at these closed shops do not let them work at the good shows. I think that the trick riders and trick ropers should join the C.T.A. This would help them. You boys can have my stock for the fee to put on a show at any of these closed shops.

Andy Jauregui and Floyd Stillings: Agreed

Reese Lockett: The Turtle will not get any place with a strike. After seeing the prize list, send in to the Committee any objections that you have.

Everett Bowman: (*This statement was marked out*) Ellensburg and Pendleton did not play fair. We gave them plenty of notice.

Irby Mundy: I want to back up Buff Brady in what he said. Stand behind E. Bowman and the six directors 100%. They will profit by it.

Rufus Ingersoll: These small shows that we have in Montana can not put up more money.

Everett Shaw: Down in Oklahoma there is a rodeo sign on every fence post.

John Bowman: Put small shows out of business.

Everett Bowman: I sent a wire to Burel Mulkey, signed by four of the Directors that no C.T.A. member could work at a closed event at the Calgary rodeo. Some of the members of the C.T.A. worked at both the open and closed events in Calgary, Canada.

Dick Truitt: I make a motion that it be left up to the Directors of the CTA whether they should be fined and what to be fined.

John Jordan: No one seemed to know about that letter sent to Calgary.

Everett Bowman: I suggest that when a Turtle works at a closed shop that he work for the Turtle Association, and that what he wins pay it into the Turtle Association.

Eddie Curtis: Seconded the motion.

John Bowman: I make a motion that the First Vice President, Herman Linder be let out as an Officer of the Organization.

Dick Truitt and Eddie Curtis: Both seconded the motion.

Dick Truitt: Suggested to have a meeting and have Herman Linder present.

Adjourned." [40]

Closed or District Events

Additionally, a new problem was brought to CTA's attention; district and closed events. Rodeos began putting area restrictions on certain events, where only those cowboys living in that area or district, would be allowed to compete. Therefore they were called 'district' or 'closed' events. CTA determined that in the case of the 'district' or 'closed' rodeos, as long as there were the same events open to everyone, in the same rodeo, it was not a problem, as long as RAA points were not given for the closed or district events. The RAA point totals at the end of the year, for each cowboy, determined who won the All-Around Champion of the World, and World Champion in each event.

The following telegram was sent by CTA to the Reno rodeo management regarding the closed events:

"As long as you have championship events in bronc riding and calf roping open to all with award of RAA points there is no objection or fine for Nevada members of the Cowboys' Turtle Association to participate in Nevada state championship bronc riding and calf roping provided no RAA points are awarded in either State championship events.

Signed: Cowboys' Turtle Association, Paul Carney, James Minotto, Directors." [50]

The following month in the RAA column in *Hoofs & Horns* the Reno Rodeo Association letter was printed, explaining that in spite of the telegram they received from Carney and Minotto problems still arose. Everett Bowman, who was at Reno, told the management team, the night before the Reno rodeo began, that two Nevada men, Cliff Gardner and Ray McGinnis, could not compete in both the Nevada events and the 'open' events against the Turtles. If they did compete they would be barred from competing at other Turtle shows and fined. These two cowboys entrance fees were refused at Vallejo and Salinas, and were told they would not be able to compete at Ogden and Cheyenne. There were other Nevada men that competed at Reno, and who were Turtles, but were overlooked by the Turtles. The Reno rodeo management team was concerned that if RAA rodeos didn't support one another there was very little benefit in the organization. [51]

As time went on the Turtles continued to work diligently with the RAA and rodeo management and things began to improve. In fact the following letter was printed in *Hoofs & Horns* August issue:

"Editor Hoofs and Horns:

Please publish this letter in the next issue of *Hoofs & Horns*. We wish everyone to know that we, managers and promoters, of rodeo contests in these southwestern states are one hundred per cent for the Cowboys' Turtle Association, and their rules and by-laws.

We have cooperated with the C.T.A. and have found that we can put on a rodeo smoother and faster with no disputes between the management and contestants.

We find that the members of the C.T.A. will stand behind their representatives' judgment.

> T. E. Robertson, promoter and mgr. Springfield, Mo; Joplin, Mo; Harrison, Arkansas.
> Florence Randolph, Mgr., Ardmore, Okla.
> Floyd Gale, Mgr., Ft Smith, Ark.
> Beutler Bros., Mgr. Amarillo, Texas; Dalhart, Teas.; Hinton, Okla.; Custer City, Okla.; Woodward, Okla.; Midland, Texas; Guthrie, Okla.; Pampa, Texas; Canadian, Texas
> Charles Tompkin, Mgr. Oklahoma State Fair Rodeo." [50]

Buttons Yonnick CTA# 359, Frank Quirk CTA# 441, ScrapIron Patch CTA# 322 and Lou Quirk CTA# 1618, and two unknown cowboys at Billings rodeo, 1938. *Photographer unknown. Courtesy of Lou Quirk.*

Buttons Yonnick CTA# 359, Frank Quirk CTA# 441, ScrapIron Patch CTA# 322 and Lou Quirk CTA# 1618, and two unknown cowboys at Billings rodeo, 1938. *Photographer unknown. Courtesy of Lou Quirk.*

CHAPTER ELEVEN

1938 – CTA's Second Year

"No Turtles Allowed"

The decision by the Pendleton RoundUp for their rodeo in 1938 was still the same as it had been in their 1937 decision. They refused to allow Turtles to pick their judges, and although the Turtles sent Carl Arnold to Pendleton to try and work out a compromise, it didn't happen. Arnold explained that the Turtles were not accusing the judges of being dishonest, just unqualified. Earlier in the year an article in the *Saturday Evening Post* about Pendleton's protest to Turtle demands showed a photograph of the sign in the Pendleton rodeo office stating "No Turtles Allowed."

CTA lost two members, reported in the October *Hoofs & Horns*, John Wilkinson, CTA #252, from Little Horse Creek, Wyo., was killed in an accident. Cecil Kennedy, CTA #66, was killed by a bucking horse at the Rocky Ford (Colorado) Rodeo, August 30, 1938. The bronc riding death brought about a new ruling for the CTA. They encouraged all members to pay an extra five dollars when paying dues. This would allow a fund to help the family of the deceased. In the past the cowboys would just 'pass the hat' when a comrade would be killed, at the rodeo where they were competing, which was a haphazard way to handle such a delicate need. [#52]

The 1939 RAA convention was to be held in Livingston, Mont., on January 6 and 7, and the decision was to invite representatives from the Cowboys' Turtle Association and the Northwest Cowboy Association (which was formed when the Turtles failed in their efforts to be allowed to compete at Pendleton RoundUp and Ellensburg, Wash. rodeo) at the convention. The agenda of the convention was changed for the year, in that there would be no set program. After the welcome, there would be a series of 'roundtable discussions' with anyone and everyone being given the privilege to discuss needs for bettering the rodeo game. [53]

The Turtles held general meetings in New York City and Chicago in the latter part of 1938. Nominations for representatives of various events were chosen and were to be voted on by the membership at an upcoming meeting to be held in Fort Worth. Votes from CTA members not able to attend the Fort Worth meeting were encouraged to be sent in by March 1.

A Little Bit of Humor

The following letter addressed to Everett Bowman was printed in the December issue of *Hoofs & Horns*:

"My Dear "Hitler" Bowman: As head Ramrod of the organization, and the guy that tells them where to spend money, please instruct Mr. Bennett to send me a check for the rent of the Stadium for three hours on Thursday morning of the past week, when the Turtles got out into the arena and 'turtled' for three or four hours. In fact, there was so G_ _ D _ _ _ _ much wind, we had to open all the ventilators or the building would have blown away.

Instead of putting on a picnic at Lewiston, we have had it here, and send us our bit, pronto.

As ever, your friend,

Fred H. Kressman" [54]

A letter to Mr. Kressman, secretary of the Chicago Stadium, was sent from Bowman and read:

"Dear Mr. Kressman: Your letter of the 22nd, received and from the tone of it I gather that you were somewhat annoyed by the Turtles meeting in the arena there and for this I am very sorry.

I realize that one at the head of such a gigantic enterprise as yours must necessarily shun many things that are apt to annoy the very busy

Winners of the World Championship Rodeo at Madison Square Garden, 1938. Left to right: Dick Truitt CTA# 5, steer wrestling; Eddie Curtis CTA# 132, bareback bronk riding; Vivian White CTA# 617, cowgirls' bronc riding; Colonel John Reed Kilpatrick, president of Madison Square Garden; Burel Mulkey CTA# 93, saddle bronc riding and RAA all-around world champion; Frank Marion CTA# 364, steer riding; and Jake McClure CTA# 142, calf roping. *Photographer Unknown. Taken from 1939 Madison Square Garden Program.*

business man and had I been present it would have been a pleasure to have had the boys meet elsewhere and save you that annoyance.

I am enclosing order for 98 cents in response of your request for rent for the meeting, and my reason for doing this is that I have no way of arriving at a conclusion as to just whom rent for the meeting space in the arena would be payable to, so the 98 cents in reality is for the extra expense of having the ventilators opened, which item I am sure you personally had charge of.

Again expressing my regrets that the Turtles have annoyed you and assuring you that I will use my best endeavors to, as far as possible, save you further annoyance from the Association, I am Very truly yours, Everett Bowman, President C.T.A." [#54]

Louis Quirk, CTA #1617, joined the Turtles in 1938 at Cleveland, Ohio at an Eskew rodeo. "The rule was that you didn't have to join until you had won $250. I didn't win that until after I got out of the service in 1946," he laughingly said. "I had the money so I joined. Eddie Curtis was a judge and I couldn't win much."

Lou later was in the Army Quartermaster Corp. in charge of everything for the Army from food to the trucks, but went right back to rodeo and bull riding when he was discharged. [131]

Faye Blackstone, CTA #1356, remembered that when she married Vick Blackstone, CTA #618, on August 27, 1937, he signed her up as a Turtle member shortly thereafter. Faye said, "all the Turtles either wore their Turtle Pin on their hat or their belt with such pride. No one would cross-over and work a rodeo that wasn't sanctioned by the Turtles either". [139]

Faye was a trick rider for many years and created several tricks of her own, including the Fly Away and the Reverse Fender Drag. She also took barrel racing to Florida for the first time from Texas where it began. Vick was a saddle bronc rider and roper for many years. They retired to Florida. [139]

Holloway Grace, CTA #13, was a bulldogger, calf roper, team roper, and a world champion steer decorator. He joined the Turtles very early and held CTA #13 and was extremely proud of his association with the Turtles. In 1938, Grace and two other Turtles – Harry Logue, CTA #155 and Bill McFarland, CTA #307, went with group of cowboys to Hawaii to put on the first professional rodeo there. The competitors went via a liner, but these three traveled on a freighter which carried the stock, so as to watch over them. During a severe storm which they encountered, Grace reported, "the bulls and horses were raising hell and we had a hard time keeping them calm. The wind blew and the ship was raise(d) up so high out of the water, and then slammed it down. But we made it and arrived safely." [136]

When 1938 came to a close the following cowboys were RAA world champions:

All Around title holder was Burel Mulkey of Salmon, ID with 8,126 points. After Mulkey next in All-Around points were: Everett Bowman with 8,039 points; Fritz Truan with 7,042; Eddie Curtis with 6,197 and Nick Knight with 6,144.

1938 CTA's Second Year

Winners of the 14th Annual World Championship Rodeo at Madison Square Garden, 1939. Left to right: Mitch Owens CTA# 179, steer riding; Paul Carney CTA# 21, bareback bronc riding; Harry Knight CTA# 37, Assistant Manager; Mildred Mix Horner CTA# 728, cowgirls' bronk riding; Col. John Reed Kilpatrick, president of Madison Square Garden Corporation; Everett Colborn CTA#1582, managing director of 1939 Rodeo; Lizzie Minnick, Sponsor Girl title winner; Mark Twain Clemens, president of World Champion Rodeo Corporation; Fritz Truan CTA# 49, saddle bronk riding; Everett Shaw CTA# 7, calf roping; and Harry Hart CTA# 246, steer wrestling. *Photographer Unknown. Taken from 1940 Madison Square Garden Program.*

RAA World Champions in their events were:
Bareback Riding – Pete Grubb of Salmon, Idaho
Steer Wrestling – Everett Bowman, Hillside, Ariz.
Team Roping – John Rhodes, Sombrero Butte, Ariz.
Saddle Bronc Riding – Burel Mulkey, Salmon, Idaho
Calf Roping – Clyde Burk, Comanche, Okla.
Bull Riding – Kid Fletcher, Hugo, Colo.
Steer Roping – Hugh Bennett, Fort Thomas, Ariz.
Steer Decorator – Warner Linder, Cardston, Alberta. [55]

CTA's Second Full Year in Operation

The organization was still struggling in its early stages and they still had much work to be done to improve the sport, but it was happening, slowly – like the Turtle. Once the contesting cowboys set their mind to making professional rodeos better there was no stopping them. But problems continued to arise that had to be solved.

The January, 1939 *Hoofs & Horns* issue had the following letter published on the CTA page:

"Dear "Ma" Hopkins: Would you please be good enough and publish this letter in *Hoofs & Horns*, as I want my friends to know, that on October 27th I resigned as a Director in the Cowboys' Turtle Association. I have so advised Everett Bowman on that date and wrote him to New York at the Madison Square Garden Rodeo.

My reasons for resigning are that the Cowboys' Turtle Association as it is now represented has plans and ideas, which are too different from my own point of view. The tendency is too professional to meet with my approval and more and more lacks the open championship spirit, which has endeared rodeos so much to my heart.

The fault is probably mine, as I am getting very likely old and cranky – and it's better for all concerned to go on without me.

As long as the Turtles don't turn to radical I shall continue to pay my dues as a regular member and my best wishes will be with them.

Will you kindly arrange that in future all communications are addressed to Mrs. Hugh Bennett at Fort Thomas, Arizona, and remove my name from the mail box of your fine publication, as far as communications from the Turtles to *Hoofs & Horns* is concerned?

With many thanks and my kindest regards,

I am – Very Sincerely Yours,

Jimmie Minotto" [55]

Also published, in that issue, was a two page article written by Guy Weadick, the cowboy who was the ramrod for the first Calgary Stampede as well as other rodeo happenings. He said the two organizations in rodeo that have attempted to organize and standardize rodeo have failed so far. He accused them both (R.A.A. and C.T.A.) of issuing contradictory statements, and had taken actions, entirely different from the announced policies of their officials. He went on to criticize 'the lack of unity in the membership of both groups, and they

1938 CTA's Second Year

Madison Square Garden Rodeo cowboys and cowgirl contestants and performers. Event was held October 7 through 30, 1938. *Photo by Knickerbocker Pictures, Brooklyn, NY. Courtesy of the Dickinson Research Center, National Cowboy & Western Heritage Museum.*

are constantly blaming one another. He detailed many errors made by both associations. In his summary he wrote:

"One can hardly imagine Joe Louis, Joe DiMaggio, Dizzy Dean, Madison Square Garden, Chicago Stadium, and of the State Fairs, or any of the big football teams fooling around in 'competitive sports' simply for the love of the sport, if they did not receive warranted profits on their investments of time, money or services.

Yes, rodeo is a business, and any time one is held and can't get by on its merits, it should fold up. It can't expect to function very long upon the free services of novices, or the honeyed words of well wishers who make their money in other business but insist upon theories in rodeo business to pay the shot.

The mistakes of the past are an open book. The eyes of the press and contest fans everywhere will be on those dealing at the coming Livingston convention (R.A.A.). Success or failure will depend upon the sort of policies, agreements, etc. concluded and lived up to." [55]

It was true, there were problems within both organizations, and it was not difficult to get discouraged with the actions happening in professional rodeo. "One step forward and two back." But improvement was happening, and in spite of the frustrations and anger that often was expressed, rodeo was becoming better than it had been.

The R.A.A. convention held in Livingston, Mont., in January, was reported to have been a success and well attended. In the *RAA Bulletin* the report said, in part:

"A general spirit of harmony and cooperation pervaded the whole Livingston Convention and through the roundtable discussion that went on at the convention it was announced contestants will be seen at various northwestern rodeos where there had been trouble in the past. It was urged that each rodeo publish their prize list at least 60 days prior to their show. The point award system was to remain the same; however it reported, that a fair basis for awarding points to be, to give a point for each dollar paid excluding added entrance fees, in all five of the major events. The five leading events were: bronc riding with saddle, calf roping, steer wrestling, steer decorating and steer riding. Points given in the other events would be seventy per cent."

"In addition to RAA convention-goers, CTA representatives, and those representing the North American Cowboys Association attended. President McNutt appointed a committee of 1 contract man, 5 rodeo managers and 5 contestants, to pick a list of fifty or more judges satisfactory to all the members of the committee, from which rodeos may (although not required) pick from. Those chosen for the committee were: Contract man, Cuff Burrell, Hanford, Calif.; Rodeo Managers: J. C. Kinney, Tucson, Ariz.; Elton B. Hebbron, Salinas, Calif.; E. L. Richardson, Calgary, Canada; J. C. Howe, Sidney, Iowa; and Frank Moore, Madison Square Garden, New York City. The five contestants picked were: Herman Linder, Cardston, Alberta, Canada; Burel Mulkey, Salmon, Idaho; Eddie Curtis, El Reno, Okla.; Everett Bowman, Hillside, Ariz.; and C. C. Coe, Hooper, Wash.. (Mr. Coe was a member of the North American Cowboys Association)."[#56]

1938 CTA's Second Year

A report of the Cowboys' Turtle Association annual meeting in Fort Worth, Texas, in March, 1939, was published in the May issue of *Hoofs & Horns*:

"Elected for the 1939 year were the following officers and Directors: Everett Bowman, President; 1st Vice President, Herbert Meyers; 2nd Vice President, Rusty McGinty; Secretary-Treasurer, Hugh Bennett. Directors and Assistants for each event were: Team Roping: Buckshot Sorrells, assisted by M. W. Del Re. Saddle Bronc Riding: Eddie Curtis and assistants, Burel Mulkey, Melvin Harper and Buck Tiffin; Calf Roping, Everett Shaw, assisted by R. R. Ingersoll, Tom Taylor and Andy Jauregui; Bulldogging Director Rusty McGinty, assisted by Hub Whiteman, Frank Van Meter and Clay Carr; Bareback Riding: Hoytt Hefner assisted by Rock Parker, Smokey Snyder and Hank Mills; and Bull Riding director Hughie Long, assisted by Paul Carney, Frank Marion and O. B. Lyman. The Assistants were elected so there would be representation in various parts of the country. It was mentioned that there was a difference between the Fort Worth rodeo and the Turtles but it was resolved two days before the show and "the Turtles went into the show with plenty of vim and vigor and helped to put it over in nice style." Two hundred Turtles were present at the business meeting. The annual banquet was held at the Hotel Texas on March 11th and began at midnight and ended at 3 A.M. No business was transacted during the banquet." [57]

CHAPTER TWELVE

CTA Starts To Hear 'Good News'

A letter to Everett Bowman, president of CTA, on the CTA page in *Hoofs & Horns*, was published, from W. A. Lee, executive director of the Houston Fat Stock Show, which said in part:

"As president of the rodeo committee I want to take time out to let you know that there was not any time during the show here when there was the slightest friction between any of the directors of the show and any member of the Turtle Association.

Your organization conducted all your business pertaining to the rodeo in a straightforward business manner and under your leadership, the boys put on a rodeo that made us proud of them and our own show.

We are proud of the fact that in two years our rodeo has taken a place in the ranking of the biggest shows of the Southwest, and we feel that you and your organization are in large measure responsible for this success.

Practically every individual of our committee was previously engaged in rodeo production and management before the organization of the C.T.A. and we cannot but compare the quibbling and squabbling of those days with the smooth businesslike manner of today, and you may rest assured that our committee are one hundred percent for the C.T.A. and that this will always be a Turtle show.

We want to express to you our appreciation of your untiring efforts put forth in the really enthusiastic cooperation you gave us. It was a pleasure to work with you and we know you now as not only president of a great organization, but a regular fellow and a real sportsman." [58]

G. K. Lewallen, a well known bull rider, had been making good shows for some time during the rodeo year and said somehow he had avoided joining and paying dues, as no one had asked him to join the Turtles. Although he believed in what they stood for, he wasn't going to 'volunteer' his dues, until he needed to. After all, that money was precious to a young cowboy. When he arrived at the Houston rodeo in 1939 he knew the bookkeeper that signed all the cowboys up for events was asking everyone to show their Turtle card. He joined and became #799 in the CTA membership ranks. [59]

Hoofs & Horns published a continuing list of new members in the C.T.A. which by the June issue totaled 750 members. The magazine also printed a list of CTA rules that had been revised at their Fort Worth meeting. [57] The following month *Hoofs & Horns* published another list of new members which now totaled 873 members. It was evident the C.T.A. was growing rapidly. [58]

Southwest Rodeo Association

A new organization called the Southwest Rodeo Association was announced. It was a rodeo group located in the south and southwest that was formed by sectional managers to guarantee purses, award titles and issue points. Rodeos held in Oklahoma, Texas, Kansas, Arkansas, Missouri, New Mexico and Tennessee would be eligible to join. It was stated since so few rodeos in those states were members of the RAA this organization would fill that void. It also stated they were working closely with the CTA and an advisory committee consisting of Everett Bowman, Everett Shaw, Eddie Curtis and Herb Myers, all Turtle office-holders. The directors of the new association which was incorporated in Oklahoma consisted of: T. E. Robertson, C. A. Studer, Charles H. Tompkins, Allyn Finch, Carl Armstrong, M. F. McClain, Dr. C. R. Donley and Lynn and Jake Beutler. The new group had barely started and all ready had commitments from over a dozen rodeos in the states listed. [58]

CTA Starts to Hear 'Good News'   Page 125

HOOFS AND HORNS

Cowboys' Turtle Association

NOTICE

Items of interest to the C. T. A. are welcomed. Please send to Jimmie Minotto, P. O. Box 2349, Phoenix, Arizona.

LIST OF NEW MEMBERS OF THE CTA
622. Geo. Robertson, 801 E. C St., Grants Pass, Oregon.
623. Diamond D. Dewey, 660 Ave. 54 St., Los Angeles, Calif.
624. Sandy Gaymon, Round Up Bar, Reno, Nevada.
625. Geo. Hatfield, Lt. Gov., Newman, Calif.
626. Ray Arano, Watsonville, Calif.
627. Ted Harmon, Rt. 3, Guthrie, Okla.
628. Joe Carey, Box 114, Guthrie, Okla.
629. Hoot Duarte, 812 P St. Rear, Sacramento, Calif.
630. Frank Duarte, 812 P St. Rear, Sacramento, Calif.
631. Lew Bassett, Box 96, El Medio, Calif.
632. Grant Marshall, Afton, Oklahoma.
633. Bill Hedge, Box 2381, Tulsa, Okla.
634. Buddy May, Star Rt., Alluwees, Okla.
635. Jack Holt, c/o Ozark Liquor Store, Lafayetteville, Oklahoma.
636. Johnnie Schrader, Town House, Reno, Nevada.
637. Jeanne Godshall, Victorville, Calif.
638. Jimmie Downs, 1052 63d St., Brooklyn, New York.
639. J. M. Getser, Round Up Bar, Reno, Nevada.
640. Jimmie Bays, Goodrich, Idaho.
641. Mrs. Alice Adams, Cloverdale, Indiana.
642. Yellow Stone Chip, Litchfield Park, Arizona.
643. Dell Smith, Klamath Falls, Oregon.
644. Dusty Doyle, Long Beach, Calif.
645. Paul Gould, c/o M. C. Sibley, Box 192, Toyah, Texas.
646. Chas. A. Shinn, Denver Dry Goods Store, Denver, Colorado.
647. Tommy Sutton, Eagle Ranch, Burbank, Calif.
648. Buff Jones, Eagle Ranch, Burbank, Calif.

649. Russell Stearns, 347 Valley St., Newhall, Calif.
650. Bob Whiting, 3707 Bellview, Bells, Calif.
651. Gordon Davis, Bryn Mawr, Calif.
652. Jun Van Horn, Eagle Ranch, Burbank, Calif.
653. Al Fletcher, Buckeye, Arizona.
654. Lee Edms, Box 38, Ft. Hall, Idaho.
655. Geo. Conwell, Laramie, Wyoming.
656. Bill Clark, Petrolia, Calif.
657. Bob Cunningham, Rt. 2, Ventura, Calif.
658. Jack Conner, c/o J. C. Sorenson, Firth, Idaho.
659. Bud Johnson, Box 180, Hope Ranch, Santa Barbara, Calif.
660. Clyde Schofield, Ft. Worth, Texas.
661. Leonard Brock, Livermore, Calif.
662. Phil Witsegar, Vernalis, Calif.
663. Pete Haverty, Benson, Arizona.
664. Joe Mendes, Visalia, Calif.
665. Mose Kruger, Prentiction, B. C.
666. Ernest Mounce, Globe, Arizona.
667. Buck Wheeler, Meridian, Idaho, Box 694.
668. Alice Greenough, Red Lodge, Mont., Box 401.
669. Margie Greenough, Red Lodge, Mont., Box 1119.
670. Jack Davis, Del Rio, Texas, 314 Greenwood St.
671. Jack Balistrari
672. Foreman Paulknar.
673. Iva Dell Jacobs, 933 Santee St., Los Angeles, Apt. 107.
674. Tex Macom, Denver, Colo.
675. Johnny Hagen.
676. Joe Cook, Trinidad, Colo.
677. Tom Wood, Molella, Oregon.
678. Pete Travis, Vallejo, Calif.
679. Jack Whatley, Tucson, Ariz., Box 244.
680. Raymond Landers, 1102 S. 29th St., Temple, Texas.
681. Ed McEuen, Ft. Thomas, Arizona. (Hon. Memb.)
682. Reva Gray, Durango, Colo. (Killed at Cheyenne in July).
683. James Like, Troy, Colo.
684. Jim Staley, Jackson, Mont., c/o Bill Carroll.
685. Dale Kennedy, Flagstaff, Ariz., Box 1031.

NOTICE!

All membership dues for the Cowboys' Turtle Association should be sent to the secretary-treasurer, Hugh Bennett, Fort Thomas, Arizona.

686. James M. Crist, Claude, Texas.
687. Pat Stewart, Castle Rock, Colo.
688. Morris Laycock, Wheatland, Wyo.
689. Mickey Hicks, Jackson, Wyo.
690. Gene Pruett, Cowiske, Wash., Rt. 1.
691. Ernest Emery, Livingston, Mont., 327 S. F. St.
692. M. A. Hollander, Longview, Wash., 1529 25th Ave.
693. John Foote, Box L. 1, Avalon, Santa Catalina Island, Calif.
694. Jack Brown Brady, Cloverdale, Ind., Box 132.
695. John Williams, Clayton, N. M.
696. Frank Cox, Avondale, Colo.
697. Bob Melville, 2027 N Chestnut St., Colorado Springs, Colo.
698. Bud Dolel, 3050 W. Bijou St., Colorado Springs, Colo.
699. Don Crain, 614½ W. Pikes Peak St., Colorado Springs, Colo.
701. Jack Salyworth, Clovis, N. M.
702. Leonard Brock, Livermore, Calif.
703. Des Burke, Comanche, Okla.

TURTLES NOTICE!

All members of the Cowboys' Turtle Association that haven't paid their 1938 dues, please get them in as soon as possible.

You have all had plenty of time to get your dues in since January 1, so don't be surprised if you go to some show and are not allowed to contest because your dues aren't paid.

EVERETT BOWMAN,
President, C. T. A.

CECIL WILLIAM KENNEDY

Cecil William Kennedy, well-known, highly respected, and great-loved cowboy who was killed by a bucking horse at Rocky Ford rodeo on August 30, was born on a farm near McDonald, Kansas, April 4, 1900.

In 1917 his parents moved to Denver, Colorado, and there Cecil learned to ride at the stock yards and to break horses at the Government Inspection Station. In 1923 he began to ride in rodeos at the age of seventeen. He won his first money in 1924 at Douglas, Wyoming, and in 1925 he won at Denver. In 1931 he won the amateur bronc riding at Cheyenne, and placed in this class year after year at the same show.

In 1933 he went with Tex Austin's show to London where he won some money, but was injured by being kicked in his back. After this he gave up contest riding.

From 1924 until 1933 he worked at the San Marcos Hotel in Chandler, Arizona, in the winters and followed rodeos in the summers.

After giving up riding, he bought cos Hotel in the winter.

This last spring he decided to go rodeoing again. His first show was Prescott early in July, then to St. Johns, Arizona; Monte Vista, Colorado; Yuma, Arizona; Durango, Loveland, Sterling, Colorado Springs, and then to Rocky Ford, Colorado—his last show.

Lillian and Cecil Kennedy

rowing family and friends laid him to rest.

Cecil Kennedy had a lovable, happy disposition. He made friends easily and held them. In the words of those who knew him well he was a "swell fellow." A good business man and a lover of horses, he had made a success of his business of raising horses. Shortly before his tragic death, he told his brother, Dale, that he fully realized the danger of riding broncs, but that he loved to do it and that if the breaks went against him, he was ready to go for he had done all the things he wanted to do.

He was a member of the Cowboys' Turtle Association.

VISALIA STOCK SADDLE C
Send for FREE Catalo
2123 Marke
SAN FRANCI

Branch Stores
10 El Paseo, Santa Ba
The Tack Room, Palm S

ESTAB 1870 **Stetson Hats**

Genuine D. E. Walker
Visalia Saddles

Patented Visalia Humane Bits

Sterling Silver Mountings

STARNES BOOT

I RAISE THE DEA
Chas. L. Evans
30 YEARS A TAXIDERMIST
THE REPTILE GARDENS
6700 E. Van Buren Street
PHOENIX, ARIZONA

Cattle Ranch

Ideal set-up for cowman. 2,000 Acre State Leases, 600 Ac Patented Land, 400 Acres Und Cultivation. Plentiful supply water for irrigation and catt Fenced and cross fenced. Win mills, tanks, pumping plant, pi lines, ranch houses, tractor a farm implements. Close to shi ping point on good road. A mon making proposition. Grazing a feeding. Priced right.

H. C. Tovrea Co
BOX 2391
TUCSON, ARIZONA

SUGGS AGENCY
REAL ESTATE
LOBBY TITLE & TRUST BLD
PHOENIX, ARIZONA

WINTER BOARDER WANTED ON A REAL CATTLE RANCH

This is not a "dude" ranch, but a genuine rawhiding cow outfit. Good board and comfortable quarters.

WIRE OR WRITE BOX 61
ORACLE, ARIZONA

Cowboys' Turtle Association page in Hoofs & Horns magazine. *Courtesy of Pro Rodeo Hall of Fame & Museum of the American Cowboy.*

An article entitled, "RODEOS OF TODAY" in the July, 1939 *Hoofs & Horns* issue included information by men in various positions of the rodeo game, giving their view of the great Western sport as it is conducted today. Remarks by E. L. Richardson, general manager of the Calgary Exhibition and Stampede; Cy Taillon, ace rodeo announcer of the day; Robert Hanesworth, secretary of Cheyenne Frontier Days; Leo Cremer, a stock contractor; and Everett Bowman, president of the CTA, just to name a few.

Bowman said:

"I have been in the rodeo business for fourteen years and there have been several cowboys' associations started, but all of them fell through until the Cowboys' Turtle Association was started in Boston, Mass., in November, 1936.

The reason for the name is that the turtle is the slowest thing the boys could think of, and they were content to go slowly but hold whatever ground they gained. This time the boys really decided to stick together and make a success of our Association.

Protection of the cowboys was the reason for forming the Association; to keep shows from holding our entrance fees and to make them pay purses according to the attendance. Also, experienced and capable judges were required. Before the Turtle Association was formed, lots of boys won bronc riding on their reputation, but now it has to be on their ability.

One thing we are trying to do within our Association is to get the cowboys to be more honest about paying their hotel and board bills.

I feel that the Cowboys' Turtle Association has accomplished a great deal during its short life. It has brought about better cooperation between the cowboys and the promoters. It is also a protection to the managements of the various shows, because when we OK a prize list, the management is sure the cowboys will put on a good show without any trouble.

In looking over my old prize lists of shows all over the country of the past four years, I notice that about 85% of them have raised their purses from 25% to 50%. This was because of the Turtle Association.

There has also been very little trouble, in proportion to the large number of shows. And, as far as I know, members of the Cowboys' Turtle Association are welcome to any show of any size with the exception of the one held at Prescott, Arizona." [60]

Jimmie Minotto, as spokesman for the CTA, was also asked to comment and he wrote:

"Whenever amateur shows take the place of real rodeos, the days of good rodeos are gone.

There is much more harmony between the Rodeo Association of America and the cowboys than there ever was before the organization of the Cowboys' Turtle Association. Each side appreciates the problems of the other and respects them, all of which tends to make better feeling and better rodeos.

I firmly believe that all good rodeos should live up to the rules of the R.A.A. and not deviate and make their own rules or set up some new trick and complicated events. Only that way will we have real champions and only that way will the rodeos survive as a fine, clean sport and an exhibition of courage and manhood.

I wish the Rodeo Association of America and my fellow Turtles the best of luck for the season of 1939." [60]

Another Non-Pro Rodeo

On the CTA page of the same issue Everett Bowman asked that no member of CTA work at Prescott's Frontier Days Rodeo this year. He wrote in the notice:

"It will be a Wild West or dud Rodeo this year and no part of it is a cowboy contest" Bowman advised members to go to Springerville, Ariz., instead. [60]

Doc Pardee was arena director for the Prescott rodeo and in 1939 he recommended to the approval of everyone that they drop out of RAA and hold a rodeo encouraging working ranch cowboys to participate. He made most of the rules for these competitions, including 5% of the gate would be held out so those not winning money would win something. The Prescott rodeo was advertised as a non-professional rodeo and continued in that vein for several years. Contestants that had won as good as second in any of the major rodeos in the past three years were ineligible. [#12]

The next month on the CTA page was a report from C. W. Gardner, the chairman of the Prescott rodeo. His statement was: "There's no future for an amateur 'be kind to animals' rodeo which Prescott held instead of the usual professional rodeo with professional contestants. Under special rules designed to prevent injuries to both livestock and performers." He reported, "The use of amateur talent slowed the show down considerably. Most of the business people of Prescott were displeased, not only with the show, but the manner in which the public received it."

It was evident the rodeos trying non-professional or amateur rodeos was a way of avoiding being 'dictated to' by outsiders, primarily CTA. All in all, most rodeo committees were finding that the professionalism of the Turtle members was more to the liking of the spectators and the sponsors. [#61]

Conflict Within the CTA Ranks

Controversy with the Ogden rodeo committee on the eve of their July, 1939, event caused quite a stir. Everett Bowman insisted they increase the purse $1,000. A lengthy discussion was held and the committee came to the conclusion it was impossible to raise the money. They admitted they could raise $750, but not $1,000.

Bowman did not give in, he gave them fifteen more minutes to raise it to $1,000. Although they were still attempting to raise the money, Bowman, Everett Shaw and some other Turtle ropers, walked out and went to Salt Lake City to compete. Left were approximately 65 other Turtles in Ogden that wanted to compete there, regardless of the lower prize money.

Bowman told the remaining Turtles that if they did stay and compete they would be fined $500 each. After Bowman left, Fritz Truan announced he would represent the Turtles remaining and approved the Turtles competing in Ogden, provided they would not be blackballed by the RAA. Meanwhile, Burel Mulkey sided with Truan, saying the bronc riders had not been consulted by Bowman in the decision, and it was Everett Bowman and Everett Shaw, ropers, that were the ones demanding the increase. The roughstock riding Turtles did stay and competed at Ogden after being approved by CTA members Mulkey and Truan.

Judge Maxwell McNutt, president of the RAA sent out a bulletin to the members of the RAA explaining the dilemma and asking for comments. Most of the comments returned were criticism of Bowman, not the Turtles, and many said they had no problems with the Turtles in the past. One or two responding members said the requests made by the Turtle representatives had been minimal and they had agreed to their requests. Rumors even spread that Everett Bowman had resigned as president. [62]

A letter on the CTA page in *Hoof & Horns*, the following month from Everett Bowman, gave an explanation of his reason for the demand. The main reason was the Ogden prize list was not circulated or submitted for CTA to see, a month in advance of their rodeo. When the list was finally circulated, only a total sum of $3,000 was announced. There was no way anyone could know how it was to be divided by event. A copy of CTA's new rules was sent to each RAA member, which included Ogden. He went on to say for everyone's interest, the Turtles were not fined for competing at Ogden and there was no dissension in the ranks. His parting comment was "On the contrary, the organization is stronger than ever before." [63]

Who Was Everett Bowman?

There was much criticism through the *RAA Bulletin* and RAA pages in *Hoofs & Horns* about Everett Bowman. No doubt there was even more criticism between cowboys and members of RAA about Bowman and how he conducted CTA business. His demeanor when representing Turtle business with representatives of various rodeos was firm and decisive.

As president of the CTA he acted in behalf of the members and presented the demands the best he could. When all information had been gathered, it appears his reasons for his actions were necessary. That doesn't mean the representatives of rodeos, especially those who had been having rodeos for some time, agreed with him, or thought the CTA had any right in dictating to them how to run their rodeos. It was not an easy job to have, being president of the Turtles. The job of president of the CTA required someone who could present demands, handle the criticism and complaints of others and not waiver. Bowman seemed to be the man for the job.

Everett Bowman was born in Hope, N.M. on July 12, 1899 and moved to Big Spring, Texas in 1907. The family then moved to Clifton, Ariz. in 1913, where he stayed the rest of his life. He was a ranch cowboy and entered his first rodeo at Salt Lake City, Utah in 1924. During his two decade rodeo career he won a significant amount of rodeos, and was the World Champion All-Around Cowboy in 1935 and 1937, plus runner-up in 1936, 1938 and 1939. He was the World Champion Bulldogger in 1930, 1933, 1935 and 1938. He held the title of Champion Calf Roper in 1929, 1935 and 1937, and Champion Steer Roper in 1937. [64]

Studio photo of Everett Bowman, taken in New York City, 1941. Many of the contesting cowboys had studio photos taken while in New York. *Photo taken by Pagano, Inc. Courtesy of Jack Long Collection.*

Bowman was no stranger to the roughstock events either, and had ridden bulls and broncs in his early years. He soon learned, however, most of his wins were at the opposite end of the arena. His titles in timed events were proof of his capabilities there.

He and his brother, Ed, made a two wheel horse trailer and pulled it to Cheyenne with an old Dodge truck in 1926. The trip from Arizona, over a thousand miles, to their destination took them a week. The trailer created quite a stir once they arrived in the Wyoming capitol as it was such a rarity. [65] Later, after he quit competing he became a field judge at Phoenix and a tie judge at Madison Square Garden rodeos.

Although he was known as a rancher and continued to ranch in later years, he ran for sheriff of Maricopa County on two different occasions, but was defeated. He was with the Arizona Highway Patrol for four years and the last year was captain of the Phoenix district. He learned to fly airplanes and in 1942 was known as Sergeant Bowman, Civil Air Patrol Number 29. His duties included flying mail and airplane parts to various airports in the state. He died in a Cessna 172 plane crash in 1971, and his body was found after a two day search southwest of Bagdad, Ariz. [66]

Is There Light at the End of the Tunnel?

After all the dissension and criticism from rodeo committees, about the very active CTA, letters started to be printed in both the CTA and RAA columns, in *Hoofs & Horns*, that complimented the Turtles instead of criticizing them. A letter received from Dr. Ralph Lovelady of Sidney, Iowa said:

"Here in this corn section of Iowa we don't know much about organized labor. About all we know is what we see in the papers and newsreels. And I am quite frank to say that seeing some of the destructive acts without knowing the details; we are rather against the whole set-up.

However, I am sure these rodeo contestants have something in this Turtle organization that is very much to their credit and exactly the reverse of the bad impressions we get from the industrial organizations.

Our rodeo has been going here fifteen years, and I have taken care of dozens of the men with both lesser and a few major injuries. They all want to work and want some sort of dressing on their injuries that will let them 'at 'em.' We get a fine chance to talk to these boys at the grounds hospital each year, to examine them, patch them up, and try to keep them in the going.

Not too many years ago when one of these boys was hurt, he was brought in with simply filthy under-clothing and a body unacquainted with soap and water. Every accident no matter how small meant a secondary infection. His bodily resistance was so low that recovery was always very much delayed, this I thought was because of their eating habits.

This year, to a man, it was an entirely different picture. No contestant showed up that was not cleanly shaven, hair cut, clothes of good quality, well pressed, and underclothing clean, good boots well polished, and a really clean body. And he had a great personal pride and his chin was up.

Years back, every man had some pet remedy for injuries that was as silly and old fashioned as a side saddle, and he was always listening to some other 'hand's' advice. Today he comes in, gets his dressing, X-ray, splinting, instructions as to how he should take care of the injury, and when to return for further treatment. In all instances he is very appreciative and follows directions really much better than our private patients. He has learned that the best of surgical treatment is the right one, and results are much quicker and better. And this is the first year I have seen no secondary infections of any kind due to a lack of soap and water.

The homes in which these boys stayed were all well satisfied, and all remarked how nice and clean they were, and this with no exceptions. Every man has the same program with this body of his and his personal appearance. A few years back these same homes were simply a wreck after our show was over and the families were through housing cowboys. Today they nearly all have arranged to have them back.

Today they are professional entertainers, take a pride in it, and are an asset to any rodeo management, and above all, I am sure they have a much higher morale that has put their chins up. Some of the credit for this big change goes to that scintillating Bowman who heads their organization, but it must be a contagious situation for every individual has the clean-up disease and has taken a complete treatment. To my way of thinking, it has been the Turtle organization that has put this change in the individual across and done the job 100 per cent.

Now don't get me wrong. With all of the above, I would not have you think for one moment that those old timers of ten or more years ago, with all their dirt and noise and hard-boiled manners, were not the salt of the earth, with the biggest of big hearts. They were simply swell, and to us who worked with them and really knew them, they were OK. Give you the shirt off their backs. They made this rodeo thing we now have and deserve the full credit despite the fact that they were a darned poor advertisement for their own profession. I know the Good Lord will be easy with them when He passes judgment.

If all the other shows have as pleasant relations with this group as we here in the tall corn country do, then rodeo is on a good solid foundation for years to come and it is these chaps that have done most of the hard work to make it so. Our people like it and want more of it." [63]

Other letters printed, even in the RAA column, such as a letter from the manager, Bob Wright, of the Lewiston RoundUp stated that although they had sent their prize list to RAA several months in advance, as required, it had NOT been printed in the *Hoofs & Horns* issue when they expected to see it, which could have caused CTA officials to not be advised in time for their rodeo. He went on to say, "As it happens, we have the approval from CTA of our prize list, but naturally it would put us in easier if it were published in the official magazine."[63]

Letters such as this began to put some of the blame on RAA officials, for failing to get information to the magazine. Rodeo managers were beginning to see the blame was not just with the CTA representatives.

There was also a letter by Pat Thomas, arena and race track manager for the San Juan Basin Rodeo Association., Inc. He wrote:

"Our committee feels that credit should be given members of the Turtle Association who contested at our show. Among them was Everett Bowman. These boys did everything possible to make the show a good one and cooperated in every manner and we feel that the Turtle Association should be given credit for a good deal of our success." [63]

Buff Douthitt, CTA #1176, rode by horseback to Carlsbad, N.M. in 1939 to enter his first rodeo. "I was young and dumb and when I entered the rodeo office, a big ole' boy said, 'are you a scab?' He scared the pants off me. I didn't know what a scab was, but I joined the Turtles. I got into the calf roping, but I didn't win anything."

Later, Buff had quite a rodeo career and not only won many roping events, he also was a performer and part of his act was to trick rope while balancing on a loose rope in cowboy boots.[#137]

1939 RAA World's Champion Cowboys Awards

The 1939 all-around cowboy and champion bareback rider was Paul Carney of Chandler, Ariz. He totaled 9,247 points in saddle bronc riding, bareback riding, steer riding, steer wrestling and calf roping. He received $500 cash from Levi Strauss & Co. He competed at 31 rodeos during the season and 28 were R.A.A. rodeos. He rode 101 saddle broncs, 76 steers, 56 bareback broncs and wrestled 16 steers. Carney, originally from Galeton, Colo., lived in Arizona.

Fritz Truan, of Lancaster, Calif., was the champion saddle bronc rider and received the Harry Rowell cash award of $200. Harry Hart, of Pocatello, Idaho, won the steer wrestling title and received $100 from the John B. Stetson Co. Dick Griffith, of Scottsdale, Ariz., was champ of steer riding and received a $200 cash award from Montgomery Wards & Co., and he also won $100 from Hamley Saddle Co., for being in 25th place in the list of cowboy standings. Dick Truitt, of Stonewall, Okla., won the 1939 single (steer) roping championship and received a $250 saddle from the Keyston Bros. Saddlery. Ray Mavity, of Helena, Mont., became steer decorating champion and was awarded $100 cash from Howard Buick Automobile Co. Toots Mansfield, of Bandera,

Paul Carney, RAA All-Around World Champion 1939, and Bareback Champ 1937 & 1939 and Saddle Bronc rider. *Photo by Max Kegley. Courtesy of Stan Searle from the Hoofs & Horns Collection.*

Texas, was the champion calf roper and received a cash award of $100 from Porter Saddle Co. Asbury Schell won the title in team tying and received $100 in cash from H. J. Justin & Sons. Schell also won this championship in 1937. [67]

CHAPTER THIRTEEN

New Year, New Rules

As the years clicked by the Cowboys' Turtle Association was making an impact on the professional rodeo world. It seemed like a slow process to those who were trying so desperately to improve the sport (*much like the movement of the turtle*). By the beginning of the fourth year, 1940, hindsight showed many demands had been met and the CTA membership had soared to 1,178. The organization was finally able to work on the rules affecting their own members, as well as rodeos.

A notice was posted:

"After January 1, 1940, no member of the CTA will be permitted to contest at any rodeo where the authority of the CTA is recognized who has not paid his dues, or who has unpaid board, doctor's, or hospital bills outstanding. This does not include personal debts."

Another edict posted:

"After January 1st, 1940, if any member of CTA is at a location where a CTA meeting is held they must attend or they will be fined. No exceptions will be made to this rule." [#67]

Ray Wharton can attest to the fact the Turtles did monitor rodeos and make sure cowboys entering CTA sanctioned rodeos had paid their dues, and had their Turtle card. He remembered being told at a Uvalde, Texas, rodeo he couldn't pay his entry fees until he joined. He was Turtle #1758. [#126] Later he became the 1956 world champion calf roper.

CTA meetings were held in Chicago and New York City during October, 1939, and the main purpose was to nominate candidates to be voted on for representatives for the six events: bulldogging, saddle bronc riding, bareback horse riding, bull or steer riding, team tying and calf and steer roping. These nominees were to be voted on by the membership by mailing in their ballot or attending the Phoenix, Ariz., meeting in February, and voting there. There was also a notice on the *Hoofs & Horns* CTA page that the dues, as of January 1, 1940, had been raised from $5.00 to $10.00.

A letter from a sixteen year old boy, named J. D. McCormick, from Council Grove, Kans., dated December 14, 1939 said he was sending in his $5.00 for 1940 dues to the Turtles. He stated he didn't make many rodeos and couldn't afford the extra $5.00 for the benefit fund.

His letter continued by saying in part:

"This summer was the first time I ever depended on what I made at shows for a living. The Turtles were good to me at all the shows. At Cheyenne I was broke and I rode over to the Turtle banquet and meeting one evening with Barton Carter. I was waiting for the meeting to start so I could go in and Mr. Bowman told me to come on in and eat. I believe I appreciated that meal as much as any I have ever eaten.

At this meeting I realized what a fine thing the Turtle Association is for the cowboys and what good work it is doing. I had been told by men who had rodeoed a long time that before the organization started there was real need for something of its nature." *(It was also mentioned in an 'Editor's Note:' that Everett Bowman paid this young man's other $5.00 for his 1940 CTA dues.)* [68]

The RAA page in the March, 1940, *Hoofs & Horns* issue had an open letter to members of RAA from president Maxwell McNutt who wrote in part:

"Rodeo Association of America was organized to foster this free and open competition spirit, to standardize rules of contest, to find a fair method of determining championships, and generally to improve conditions for all involved..."

After continuing to summarize what had been accomplished by RAA he said:

"On the other hand, if an organization of contestants is to name the purses, name the judges, and name the contestants, the members of R.A.A. will become instruments in a purse-splitting, money-distributing business. To many of the contestants who have in confidence expressed their opinions to me, this sort of spectacle is quite as obnoxious as it ought to be to every member and to every officer of R.A.A. Obviously the R.A.A. as such is powerless to remedy this condition unless every member thereof insist that point award events be open to all, and refuse to bar anyone at the behest of any person or of any body of persons." [#69]

Fritz Truan, Paul Carney, and Burel Mulkey waiting for the rodeo to begin.
Photographer unknown. Courtesy of the Jack Long Collection.

Election of Officers and Representatives for 1940

The election of CTA officers for 1940 were Everett Bowman, president; 1st vice-president, Herbert Meyers; 2nd vice-president, Rusty McGinty; and Hugh Bennett secretary-treasurer. The following representatives-directors were also elected: saddle bronc riding – Alvin Gordon; bareback bronc riding – Chet McCarty; steer riding – Ken Roberts; bulldogging — Tom Hogan; calf roping – Cecil Owsley; and team roping – Buckshot Sorrells. assistant representatives would be elected later. [#69]

The Rodeo Association of America convention was held in Houston, Texas, March 21 to 23, 1940. CTA representatives also attended and read their 1940 revised rules. From all reports it appeared the two organizations cooperated with one another in every way, and no rules were questioned. The CTA then adopted the RAA rules for contests. The RAA Rules & Regulations were printed entirely in the April issue of *Hoofs & Horns. (See Appendix; RAA Rodeo Rules)*[#70]

CTA 1940 Rules Sent

Everett Bowman, as president of CTA, wrote a letter to every promoter and stockman in the country:

"Dear Sir:

The Cowboys' Turtle Association takes pleasure in sending you their 1940 rules and membership list. This year the Association has enlarged its membership to include the following contract performers: cowgirl bronc riders, trick riders, trick ropers, clowns and announcers. In the back of the book you will find a list of members who have been dropped from the CTA for having failed to pay their 1939 dues. These members may enter only if they can show a 1940 card.

The CTA has already notified stockmen that its members will not contest at a rodeo where stock is furnished by a contractor who also furnishes stock to amateur shows, therefore we request your cooperation in this matter.

At the 1940 RAA meeting at Houston the CTA agreed to adopt the RAA rules for contests. Both organizations are anxious to see these rules put into effect and hope that all rodeo managements will adhere strictly to them.

The CTA requests that all shows furnish an ambulance and first aid equipment at the arena during each performance for the injured contestants. And the CTA hopes that the rodeos will see their way clear to paying doctors' and hospital bills, or as large a percentage of them as possible. A number of the foremost rodeos of the country have undertaken this responsibility which is appreciated by every member of the CTA. This is particularly important as the contestants are unable to secure accident insurance and the death benefit fund of the Association does not cover accidents.

The CTA feels assured of your cooperation and wishes your rodeo the best of luck. Our members will do everything to make your show a success, for as you know, mutual trust makes for mutual advantage.

Yours very truly,

Everett Bowman, President."[71]

Ellensburg "Golden Jubilee" rodeo, held the latter part of summer, was advertised as "three successive days of thrills," Saturday, Sunday and Labor Day. When the CTA first formed they were at odds with this rodeo for several years. According to the following letter written to Everett Bowman, president of CTA, by their secretary their feelings toward CTA had changed. It said:

"May 9, 1940 Dear Everett: Arena Director Lou Richards and the directors have asked me to write you relative to plan of selection of cowboy judges for the 18th annual Rodeo, Saturday, Sunday and Labor Day.

The plan agreed upon a year ago, was to have you the official Turtle representative and our arena director to each select five men from the Turtle approved list; who were on the scene and available, and then draw the required number of names out of the hat, two each for the bronc and bull riding events, and flag and barrier judges for the dogging and calf roping events. We paid $50.00 each for the riding judges and $25.00 each for the flag and barrier men. If I remember correctly last year Lou did not even put any names in the hat but simply approved the men the Turtles selected, because he figured all these men were perfectly satisfactory to our management, especially as they met with the approval of the contestants.

We have had several letters of application for the judging work from men on your list, but so far have answered these men, that we were largely leaving this to agreement with the contestants, after they reach Ellensburg.

Does the above last year's plan meet with your approval and that of your organization? Our rules and regulations will be ready for the press in a few days, and we want to be able to publish the manner of selecting judges. If the above plan is not satisfactory, please suggest any changes.

We have also added bareback riding as a contest this year. Our purses will be as follows:

Final Money divided 40 per cent to winner, 30 per cent to second, 20 per cent to third and 10 per cent to fourth.

Saddle Bronc Riding	$600
Calf roping	$600
Bulldogging	$600
Bull Riding	$400
Bareback riding	$300

We realize the bareback is down to the minimum for a three day show, but if the boys will play with us on that amount this year we will endeavor to raise it some next, providing we make any money. Last year we lost $2500, but as you know paid off in full during the show, and raised the money afterwards. By having a $400 purse for bull riding and $300 for bareback riding, we figure the bareback boys will have a chance at good money here.

All entrance fees to be put into day money prizes. Wild horse race will also be open to all this year.

As soon as the premium lists are off the press will forward to all members of the official family of the Turtles. For that reason we are anxious to have your approval on the judges and your suggestions on any other points. In the rules for each event, we are eliminating all local conditions, simply stating that each of those events will be run under RAA rules, which have been approved by Turtles.

Can you tell us where Jaswell (*I believe they are meaning Jasbo Fulkerson)*, the clown, is now. We want to use him again this year as we did last year, but understand he has been in Australia. Johnny Jordan will announce.

Note your request in bulletin to have shows use only members of Turtles in trick riding and roping. Are the following in good standing with your organization? Dick Griffith, Fay Dennis Knight and Paul and Marie St. Croy.

New Year, New Rules Page 143

Dorothy Looney, the little local girl we used last year, wants to ride again. It is the only show she makes and because of the local angle and the color of such a little tot, we are anxious to use her if your organization has no objection. Sincerely, (signed) Fred T. Hofmann, Secretary, The Ellensburg Rodeo Copy sent to: Hugh Bennett" [72]

After the earlier problems with Ellensburg refusing to comply with demands made by the CTA, it appears that just as some of the other resistant rodeo managements, such as Pendleton RoundUp, they had a change of heart. More and more rodeos were complying with CTA requirements because they knew the best rodeo cowboys were members of the Cowboys' Turtle Association. If Turtles were going to compete at their rodeo their crowds would be larger and therefore they would make a bigger profit. Who could complain about that?

Competition 'Down Under'

The Australian Rodeo Association held an International Tournament including Australian rodeo cowboys plus cowboys from the United States and Canada during this time. It was called The Royal Easter Show and had been held annually in March at Sidney. The cowboys who represented the United States in 1940 were: Hank Mills, CTA #222, from Colorado, and Cecil Jones, CTA #299, from Idaho. Cowgirls attending were Tad Lucas, CTA #601, from Texas, known as a champion bronc rider, and Trixie McCormick, CTA #1881, of Chicago, who trick rode and spun the ropes. Jasbo Fulkerson, CTA #1252, from Texas, was the cowboy clown, and was quite popular in Australia as he had performed there for several years.

The Canadian representatives were Waldo Ross, from Alberta, and Harley Walsh, of Madden. The Canadians won the 'buck-jumping (saddle bronc riding), followed by Jones and Mills from the U. S.

Bulldogging was a new competition 'down under' and surprisingly the Australian team out-'dogged' their visitors. Jones tied with two Australians Ken Edwards and Grove McDonald for first place in the bull riding event. [73]

Cecil remembered that he rode a bull that had never been ridden and they were so impressed they presented him with a wristwatch that he still has today. [74]

Amateur Versus Professional

As the Turtles continued to make inroads in the world of professional rodeo there were always rodeos reluctant to comply with the rules the CTA demanded. The following article was placed in *Hoofs & Horns* by president Bowman:

"TURTLES, ATTENTION! I have just read in the newspaper about Prescott going amateur again this year. It seems a pity that it, being the oldest rodeo in history and at one time a really good show, has now gone down to nothing. I really thought they would be through with an amateur show after having such a mess of a rodeo there last year. I went to see the Chairman of the Board, Clarence Jackson, and suggested that they have an open show with the amateur events along with the professional events. He seemed to think it was a good idea.

I want to advise the contract people such as trick riders, trick ropers, announcer, and clown that they had better not work at Prescott, as it is advertised as strictly an amateur show, and working there would put them in bad with the CTA at all professional rodeos. Also the stock that is used at Prescott will be boycotted by the CTA at all professional shows.

In the last few weeks I have OK'ed lots of prize lists, but have refused two on account of the purses being so uneven. These two were Livingston, Montana, and Reno, Nevada." [75]

CTA Gets Some Much Needed Praise

Ethel A. Hopkins, editor of *Hoofs and Horns*, was one of the strongest supporters of the Turtle association. She wrote an article applauding the CTA and what it had accomplished. With huge headlines, on page 5 of her July issue:

"Risking Their Necks for Glory!

Risking their necks for glory!

Yes, literally that!

For Rodeo is the most dangerous of sports. The cowboys are pitting their strength and technique against the brute strength and trickiness of the broncs, bulls, steers, and calves they work with in the arena. And the battle many times goes to the animal.

That Rodeo is a sport with a capital "S" cannot be denied, for in no other one do those engaged in it pay for the privilege of contesting for prize money. Rodeo is strictly a contest – no salaries are paid the contestants, and if they do not win, all they get is the glory of having tried.

Rodeoing, from the cowboy's standpoint, is no mere child's play, but danger and drama – the drama of the range.

The cowboys do not just "up and do it" in any of their work. Back of every exhibition of skill lie long months and years of learning and practice.

It looks easy, but could YOU do it?

The cowboys you see at the good rodeos are professionals—ten chances to one they're Turtles.

'Turtles?' you ask. 'They don't look like turtles, they're too fast.'

And fast they are! The Cowboys' Turtle Association didn't select the name because of the speed of the creature which is their symbol, but because of its tenacity and perseverance. And looking at it that way, it suits them to a 'T.'

The C.T.A. came into being in 1936 because there was a great need for such an organization – for cowboys. The aims of the Association were to raise the standards of cowboy contests from the standpoints of both managements and contestants and to protect the interests of professional contestants by having larger purses offered with the cowboy's entrance fees added to them, and by having competent judges for the events.

These Turtles are professionals and they are as jealous of their standing as are professionals in any other line.

Within the Association the standards of honesty, fair play, financial responsibility, and fair representation are high. Individuals who are unable to maintain these standards are gradually disappearing from the membership list.

As a result of the policy of the C.T.A. being put into effect and through cooperation with the managements of rodeos, better shows are being given with more satisfaction to all concerned.

In the less than four years of its existence, the Cowboys' Turtle Association has attained a membership of more than 1,100 and has become a power in the rodeo world. Much credit is due these cowboys who are working to perfect an organization to benefit not only themselves but the great sport of Rodeo as well."[#62]

In the following issue, Hopkins included another page long article she wrote touting "IT'S A TURTLE SHOW!" and told more in detail how the sport had improved in so many ways since the CTA had been formed. [#73]

Ethel "Ma" Hopkins, First Lady of Rodeo

"Ma" Ethel A. Hopkins was called the 'First Lady of Rodeo' when she died at the age of 85, in November of 1964. She had been a teacher for many years. She moved from Missouri to Oklahoma, but when it was necessary to move to Arizona for her husband's health they settled in Tucson and she was the secretary to the dean of the college of agriculture. She also became editor of the University of Arizona faculty publications. Her husband, an attorney, died in 1923. She later married Joseph Hopkins, in 1930, a printing company official. At his request in 1933 she took over *Hoofs & Horns*, a slumping magazine, which published only 1,000 copies. She changed the format to cover rodeo and it became the "bible" to the world of rodeo. The circulation soared to 10,000 copies an issue. When she came to *Hoofs & Horns* she didn't know a surcingle from a saddle but it didn't take her long to learn the lingo and learn to love 'her' cowboys and cowgirls. It was evident her magazine was a labor of love and she took care of the rough and tumble fellows that called themselves cowboys.

One day a fox terrier crated and addressed to her arrived by mail in her office. "I know no one who would send me a dog," she thought wondering about him. A few days later a cowboy from Texas, that Ma didn't know, arrived asking for his dog. He admitted he was moving to Tucson and didn't know a soul who he could keep his dog until he got there, but he read *Hoofs & Horns* religiously and decided she was a good woman and he knew she would care for his dog until he got there." Ma finally retired, at age 76, and sold the magazine.[77,#78,#79]

"Ma" Hopkins, editor of the Hoofs & Horns magazine receives a gift from Mrs. Jones, at the Cow Palace, for her service to CTA and to rodeo in general on the 17th anniversary of the magazine, 1950. In the background is Carl Sheppard on the left and Eddie Akridge on the right. *Photographer unknown. Courtesy of Stan Searle from the Hoofs & Horns Collection.*

McNutt Resigns

In the July *Hoofs & Horns* issue was a letter from president Maxwell McNutt, of the Rodeo Association of America, dated June 6, 1940, to all members, directors, and officers of the RAA, announcing his resignation from the offices of director and president. He apparently decided it was time to resign because of the lack of response from his letter printed previously in the March issue to all RAA member rodeos, and specifically due to the lack of response from rodeos in his home state of California.

He determined that the "California members have accepted 'the ordination' of the Turtles." Since this was in opposition to his feelings about rodeo he completed the letter by writing:

"I am not to be understood as expressing any criticism, but I feel that where there exists such a divergence of opinion upon a subject so fundamentally affecting the institution of the Rodeo, as I view it, my further participation in such capacity would avail nothing.

McNutt had been a strong supporter to the members of CTA, at its beginning. He had even written the original articles of the association, by-laws, and rules, for the Turtles, based on his experience as a director of the RAA and as his professional background as an attorney and a Superior Court judge in California.

There were times, however, when he opposed the manner in which CTA members went about making their demands to rodeo. But he always handled each situation with an open mind. Where and when he began to disagree with the Turtle's advances in professional rodeo one can only guess. His importance and support of CTA in the beginning of the cowboy's organization should be respected and appreciated.

L. B. Sylvester took McNutt's place as president of the RAA. He was born in the state of Wisconsin, but moved to Colorado fifty years earlier. He served as president of the Colorado State Cattle Board for nine years, started and named the Ski-Hi Stampede, in Monte Vista, Colo. over twenty years earlier, and since the beginning of the RAA had served as a member of the board of directors. [76]

The Billboard Publishing Company, which included a column entitled The Corral, and reported on Wild West and rodeo people, received a letter by Pat Thomas, secretary of the San Juan Basin Rodeo Association, Inc. that was printed in that column and said:

"Dear Sir: In the July 6th issue of *The Billboard* on page one appeared an article about Judge Maxwell McNutt resigning as President of the RAA in which he remarks that rodeos have descended to the level of a racket and are under the control of a certain group of union riders. In fairness to the cowboy contestants and the Turtle Association, exception should be taken to this, as rodeo today is on a much higher plane than it was several years back when there was no Cowboys' Turtle Association or Rodeo Association of America.

I have been in the rodeo business approximately fifteen years working on committees and with the promotion, and have found that in the last three or four years since the organization of the Turtles that the shows have improved both in the type of performers and in the ease of management due to the fine cooperation given to our show by the members of the Cowboys' Turtle Association.

Rodeo is a tough game and there is no protection granted any cowboy contestant. He has to put up money to enter a contest, and the rules of the game have become so strict that in every sense the advantage

Buck Echols CTA #104, roping at the Dublin Rodeo, home of Lightning C Ranch, owned by Everett Colborn, of World Championship Rodeo. *Photographer R. R. Doubleday, from the Dickinson Research Center, National Cowboy & Western Heritage Museum. Courtesy of the Echols Family of Liberty, Texas.*

is given to the animal he competes upon. I was at the Houston Convention (RAA), and the Turtle Association, under their president, Everett Bowman, made it known that they were willing to cooperate in every way with members of the RAA.

The Spanish Trails Fiesta of Durango (CO) is an RAA show, and is also a Turtle show, which means it is open to the world for competition, but it does abide by the rules and regulations as set down by the Turtle Association. We have operated this way for the last five years and each year our show has grown, and due to the fine cooperation of the cowboys, it is making it possible to be one of the best shows in the Southwest.

Would appreciate your publishing this letter as I feel that the cowboys need someone to take their part as they are receiving far too much criticism from too many sources, and the real success of the rodeo game is dependent upon these fine performers." [80]

Bob Chambers, CTA #261, remembers vividly when Everett Bowman asked him if he wanted to be a Turtle. Bob said, "It was like God speaking to you. Everett was the main man. We were at Puyallup, Wash. and they let out twenty broncs, bulls, steers with guys on them. I was signed up to ride. It was quite a thing to watch. I was only 17 and not much of a rider and when he asked me, I was honored and paid my $10 right then."

Chambers became a well known rodeo announcer and spent many years in the announcer's stand, including announcing the National Finals Rodeos for 1967, 1973, and 1981. [130]

John D. Holleyman, Turtle #1404, of Corona, N.M., told the following when queried about the Turtles: "I was just a poor working cowboy. I joined the Turtles at Cheyenne in 1940 because they wouldn't let us enter if we didn't join. But we didn't put up much of a fuss. It cost $5.00 and in those days that was as big as a wagon wheel!" [153]

Holleyman was a roper. In addition to his rodeo competition, he also was in numerous 'matched ropings'. He was matched against Toots Mansfield at Pecos, Texas in 1949, and after they both roped ten head of snuffy brahma steers, they were tied—both had a score of 155.5 seconds. [154]

Don "Jug" Reynolds, CTA #216, is the son of well known rodeo clown and animal trainer of the Turtles era, Fess Reynolds, CTA #196. When Don was just shy of three years old, he performed in his first rodeo at Erick, Okla. in 1939 with a trained Shetland pony and an Angora goat. He continued to perform with his dad and became a trick rider, trick roper, and a Roman rider. "Jug" said he doesn't remember becoming a Turtle, but obviously, Fess made sure he was a member. [133] He may have been the youngest cowboy at the age of three 3 or 4 to become a Turtle. The CTA numbers Fess and Don were assigned had been CTA numbers originally for other cowboys. It can be surmised that Fess and Don joined after the 1940 CTA book was printed and were assigned numbers from cowboys who dropped out of the Turtle group. Later when "Jug" was around twelve years old he became Red Ryder's sidekick, Little Beaver, in movies released in 1949. In addition to his acting in movies and later in his career he also trained animals, like his dad, and had quite a movie career. [134]

The CTA annual meeting was held in the Belvedere Hotel in New York City during the October rodeo there. The following men were elected to serve in official capacities for the 1941 year. Officers elected were:

Everett Bowman remained President;
Rusty McGinty, Vice President
Bill Clemans, Secretary-Treasurer
Event Representatives:
Bareback Riding – Chet McCarty
Saddle Bronc Riding – Alvin Gordon
Calf Roping – Buckshot Sorrells
Bulldogging – Tom Hogan
Bull Riding – Hughie Long
Steer Roping – King Merritt

The following donations were made to the Turtle Benefit Fund: Jack Kriendler of 21 Club (New York City) donated $200, Gene Autry donated $150 and Sears-Roebuck gave $200. [81]

R.A.A. World Champions for 1940

The RAA world champions were: all-around went to Fritz Truan, of Salinas, Calif., who also won the title for saddle bronc riding. He had also won the saddle bronc riding championship in 1939. Carl Dossey, of Phoenix, Ariz., was the champion bareback rider. Clay Carr, of Visalia, Calif., won the title for steer roping. He held this title in 1930, and also won the saddle bronc and all-around titles that year, too. Homer Pettigrew, of Grady, N.M., was the world champion steer wrestler. Pete Grubb, of Florence, Ariz., was the team roping champion.

He had won the bareback riding title in 1938. Dick Griffith, of Scottsdale, Ariz., was the world champion bull rider, and held the same title in 1939. He had also been an International champion trick rider. Toots Mansfield, of Bandera, Texas, was the calf roping title holder, and he also held that same title in 1939. Jack Wade, of Chandler, Ariz., was the world's champion steer decorator.

The following competitors were runners-up in these events: Nick Knight, of Cody, Wyo., was second in saddle bronc riding. Kid Fletcher, of Hugo, Colo., won second in bull riding and Smokey Snyder, of Buena Park, Calif., won third. Frank Finley, of Phoenix, Ariz., was second in bareback riding. Waldo Ross, of Warner, Alberta, Canada, won second in steer decorating. Charles Whitlow, of Florence, Ariz., was second in team roping. Gene Ross, of Sayre, Okla. was second in steer wrestling. Jess Goodspeed, of Okemah, Okla., was second in calf roping. Buck Goodspeed, of Okemah, Okla., was second in single steer roping. [82]

CHAPTER FOURTEEN
1941 – A Spirit of Cooperation

The RAA Convention was held in Salinas, Calif., in January, 1941. Due to an automobile accident incurred by the new president, L. B. Sylvester, R. J. Hofmann, of Cheyenne, Wyo. was elected president. Included in his resume was his association with Frontier Days since 1926 and he had been chairman of Frontier Days since 1938. His dad had been involved in the management since the first Frontier Days in 1897.

Other important items handled at this meeting included the CTA announcing they were releasing stock contractors from the requirement they could not furnish stock to an amateur show. CTA also got RAA to agree that "no member of the RAA would accept, for contesting, any person who was unsatisfactory to both the Turtles and the RAA" It was also agreed that all member rodeos (of RAA) must send in its results of the rodeo immediately after the show, and on the blank form furnished by the RAA, including the names of the announcer, trick ropers, and riders, the clown, arena judges, and the name of the stock contractors which would be printed in the *RAA News*. Another change that was made by RAA was that: "one point would be given for each dollar won, not including added entrance fees, instead of the two points as heretofore." There were also some individual event rule changes. (*Found in the Appendix, under RAA rules*). [82]

An article by Bill Clemans, the new secretary of CTA, in the February issue of *Hoofs & Horns*, said:

"There have been a lot of conflicting stories about the Denver Rodeo (*part of the National Western Stock Show & Rodeo held annually in January*), and in order to clear the matter up, I will give the outstanding points.

The Cowboys' Turtle Association asked Denver to add calf roping to their program, and although they did not actually refuse, the Denver officials stated they did not like to add this event. The CTA representatives (board of directors) then took a vote as to whether or not they should work the Denver show. The vote was 5 to 2 not to work there unless calf roping was added. The Denver officials were advised of this fact, and calf roping was added to the program, and OK'ed by the CTA. So the Denver rodeo of 1941 is now accredited for CTA members." [16]

An editorial by Lou Richards, of Ellensburg, Wash., vice president of District No. 2 of the RAA wrote:

"On the whole the RAA Convention in Salinas last January was the best I have ever attended. There were several factors that contributed towards making this convention outstanding.

First – was the vastly improved spirit of cooperation that seemed to prevail. Rodeo directors and managers, stockmen, contract people and contestants alike showed a broader attitude toward common problems. There seemed to be a growing realization that we must all work together in perpetuating the spirit of the Old West, preserving its ideals and traditions, and uniting in putting over a program that will mean a better understanding of the West and for better attendance, better showmanship and better publicity.

Throughout this Convention there seemed to be a growing realization that we are all selfishly interested in the same general results, and that we must give as well as take and, above all, we must realize that others undoubtedly have good and sound reasons for the positions they have taken.

We, of the Ellensburg delegation at Salinas, came home enthusiastic about this better understanding and cooperation. We feel the Rodeo

1941 - A Spirit of Cooperation

Winners of 1940 Madison Square Garden Rodeo. Left to right: Dick Griffith, Steer riding; Hank Mills, Bareback bronk riding; Jackie Cooper, Saddle bronk riding; Bill Clemens, Secretary CTA; Gene Autry, rodeo guest artist; Cherrie Lee Osborne, Winning ranch girl sponsor contest; Alice Greenough, Cowgirl Bronk Riding; Colonel John Reed Kilpatrick, President of Madison Square Garden Corporation; Everett E. Colborn, Managing Director of Rodeo; Toots Mansfield, Calf roping; Howard McCrory, Steer wrestling. *Photo from 1941 Madison Square Garden Program, photographer unknown. Courtesy of the Jack Long Collection.*

today is on a far better footing than ever before, and that with the knowledge that all the groups that have a part in Rodeo, at last have united, we can go ahead and build our shows on a much sounder basis.

The contestants and the contract men are losers when the shows are not financially strong and I know they realize this.

The rodeos which deal fairly and squarely with the contestants and the contract people are the ones which will attract the best contestants and put on the best performances.

I believe that we on the management end have at times been too stubborn, and that some of the changes the Turtles have brought about have been a mighty good thing for the rodeos. I believe today we have better judging and I know the contestants have cooperated with me as arena director in helping to speed up the show. I believe the contestants are entitled to good purses. I certainly believe they are entitled to have a real voice in the contest rules.

We, as managers, are interested in fast, thrilling shows that please the crowd. We, in the old cattle districts, are also interested in preserving some of the best traditions. Many of us are working solely as a community job, and the community wants top quality and little thought of any financial returns other than a sinking fund.

I feel some bad mistakes have been made on both sides in the past. I am most hopeful, after the Salinas Convention of better understanding and the elimination of any strife in the future. Let us all help in keeping up the good work and in preventing any misunderstandings or strife. It is to the selfish interests of everyone of us to follow that course." [83]

An article entitled "RODEO TODAY" in the July issue of *Hoofs & Horns* had statements made by various people representing various phases of the sport. Those included were L. B. Sylvester, president emeritus of RAA; Fred S. McCargar, secretary of RAA; Richard Merchant, as a contestant; C. A. Studer of the Southwest Rodeo Association; John Jordan, an announcer; Jack M. Dillon, on rodeo in Canada; Foghorn Clancy on famous bucking horses; Leland Rice for the Cowboys' Amateur Association of America; and Bill Clemans, secretary-treasurer of the CTA.

Clemans wrote:

"The Cowboys' Turtle Association was originally formed as a protection for the cowboys against what the cowboys considered at the time, unjust conditions in rodeos. Later at the formal organization of this Association the scope of the CTA was enlarged, and in the Articles of Association the following were some of the desires and ambitions outlined:

To organize the professional rodeo contestants of the USA for their mutual protection and benefit.

To raise the standards of cowboy contests so they rank among the foremost American sports.

To cooperate insofar as possible with the management of all rodeos at which the members contest.

To protect members against unfairness on the part of any rodeo management.

To bring about honest advertising by the rodeo associations so that the public may rely upon the truth of advertised events in which it is claimed that members of the CTA will participate.

To work for the betterment of conditions and of the rules governing rodeo events in which the members of the CTA take part.

Now as a full fledged organization of approximately 1500 members the CTA can look back over the past with few regrets. True, mistakes have been made but most of these mistakes can be traced to overzealousness and misunderstanding, and in few instances can the mistakes be traced to malicious or intentional desire to show power.

Many of the ambitions as originally outlined have been accomplished but the desire of the members of the CTA to continue to better their organization, as well as rodeo conditions in general, has not slackened. This can be more clearly emphasized by citing the action of the Board of Directors at a recent meeting in Fort Worth. At this meeting it was unanimously voted to pay bad bills run up by members in connection with a rodeo. Second and third offenders are to be penalized and fourth offenders will be suspended.

Fritz Truan, Toots Mansfield, Buckshot Sorrels and Homer Pettigrew hanging on a corral. *Photographer unknown.*

The Cowboys' Turtle Association has not devoted much time toward an effort to bring about honest advertising nor have they been particularly successful in having rodeo recognized as a national sport. These are problems that still lie ahead and will eventually receive the Turtle attention they merit. Seldom a week passes but this office receives a letter commending the CTA upon its honest desire to improve rodeo and the spirit of cooperation the Turtles have shown in an attempt to achieve this end.

All credit for the success of this organization must be given to the men that have worked as officers and directors of the CTA. It is men like Everett Bowman, who in the afternoon of his rodeo career, can look back over an enviable record as a rodeo contestant and see the Association nurtured from an immature and unpredictable body having grown into an organization of national importance in the rodeo world." [84]

In that same issue on the CTA page was a notice to all contractors that stated: "The CTA is not attempting to deny any stockman the privilege of furnishing stock to any show. However, the CTA does reserve the right of advising its members what shows they can work and the CTA will continue to exercise that privilege."

The annual meeting held in New York during the Madison Square Garden rodeo in October 1941 was time for election of new officers, representatives, directors and spokesmen. Everett Bowman continued as president. Floyd Stillings, of Cody, Wyo., was vice president, and Emily K. Knight, of Florence, Ariz., was elected secretary-treasurer. The representatives of each event were: Buck Sorrells, of Tucson, Ariz., for calf roping; Hub Whiteman, of Clarksville, Texas, for bulldogging; Smokey Snyder, of Fullerton, Calif., for bull riding; Carl Dossey, of Phoenix, Ariz., for bareback riding; Nick Knight, of Cody, Wyo., for saddle bronc riding; and King Merritt, of Federal, Wyo., for steer roping.

The CTA spokesmen elected were: Clay Carr, Visalia, Calif.; Doff Aber, of Newhall, Calif.; Hoytt Hefner, of Wichita Falls, Texas; Clinton Booth, of Manvel, Texas; Everett Shaw, of Stonewall, Okla.; Stub Bartlemay, of Arlington, Ore.; Harry Hart, of Pocatello, Idaho; Pete Kerscher, of Blackfoot, Idaho; Dave Campbell of Reno, Nev.; Buck Echols, of Liberty, Texas; and Joe Bassett of Payson, Ariz.. [85]

A small notice in *Hoofs & Horns* from Hughie Long, representative of the CTA bull riders wrote asking bull riders:

"Do you want to spur bulls once out of first three jumps in 1941? Let me hear from all of you real soon, as it isn't long 'till the RAA

Unidentified boy playing guitar and singing with Everett Bowman, Everett Shaw and Shorty Creed listening in the basement of Madison Square Garden. *Photographer unknown.*

Convention. Please sign your name to letter or postcard. Hughie Long, Box 122, Cresson, Texas". [88]

The RAA world champions for 1941 were: all-around champion, Homer Pettigrew, from Grady, N. M., with 5,027 points. He was the world champion steer wrestler in 1940 and second place in the steer wrestling and calf roping in 1941; saddle bronc champ, Doff Aber, Newhall, Calif.; top bull rider, Dick Griffith, of Scottsdale, Ariz., won the title for the third consecutive year. Bareback riding world titleholder, George Mills, Montrose, Colo.; calf roping champ for the third year in a row, Toots Mansfield, Bandera, Texas; steer wrestling champion, Hub Whiteman, Clarksville, Texas; steer decorating champ, Frank McDonald, Stavely, Alberta., Canada; single (steer) roping champion, Ike Rude, Mangum, Okla.; team roping champion, Jim Hudson, Dos Cabezos, Ariz.. [86, 87]

Laurence T. Heron, of the *Chicago Tribune*, wrote to the RAA asking specific questions about rodeo, and the RAA secretary, Fred S. McCargar not only answered his questions, but also posted his answers in an issue of *Hoofs & Horns* for everyone's benefit. It was quite informative and gave an overall perspective of rodeo in 1942.

McCargar explained that the RAA had been selecting the world champions in the major events for the past 12 years under a system of points awarded at RAA member rodeos. Points were based on the amount of money earned by the contestant, less the money known as 'added entrance fees'. "To date we have found no system which is better than this, although even this system has this flaw – it gives the contestant who attends the most shows a decided advantage over the contestant who may have won by competing only at a few shows. In other words, there is no average."

Contract performers; Dick Griffith, Polly Burson, Faye Blessing, Myrtle Goodrich, Bernice Dossey and Buff Brady, 1942. *Photographer unknown. Courtesy of Jack Long Collection.*

Heron asked how many rodeos are held each year in the United States and Canada, and McCargar's answer was: "There are approximately 150 recognized rodeos. Some of these are exclusively rodeos, some are held in conjunction with fairs and stock shows."

Secretary McCargar said the question asked about attendance was impossible to answer because although 260,000 attended the Calgary fair and rodeo each year, how many attended the rodeo was uncertain. The question about how many contestants enter a rodeo was answered that generally around one hundred contestants would enter. He explained that rodeos that had low entrance fees often attracted local cowboys to compete against champions. For example, as many as 350 contestants entered the Salinas rodeo the last few years.

Which and where are the ten biggest rodeos?
By the amount of money paid to contestants per event per performance. They were:
1. Los Angeles, (California) Coliseum Rodeo, one performance
2. Cheyenne (Wyoming) Frontier Days, five performances
3. San Bernadino, (California) National Rodeo, two performances
4. California Rodeo, (Salinas) four performances
5. Madison Square Garden Rodeo (New York), twenty-six performances
6. Tucson (Arizona) Fiesta de los Vaqueros, three performances
7. Iowa Championship Rodeo (Sidney) four performances
8. Reno (Nevada) Rodeo, three performances
9. Klamath Falls (Oregon) Rodeo, three performances
10. Pendleton (Oregon) RoundUp, four performances, and Lewiston (Idaho) RoundUp, three performances (tied)

Taking the rodeos according to the total purse paid to the contestants, they rate as follows:
1. Madison Square Garden, N.Y.

2. Chicago Stadium Rodeo
3. Boston Garden Rodeo
4. Minneapolis Aquatennial Rodeo
5. Cheyenne Frontier Days
6. Houston Fat Stock Show Rodeo
7. Grand National Exposition, San Francisco, California
8. California Rodeo, Salinas, California
9. Calgary Exposition and Stampede
10. Iowa's Championship Rodeo, Sidney, Iowa
Auditorium Rodeo, Buffalo, New York
Cleveland Arena Rodeo, Ohio (these three tied) [87]

The end of 1940 Hugh Bennett gave up his job as secretary-treasurer of the organization. Bill Clemans, of Florence, Ariz., held the office for 1941 until the December, 1941, *Hoofs & Horns* issue announced CTA dues should be sent to secretary-treasurer, Emily Knight at Florence, Ariz.. CTA Headquarters moved to 1613 North Laurel Avenue in Phoenix, Ariz. in 1942 and Fannye Jones was announced as secretary-treasurer. [87] A position she held until the CTA became the Rodeo Cowboys Association.

CHAPTER FIFTEEN

World War II Affects Everyone

World War II began in 1939 when Germany invaded Poland. A little later Britain and France were in the battle, shortly followed by Australia, New Zealand, Canada and South Africa. Japan had been at war with China since 1937, but on December 7, 1941, they bombed an unsuspecting Pearl Harbor, Hawaii, as well as some British Islands in the Pacific. It didn't take long once the fighting began for United States citizens to get involved.

Cowboys, especially, don't have to have much of a reason to get involved in a fight, and it was evident this war was going to be the biggest 'fight' of the century. Some cowboys were drafted, but many enlisted. Some went to Europe to fight, while others were sent to the Pacific.

Rodeo Important to National Defense

One of the major concerns by 1942 was the war and the part played by American citizens. Chuck Martin, long time rodeo reporter, wrote in the March issue of *Hoofs & Horns* about the situation. He said, in part:

"Rodeo has already contributed to National Defense until it HURTS. Many of our top hand contestants now wear Uncle Sam's uniform, and many more will be called. Nearly all are physically fit, because they have to keep that way in order to compete in their chosen profession."

Martin also encouraged rodeos to continue to be held, during wartime, especially during the daylight hours, as rodeo was a builder of morale. He knew concessions would be made by the CTA, in their stringent rules and regulations, but it would mean an increase in Turtle membership. Defense workers were working overtime and their nerves were strained. They needed recreation to relax and rodeo would give both. [#89]

At the RAA Convention in Colorado Springs, January, 1942, most of the discussions were about the role of rodeo in national defense. It was encouraged that rodeos be held near military bases whenever possible. It was also reiterated that rodeo was one of the most important ways to keep morale at an all time high, not just with soldiers, but with the general public. [#89]

The CTA purchased $10,000 worth of United States Defense Bonds. [#90] Some rodeos were canceling their annual event in anticipation of poor attendance. Although rodeos were encouraged to continue several factors had to be determined before rodeos could make their final decision. Both east and west coasts were encouraged not to hold large gatherings under lights at night, due to the possibility of attack. In fact, the west coast had a mandatory blackout.

Restrictions were put on travel, and gas and tires were precious commodities. What with gas rationing and all, many rodeo locations were short on men, for those who didn't enter the military, were either left at home to take care of business, or working in defense plants.

Hoofs & Horns, which had all ready become known as the cowboy's 'bible' became more important during war-time and was full of patriotic comments. The July issue's cover was the American flag, and "Ma" Hopkins, editor, wrote on the first page:

"The American Flag on our cover is the symbol of the freedom which we have always enjoyed – freedom to think and speak and write; freedom to work; freedom to play; and freedom to worship in the way our conscience and beliefs dictate – individual freedom which is the basis of national freedom.

And to the ideals of which our American Flag is the symbol we dedicate ourselves anew.

We will work, fight, and pray until the menace to our freedom is removed.

As Joe Louis said lately, 'We will win this war because we are on God's side.' Not that 'God is on our side.'

Rodeo would get short shrift under an axis regime. So Rodeo is one thing we are fighting for, and it must be kept alive, as an integral part of our American way of living, for the duration. Wherever it's practicable the shows should go on. And after the active fighting is ended, it will again come into its own, for there is no other sport that so appeals to red blooded Americans.

WE WILL WIN THE WAR.
WE WILL HAVE RODEO." [91]

When cowboys began joining the military and being drafted in to the Army the magazine and "Ma" were the first to be notified. Servicemen appreciate letters and "Ma" encouraged everyone to send mail to those Cowboy Soldiers, that were listed in the magazine, to her address, and she in turn, would see the letters were forwarded immediately from her office.

The very first list of servicemen included the following cowboys:

Pvt. Marion Getzwiller
Pvt. Spud Richardson
Pvt. George F. Green
Pvt. Elio Reale
Pvt. Paul C. Densmore
Pvt. Phil A. Manix
PFC Cecil Friend
Frank Kitchens, Jr.
Pvt. Vernon Whitaker
Pvt. Glenn I. Soward
Joseph Bessler
Pvt. John F. Oldenburg
Pvt. Cecil Jones
Pvt. John Segleski (Buttons Yonnick)
S. Sgt. L. L. Chiles
Pvt. John Taylor (Buck)
Pvt. Alan Pattee
Turk Greenough
Pvt. Eddie Boysen
Pfc. E. V. Dorsey
John Krashovitz
F. R. Blasingame
Pvt. Garner B. (Bud) Fisher

Fannye Jones, CTA secretary, reported by July, 1942 nearly one hundred Turtles were serving Uncle Sam in various branches of the service. Others that weren't in the military served the country in other ways, like Civil Air Patrol, as Everett Bowman did. Civil Air Patrol was a volunteer group of men and women owning their own planes, who learned to fly in peace time, and now had the opportunity to serve their country in war time. She also reported CTA was considering buying an additional $5,000 in war bonds. [91]

From Broncs to Bombers

"From Broncs to Bombers" was an article published in *Hoofs & Horns*, written by Private Bob Hart. It said:

"A bronc-bustin' waddie from the brakes of Wyoming who has collected rodeo 'day' money from Pendleton, Oregon to Miami Beach (and who has collected his share of spills enroute), has traded his chaps for a set of O. D. suntans and his spurs for a bomber gunsight.

Steer rider, Buttons Yonnick, CTA # 359, at Strong City, Kansas rodeo. *Photographer unknown. Courtesy of Imogene Veach Beals.*

Not that Pvt. Mickey Hicks, of Davis-Monthan Field, Tucson, Arizona, is the only rodeo rider in the West to sign up with the U. S. Air Corps. Plenty of saddle-wise Westerners have made public their preferences for the flying forces instead of joining the cavalry.

But Mickey typifies that horizon-hunting breed of Americans who have opened new lands, planted the flag on them, and died for it when their freedom became involved. His grandfather came west with Brigham Young.

His Dad staked out range-land near Big Piney, Wyoming, when most western states were still in their infancy and the six-gun was an article of clothing.

He himself started riding a horse practically as soon as he could sit upright on one. On the range of Wyoming, claims Private Hicks, you learn to say 'giddap!' and then words like 'Mama' and 'milk.'

At 11, when most kids are learning how to shoot marbles, Mickey climbed on the back of a wild Brahma calf, got thrown 239 feet by his own estimate, and climbed back on to try it again. He is 26 now (just under the age limit for the aviation cadet school he hopes to make) and for the past five years he has earned a substantial income for himself and his wife by following the rodeos to 32 states. And that word 'substantial' wasn't dropped in at this point too lightly. In the summer season of '40, Mickey collected $2,600 in 'average' and 'day' money.

That was for three short months; the full rodeo season lasts practically year round – and should be of interest to income tax collectors. Since the bronc-riders get two and three rides at each rodeo, Mickey estimates that he has been on the backs of some 500 twisting, kicking spinning mounts in the last five years. He doesn't think he'll be troubled with air-sickness, and he's sure he'll be able to ride out a Link Trainer.

That is, if the Link Trainers aren't any wilder than that seven-second cruise he got aboard 'Five Minutes to Midnight', at Pendleton in 1940. 'I've ridden 'em in Cheyenne, Fort Worth, Calgary, and in Cleveland, Washington D. C. and Boston," said Mickey, 'but that was the craziest piece of horse-flesh I ever tackled – and you can quote me.' He was on the bronc seven seconds, as we said, and the time limit is 10 seconds. Mick didn't enlarge on his where-abouts in the remaining interval.

Another one that he remembers distinctly is a stiff-legged artist named 'Black Evans.' Mick was on 'Black Evans' 13 times in 1932, but the two couldn't seem to zig and zag at the same time because he was thrown 13 times, too . . . The bronc he wants to saddle some day is 'Hell's Angel,' leading rodeo performer in the nation. And he doesn't think the horse will have slowed down by the time we've won this war.

He won day money at Dodge City, Kans., June 26, last year. And when he returned to his hotel they handed him his selective service questionnaire.

So Mickey went back to Big Piney to help his Dad through the fall and winter business of ranching. On the Sunday of Pearl Harbor he decided on the Air Corps. Business concluded, he enlisted at Cheyenne in early January.

He believes he'll have more of a chance to see real action in the Air Corps than he would have had in the cavalry, and he didn't like the idea of learning how to ride army style, anyway.

'One of the gang who signed up for the cavalry in Kansas,' Mickey claimed, 'had to spend three days sitting on a barrel to learn how to sit on a horse. He had been sitting on broncs as long as I can remember, so I thought I'd take the airplanes.'

It's quite a saddle-jump from the loose, rambling, poker-playing life of a follower of rodeos, to the rigid discipline of the army. There'll be no more get-togethers with fellow members of the Cowboys' Turtle Association, and the heavy-handed practical jokes are things of the past.

For with his buddy, Pvt. Billy McGinnis, also of Big Piney, Wyo., who enlisted with him, Mickey has settled down to the more serious business of riding the horses of War. Like the Westerner of the days of Wyatt Earp, the Westerners of 1942 have moved in the van of trouble and are waiting their crack at the Japs.

'And if the Air Corps don't take all th' bow out of my legs,' says Mickey, 'I'll be back in a rodeo saddle when the fightin's done.'" [92]

A letter from F. Leslie Herrick, M. D. on the board of directors of the Livermore, Cailf. rodeo wrote to president Bowman telling him that their announcer said "the C.T.A. extended thanks to the board of directors for having been as courageous as to go ahead, and also for the show and the kind treatment they had received there." He was not sure whether the announcer had 'manufactured' the statement or if it had come from the Turtles or headquarters. He went on to say:

"However, I do believe that such spirit and friendliness between cowboys and managements is a wonderful thing to cultivate and that this was a fine way to cultivate it and was a most gracious move. The public liked it very much also. So on behalf of myself and the Board of Directors, may I thank you or your representative most graciously for such, and with all good wishes to you for the future success and more of such cooperation in the future." [93]

World Champion Cowboys for 1942 were:

Gerald Roberts of Strong City, Kans., winning 7,260 points became the RAA World's Champion All-Around Cowboy. He also placed second in bull riding. Homer Pettigrew of Grady, N. M., was the steer wrestling champion. Dick Griffith, of Scottsdale, Ariz., captured the bull riding title for the fourth consecutive year. Louis Brooks, Pawhuska, Okla., was the world's champion bareback rider, and won the 1941 N.R.A. (formerly the Southwest Rodeo Association) Champion Cowboy award. Vic and Vern Castro (brothers), of Richmond, Calif., were the champion team roping team. Clyde Burk of Comanche, Okla., was the champ in calf roping, which he captured earlier in 1936 and 1938. King Merritt, of Federal Wyo., was world's champion single (steer) roper. Doff Aber won the saddle bronc championship again for the second year. Joe Bassett, of Payson, Ariz., was the world champion team tyer.

Second place winners were Buckshot Sorrells, Tucson, Ariz., in single (steer) roping; Bill McMackin, of Trail City, S. D., in saddle bronc riding; Toots Mansfield, of Bandera, Texas, in calf roping; Dave Campbell, Las Vegas, Nev., in steer wrestling; Hank Mills, Van Nuys, Calif., in bareback riding; Dick Andrews, of Claresholm, Alb., Canada,

Winners of the Boston 1942 Garden Rodeo: Standing, left to right: Bud Linderman, bareback bronc riding; Ken Roberts, bull riding; Bill Clemans, assistant rodeo manager; Brigadier General John Reed Fitzpatrick, president, Madison Square Garden Corp.; Everett Colborn, rodeo manager; Homer Pettigrew, steer wrestler. Kneeling, left to right, Jerry Ambler, saddle bronc riding; and Buck Echols, calf roping. *Photographer unknown. Courtesy of the Echols Family, Liberty, TX.*

in steer decorating; and Asbury Schell, of Tempe, Ariz., in team tying.
[#94]

Seventh Year for CTA

CTA Officers for 1943 were: Everett Bowman, president; first vice-president was Rusty McGinty.

The elected representatives for their events were: bareback riding, Carl Dossey; saddle bronc riding, Doff Aber; steer roping, King Merritt; calf roping, Buckshot Sorrells; bulldogging, Hub Whiteman; bull riding, Smoky Snyder; trick riding, Dick Griffith. The following spokesmen were elected: Clay Carr, Hoytt Hefner, Clinton Booth, Everett Shaw, Stub Bartlemay, Harry Hart, Pete Kerscher, Dave Campbell, Buck Echols and Joe Bassett. [#95]

World War II Affects Everyone Page 171

Tater Decker joined February, 1943 at El Paso, Texas. Doff Aber, a director for CTA, walked up to him and said, "Hey, you dirty little sneak. You're not going to slide by another year without joining the Turtles!"

Tater had ten dollars and some change. He paid his dues and had 'some change' left. When asked if he won anything at El Paso, he said, "No". [132]

Bud Fitzpatrick, CTA #1114, recalled that he was forced to join the Turtles, too, but couldn't remember the place. [146]

Fannye Jones, secretary, for CTA diligently tried to get CTA service cards to all military Turtles. Some rodeos were put on hold due to the war, and everyone was doing their bit for the war effort. The mounting list of Turtles in the military was posted in most issues of the *Hoofs & Horns*. Issues of the magazine, which cowboys considered their 'Bible' was sent to every cowboy soldier. Most military cowboys' subscriptions were paid for by several donors, including Harry Rowell, well known stock contractor and rodeo producer, and Harold Busick on behalf of Sears Roebuck Company. [91]

Some of the eastern rodeos were called off, even though Washington D.C. powers had given them the 'go ahead,' managements worried that fans had found other sports to attend instead of rodeo. It was also a major concern to cowboy competitors because if the fans didn't attend rodeos those dollars paid at the gate would not be available to add to the purse for those who did get in the money. [96]

RAA president R. J. Hoffmann wrote:

"The hope of everyone is that 1944 will bring happier days to those connected with rodeos which afford so much clean entertainment to thousands of American people. To those shows that carried on during the past year, we offer our congratulations, and the hope that the New Year will bring greater success than the years that have gone before. To those shows that for one reason or another, were unable to function in 1942, we offer the hope that things will be such in 1944 that they may resume their celebrations and help the morale of the men and women in the Services and the folks at home who are doing such a grand job of backing up our Armed Forces." [97]

The 1943 RAA World's Champion Cowboys were:

Louis Brooks, of Pittsburg, Okla., all-around champ with 6,924 points. He also won the world's champion bronc riding title, plus he also accumulated enough points in the National Rodeo Association, formerly the Southwest Rodeo Association, to win their all-around title and bareback riding title. Toots Mansfield, of Bandera, Texas, was the calf roping title holder, which was his fourth time, winning it in 1939, 1940 and 1941. Homer Pettigrew, of Mills, N. M., was world's champion steer wrestler, which he also won in 1940 and 1942. World champ in bareback riding was Bill Linderman, of Red Lodge, Mont.. Tom Rhodes, of Sombrero Butte, Ariz., won the single (steer) roper title. Gordon McFadden, Globe, Ariz., was the champion team tyer. Arnold Montgomery, of Dorothy, Alb., Canada, was the world's champion steer decorator. Ken Roberts, of Strong City, Kans, was the world's champion bull rider. Leonard Block of Livermore, Calif., and Mark Hull, of Hayward, Calif., were the world's champion team ropers. [97]

Doff Aber on "Brown Jug", 1941 RAA World Champion Saddle Bronc Rider. *Photographer unknown. Courtesy of Jack Long Collection.*

CHAPTER SIXTEEN
Hoofs & Horns Goes Abroad

The cowboys in service were conscientious in writing the CTA and RAA through letters to "Ma" Hopkins, editor of *Hoofs & Horns*, about where they were and what they were enduring during their tours of duty.

Some of 'Ma's' comments made were:

"Cecil Jones, now at Camp Swift, Texas, says he got to go to the Houston rodeo and sure had a fine time visiting with friends around the chutes. Says he wishes the war was over so 'a guy could rodeo again' but that he's doing all right."

"Pat Smith, in Africa, wrote his wife and said he had one Sunday off, and an old cow wandered near the village where he was stationed, so Pat rode her, and was she surprised – really acted up."

"Out of 163 boys trying for the Marines Frank Finley was one of only three chosen. The Phoenix paper carried a picture of him turning in his cowboy clothes in trade for some of Uncle Sam's."

Letters from some of the soldiers said:

"A delayed letter from Chili Cole, written December 7, 1942, says: 'One year ago today the Japs fixed the first go around in this contest. They cut our loose ropes on the sly and let a little slack in our riggin' when we weren't looking. Lots of boys whammed the ground without a chance to qualify. Some of these boys had set their last Hamleys. Others just got up, knocked the dust and blood out of their manes and come out hookin' 'em high at the next performance. This is one show that didn't close the entry books on the opening day, so lots of us boys were able to enter for the duration. None of us know how many performances there will be. So please take my name off the *Hoofs & Horns* books and sort of retire me, and when I get out I'll pay up again, and we can all go to another show that we don't want to win quite as much as we do this one'." #96

"Dear Ma: I couldn't help but write and tell you how glad I was to receive my first copy of Hoofs & Horns the other day. You should have seen me, huddled up in my fox hole reading it while the planes were buzzing overhead. It will take more than Tojo to keep me from reading about the boys. I want to thank you for forwarding my mail on to me. I received a letter through your office from a boy I hadn't heard from in three years. Again I say thanks a lot. Say hello for me to any of the cowboys you see. Here's hoping to see you in Tucson in 1944.

Sincerely yours,
Pfc. Wendell W. Elzig."

"From out in the Pacific, Sgt. Luther Finley writes, 'Imagine my surprise to get a telephone call this morning asking did I know a 'Fritz.' So I went about a mile from my place and old Truan was so well concealed (escape work party) that it took over an hour for his sergeant and me to find his hiding place. Fritz says he hopes there will be only two cowboys unfortunate enough to land here, but there are three, he

Luther Finley, CTA#396, proudly displays his Turtle pin on his hat. *Photo by Milton Photo, NYC. Courtesy of Stan Searle from the Hoofs & Horns Collection.*

hopes the next one is Frank (Finley)." [#98]

"Pvt. Robert G. Fetters over in Fresno, Calif. writes: " I was pretty lucky getting into the Air Corps, but I would rather have drawn the same outfit as Kid Fletcher or Ward Watkins or Freckles Brown, cause it shore gets tiresome telling a bunch of greenhorns about bulls and broncs that have bucked the country over. Please send my *Hoofs & Horns* to me here."

"Jesse D. Merritt, son of King Merritt, of Federal, Wyo. has been advanced in rank to Sergeant in the Bombardier School at Big Spring, Texas. His brother, Pvt. James K. (Hyde) Merritt, Jr., is an aviation cadet at Springfield, Missouri. Both boys are Turtles." [#99]

Bern Gregory recalled his training at Fort Francis E. Warren, in Cheyenne, Wyo. In a letter to "Ma" Hopkins, he wrote: "I've been moved to a spot where I can see Frontier Park from my barracks window." [#84] Bern remembered that King Merritt, whom he had met earlier at a rodeo in Woodward, Okla., told him if he could get a weekend pass, he'd come and get Bern and take him to the Merritt ranch at Federal, Wyo. He remembered fondly his weekend on the ranch. [#100]

"Cpl. Johnny Becker says he had just been handed a copy of *Hoofs & Horns* by a friend, the first copy he had ever seen since he left the States eighteen months ago. Said censorship would not allow him to tell where he was, but it was the home of the ancestors of the Brahma bulls." [#101]

T/Sgt. Don Wilkins wrote, in part: "There wasn't anything I enjoyed more than reading *Hoofs & Horns* while I was sweating out those 88s in fox holes. It looked for a while that maybe I wouldn't see the other side or make the next show, but I did. As long as they don't get any closer than they did (18 inches) I guess I shouldn't sweat. No doubt during the Big Push you read of the battles of El Guettar and Maknassy. Well, what I mean, we were right in the thick of it. The Jerries couldn't do any good there and pulled out, going north. Then of course we couldn't stop, so we went up in the mountains and pushed them out. This wasn't as big a snap as it seemed, but with the combination that

Uncle Sam has got, it's pretty hard to beat – No? We had the worst counter battery fire an outfit ever got, but we got off very light. They shelled us during the day and bombed us off and on during the night, but you know us – no quitters." #102

A clipping from a Chicago newspaper tells how S/Sgt. Henry "Steve" Brody, cowboy from Bloomfield, Mont., and now Ball Turret Gunner in a bomber named Hell's Angel, and the other gunners sent some Messerschmidts on their long last ride. Which goes to show, that even though that grand bucking horse, Hell's Angel, was laid to rest last fall, his fame goes on, and that the 'never-quit' spirit of the rodeo contestants is just as much a part of the war as it was of the arena contests?"

Turtles stationed in various places as soldiers in 1944, wrote 'Ma' the following:

Pvt. N. E. Barron got his first *Hoofs & Horns* issue and said he didn't bother anyone until he had read it through.

Sgt Lyndon E. 'Frank' Marshall was somewhere in Italy, and was cited for gallantry in action and awarded the Silver Star. He tried sending the citation to his father but the censor stopped it, so he sent his dad the medal. "I am very proud of him," wrote his dad.

S/Sgt. Joe Bessler was somewhere in the Aleutians and said H&H means as much to the boys as letters from home.

Luther Finley was on Mare Island, but had been in the South Pacific and was wounded, but anxious to get back in the fighting!

A photograph of Pfc. Clifford 'Montana' Longacre, of Billings, Montana, was included, in a jeep somewhere in the South Pacific proudly wearing his cowboy boots. He is a veteran of Guadalcanal.

Pvt. Gayle A. 'Red' Millet was getting to like England better all the time. "But there will never be a place like our States and our West. It's really worth the hell and high water we are going through to save our freedom."

Pvt. Harvey A. Luer was in New Caledonia. "This is a beautiful island" he wrote, "but I'd rather be vacationing on it. These natives sure have some sorry looking cattle and horses."

Event winners at 1944 Madison Square Garden rodeo. (Left to right) Jiggs Burk, steer wrestling; Jack Shaw, special prize for fastest time in calf roping, 13 2/5 seconds; Clyde Burk, calf roping; Bill Clemans, assistant managing director; Louis Brooks, bareback bronc riding; Everett Colborn, managing director; Ned Irish, acting president of Madison Square Garden; Dick Griffith, bull riding; Roy Rogers, Republic pictures star; Shirley Hussey, saddle bronc rider; and Hugh Bennett, wild cow milking. *Photo taken from 1945 Madison Square Garden Program. Courtesy of Jack Long Collection.*

Pfc. Sonny Tureman was recently given a medical discharge from the service due to a leg injury received while bronc riding. #103

Pvt. Howard O'Neill, one of the O'Neill Twins, rodeo clowns, spent seventeen months fighting Japs in the South Pacific. He is now in the States suffering from malaria and shell shock. A letter from him, said in part: "My last campaign was in the New Garagos. It's grim terrain, among the worst in the world . . . We went into the jungle this way, patrols first, bulldozers next, followed by jeeps and artillery. To go seven miles took one month. Though we laid down heavy artillery barrage, the Japs crawled through it and dropped grenades in our fox holes or struck with knives in the dark. It was severe to say the least."
#104

Bob Chambers was proud to be part of the 129th Horse Cavalry, the very last Cavalry Unit at Fort Riley, Kans. He spent a year and a half there. The boys built a little arena there so they could practice and put on rodeos. The hillside next to the arena made a great place from which spectators could watch. At one rodeo he drew a well known bull from Sidney, Iowa named Fiddle Face. The stock contractor told him that he was rank and why didn't he turn him out and draw another bull. Bob replied, "If I start turning out rank bulls I don't think I deserve to ride bulls." He rode Fiddle Face and won the bull riding and got a home made buckle, made by a buddy, and $50.

Eventually, when the 129th was closed down for good, Bob was sent to California and his group was sent overseas. They spent 46 days on a ship headed for India dodging submarines on the way. They ran out of food and were served beans and ketchup once a day. After arriving in India they were sent by plane to Burma. As they were landing, the Japanese were simultaneously attacking the airfield. His Sergeant, a man named Parker from the famous Parker Ranch in Hawaii, was wounded as they opened the door of the plane. Soon afterwards they were sent by train to an infantry battalion. They were given the assignment to 'knock off' the Japs who were controlling the Burma Road, and to regain control from them. "We walked over five hundred miles leading mules before we ever heard a shot. I was part of the well known Merrill's Marauders. Fortunately, I was never wounded, but found many of my buddies were; I was just lucky." [#130]

C. E. Tooke, rodeo stock contractor of Ekalaka, Mont., wrote "Ma" to report: "Rodeos are scarce here now as practically everyone is in the service or defense work, and ranch hands are too busy to get away. We have our top horses and a lot of new ones on pasture for the shows when the big one is over. We are having a mild winter and all stock is fat. The three younger brothers are in active service overseas in the Navy and the Air Force. [#104]

A notice to all CTA boys in the Armed Forces said to disregard payment of dues if they were in any branch of the armed forces as they were exempt from paying dues for the duration of the war.

Some of the CTA approved rodeos for 1944 were: Baton Rouge, La.; Phoenix, Ariz.; Oklahoma City, Okla.; Newhall, Calif.; San Francisco, Calif.; Los Angeles, Calif.; Lodi, Calif.; Fort Smith, Ark.; Sacramento, Calif.; Bay City, Texas; Los Angeles Coliseum, Calif.; Mandan Rodeo Association; Caldwell, Idaho; Billings, Mont.; and Pueblo, Colo. [#105]

A statement from Commanding General, General Fegan, United States Marine Corps, Camp Joseph H. Pendleton, Oceanside, Calif., wrote:

"Dear Cowhands: Today you are riding herd on a pack of devils instead of steers. While riding the battle ranges thoughts of what you were doing not so long ago may leave you lonesome for the clear skies and doggie stews. You've traded your past Pinto for a jeep – a war bronc whose cold steel could never compare with the soft nose of your pony. You'll long for your horse and chaps, but the jeeps and half-tracks will ease your dogs. I know the bugle calls will haunt you more than the howl of coyotes. Now, instead, you will hear the loud thunder of planes and long-range guns. That chow line doesn't appeal to your hunger like an open air chuck wagon with its smell of crisp bacon frying did. But canned bill and beans will keep your belt tight.

When this war is won you can go back to your home on the range where you'll find your saddle in the barn. You can dust it off and throw it over your Pinto who stands underneath that old cottonwood tree. When you go to town and into the old Silver Dollar bar, you'll be welcomed by howls from the old gang. And, as you have one on the house, you can say 'It was damn well worth while after all!'

I'll be seein' ya at the old bunk-house so we can finish whittlin' on that corral post.

Joseph C. Fegan, USMC, Major General." [103]

Soldiers Rodeos Held in the Strangest Places

From 'down under' Corporal Merle Skelton wrote: "Dear Ma: I was at a rodeo last month (October) an all-soldier show with Aussies and Yanks competing. Bill Keas of Elko, Nev., win the bronc riding – 'buck jumpin' they call it here; Bill Morrison from Pendleton win the bull riding – here it's called 'bullock clinging!' Doc Blackstone dogged a steer from a jeep; Red Goodspeed and Jack Dupree were also there and a lot of good cowboys in uniform. Keep the *Hoofs & Horns* coming. It's a life saver. I'm the only one in my outfit that takes it but a lot of the boys get it when I'm through." [106]

Cecil Jones was a 1st Sergeant in the Army, and was sent north of Tokyo when the war was over. He was contacted by a rodeo promoter, Lieutenant Dick Ryan, of Fort Riley, Kans, who wanted to put on a two day G.I. rodeo in Tokyo, in November, 1945.

Ryan was aware Cecil knew the workings of a rodeo and asked if Cecil would help him accomplish this plan. Ryan promised he would see that Cecil got out of the Army early. Cecil contacted his good friend, Harry Rowell, rodeo producer, in Hayward, Calif., and asked him to send a set of plans for building chutes and an arena. Cecil was assigned a company of engineers and under his direction they built an arena and chutes in Meiji Stadium in Tokyo. They had brand new lumber, Cecil remembered.

The rodeo went off without a hitch; [74] it was called 'National Allied Championship Rodeo', and included British, Aussies, New Zealanders and Americans. 55,000 allied personnel attended. Those willing to ride were offered free passes to the rodeo if they had any experience or wanted to ride in the rodeo. There were marines, navy men, as well as the Army represented. Some of the events were: saddle bronc riding, steer riding, pony express relay race, dressage exhibition, wild cow milking, and a few other venues such as an air circus, military band contest and a flaming motorcycle event.

Ryan rode the Emperor's white horse, 'First Frost' and it was said he was the first person other than the Emperor to ride him. Bud Antone reported to *Hoofs & Horns* about the Tokyo rodeo, "After people began to leave, one of the boys decided to try out a bull that was left in the chute. He was a big black one and hadn't been used in the bull riding. He left the chute with his rider, went through the side gate which was left open, hit the ambulance and lost his rider, but continued on through the aisles of the stadium and you should have seen the people scatter. Nobody was reported injured."[#107]

Cecil remembered the stock wasn't bad, but he couldn't remember who supplied it. Ryan had also held rodeos for servicemen in Australia, New Guinea, the Philippines, as well as Japan. After the rodeo was over Cecil got his orders, was sent back to the States, and was discharged at San Antonio, Texas in December 1945, just as Ryan had promised. [74]

Bern Gregory was stationed in Furth, Germany, at war's end and the Red Cross wanted to hold a rodeo for the military men still abroad. It was to be held at Wurzburg, a city in disrepair due to heavy bombing. Bern assisted, as did Dee Burk, who was in the same group. Bern related that trees were cut from the forest, to make planks for the chutes by Army engineers. Airplane landing mats were used for fencing around the arena. Local horses were used for bronc riding, and the bronc saddles were World War II cavalry saddles, with horns. For the bull riding event they borrowed work oxen, and Bern said, "they used a hot shot on them to get them to buck, and I understand they weren't much good for work after the rodeo." [100]

The cover of the rodeo program for the rodeo held in Tokyo, Japan. Lieutenant Dick Ryan is astride Emperor Hirohito's horse. *Courtesy of Billy Huckaby Collection*

CHAPTER SEVENTEEN

Meanwhile Back In The States

Some of the Turtles who did not join the military, but worked in defense in the States were;

Doff Aber worked at Timmons Aircraft plant in Van Nuys, Calif., and his wife Marie worked nearby at an instrument manufacturing plant. Bob Haverty worked at an airplane factory in Wichita, Kans. [98] Hughie Long was a mounted guard at an Ordinance plant in Texas. [108] Nick and Fay Knight were employed at Kaisers Vancouver Shipyard in Washington. [105] Murray Riggs went to work for Consolidated Vultee Aircraft in San Diego, Calif. [109] Jimmy Hazen and his wife worked at Consolidated Aircraft in Tucson, Ariz. [110] Charley and Imogene Beals went from Missouri to Spokane, Wash. and worked for Boeing Aircraft. [111] Holloway Grace put his rodeo career on hold for three years to work during the war at Douglas Aircraft in El Segundo, Calif. [136]

Elected CTA officers for 1944 were: Everett Bowman, president; Toots Mansfield, vice president; and Fannye Lovelady, secretary-treasurer. Event directors elected were: Hugh Bennett – bull dogging; Louis Brooks – bronc riding; Dick Griffith – contract personnel; King Merritt – steer roping; George Mills – bareback riding; Gerald Roberts – bull riding; Everett Shaw – calf roping; and Buck Sorrells – team tying.

Spokesmen for 1944 were: Carl Arnold, Fritz Becker, Dave Campbell, Ralph Collier, Jackie Cooper, Carl Dossey, Bobby Estes, Vern Goodrich, J. K. Harris, Harry Hart, Clyde Hebert, Shirley Hussey,

Maurice Laycock, Roy Lewis, Shorty McCrory, Buddie Mefford, Vic Montgomery, Fox O'Callahan, Dub Phillips, Walton Poage, Gene Rambo, Ken Roberts, Tony Salinas, Chuck Sheppard, Marvin Shoulders, Wally Squires, John Tubbs, Arnie Wills, Charlie Smith, Tom Hogan and Cecil Bedford. [#112]

Fannye Lovelady (formerly Fannye Jones before she married Sam 'Shorty' Lovelady, CTA #1999) secretary of the CTA kept sending information of military Turtles, and what was happening at home through *Hoof & Horns*. She announced that 167 Turtles were in the armed forces, including her husband Shorty, by February, 1944. She also reported that Jack Knight, in U. S. Marines, from Goose Creek, Texas was reported missing in action. Knight was the first CTA member to be reported missing. [#97]

To all managements of rodeos Fannye reported: "If a rodeo management wishes an absolute guarantee that members of the C.T.A. will contest at given rodeo after their arrival at said rodeo, they must submit their prize list no later than thirty days prior to show dates to the office of the Cowboys' Turtle Association, 733 West McDowell Rd, Phoenix, Arizona." [#104]

Cowboys' Turtle Association rules and regulations for 1944 were posted in *Hoofs & Horns*. The following were in various issues during the year:

"Rules Affecting Stock Contractors adopted by the CTA said: "Stock contractors are requested to make sure all prize lists have been approved by the CTA before signing a contract to furnish stock for a show. (All prize lists must be submitted to the CTA office, address added, not later than thirty days prior to show dates.)

Rodeo stock contractors cannot furnish stock to both professional and amateur shows. If stock contractors furnish stock to an amateur show, they must stay amateur."

To All Show Managements:

"Any contract event held prior to 1941 and during 1941 can not be cut from any show now. This includes Trick Riding, Trick Roping, Clowning, and any contract event considered pertinent to the rodeo."[#110]

In a later issue a notice of the CTA meeting held in Denver in January prior to the rodeo encouraged all stock contractors and promoters the opportunity to meet with members and representatives of CTA to lend any suggestions or criticism that would enable all concerned to promote 'bigger and better' rodeos.[#112]

"Notice to All Members of the CTA: Any member of the CTA who works a show that has not had its prize list approved by the CTA is automatically blacklisted." [#97]

A notice of rule changes and new rules adopted by CTA were posted in *Hoofs & Horns*, and included:

"If more than two events are held a show will not be considered a jackpot, and to qualify as a jack pot it must be advertised as such and not advertised as a rodeo.

If any decision is made by any spokesman, report of such a decision must be sent into the CTA office.

When a prize list has been approved by five Directors or four Directors and the President, the remaining Directors are to be notified of such action."[#112]

Additional rodeos for the 1944 season approved by the Turtles were: Cheyenne, Wyo.; Salt Lake City, Utah; Ogden, Utah; Price, Utah; Jantzen Beach, Portland, Ore.; Boise, Idaho; Las Vegas, N. M.; Dodge City, Kans.; Great Falls, Mont.; Albuquerque, N. M.; Anadarko, Okla.; XIT Rodeo, Dalhart, Texas; Pretty Prairie, Kans.; Milwaukee, Wis.; St Paul, Minn.; Topeka, Kans.; Oklahoma City, Okla.; Elk City, Okla.; Billings, Mont. (The prize money and events were also listed.)

Here's the Real Story

A response to an article in the *RAA Bulletin* regarding the Turtles was answered by the directors of CTA:

"In a recent issue of the RAA bulletin the CTA was a subject of great and confusing criticism. We do not object to being criticized, in some cases it has helped us to correct our mistakes and improve our association. We would, however, be very grateful if our critics would study our rules so they might have a better understanding of what we are trying to do.

It is only natural that some shows would have a surplus of contestants and others only a few. With transportation as it is today, the boys can't make long jumps to shows they would patronize in normal times. Today they are forced to go to parts of the country that have the best shows close together.

There has been much comment about the Turtles asking for raises in prize money. Why this has to be done is obvious to everyone, and should require no explanation. Comparatively few of the shows have lost money in recent years. It is doubtful that exorbitant prize money was responsible for their loss. There can be other reasons such as, an act of God, poor management, inadequate advertising, and location. It isn't the policy or aim of the Turtles to make unfair demands on any show. There are many shows, and hundreds of cowboys, and our association is working for the betterment of everyone concerned.

It has been suggested by some that the cowboys should give up the rodeos and take jobs in war plants. A few with previous training have done this. An office employee might be able to give up his work and take a better paying war job, and still be able to go back to his profession after the duration. It has been proved that a rodeo contestant isn't so fortunate. Judging from letters received from our boys in the service, they want us to keep the shows going bigger and better. Rodeos have been the means of entertainment for many service men, and considerable sums of money have gone to them.

Some shows have been approved for very small prize money, because their crowds were mostly service men, who were to be admitted at a small cost. Once the Directors were surprised when they arrived at such a show, and found that the service men were charged double the amount submitted to our office.

No individual or stock contractor has been blacklisted by our association unless he chose to be so himself. Everyone on this list is familiar with the rules of our association. If he chooses to go against them that is his business.

In gate receipts, rodeo ranks with the three leading sports of this country. Yet it has only been in the last few years the cowboys have had any say concerning their own profession. In the past they have taken every kind of beating imaginable from fly-by-night promoters and selfish committees. It was only through the honest stock contractors and committees that rodeos were able to survive.

A few poor shows in a town can ruin it for that town for years to come. We are trying to cooperate with and help all stock contractors, committees, and promoters, who want to put on shows that will be a build-up to our profession. We invite all producers to contact our office for any information concerning their show. If any difficulties arise at a show, you can always receive our consideration by calling our office.

Photograph of Pete Kerscher, CTA#295, his hat, Turtle Pin, PRCA card and Rodeo Historical Society membership card. *Photo courtesy of D'Lyla Kerscher Longo.*

If we can have the cooperation of the cowboys, committees, and stock contractors, all working for the good of the sport, then we can convince the public that it is a sport worthy of their support.

Signed: THE DIRECTORS OF THE CTA." [114]

1944 RAA World's Champion Cowboys were: Louis Brooks, of Sweetwater, Texas, all around champ with 11,144 points. He also won the saddle bronc title and the bareback title. Homer Pettigrew, of Mills, N. M., was champion steer wrestler, and held this title in 1940, '42, and '43. Tommy Rhodes, of Mammoth, Ariz., was the world's champion team tyer. John Rhodes, of Oracle, Ariz., was the single (steer) roper title-holder. Murphy Chaney, of Cholame, Calif., was the champion team roper. Everett Shaw, of Stonewall, Okla., was the champion wild cow milker. Padgett Berry, of Phoenix, Ariz. was the steer decorating champ. Ken Roberts of Strong City, Kans., was the world's champion bull rider, and won it in 1943, too. Clyde Burk, of Comanche, Okla., was world's champion calf roper. [115]

So Long Cowboys

The following month Clyde Burk died in a fatal accident while hazing for steer wrestler, Bill Hancock, at the Denver rodeo. The horse ran into the steer and horse, steer and Burk all went down. He died in the hospital January 22 when all attempts to save him failed. Hugh Bennett took Burk to the rodeo at Madison Square Garden the first time and said of him, "For a small guy he was the best roper I know of." [64]

The supreme sacrifice was made by Fritz Truan, in the service of his country, when he was killed in a bloody Battle at Iwo Jima, February 28, 1945. He entered the U.S. Marine Corp in 1942 and attained the rank of Sergeant. He was a well known saddle bronc riding champion and the all-around world champion in 1940. It was said he fought in war, as he competed, asking no quarter and giving none. [64]

Mr. & Mrs. Thomas Quirk, of Woodstown, N. J., were unique in that they had twenty children. During World War II nine sons joined the military to defend our country, including the three boys that were cowboys, Frank Q, CTA #441, Louis, CTA #1618, and Robert (better known as Rabbit), CTA #1619, that joined the Army. Robert 'Rabbit' was killed on April 16, 1944, in the South Pacific. On June 8, 1944, President Franklin D. Roosevelt wrote a personal letter to the Quirks, and in it he said: . . . "as parents of eight children who are serving their country and one who has given his life for his country, you stand as a real inspiration to the parents of all our soldiers and sailors."

The other six brothers were; Walter J – Army; William F – Army; Joseph L.– Army; John – Army; Richard – Navy; and Wilbert – Navy. After the war five more Quirks joined the Armed Forces. [145]

On May 8, 1945, the European battle was over when Soviet and American troops captured Berlin. V-J Day, September 2, 1945, Japan

THE WHITE HOUSE
WASHINGTON

PERSONAL
Dear Mr. and Mrs. Quirk:

June 8, 1944

My attention was recently called to the fact that you had nine sons in the Armed Forces of the United States, and as Commander-in-Chief, I take this opportunity to extend to you my heartiest congratulations.

I am told that the records of the War and Navy Departments contain the names of the following boys who have listed you as their parents: Robert Quirk, Army of the United States; Walter J. Quirk, Army of the United States; William F. Quirk, Army of the United States; Joseph L. Quirk, Army of the United States; Frank Quirk, Army of the United States; Louis Quirk, Army of the United States; John Quirk, Army of the United States; Richard Quirk, United States Navy; and Wilbert Quirk, United States Navy.

It must be a great satisfaction to you to know that you have so many sons able to serve in the Armed Forces of their country at such a critical time. I know that the boys, too, receive inspiration in the performance of their duties when they think of all their brothers in the service.

You have my deepest sympathy in the loss of your son Robert, who I am told was killed in action in the South Pacific area on April 16. However, his death in his country's service is something for which you can justly be proud, and I know it has served to increase the determination of yourselves and the other members of your family to bring this war to an early and victorious conclusion. As the parents of eight children who are serving their country and one who has given his life for his country, you stand as a real inspiration to the parents of all our soldiers and sailors.

Very sincerely yours,

Franklin D. Roosevelt

Mr. and Mrs. Thomas F. Quirk,
Woodstown, New Jersey.

Letter from President F. D. Roosevelt to the Thomas Quirk family concerning their nine sons in World War II, and the death of one son, Rabbit Quirk. *Courtesy of Louis Quirk.*

surrendered, but the Treaty of Peace with Japan was not signed until 1951. Although the fighting had ended it would take awhile before the American soldiers would get back home as there was much more to do once the fighting ended. [116]

Pete Kerscher, CTA #295, was working for Everett Colborn, rodeo producer, after he returned from the Army Air Corp. A representative of the popular radio show, "Truth or Consequences" came to Everett Colborn, at Madison Square Garden rodeo, and said they wanted a cowboy that had been in the military to be on the show. Colborn pointed at Kerscher and said, "There's your man."

Kerscher's daughter, D'Lyla remembered listening to the radio, on November 16, 1946, and hearing him on "Truth or Consequences." The premise of the show was when a contestant didn't get the answer to a question and 'tell the truth' they were given a consequence. Pete had the consequence of being asked to sing a song, and he sang the ever-famous, "Tumbling Tumbleweeds." As his prize, the president of Southwest Aircraft, Inc. presented Pete with an Aeronca Chief airplane. This prize encouraged him to go to school and earn his airplane mechanic license, but he never quit rodeo. [47]

In a conversation with D'Lyla Kerscher Longo, daughter of Pete Kerscher, CTA #295, who had been a member almost from the beginning and he was very active in early CTA meetings. She recalled her dad having much pride in being a Turtle.

"He could do almost anything in rodeo," she said. "He worked for Everett Colborn, when he was still in Blackfoot, Idaho." She remembered "Dad was from a family of thirteen children and when their mother died birthing the last child, it was necessary to 'farm the children out.' Dad and his brother, Jack, ran away and began to rodeo when he was only 13 years old. He competed as a bulldogger and bull rider. He also learned to be a rodeo secretary, an announcer, he could build chutes, shoe horses, and take care of the stock." She said, "Dad said if anyone asked you if you were a Turtle you always answered by saying, 'You bet your sweet ass I am!'" [47]

Imogene Veach Beals confirmed Longo's statement on the pride cowboys had in being a Turtle. She remembered husband, Charley

Beals, CTA #1058, also felt pride in being a Turtle. She said, "He always 'rode for the brand'. He wouldn't think of competing at a rodeo that was not approved by the CTA."[#111]

Tom Taylor was Turtle # 162. He was very proud of his Turtle pin and often wore it on his lapel. His young son, Tom, Jr, age 6, knew this was an important pin to his dad, and took the pin, but lost it. Tom, Jr. said "I got a thrashing for losing the pin, and I remember it well, to this day." He also said he knew his dad wanted to do more to help the Turtles, but they lived quite a distance in the country near Bronte, Texas, and did not have a telephone. [#129]

As cowboys continued to rodeo, after the war, some tried to avoid joining the Turtles, as long as they could. It wasn't that they didn't believe in the organization and what they were accomplishing nor was it because they didn't consider themselves a professional cowboy. It was because that amount of money, for a young man, was hard to come by, and he hated to part with it. Some cowboys have told about competing in a rodeo, and if they happened to win they were told they couldn't collect their money until they joined the CTA.

Bill Fedderson recalled that he had gone to rodeos for over a year before he joined. He arrived at the Denver rodeo in January, 1945, and Eddie Curtis, a director of the Turtles, told him he couldn't enter without joining, and took his dues. [#125]

Jim Shoulders was just breaking out in rodeo, as far as the 'big' rodeos were concerned. He had been rodeoing around his home turf for awhile, but his first big rodeo was Houston in February 1945. He was told he couldn't enter if he didn't join the Turtles. He paid his dues, but he hesitated because it was going to take all the money he had left after he entered, and he planned to use that money to eat on. But nothing was going to stop Jim Shoulders from competing. According to the Houston rodeo results Jim didn't win any money, but big brother Marvin Shoulders won a third in the 2nd go-round. Those winning the 'big marbles' in the bull riding were: Todd Whatley first place, Ken Roberts, second, Fritz Becker was third, and Wart Baughman was fourth. [#120, #121]

In the Appendix you will find all three books published by the CTA of Articles, By-Laws and Rules, and also included a list of members. However there is at least a year of members that joined after the last book, dated 1944, was published. By 1944 Turtle-sanctioned rodeos insisted dues were paid before cowboys could compete. Also dues were gathered at rodeos across the country by representatives of the Turtles and there is no telling how soon the secretary, Fannye Lovelady, received them and was able to record them. Some of the last members to join do not recall ever receiving a Turtle number, because of the transition from CTA to RCA. Numerous efforts are being made to find that last and final list of Turtles, however to date we have come up empty-handed.

Some of the cowboys that were members, and never listed in one of the three printed CTA books of membership were:

Tater Decker	Bill Fedderson	Dude Smith
Clyde Allred	Buff Douthitt	Jim Shoulders
Frenchie Collell	Lloyd Palmer	T. B. Porter
Phil Stadtler		

As this book goes to the printer the following known CTA members are still living:

Clyde Allred - Thatcher, Ariz.	Uknown
Don Bandy - Stapleton, Neb.	CTA# 1699
Endre 'Kid' Barr - Apple Valley, Calif.	CTA #145
Faye Blackstone - Parrish, Fla.	CTA #1356
Mrs. Ken Boen - Calif.	CTA #63
Paul Bond - Nogales, Ariz.	CTA # 395
Nancy Bragg (Witmer) - Winfield, Kans.	CTA #1914
Emma 'PeeWee' Burge (Ott) - Modesto, Calif.	CTA #1911
Jack Buschbom - Green Forest, Ark.	Unknown
Bob Chambers - Athena, Ore.	CTA #261
Bart Clennon - Tucson, Ariz.	CTA #418
John 'Frenchie' Collell - Salem, Oregon	Unknown
Tater Decker - Clayton, Okla.	Unknown
Buff Douthitt - Santa Fe, N. M.	Unknown
Buford Dugger - Three Rivers, Texas	CTA #1276

Bill Fedderson - El Reno, Okla.	Unknown
Bud Fitzpatrick - Bandera, Texas	CTA #1114
Bern Gregory - Florissant, Missouri	CTA #1796
Gus Gruwell - Rolling Hills, Wyo.	CTA #454
John D. Holleyman - Corona, N. M.	CTA #1404
Cecil Jones - Garden Valley, Calif.	CTA #299
G. K. Lewallen - Stephenville, Texas	CTA #799
Mitzi Lucas Riley - Aledo, Texas	CTA #479
Montie Montana, Jr. - Springville, Calif.	CTA #1251
Gene McLaughlin - Moorpark, Calif.	CTA #277
Joe Murray - Shreveport, La.	CTA #2024
Lloyd Palmer - Kremmling, Colo.	Unknown
T. B. Porter - Leesville, La.	Unknown
Frank Quirk - Fort Worth, Texas	CTA #441
Louis Quirk - Fort Worth, Texas	CTA #1618
"Brown Jug" Reynolds - Bowie, Texas	CTA #216
Lester Rosaschi - Wellington, Nev.	Unknown
"Dude" Smith - Burkburnett, Texas	Unknown
Jane Burnett Smith - Tempe, Ariz.	CTA #1144
Shoat Webster - Lenepah, Okla.	CTA #1930
Ray Wharton - Bandera, Texas	CTA #1758
Delbert Wise - Stephenville, Texas	CTA #1761

CHAPTER EIGHTEEN

Farewell Cowboys' Turtle Association

"NOTICE OF SPECIAL MEETING OF BOARD OF DIRECTORS OF THE COWBOYS' TURTLE ASSOCIATION.

Notice is hereby given that a special meeting of the Board of Directors of the Cowboys' Turtle Association will be held at the Blackstone Hotel, in Fort Worth, Texas, on Friday, March 16, 1945, at the hour of 11:00 A.M. for the purpose of transacting the following business:

1. Election of a Vice President
2. Moving the business office from its present location in Phoenix, Arizona.
3. Amend by-laws of the Association to authorize Earl Lindsey to sign checks on the treasury fund.
4. - Change the name of the Association from 'Cowboys' Turtle Association' to 'Rodeo Cowboys' Association'.
5. To take action on any and all matters that may come before the meeting.

Dated this 8th Day of March, 1945

Signed by: COWBOYS' TURTLE ASSOCIATION
                         Dick Griffith
                         Gerald Roberts
                         George Mills" [117]

Turtles: (Front, left to right): George Mills, Doff Aber, Carl Dossey, (behind is Homer Pettigrew), Everett Bowman, Hub Whiteman, (between & behind is Buckshot Sorrels) and Dick Griffith with The Sons of The Pioneers and Roy Rogers. *Photographer unknown. Courtesy of the Jack Long Collection.*

Approximately one hundred Turtles met at an open meeting in Fort Worth, Texas, on March 15, 1945. Big changes were made. The organization changed their name. It was also decided to hire business manager, Earl Lindsey and setting up an official business office.

The following day the board of directors met, as the notice indicated. Louis Brooks was elected vice president, succeeding Toots Mansfield, elevated to president, replacing Everett Bowman; and George Yardley, Roswell, N.M., was elected saddle bronc representative succeeding Louis Brooks. It was also decided to move the general office to Fort Worth after April 15t. The new address would be: 1116 Sinclair Bldg. Fort Worth, Texas. [119]

Resignation of Bowman

Not everyone in attendance agreed with these recommendations and consequently that also caused some additional changes. Everett Bowman resigned. A statement from Everett Bowman was printed in the June, 1945 *Hoofs & Horns* issue:

"I wish to take this means of answering the many questions I have been swamped with the past few weeks in letters from rodeo committees, stock contractors and members of the Cowboys' Turtle Association, the main question being 'What has happened to the Turtles?'

If you will refer to the write up in the May issue of *Hoofs and Horns* by the Rodeo Cowboys' Association you will get a clearer picture of just what has been taking place. First, I wish to call your attention to a paragraph in which you find a statement mentioning a meeting where approximately one hundred boys (members of the CTA) were present and it was decided to change the name of the organization and to hire Earl Lindsey. One would get the impression the hundred boys were allowed to vote on both issues mentioned. No vote was taken by the members – the changing of the name and the hiring of Lindsey was done by the six directors.

I told the boys at New York when it was suggested that we hire a business representative that they could count me out. I was never in favor of such an extravagant idea, and I did not think it would work. I always felt that any time the boys could not run their own business it was time to quit. Any time we had to go outside of the Cowboys to get someone to run the business, the thing was sunk, according to my way of thinking. I still think our cowboys are plenty capable of running their own business. To me, every boy who has paid as much as $10.00 in dues should certainly be considered a stockholder and deserves the right to his opinion and should be allowed to vote on such issues as vital to the association as the two mentioned above. The dues accumulated belong to the boys who were members of the CTA, and I certainly think they should have had some voice in how that money was going to be used.

As a member of the Cowboys' Turtle Association, and since there are a great number of the boys who already know what the business manager is being paid, I see no reason why those who have not been told should be kept in the dark. The salary is $7,500 a year, plus all expenses of traveling, hotels and meals. There is no limit placed on these expenses. I also want the boys to know that at the time I resigned we had on checking account $7,497.00. We also had $20,000 invested in United States Government War Bonds.

Following the Phoenix rodeo King Merritt and Hugh Bennett received letters from Earl Lindsey telling them they had been removed as Team Tying and Bulldogging directors respectively, and such action was taken at a meeting of the board of directors at Phoenix, Arizona. I wish to call your attention to the directors who were at Phoenix at that time: Dick Griffith, Gerald Roberts, George Yardley and Buck Sorrells. You will note that there was only one roping and dogging representative present. In the first place, I am wondering if Mr. Lindsey did not know that Merritt WAS NOT a team tying director, but was a steer roping director. There were no reasons given why Merritt and Bennett were being removed, but one would naturally suppose it was because they had not been 'yes' men to such drastic changes. I think the ropers and doggers are still capable of taking care of their portion of the business. I am wondering how the boys who had enough confidence in Merritt and Bennett to nominate them, then to elect them to office, feel about the situation. Is this another one of those things where a few try to cram something down your throat and make you like it?

I would say that what has really happened to the Turtles is that a small group, spurred on by their own selfish interests, undertook in this high-handed manner to change the entire set up without bothering to contact the members who were unable to attend the meeting because they were tied down on their ranches due to war conditions, working in defense plants, or away at war. To me, these boys certainly should have some consideration as they have always contributed their bit toward the success of the Turtles, and may well be called the backbone of the association.

(Signed) Everett Bowman" [118]

In spite of his comments, plans continued with the Rodeo Cowboys Association. Before his resignation Bowman had all ready accepted a position with the Arizona Highway Patrol. [#119]

The following report was sent to Bennett and Merritt regarding the meeting:

"The undersigned representatives of the Cowboys' Turtle Association have met here and discussed hiring a business representative, changing the name of our organization, setting up a business office, and streamlining our activities so it will go forward in promotion of the cowboys' interest, as well as build goodwill by the organization with the various rodeos we participate in during the year.

Briefly we will outline what has been discussed and agreed upon here. We have all voted in favor of this move, and you, as a representative, now have the privilege of casting your vote.

We agreed to hire Earl Lindsey whom you no doubt know has being around the shows the past several years as Gene Autry's representative, to act as our business representative, his duties will consist of running the office, making contact with the various stock show and rodeo committees in regard to prize lists to be approved by the representatives before final acceptance, build goodwill for the organization and sell the stock show and rodeo committees the idea that the cowboys are eager and anxious to make their shows a success, as well as them being an asset to their shows.

Regarding changing the name of our organization; as you are well aware, the Turtle name has been abused in many instances. In some instances differences have been forgiven and forgotten, but in other cases there is still a feeling of resentment. Too, the name 'Turtle' does not have any connection with rodeo business, cowboys, nor anything connected with the West; is confusing to the public, and is entirely out of place for the purpose of our organization. Inasmuch as we are going to revamp our entire setup, we agree that a change in the name of our organization is in order. Therefore, we have selected for our new name the 'RODEO COWBOYS ASSOCIATION'; which is what our organization will be known and referred to from this date on.

We know there is going to be some opposition to our move, but if we are going to survive as an organization we must have someone to protect our interests at all times. After careful consideration and discussion, we agree that the time has arrived for us to take this step.

We have also agreed that there is no personal criticism toward anyone in our group in making this move, but we feel that we are justified in our actions for the betterment of our organization and the rodeo business as a whole, which after all, is how the most of us make our living.

Kindly mail in your vote promptly upon receipt of this letter – either YES or NO.

If this plan works out as we have planned, this will be the greatest thing that ever happened for the benefit of the cowboys, and in a period of twelve to eighteen months we will have firmly established our organization as trustworthy, desirable, and in demand at all rodeos in this country. Signed: George Mills, Louis Brooks, Buck Sorrells, Gerald Roberts, Everett Shaw and Dick Griffith."[#119]

Fannye Lovelady, CTA #77, secretary treasurer of the CTA also resigned as of March 15, and although no action was taken on it she severed her ties with the organization on March 31. She had been an excellent member of the board and served them well. She had endeared herself to the entire organization by her whole-hearted devotion to the interests of the individual boys and to the association. The CTA office was in her home and she often worked through the night when necessary. "No hours too long, no work was too hard for her when her Turtles were concerned." [#119]

1985 Fannye Lovelady Becomes
Rodeo Historical Society Woman of the Year

Going forward forty years the following letter was written by Lovelady to Willard Porter, with the National Cowboy Hall of Fame, which explains and clears up some of the concerns about the demise of the CTA and the beginning of the Rodeo Cowboys Association. It read:

"629 East Boca Raton Road
Phoenix, Arizona 85022

May 31, 1985

Willard H. Porter
Director, Rodeo Division
1700 Northeast 63rd Street
Oklahoma City, Oklahoma 73111

Dear Mr. Porter:

 I enjoyed talking to you on the phone and am still excited about being named the Rodeo Historical Society Woman of the Year in 1985. Now I'll answer your letter as best I can, with a little history of my involvement with the Turtles.

 It was during the summer of 1940 when some of the directors and representatives of the Turtles were on the rodeo circuit that they got to discussing the problems they were experiencing with their mail not being able to catch up to them until months later. The boys who were sending in their membership dues through the mails weren't getting their membership cards sent to them until months later. The directors and representatives then decided the Turtles should finally get a permanent address and hire someone to take care of the mail and then send out the membership cards and buttons.

 It was at that time that Everett Bowman called me from Colorado Springs to see if I was interested in doing this and if I would take the job. He said he would be in Phoenix in a few days and for me to think about it until then.

 I already had a good job with the Arizona State Industrial Commission and I knew my monthly salary with the Turtles still wouldn't equal my one weeks salary with the State, but I was terribly interested in the Turtles because of its possibilities.

 When Everett arrived in Phoenix, I resigned from my State job and proceeded to set up an office in the sunroom of my home for the Cowboy Turtle Association. The office consisted of one file cabinet, a cardex file and a little brown book with the names of some of the cowboys and the dues they paid. They also gave me a half filled box of membership cards and buttons. The checking account amounting to about $6,000.00 and savings account with about $16,000.00 were then turned over to me and work was underway.

The war was in full swing at the time I took over the Turtles and the odds were really against the rodeo cowboys. For example, gasoline and tires were being rationed and you needed coupons to get them. If you ran out of your gasoline coupons, you were out of luck. The life of the rodeo cowboy with so much traveling going on, would frequently use up his coupons way too fast. I used to get many calls from stranded cowboys who had run out of gasoline and the coupons to get it with. Luckily I knew a lot of farmers who would give me their coupons and then I would call the service station guaranteeing that I would send them the coupons and to give the cowboy some gas to get to the rodeo.

Scheduling rodeos was quite difficult due to the telephone priorities. All the calls to the directors and committees to get rodeo approvals and prize lists had to be done late at night.

The media also projected an almost anti-American image against the rodeo cowboy insinuating they should be on the front line and not in a rodeo. It was amazing to me how many of the boys that were in the rodeos were in the service and others worked in defense plants. Yet the general public, because of the press, were fighting the rodeos even to the point of calling the boys "four 'F'ers'. The turnouts for the rodeos, however, especially if they were held by a base, were very good and the fans and servicemen considered seeing a rodeo great entertainment.

It was a difficult time, but we made it despite the media and to the delight of the fans. It was a good outlet for everyone, especially at that time.

You asked about the changes after January of 1945. There was a general meeting in Denver, as was usually done every year during the Denver Stock Show and Rodeo. It was at these times that many of the larger rodeos would have representatives from their committees present their prize lists to our directors for approval. Should there be any new rules, any unfair business practices or new business, they were all taken care of at these meetings. At this particular meeting, the subject of changing the Turtle's name was brought up. Some boys felt that the name was too confusing and that it might be better to change it.

Since this meeting consisted of only directors, representatives and committee-men, I suggested we have a luncheon so that all the members could attend and express their views on changing the name. We then had the announcer make an announcement during the rodeo that evening that a luncheon would be held the next day and that all members were invited.

Also, during the business meeting, I suggested that the association hire a field man who was familiar with rodeos, who could get along with people and who could travel to the different rodeos throughout the country to keep track of what was going on, to resolve any differences and to make sure the rodeos were operating smoothly. Operating the office limited the amount of traveling I could do and the rodeos were getting to a point where cowboy representation was needed on the spot. The field man would report his findings to my office or to the directors of the association so that corrections could be made as needed.

We held a luncheon the next day at a hotel and had a rather large turnout. Toots Mansfield served as president since Everett Bowman was not present. What was discussed most, of course, was the changing of the name. RCA was suggested and there was much pros and cons about it, as such deals are. Most seemed to think that RCA was the most fitting but agreed it was too confusing with the Radio Corporation of America, also called RCA. The members decided then and there to wait with any decision until the rodeo in Houston, which was to take place in a couple of weeks. They felt there would be many more boys there than at Denver and that there would be more votes.

After the Houston rodeo, RCA was used until a few months later, in Denver again, the name was changed to the Professional Rodeo Cowboy Association. *(This is confusing as the official RCA name was **not changed** to PRCA until 1975.)*

I could feel, at this time that politics were starting to creep in for the first time. One of the cowboys, (who dreamed of becoming the president of RCA), called me from Houston and told me he thought Everett Bowman should resign since Everett had accepted a job with the sheriff's office in Phoenix and would no longer be in the rodeos. He wanted me to pass the word to Everett and went on to say how much he liked Everett and felt his resigning would be better than being replaced.

I told him I would talk with Everett and I would let him know what Everett said.

He then added that they had approved my suggestion of hiring a field man and were going to hire Earl Lindsey for that position.

The next morning I called Everett at the sheriff's office and asked him to come by the office when he had some spare time that I had something very important to discuss. When he arrived I poured him a cup of coffee and we sat at the desk. I can truly say this was one of the hardest things I had to do in my entire life. I told Everett about the call from Houston and exactly what had been said.

I cried while Everett swore something he rarely did. We were both silent for a few minutes and then Everett said, 'Good! I fought all these years and its done well. I'm tired and there's no more fight in me. I'd rather fight for the law than fight rodeos any longer.' Then he turned to me and said, 'you have such a good way of saying things . . . you answer this in your way, but be sure to say that I've resigned.'

It had also been decided, in that Houston meeting when the name was changed, that the main headquarters be changed from Phoenix to a more centralized location in the United States to also accommodate the Canadian boys. It would temporarily be moved to Denver until a suitable location could be found. Toots Mansfield wanted me to move with the office to Denver but I told him, 'No.'

He then called me again, a few days after Everett's 'resignation', and asked me to stay on long enough, at least, to show the new field man something about the business, which I did agree to do.

The new man showed up and immediately wanted me to turn over the books, checking and savings accounts to him. I told him I wasn't turning over anything to him until I received a telegram from each and every one of my directors giving me permission to do so. I was determined to take good care of those books and the money, which then was up to $8,000.00 in checking and $19,000.00 which was invested in U. S. Government War Bonds. (I had suggested taking the savings account and investing it in the war bonds to Everett and he received full approval from the directors to do so.)

The new field man immediately called for an audit of all the books and money from the inception of the association in 1936!

The audit was completed and the auditors gave their report with amazement. Even with the mail problems and dues being hauled around for four years all over the country until an office was established, they only found a seven cent, (7 cent) error. That, in itself, said so very much for the boys and the integrity they had. They had turned in every dime.

It was a lively, busy time, and I am proud to have worked for such an association, and now I'm even prouder over being honored by you.

I look forward to attending the ceremony.

Sincerely,
Fannye Lovelady

FL/rh" [140]

Rodeo Cowboys Association
Form Point System for World Champions

The Rodeo Cowboys Association (RCA) formed their own point awarding system, starting January 1, 1945, and would announce their World Champions in each event from that date forward. (*The RAA continued to also select World Champions under their rules until 1955. RAA rules never include entrance fees in their point system.*)

The RCA point system was:

"Points are awarded for each dollar won in contest. No all around champion cowboy will be named, but the high point winner in each event will be adjudged champion in that event. Therefore, all rodeos are requested to mail in their prize lists for O. K. and then send in the list of winners at each show so respective boys can be credited with their points.

Fees for joining the R.C.A. point award are a minimum of $10.00 for small shows with $75.00 or less for each event; $25.00 minimum for shows of over $75.00 an event, or 1% of the prize money in the highest major event, whichever is the larger.

All fees collected over and above expense of keeping records, will go towards prizes for champions in each of the events. Several nice donations have already been pledged and it is the aim of the RCA to have a substantial sum for these awards by the end of the year.

Membership is voluntary this first year, but beginning January 1, 1946, when a prize list is OK'd the rodeo automatically becomes a member of the RCA Point Awarding System. However, all shows are urged to join this year."[119]

Meanwhile, as things were changing drastically in the world of the rodeo cowboys, so was the Rodeo Association of America. Dated April 1945 the following was written:

"At the meeting of the President and Secretary of the National Rodeo Association (which was originally the Southwest Rodeo Association) and of the Executive Committee of the Rodeo Association of America at the Tucson, Arizona, rodeo, it was decided that it probably might be a good thing to merge the two associations, thereby increasing the amount of trophy money for each event, but it was also agreed that it would be impossible to do this without a convention of the members of each organization probably being held at the same time and at the same place to work out such a merger." [119]

The Rodeo Cowboys' Association (RCA) didn't take long to make changes. At a meeting held April 14, 1945, in Phoenix, Arizona, several changes were made:

New Officers and Directors were:
Toots Mansfield, of Bandera, Texas, President;
Louis Brooks, of Sweetwater, Texas, Vice President;
Earl Lindsey, of Fort Worth, Texas, Business Representative.
Directors were: Dave Campbell, Las Vegas, Nev., Bulldogging;
George Yardley, Roswell, N.M., Saddle Bronc Riding;
Dick Griffith, Scottsdale, Ariz., Contract Performers;
Jiggs Burk, Comanche, Okla., Steer Roping;
Carl Dossey, Chandler, Ariz., Bareback Riding;
Gerald Roberts, Young, Ariz., Bull Riding;

Everett Shaw, Bethel, Okla., Calf Roping;
Buckshot Sorrells, Tucson, Ariz., Team Tying

The new location for the office was moved to 1116 Sinclair Building, Fort Worth, Texas. [118]

The following list named 34 Spokesmen for RCA. They were:

Carl Arnold, Buckeye, Ariz.   Fritz Becker, Alamosa, Colo.
Tom Bride, Faucet, Ore.   Cecil Bedford, Walla Walla, Wash.
Clinton Booth, Manvel, Texas   Dave Campbell, Las Vegas, Nev.
Bo Chesson, Beaumont, Texas   Ralph Collier, Coleman, Texas;
Jackie Cooper, Newhall, Calif.   Bobby Estes, Baird, Texas
Vern Goodrich, Newhall, Calif.   J. K. Harris, Longview, Texas;
Tom Hogan, Tulsa, Okla.   Harry Hart, Pocatello, Idaho
Bob Henson, Crosby, Texas   Shirley Hussey, Moses Lake. Wash.
Maurice Laycock, Wheatland, Wyo.   Roy Lewis, House, N.M.
Shorty McCrory, Waverly, N.Y.   Buddy Mefford, Kissimmee, Fla.
Vic Montgomery, Ozona, Texas   Fox O'Callahan, Newhall, Calif.
Dub Phillips, San Angelo, Texas   Walton Poage, Rankin, Texas
Gene Rambo, Shandon, Calif.   Ken Roberts, Strong City, Kans.
Tony Salinas, Encinal, Texas   Chuck Sheppard, Kirkland, Ariz.
Marvin Shoulders, Tulsa, Okla.   Charlie Smith, Rifle, Colo.
Wallis Squires, Tacoma, Wash.   John Tubbs, Valley, Wash.
Arnie Wills, Kartar, Wash.   Oral Zumwalt, Wolf Creek, Mont. [122]

Forty-five approved rodeos for RCA were posted by the May issue in the *Hoofs and Horns*. Additionally recent application by rodeos for membership included: Houston, Texas; Fort Worth, Texas; El Paso, Texas; Beaumont,Texas; San Diego, Calif., Los Angeles, Calif., Ada, Okla., Gladewater, Texas, Cheyenne Frontier Days, Orange, Texas, Dublin, Texas and others.

New sterling silver buttons of a bucking horse design were selected by the board for the RCA emblem, at a cost of $2.25 each. [118]

The 1945 world's champion cowboys chosen by the R.A.A. were: Bill Linderman, the all-around champion cowboy with 15,303 points. He also won the saddle bronc championship. Amye Gamblin held the single tyer (steer tripping) title. Bud Linderman was the champion bareback rider; Ken Roberts won the bull riding title; Floyd Peters, was the world's champion steer decorator; Tom Rhodes, won the title for team tyer; Lane Falk the title for champion team roper; John Bowman champion steer roper; Toots Mansfield, world's champion calf roper; Shoat Webster as world titlist in cow milking; and Homer Pettigrew, world's champ for steer wrestling. [123]

> The 1945 Rodeo Cowboys' Association World Champions were:
> Bud Linderman, bareback riding with $8,313 won
> Homer Pettigrew, steer wrestling with $6,630 points
> Ernest Gill, team roping with $1,112 points
> Bill Linderman, saddle bronc riding with $7,104
> Toots Mansfield, calf roping with $14,180 points
> Ken Roberts, bull riding with $9,332 points
> Everett Shaw, steer roping, with $2,573 points
> *(Note: RCA did NOT award an All-Around winner until 1947)* [20]

Also in the mix were National Rodeo Association (Formerly Southwest Rodeo Association) 1945 Champion Cowboys. They were: All-Around and bull Rider, Kid Fletcher of El Reno, Okla.; steer wrestler, Dub Phillips of San Angelo, Texas; saddle bronc rider, Eddie Curtis, of El Reno, Okla.; bareback rider, Louis Brooks, of Sweetwater, Texas; calf roper, Slim Whaley, of Duncan, Okla.; and single steer roper, Dick Truitt, of Stonewall, Okla.[124]

The Finale

And the final chapter on The Cowboys' Turtle Association comes to a close. In nine short years the organization of rodeo cowboys made the sport better for everyone involved, especially the cowboys, who had no say prior to its formation. This did not happen easily. There were many barriers in the way and trying to enforce the demands that were so important to the cowboys' success often met with much criticism and sometimes downright refusals. It took some very dedicated members to stand by their beliefs. The RAA was anxious to have an organization to represent the cowboy, as RAA supported rodeo management, but often they were extremely discouraged when the fledgling cowboy group went about their business in ways RAA considered 'unprofessional.'

Regardless of the criticism and the complaints, it didn't take long before rodeos began to realize what the Turtles were asking for was good for rodeos, too. As the spectator numbers increased the CTA began to get support from various rodeos across the country. It was evident fans wanted to see the best cowboys compete and to have the best meant complying with CTA rules and demands. The Turtles definitely proved they were on the right path to improve the world of rodeo for the professional cowboy but also for everyone involved in rodeo. Letters of thanks and appreciation from rodeo managements were being received in the CTA office.

If it weren't for these early day 'Turtles' who had the guts and grit, determination and willingness to stand up to complaints and fight for what they knew was right, professional rodeo wouldn't be the outstanding sport it is today. God Bless the Cowboys' Turtle Association!

Turtles These

The boys in spurs and boots and chaps,
A picture bright in these gay traps,
You'll find them frolicsome, jolly chaps,
They're ready for work, or fun, perhaps,
These boys that ride and rope and tie,
These daring Western sons!

There's Oral and Rufe and Alvin and Hugh
Mickey and Jimmie and Johnnie too,
They belong to the Turtles, all of this crew,
They and a host of others too,
These boys that ride and rope and tie,
These daring Western sons!

Now if you think these Turtles slow,
It's time for you to get ready and go
To the next rodeo your city will show
And to see them work to the whistle's blow,
These boys that ride and rope and tie,
These daring Western sons!

Just watch them at their dangerous game,
Winning their way to glory and fame,
They play it straight and they play it game
For they are Turtles, always the same,
These boys that ride and rope and tie,
These daring Western sons!

Tillie Hicks Murphy [103]

The Turtles

It was Boston boys in '36
The battle lines were drawn
Rodeo was a wild west show
And the cowboys had been done wrong.
The purses were light and you 'bout had a fight
The judges to get a check.
It was a crooked draw and most had saw
That to continue this was a wreck.
They drew the line, decided the time
Was right to make a stand
And they had a strike that changed our world,
United to the very last man.
They called them Turtles 'cause they's slow to start
And wasn't sure which way to go.
But because of their guts and leadership,
You and I got rodeo.
They faded away to the R.C.A.
A symbol that we recognize,
Then the P.R.C.A. as it is today.
And the purses have grown to their size
The new breed should stop and look around,
At this game and where its been led.
And not get so busy a fluffin' their pillows,
That they forget just who made the bed. [147]

This poem was written by Dan Willis, at a Turtle Reunion, when June Ivory asked if he would write a poem for the gathering. When he asked June when she needed it, she replied, "About ten." That was an hour and a half away. Dan had been told all about the brave men who had been Turtles, and in that small segment of time, Dan meted out the above. At 10 o'clock, Dan recited the poem. Willis was a roughstock competitor, a RCA bullfighter and the 1965 Rookie of the Year.

The Cowboys' Turtle Association & Wild Bunch Reunion, held in Oklahoma City, Okla. in 1977 at the National Cowboy & Western Heritage Museum. *Photograph by Bern Gregory. From the Dickinson Research Center, National Cowboy & Western Heritage Museum. Courtesy of Imogene Veach Beals.*

CTA members at Cowboy Reunion, National Finals, Las Vegas, 1996. Standing left to right: Phil Stadtler, Orie Dooley, Frank Mendes, Gus Bartley, Stub Johnson, Tex Smith, Walt LaRue, Warren Gunn, Adoph Ebner, Jimmy Schumacher, Tater Decker, Billy Bachman, Cecil Jones. Front Row: Frank Marshall, John Mendes, Homer Pettigrew, Chuck Sheppard, Paul de Fonville, Jim Like, Margie Greenough Henson, Herman Linder, Ed Rucker, Pat Torrance Kilts, "PeeWee" Burge Ott, Buster Ivory. Not pictured but attending were: Polly Burson, Marion Getzweiller, Dale Kennedy, Holloway Grace, Dave Crocker, Faye Blackstone. *Photography by Bill Cheshire. Courtesy of The Cowboy Reunion.*

Appendix

ARTICLES OF ASSOCIATION AND BY-LAWS OF THE COWBOYS' TURTLE ASSOCIATION

(This was the first Articles, etc., written by Maxwell McNutt for the C.T.A. when it began)

The undersigned and those who may sign hereafter hereby form the Cowboys' Turtle Association, and hereby certify that:

FIRST:

The name of this association is and shall be

COWBOYS' TURTLE ASSOCIATION

SECOND:

That the purposes for which this association is formed are:

To raise the standard of Rodeos as a whole and to give them undisputed place in the foremost rank of American sports.

To advocate and work for the bettering of conditions and rules under which the members of this association are governed in the rodeo events in which they participate.

To adopt such rules and regulations for the benefit of the members as will tend to elevate not only the class of the participants but the sport itself.

To protect the members of this association in seeing to it that they are paid or compensated according to the contract or arrangement which any of the members may have with any rodeo.

To bring about honest and fair advertising by the rodeo associations in order that the public be fairly dealt with and may rely upon the truth of advertised events in which the members shall participate.

To do away with all strikes by cowboys and participants in rodeos and in lieu thereof through this organization by peaceful persuasion reach amicable understandings with rodeos to the end that members of this association have a larger participation in the moneys paid in by the public as a result of the advertising benefits obtained by shows because of the standing which members have in the eyes of the public.

To bring about a central place of registration of its members to the end that the Rodeo Association of America and the various members thereof can readily communicate with the members hereof.

To provide through a bulletin to be issued, or otherwise, exact information concerning the time of holding rodeos, the participants therein, the prize money, day money, and other particulars thereof, in which the members hereof are interested.

To advocate the cause of any member of this association who may be wronged by any decision of the Rodeo Association of America or by any of its members.

To obtain if possible group accident insurance for the protection of members, and to accumulate a fund to be used for such purposes as will in the judgment of the board of directors advance the interests of the association and of its members.

ARTICLE I

Section 1. The legislative or rule-making power shall be vested in a board of directors which shall consist of five members, and the board shall be so chosen that in the membership thereof the following rodeo contest events shall be represented: roping, bull-dogging, saddle bronc riding, bareback horse riding, and steer (or bull) riding. The board of directors shall have general supervision over the business and affairs of the association and with power to make, and adopt, alter or amend the by-laws of this association and all rules which it deems proper to carry out the purposes of this organization, and to make any contracts incidental thereto.

The board of directors shall have the power to fill vacancies caused by the death or resignation of any of the officers and directors of this association.

Section 2. The board of directors shall be chosen at the annual meeting of the members of this association and shall hold office for one year and until their successors are elected and qualified, in the following manner: Each member of this association in good standing shall be entitled to cast one vote and those five persons receiving a majority of the votes cast shall be the directors for the ensuing year and until their successors are elected. Members may vote in person or those unable to attend by proxy, on forms furnished by the secretary of this association for that purpose.

Section 3. The officers of this association shall be President, First and Second Vice President, Secretary and Treasurer. The president and the two vice presidents shall be elected from the board of directors at the annual meeting thereof and it will not be necessary that the secretary and treasurer be elected from members of the board of directors.

Section 4. The home office and principal place of business shall be County of _____, State of _____;
provided, however, that meetings of the board of directors and meetings of the members of this association may be held in any place designated therefore by the board of directors.

Section 5. The by-laws of this association may be amended as hereinafter provided.

ARTICLE II

Section 1. Membership in Cowboys' Turtle Association shall be confined to bona fide contestants in such rodeo events as the by-laws of this association may provide.

Section 2. This association, through its board of directors, shall adopt a suitable card by which membership in this association will be certified, and, further, shall require its members to carry and to exhibit the membership card before participating in rodeo events.

BY-LAWS
ARTICLE I

Section 1. Any bona fide contestant or person desirous of becoming such in those events generally known as contest events conducted at rodeos shall be eligible for membership upon the vote of the board of directors, and the payment of the annual dues of members which shall have been fixed and required by the board of directors. The annual dues of membership is hereby fixed at $ per year, provided, however, that all those persons who originally met though in an informal manner, to form this association shall remain members hereof; provided, however that since their induction into this association they, or any of them, have not been expelled therefrom by the board of directors hereof, or otherwise.

Section 2. Hereafter all applications for election to membership in the association must be in writing, seconded by a member hereof in good standing, and the annual dues for that year must accompany the application. The annual dues shall be payable during the month of January of each year. The annual dues shall become delinquent on the first Monday of February of each year and the secretary of the association shall notify the delinquent member, in writing, of his delinquency for non-payment of dues, and if the member so delinquent shall not have paid the said annual dues by the   day of   , of said year, the board of directors may, in its judgment, terminate the membership of the member for so failing to pay.

Section 3. Membership in this association may be terminated by the board of directors—
   (a) by a voluntary resignation tendered in writing addressed to the secretary;
   (b) for failure to pay dues as hereinabove provided;
   (c) a termination of membership for cause by the board of directors.

Section 4. No person can become a member of this association unless he shall subscribe to the Articles of the association and By-Laws and agree to be bound by the same.

Section 5. If any member hereof shall be charged, in writing, addressed to the President with conduct injurious to the welfare of this association, or at variance with its by-laws and rules, the board of directors shall inform him thereof in writing, furnishing him a copy of such charge, and giving him at least thirty days' notice to appear before the board of directors to answer thereto. The member so charged shall have the right to appear before the board, either in person or by counsel, and shall have the right to be confronted by the witnesses and to cross-examine them. If upon hearing the board of directors shall be satisfied of the truth of the charge they may censure, suspend, admit to probation, or otherwise deal with the member as in their judgment the interest of the association demands.

Section 6. Any member who shall willfully violate any rules of the association, or who shall be guilty of such misconduct as to bring the same into disrepute, may be expelled from membership by the board of directors. What constitutes misconduct shall be determined by the board of directors with finality. Proceedings to expel any member for the alleged willful violation of any rules of this association shall be instituted upon written complaint, preferred by one or more members, and notice thereof and of the time and place of hearing shall be given to the accused member, who shall be permitted to appear before the board to testify with reference to the charges and cross-examine any person bringing the same. The board may render judgment for either expulsion or suspension.

Section 7. Any action of the board of directors concurred in by a majority, either in person or in writing, shall constitute legal action by the board. The by-laws of this association may be amended, altered or modified by the board of directors at any regular meeting or at any special meeting called for that purpose, notice of which and of the purpose thereof to be given for such time as the board of directors may determine.

Section 8. All persons may become members hereof by signing the articles of the association and by-laws hereof and agreeing to be bound by the same, and the signing and lodgment with the secretary of a copy of the articles and by-laws shall be deemed the equivalent of the signing of the original articles and by-laws.

ARTICLE II

Section 1. The president shall preside at all meetings of the association and board of directors, and enforce all laws and regulations of the association. He shall perform such other duties as shall be imposed upon him by a resolution of the board of directors. The president shall, with the secretary, sign all written contracts and/or any obligations of the association.

Section 2. In the absence of the president, either of the vice-presidents shall perform his duties. In the event of death or disability of the president, either of the vice-presidents shall act until the board of directors fill the office.

Section 3. The secretary shall keep the minutes and other official reports of the association; he shall conduct the official correspondence of the association; he shall keep all records, books, documents and papers relating to the association at such place as shall be designated by the board of directors; he shall perform such other duties as may be assigned to him by direction of the board of directors.

Section 4. The treasurer shall keep account of all moneys received by him and deposit the same in the name of the association in such depository as shall be designated by the board of directors. He shall not pay out or disburse any of the moneys of the association except by check signed by the president and countersigned by the secretary of the association. At each annual meeting of the board of directors, he shall make a statement of the financial condition of the association, and at the annual meeting of the association he shall submit a detailed report of the financial condition of the association for the preceding fiscal year.

ARTICLE III

Section 1. The board of directors shall meet for the transaction of business on the last Monday of January of each year, and at any other time at the call, in writing, by the president, or any three members thereof, provided written notice shall be given to each member of the board ten days before the time appointed for said meeting. At any meeting of the board of directors a quorum shall consist of three members.

Section 2. At the annual meeting of the association on the last Monday of January of each year the board of directors shall make a full report of their proceedings during the preceding fiscal year, and recommend such measures as they may deem advisable.

Section 3. The board of directors may fill any vacancy among the officers or directors by vote of the majority of those present at any meeting, such board and such election to be for the unexpired term.

ARTICLE IV

Section 1. The board of directors is empowered to make all rules and regulations in its judgment necessary to advance the interests of this organization, and to accomplish the purposes for which it is formed, including the power to adopt all rules necessary for the discipline of its members.

KNOW ALL MEN BY THESE PRESENTS: That we, the undersigned, members of Cowboys' Turtle Association do hereby assent to the foregoing articles of association and by-laws and adopt the same as the articles of association and by-laws of said association and agree to be bound by the same.

IN WITNESS WHEREOF, we have hereunto subscribed our names this:

_____ day of _____ , 1937.

MEMBERS
DIRECTORS
#28

Cowboys' Turtle Association
Articles of Association, By-Laws, Rules
(These were printed in the first book published for the CTA, 1938)

The undersigned and those who may sign hereafter for the Cowboys' Turtle Association, and hereby certify that:

FIRST:
>The name of this association is and shall be
>THE COWBOYS' TURTLE ASSOCIATION

SECOND:
The purposes for which this Association is formed are:

To raise the standard of rodeos as a whole, and to give them undisputed place in the foremost rank of American sports.

To advocate and work for the bettering of conditions and rules under which the members of this Association are governed in the rodeo events in which they participate.

To adopt such rules and regulations for the benefit of the members as will tend to elevate not only the class of the participants but the sport itself.

To protect the members of this Association in seeing to it that they are paid or compensated according to the contract or arrangement which any of the members may have with any rodeo.

To bring about honest and fair advertising by the rodeo associations in order that the public be fairly dealt with and may rely upon the truth of advertised events in which the members shall participate.

To do away with all strikes by cowboys and participants in rodeos and in lieu thereof through this organization by peaceful persuasion reach amicable understandings with rodeos to the end that the members of this Association have a larger participation in the moneys paid in by the public as a result of the advertising benefits obtained by shows because of the standing which members have in the eyes of the public.

To bring about a central place of registration of its members to the end that the Rodeo Association of America and the various members thereof can readily communicate with the members hereof.

To provide through a bulletin to be issued, or otherwise, exact information concerning the time of holding rodeos, the participants therein, the prize money, day money, and other particulars thereof, in which the members hereof are interested.

To obtain, if possible, group accident insurance for the protection of members, and to accumulate a fund to be used for such purposes as will, in the judgment of the Board of Directors, advance the interests of the Association and of its members.

To advocate the cause of any member of the Association who may be wronged by any decision of the Rodeo Association of America or by any of its members.

ARTICLE I

Section 1 – The legislative or rule-making power shall be vested in a Board of Directors which shall consist of seven members, and the Board shall be so chosen that in the membership thereof the following rodeo contest events shall be represented: roping, bull-dogging, saddle bronc riding, bareback horse riding, steer (or bull) riding, and team tying. The President shall be a member of the Board of Directors. The Board of Directors shall have general supervision over the business and affairs of the Association and with power to make, and adopt, alter, or amend the By-laws of the Association and all rules which it deems proper to carry out the purposes of this organization, and to make any contracts incidental thereto.

The Board of Directors shall have the power to fill vacancies caused by the death or resignation of any of the officers and directors of this Association.

Section 2 - The Board of Directors shall be chosen at the annual meeting of the members of this Association and shall hold office for one year and until their successors are elected and qualified, in the following manner: Each member of this Association in good standing shall be entitled to cast one vote for a Director, who will represent the group that this member is contesting in, and if this member is contesting in more than one event he may cast a vote for Director in each event that this member contests in. The six persons receiving the highest number of votes cast in each group, namely, roping, bull-dogging, saddle bronc riding, bareback horse riding, steer (or bull) riding, and team tying, and who have so been elected by the members who are contestants in these groups, shall be the Directors for the ensuing year and until their successors are elected.

Section 3 -The officers of this Association shall be President, First and Second Vice- Presidents, Secretary and Treasurer and they shall be elected by the Board of Directors.

Section 4 - The home office and principal place of business shall be Phoenix, County of Maricopa, State of Arizona; provided, however, that meetings of the

Board of Directors and meetings of the members of this Association may be held in any place designated therefore by the Board of Directors.

Section 5 - The By-laws of this Association may be amended as hereinafter provided.

ARTICLE II

Section 1 – Regular and voting membership in Cowboys' Turtle Association shall be confined to bona fide contestants in such rodeo events as the By-laws of this Association may provide.

Section 2 - This Association, through its Board of Directors, shall adopt a suitable card by which regular and voting or honorary and non-voting membership in this Association will be certified. The insignia for regular voting membership shall be different from the insignia of honorary non-voting membership.

Section 3 - Honorary non-voting membership shall be subject to approval of two members of the Board of Directors.

BY-LAWS
ARTICLE I

Section 1 - Any bona fide contestant or person desirous of becoming such in those events generally known as contest events conducted at rodeos shall be eligible for membership upon the vote of the Board of Directors, and the payment of the annual dues of members which shall have been fixed and required by the Board of Directors. The annual dues of membership are hereby fixed at five dollars ($5.00) per year.

Section 2 - Applications for election to membership in the Association must be in writing, seconded by a member hereof in good standing, and the annual dues for that year must accompany the application. The annual dues shall be payable during the first six months of the year. The annual dues shall become delinquent on the first Monday in August of each year and the Secretary of the Association shall notify the delinquent member in writing, of his delinquency for non-payment of dues, and if the member so delinquent shall not have paid the said annual dues by the 1st day of September, of said year, the Board of Directors may, in its judgment, terminate the membership of the member for so failing to pay.

Section 3 - Membership in this Association may be terminated by the Board of Directors
        (a) By a voluntary resignation tendered in writing addressed to the Secretary.
        (b) For failure to pay dues as hereinabove provided.
        (c) A termination of membership for cause by the Board of Directors.

Section 4 - No person can become a member of this Association unless he shall subscribe to the Articles of the Association and by-laws and agree to be bound by the same.

Section 5 - Any member who shall willfully violate any rules of the Association, or who shall be guilty of such misconduct as to bring the same into disrepute, may be expelled from membership by the Board of Directors. What constitutes misconduct shall be determined by the Board of Directors in finality. Proceedings to expel any member for the alleged willful violation of any rules of this Association shall be instituted upon written complaint, preferred by one or more members, and notice thereof and of the time and place of hearing shall be given to the accused member, who shall be permitted to appear before the Board to testify with reference to the charges and cross-examine any person bringing the same. The Board may render judgment for either expulsion or suspension.

Section 6 - Any action of the Board of Directors concurred in by a majority, either in person or in writing, shall constitute legal action by the Board. The By-laws of this Association may be amended, altered, or modified by the Board of Directors at any regular meeting or at any special meeting called for that purpose, notice of which and of the purpose thereof to be given for such time as the Board of Directors may determine.

ARTICLE II

Section 1. The President shall preside at all meetings of the Association and of the Board of Directors, and enforce all laws and regulations of the Association. He shall perform such other duties as shall be imposed upon him by a resolution of the Board of Directors. The President shall, with the Secretary, sign all written contracts and/or any obligations of the Association.

Section 2. In the absence of the President, either of the Vice-Presidents shall perform his duties. In the event of death or disability of the President, either of the Vice-Presidents shall act until the Board of Directors fills the office.

Section 3. The Secretary shall keep the minutes and other official reports of the Association; he shall conduct the official correspondence of the Association; he shall keep all records, books, documents, and papers relating to the Association at such place as shall be designated by the Board of Directors; he shall perform such other duties as may be assigned to him by direction of the Board of Directors.

Section 4. The Treasurer shall keep account of all money received by him and deposit the same in the name of the Association in such depositary as shall be designated by the Board of Directors. He shall not pay out or disburse any of the moneys of the Association except by check signed by the President and counter-signed by the Secretary of the Association. At each annual meeting of the Board of Directors, he shall make a statement of the financial condition of the Association and at the annual meeting of the Association he shall submit a detailed report of the financial condition of the Association for the preceding fiscal year.

ARTICLE III

Section 1. The Board of Directors shall meet for the transaction of business on the last Monday of January of each year, and at any other time at the call, in writing, by the President, or any three members thereof, provided written notice shall be given to each member of the Board ten days before the time appointed for said meeting. At any meeting of the Board of Directors a quorum shall consist of four members.

Section 2. At the annual meeting of the Association on the last Monday of January of each year the Board of Directors shall make a full report of their proceedings during the preceding fiscal year and recommend such measures as they may deem advisable.

Section 3. The Board of Directors may fill any vacancy among the Officers or Directors by vote of the majority of those present at any meeting; such Board and such election to be for the unexpired term.

ARTICLE IV

Section 1. The Board of Directors is empowered to make all rules and regulations in its judgment necessary to advance the interests of this organization, and to accomplish the purposes for which it is formed, including the power to adopt all rules necessary for the discipline of its members.

The foregoing Articles of Association and By-laws were adopted as the Articles of Association and By-laws of said Association at the annual meeting of the Cowboys' Turtle Association at Fort Worth, Texas, March 10, 1938, and the members of the Association agree to be bound by same.

RULES OF THE
COWBOYS' TURTLE ASSOCIATION

Adopted by the Board of Directors, Phoenix, Arizona, January 3, 1938, and approved by members at the annual meeting at Fort Worth, Texas, March 10, 1938.

Rule I. - At all cowboy contests held during the year 1938, all entrance fees in each event must be added to the guaranteed prize money of each event. Such entrance fees are to be added either to the daily prize money or to the final purse, or maybe both.

Rule II. - No C.T.A. member shall be allowed to compete at an amateur rodeo. An amateur rodeo is one which is advertised as such and held for the benefit of cowboys with limited rodeo experience, and in which they are protected by excluding any cowboys because of experience in other rodeos or in which handicaps are placed on any persons entering. However, a rodeo having special events for amateurs shall not be classified as an amateur rodeo by virtue of such fact alone.

Rule III. - If a member of the C.T.A. has entered as a contestant or worker in any rodeo that has been approved by the C.T.A. and if such member of the C.T.A. owes a room or board bill which was incurred during the time of the contest, or any other reasonable expense in connection with the contest, then the C.T.A. upon investigation of facts and subject to the final approval by the Board of Directors of the C.T.A. will pay such room or board bill, or any other reasonable bill incurred at that time. Members of the C.T.A. whose obligations have been paid by the C.T.A. will not be permitted to contest or work at any rodeo until the C.T.A. has been reimbursed in full for the money paid out in his behalf, and also has received payment in full for the fine that has been assessed against him.

Rule IV. - The R.A.A. will notify the Secretary of the C.T.A. at least sixty (60) days in advance of any rodeo held under auspices of the R.A.A. giving full details as to rules and regulations, events, prize list, and judges of that particular rodeo, and such rules and regulations and prize list must be approved by the C.T.A. Approval or rejection must be given by the C.T.A. in writing to R.A.A. and to the local rodeo authorities within thirty days from receipt of the above by C.T.A.

Rule V. - Any member of the C.T.A. who either competes or works at a rodeo which has been disapproved by the C.T.A. is subject to fine and suspension or both by the C.T.A.

Rule VI. - In the event the governing body imposes a fine on a member of the C.T.A. for infraction of rules, such fine must be paid in full before any such member can participate in any future contests except when the Board of Directors of the C.T.A. permits such contestant to pay such fine in installments, provided, however, that such installments shall never be less than ten per cent of the original amount of such fine and provided, further, that twenty-five per cent of all prizes won by such contestant must be applied to such fine until paid in full. If any contestant fails to either pay his fine in full or a percentage of such fine as stipulated by the Board of Directors or a percentage of his winnings in accordance with the above, such member shall be immediately suspended from the C.T.A. and forfeit all money that has been paid up until that time.

Rule VII. - It is understood that no officer, director, member, or employee of the C.T.A. shall be liable individually or otherwise for any breach of the above rules or of any understanding or agreement between the C.T.A. and the R.A.A. or with any other rodeo association.

The above amended rules of the C.T.A. were unanimously adopted at a special meeting held by the Board of Directors of the C.T.A. in Phoenix, Arizona, on Monday, January 3, 1938.

COWBOY TURTLE ASSOCIATION

EVERETT BOWMAN, *President*
HUGH BENNETT, *Secretary*
DICK TRUITT, *Director*
HUGHIE LONG, *Director*
EDDIE CURTIS, *Director*

EVERETT SHAW, *Director*
BUREL MULKEY, *Director*

Roster Of
Cowboy's Turtle Association Members By April 1, 1938

C.T.A. # Name Hometown

1. Jimmie Nesbitt, Ft Worth, TX
2. Rusty McGinty, Plains, TX
3. Dick Griffith, Ft Worth, TX
4. Red Thompson, Springtown, TX
5. Dick Truitt, Stonewall, OK
6. Leo Murray, Benson, AZ
7. Everett Shaw, Stonewall, OK
8. Hugh Bennett, Ft Thomas, AZ
9. Ralph Bennett, Abilene, TX
10. John Bowman, Salida, CA
11. Hub Whiteman, Clarksville, TX
12. Joe Welch, Carlsbad, NM
13. Holloway Grace, Compton, CA
14. Hughie Long, Ft Worth, TX
15. Everett Bowman, Hillside, AZ
16. Melvin Harper, Markham, TX
17. Joel Fleming, Center, TX
18. Whitey Koed, Garden Valley, ID
19. Ralph Stanton, Missoula, MT
20. Howard McCrorey, Deadwood, SD
21. Paul Carney, Galeton, CO
22. Herman Linder, Cardston, Alta, Can
23. Turk Greenough, Red Lodge, MT
24. Frank Martz, Midland, TX
25. Jonas De Arman, Sayre, OK
26. Earl Moore, Olton, TX
27. Homer Pettigrew, Grady, NM
28. Sonny Hancock, Roswell, NM
29. Doff Aber, Cooke City, MT
30. Floyd Stillings, Cody, WY
31. Donald Nesbitt, Snowflake, AZ
32. Andy Jauregui, Newhall, CA
33. James Kenney, Midland, TX
34. Chic Dayton, Durango, CO
35. Pat Woods, Newhall, CA
36. Earl Thode, Casa Grande, AZ
37. Harry Knight, Calgary, Canada
38. David Stout, Oracle, AZ
39. Jimmie McGee, Phoenix, AZ

C.T.A. # Name Hometown

40. Smoky Snyder, Kimberly, B.C.
41. Shorty Hill, Venus, TX
42. Asbury Schell, Tempe, AZ
43. Lee Barkdoll, Scottsdale, AZ
44. Breezy Cox, Pine Top, AZ
45. Alvin Gordon, N. Hollywood CA
46. Tom Rhodes, Tucson, AZ
47. Fox O'Callahan, Newhall, CA
48. Jackie Cooper, Jasper Park, Canada
49. Fritz Truan, Long Beach, CA.
50. Perry Henderson, Dewey, AZ
51. Charley Turk, Sanderson, TX
52. Cecil Owsley, New Laguna, NM
53. Bud Parker, Tucson, AZ
54. Marion Getzweller, Benson, AZ
55. Clay Carr, Visalia, CA
56. John Rhodes, Tucson, AZ
57. Ike Rude, Mangum, OK
58. Oral Zumwalt, Wolf Creek, MT
59. Joe Burrell, Hanford, CA
60. E. Pardee, Lamar, CO
61. Buck Sorrells, Tucson, AZ
62. Milt Moe, Beggs, OK
63. R. R. Ingersoll, Wolf Creek, MT
64. Carl Shepard, Phoenix, AZ
65. Kenneth Gunter, Benson, AZ
66. Cecil Kennedy, Chandler, AZ
67. Albert McEuen, Hillside, AZ
68. Rex Glenn, Tucson, AZ
69. Arthur Beloat, Buckeye, AZ
70. Carl Arnold, Buckeye, AZ
71. Steve Heacock, Phoenix, AZ
72. Melvin Cropper, Deseret, UT
73. Jack Sellars, Del Rio, TX
74. Hugh Clingman, Wickenburg, AZ
75. Tom Hogan, Tulsa, OK
76. "Ma" Hopkins, Tucson, AZ (Hon.)
77. "Pa" Hopkins, Tucson, AZ (Hon.)
78. "Babe" Knight (Mrs. Pete Knight)(Hon)

79. Eddie Woods, Emmett, ID
80. Dave Campbell, Las Vegas, NV
81. Vic Schwartz, Wichita Falls, TX
82. Paul Crain, Denver, CO
83. Earl Blevins, Denver, CO
84. Ted McCrory, Bozeman, MT
85. Mickey McCrory, Deadwood, SD
86. Slats Jacobs, St. Thomas, AZ
87. Kid Fletcher, Hugo, CO
88. Dan Fernamburg, Denver, CO
89. Stub Bartlemay, Arlington, OR
90. Al Allen, Burbank, CA
91. Pete Grubb, Blackfoot, ID
92. Cliff Gardner, Reno, NV
93. Burel Mulkey, Salmon, ID
94. Dell Mercer, Tucson, AZ
95. Hugh Strickland, Bakersfield, CA
96. Bill Horton, Buffalo, WY
97. Charles Jones, Van Horn, TX
98. Wesley Walls, Carmel, CA
99. John Jordan, Florence, AZ
100. Earl Sellers, Del Rio, TX
101. Clinton Booth, Manvel, TX
102. Nick Knight, Cody, WY
103. Rube Roberts, Ft Worth, TX
104. Buck Eckols, Liberty, TX
105. Bill Nix, Rankin, TX
106. Lonnie Rooney, Wilson, OK
107. King Merritt, Federal, WY
108. Roy Lewis, House, NM
109. Herbert Meyers, Okmulgee, OK
110. Barton Carter, Pawhuska, OK
111. Richard Merchant, Tucson, AZ
112. Andrew Bode, Rock Springs, TX
113. Raymond Quigg, Vinegarone, TX
114. Ted Powers, Coleman, TX
115. Dad Turk, Sanderson, TX (Hon.)
116. Juan Salinas, Encinal, TX
117. Gene Ross, Sayre, OK
118. Roy Kirk, Rayville, LA
119. Herb Dahl, Murdo, SD
120. Roy Matthews, Ft Worth, TX
121. Dalton Parrish, Bridgeport, TX
122. Andy Curtis, El Reno, OK
123. George McIntosh, Ft Worth, TX
124. Hoyt Hefner, Wichita Falls, TX
125. Ken Hargis, Utleyville, CO
126. Ward Watkins, Model, CO
127. Shorty Creed, Rye, CO
128. Jim Whiteman, Clarksville, TX
129. Weldon Bascom, Raymond, Alberta
130. Junior Caldwell, Ft Worth, TX (dec.)
131. Shorty Ricker, Ranger, TX
132. Eddie Curtis, El Reno, OK
133. Joe Thompson, Coweta, OK
134. George Wilderspin, Ft Worth, TX
135. C. O. Leuschner, Tilden, TX
136. Cleve Kelley, Ft Worth, TX
137. Dick Slappert, Miles City, MT
138. Dick Anderson, Ft Worth, TX
139. Howard Westfall, Ft Worth, TX
140. Claude Wallace, Atoka, OK
141. Fred Barrett, Del Rio, TX
142. Jake McClure, Lovington, NM
143. Reese B. Lockett, Brenham, TX
144. Clyde Burk, Comanche, OK
145. Endre Barr, Hemet, CA
146. Omer Maxwell, Wagoner, AZ
147. Lee Simon, Pueblo, CO
148. Doc Simon, Pueblo, CO
149. Gordon Ferris, Reno, NV
150. Willie Clay, Visalia, CA
151. Leslie Jenkins, Camp Wood, AZ
152. Joe Edwards, Irvine, CA
153. Lloyd Saunders, Burbank, CA
154. Floyd Peters, Browning, MT

155. Harry Logue, Burbank, CA
156. Bill Truan, Long Beach, CA (dec)
157. Ace Gardner, Keene, CA
158. Dick Shelton, Tilden, TX
159. Wayne Cutler, Sutcliffe, NV
160. Perry Ivory, Alturas, CA
161. H. T. Miller, Monticello, CA.
162. Tom Taylor, Spofford, TX
163. Vic Rogers, Kerrville, TX
164. Jim Lucas, Lewistown, PA
165. Al Skelton, San Jose, CA
166. Johnnie Schneider, Livermore, CA
167. John A. Beach, Santa Cruz, CA
168. M. W. Del Ray, Tipton, CA
169. Led Engelsman, Santa Cruz, CA
170. Cliff Kilfoyl, Santa Cruz, CA
171. A. A. Horton, Santa Cruz, CA
172. D. R. Wilder, Santa Cruz, CA
173. Earl Batteate, Oakland, CA
174. Al Landon, Escalon, CA
175. Dick Robbins, Tempe, AZ
176. Jim Irwin, Azle, TX
177. Archie McIntosh, Reno, NV
178. Ray McGinnis, Reno, NV
179. Mitchell Owens, Alturus, CA.
180. Chuck Sheppard, Reno, NV
181. Bill Eaton, Jal, NM
182. John Barton, Hayward, CA
183. Cecil Henley, Hayward, CA
184. Girard Davis, Woodlake, CA
185. Bob Crosby, Roswell, NM
186. Frankie Schneider, Livermore, CA
187. Howard Brown, Hollywood, CA
188. Charles J. Lyne, Blue Jay, CA
189. Leonard Ward, Saugus, CA
190. Adolph Gill, Exeter, CA
191. Joe H. Wade, Brea, CA
192. Emmett Gill, Exeter, CA
193. Roy Stewart, Corcoran, CA
194. Walt Stewart, Corcoran, CA
195. Jess Kell, N. Hollywood, CA
196. Blondy Brunzell, Gardena, CA
197. Martin Deal, Del Rio, TX
198. Ned Winegar, Los Banos, CA
199. Shorty Sisco, Exeter, CA
200. Dick Hunter, Santa Rosa, NM
201. Felix Cooper, Los Angeles, CA
202. Charlie Maggini, Gilroy, CA
203. Arnil Ferrario, Livermore, CA
204. Carl Dossey, Phoenix, AZ
205. Dutch Bartrum, Hayward, CA
206. Merle Vincent, Glennville, CA
207. Bob Fisher, Chowchilla, CA
208. John Mendes, Visalia, CA
209. H. H. Mueller, San Fernando, CA
210. Ned Ferraro, Maywood, CA.
211. Neil Wagner, Maywood, CA
212. Roland Curry, Casa Grande, AZ
213. Russell McGinnis, Reno, NV
214. Everett Chetham, Reno, NV
215. Charlie Lattemore, Reno, NV
216. Frank Borges, Reno, NV
217. Glen Shaw, Escalon, CA
218. Jack Kerscher, Blackfoot, ID
219. Jim Massey, Ft Worth, TX
220. George Mills, Montrose, CO
221. Wes Hamilton, Reno, NV
222. Hank Mills, Montrose, CO
223. Tom Breedon, Tucson, AZ
224. Jimmie Wilkinson, Meriden, WY
225. Charlie Duckett, Rio Blanco, CO
226. Mike Hastings, Spofford, TX
227. Fred Alvord, Baird, TX
228. Hayden Rucker, Okmulgee, OK
229. Floyd Gale, Morris, OK
230. Buck Davis, Moro, OR
231. Melvin Tivis, Faith, SD
232. Fred Lowry, Lenapah, OK
233. A. J. Holder, Rankin, TX
234. Roy Sewalt, Brooksmith, TX
235. E. H. Blacky Johnson, Marques, TX
236. Charlie Bennett, Meriden, WY
237. Toots Mansfield, Bandera, TX
238. Andy Gibson, Havre, MT
239. Irby Mundy, Shamrock, TX
240. Ed Osborne, Niles, CA

1938 CTA Rulebook & Membership Page 231

241. Alford Hayhurst, Coalgate, OK
242. Lee Farris (Canada Kid) Newhall, CA
243. John McIntyre, OK
244. Richard Miller, Westhoff, TX.
245. Red Allen, Helena, MT
246. Harry Hart, Pocatello, ID
247. Guy Cash, White Bird, ID
248. Bud Evans, Sheridan, WY
249. Jay Snively, Wynono, OK
250. Herschell Ross, Sayre, OK
251. Chick Martindale, Phoenix, AZ
252. Johnnie Wilkinson, Divide, WY
253. Art Casteel, Cheyenne, WY
254. Elmo Walls, Blum, TX
255. Geo. Cline, Roosevelt, AZ
256. Durant Ryan, Duncan, OK
257. Eddie Jones, Ft Hall, ID
258. Doc Cline, Roosevelt, AZ
259. Ken Roberts, Strong City, KS
260. Bill Sievers, Glenwood Sprg, CO
261. Walter Cravens, Butler, OK (Killed at New York City, N.Y.)
262. Billy Wilkinson, Meriden, WY
263. Buck Goodspeed, Wetumka, OK
264. Ted Youchum, Porter, OK
265. Jess Goodspeed, Wetumka, OK
266. Rube Nelson, Ross, WY
267. Cliff Helm, Dallas, TX
268. O. C. Glenn, Benson, AZ
269. Dave Starr, Deming, NM
270. Lawrence Conley, Casa Grande, AZ
271. Jimmie Minotto, Phoenix, AZ
272. Sie Elliot, Burns, OR
273. Herb Benden, Collbran, CO
274. Bob Lockie, Red Bluff, CA
275. Jack Myers, Red Bluff, CA
276. Jack Case, Reno, NV
277. Roy Gafford, Casper, WY
278. Dee Hinton, Geronimo, AZ
279. Bob Boden, Ismay, MT
280. Joe Orr
281. Maurice Rielly, N. Platte, NE
282. Terry Lockyer, Firth ID
283. Harold Piper, Jelm, WY.
284. Justin Peak, Encampment, WY
285. Jack Wade, Bymoor, AB
286. Jerry Ambler, Byemoor, AB
287. Cecil Bedford, Givenlock, SK
288. Doug Bruce, Colfax, WA
289. Ross Greenwood
290. Maynard Gaylor, Odessa, TX
291. Mike Fisher, Dunning, NE
292. Vern Meeks, Jackson, WY
293. Ed Harrington, Meriden, WY
294. Tom Knight, Cody, WY
295. Pete Kerscher, Blackfoot, ID
296. Harold Emory, Livingston, MT
297. Carl McCullough, La Crosse, WA
298. Lonnie Allen, Magdalena, NM
299. Cecil W. Jones, Menan, ID
300. Walter Heacock, Twin Falls, ID
301. Dave Shipp, Cody, WY
302. Larry Daniels, Homestead, OR
303. Ray Mavity, Helena, MT
304. H. L. Dyer, Bartlesville, OK
305. Hugh Ridley, Redrock, OK
306. Buff Brady, Ellensburg, WA
307. Bill McFarlan, Lynwood, CA
308. Bill Taylor, Payson, AZ
309. Paul Luffman, Lewiston, ID
310. Norman Stewart, Clarkston, WA.
311. Hugh McAdam, Perma, MT
312. Howard Peelgren, Colfax, WA
313. Buck Tiffin, Dayton, WA
314. Bob Hougton, Eugene, OR
315. Cherokee Alcorn, Hollywood, CA
316. A. J. Anderson, Hollywood, CA
317. Phil Armstrong, Meeker, CO
318. Tom Wood, Molalla, OR
319. Hubert Sandall, Tremonton, NV
320. Buck Petersen, Silver Peak, NV
321. John Elfic, Noxon, MT
322. Scrap Iron, Miles City, MT
323. Oran Fore, Pasadena, CA
324. Marvin Paul, Billings, MT

325. Keith Hunsaker, Tremonton, UT
326. Mel Stonehouse, Chugwater, WY
327. Frank Van Meter, Weiser, ID
328. John Tubbs, Spokane, WA
329. Gale Anderson, Twin Falls, ID
330. John Drayer, Redmond, OR
331. Bert F. Morrison, Portland, OR
332. Don Thompson, Calgary, AB
333. Arnie Wills, Kartar, WA
334. Frank Campadore, Spokane, WA
335. Carl Lee, Beswick, CA
336. I. W. Young, Odessa, TX
337. Hans Starr, Witch Creek, CA
338. Chick Hannon, San Fernando, CA
339. Art Deck, Livermore, CA
340. Bob Walden, Cheyenne, WA
341. Speedy Densmore, Tekamah, NE
342. Dale Adams, Odell, TX
343. Charles Tompkins, El Reno, OK
344. Jimmie Olsen, Pampa, TX
345. Slim Whaley, Petrolia, TX
346. Ace Soward, Buffalo, OK
347. Elmer Martin, Okmulgee, OK
348. C. J. Shellenberger,
349. John Lindsey, Wichita Falls, TX
350. Amye Gamblin, Petrolia, TX
351. Whitey Stewart, Anadarko, OK
352. Tommy Horner, Brady, TX
353. Shorty McCrory, Springtown, TX
354. Floyd Shumaker
355. H. D. Binns, Coalgate, OK
356. Lee Sanborn, Reno, NV
357. Buck Buckley, Oklahoma City, OK
358. Tom Foreman, Oklahoma City, OK
359. Buttons Yonnick, Ft Worth, TX
360. Earl May, Butte, MT
361. Bob Askins, Ismay, MT
362. Bob Estes, Baird, TX
363. Joe McMackin, Java, SD
364. Frank Marion, Velasco, TX
365. Ralph Warren
366. Leslie Karstad, Browning, MT
367. Tom Shipman, Bozeman, MT
368. Doc Foust, N. Platte, NE
369. John Strachan, Wolf Point, MT
370. Eddie Boysen, Strong City, KS
371. Al Wilkinson, Douglas, WY
372. Smokey Ballard, Miami, OK
373. Sam Proctor, Okema, OK
374. Lyle Cottrell, Monte Vista, CO
375. Jim Brister, Lordsburg, NM
376. Jim Hudson, Dos Cabezos, AZ
377. Bill Hancock, Roswell, NM
378. Orville Stanton, Wyandotte, OK
379. Walter Haythorn, Arthur, NE
380. Waldo Haythorn, Arthur, NE
381. Pat Plaskett, Woodstown, NJ
382. Bob Matthews, Phoenix, AZ
383. Larry Cullen,
384. Walter Stevenson, Reno, NV
385. Eddie Hovenkamp, Ft Worth, TX
386. Jack Avery, Paris, TX
387. Emile Avery, Paris, TX
388. David Longricker, Scenic, SD
389. Rock Parker, Myakka City, FL
390. Bill Parks, Gordon, NE
391. Jess J. Rhodes, Dalhart, TX
392. Curley Hatchel, Alpine, TX
393. Jack Quait, Marland, OK
394. Charley Whitlow, Florence, AZ
395. Paul Bond, Carlsbad, NM
396. Luther Finley, Mesa, AZ
397. Glen Lowry, Lenapah, OK
398. Curley Bell, Ft Worth, TX
399. George Ward, Stevens, SD
400. Buck Edwards, Tucson, AZ
401. Heavy Henson, Red Lodge, MT
402. Frank Finley, Mesa, AZ
403. Jimmie Wallace, Montrose, CO
404. Carl Beasley, Ada, OK
405. Tom Perkins, Walkill, NY
406. Charles Colbert, Byers, TX
407. Art Jones, Ft Hall, ID
408. Casey Davis, Cheyenne, WY
409. Chet McCarty, Hotchkiss, CO
410. Ted Buschbaum, Topeka, KS

1938 CTA Rulebook & Membership Page 233

411. Bill Buschbaum, Bloomington, WI
412. Raymond Al Garrett, Alliance, NE
413. Buck Wyatt, Kendrick, OK
414. Raymond L. J. Riling, Philadelphia, PA, (Hon.)
415. Charles Aldridge, New York City NY (Hon.)
416. Deafie Scott, Ft Worth, TX
417. Bud Keenan, Newhall, CA
418. Bart Clennon, Deadwood, SD
419. Texas Kid Jr., Knott, TX
420. Prosser Martin, Del Rio, TX (Hon.)
421. Joe Teague, Ft Smith, AR
422. Jimmie Hazen, Los Angeles, CA
423. Pete Martinez, Tucson, AZ
424. Dick Johnson, Hatfield, AR
425. Homer Todd, Ft Smith, AR
426. Skip Goodson, Broken Arrow, OK
427. Eddie Smith, Wellington, TX
428. Jack Yale, Amarillo, TX
429. Clyde Cline, Muskogee, OK
430. Wiley Elliott, Guthrie, OK
431. Sam Stuart, Ft Worth, TX
432. Frank Autry, Tulsa, OK
433. Johnny Marz, Sapulpa, OK
434. Dude Teague, Ft Smith, AR
435. Louie Collins, Ft Tosson, OK
436. Ralph Stockwell, Nowata, OK
437. Glen Harp, Springdale, AR
438. Harry Williams, Vinita, OK
439. Jack Sherman, Calgary, AB
440. Leonard Murray, New Paltz, NY
441. Frank Quirk, Woodstown, NJ
442. Eddie Cameron, Houston, TX
443. Rube Hubbell, Denver, CO
444. Johnny Geist, New York City, NY
445. Walter Hannum, St Louis, MO
446. Joe Farrell, Lancaster, MO
447. Len Jacobs, Rushville, NE
448. Fred Beeson, Arkansas City, KS
449. Jim Snively, Pawhuska, OK
450. Dan Wilder, Clear Lake, IA
451. Eddie Collins, Sisseton, SD
452. Bennie Bender, Trail City, SD
453. George Danials, Bentonsport, IA
454. Handy Henderson, Wetumka, OK(dec.)
455. Fred Ryser, Muskogee, OK
456. Bob Elliott, Muskogee, OK
457. Jimmie French, Muskogee, OK
458. George Elliott, Muskogee, OK
459. George Bailey, Ft Gibson, OK
460. Barney Burcham, Muskogee, OK
461. Owen Buffington, Westville, TX
462. E. E. Buffington, Westville, TX
463. Bob Wilkinson, Throckmorton, TX
464. Ross Lund, Scottsdale, AR
465. Lynn Heskey, Ft Towson, OK
466. Tony Salinas, Encinal, TX
467. Clyde Ford, Olney Springs, CO
468. Henry Snively, Pawhuska, OK
469. Buck Standifer, Plainview, TX
470. Milo Lines, Sacaton, AZ
471. A. Altamarino, Sombrero Butte, AZ
472. Allan Jesperson, Cholame, CA
473. Bill Lyon, Cholame, CA
474. Austin Ranny, Stanford, CA
475. Lee Webb, Dubois, WY
476. Tex Cutler, Ft Hall, ID
477. Fritz Taylor, Rimrock, AZ
478. Jerry Littrell, Sacramento, CA
479. Joe Schell, Camp Wood, AZ
480. James McGowan, Nespelem, WA
481. Bill Bisaro, San Francisco, CA
482. Beverly Conners, Tonasket, WA
483. Jack Streeter, Stavely, AB
484. Bill Hanna, Muskogee, OK
485. Tom Bride, McMinnville, OR
486. Ed Jauregui, Newhall, CA
487. John Gerig, Hayward, CA
488. B. P. Rosenberg, Wibaux, MT
489. Ray Kohrs, Malaga, CA
490. Johnny Gardner, Palm Springs, CA
491. Al Kay, Palm Springs, CA
492. George Guen, Hershey, NE
493. Frank Compadore, Spokane, WA
494. Carl Bisaro, San Francisco, CA

495. George Garbarino, San Francisco, CA
496. Lester Vance,
497. Johnnie Vance,
498. Chuck Williams, Cheyenne, WY
499. Padgett Berry, San Antonio, NM
500. E. Felts, Orange, TX
501. Dan Hines, Orange, TX
502. Art Manning, Victorville, CA (Hon.)
503. Goldie Corbin, Ft Worth, TX
504. Albert Barnhart, Butte, MT
505. Len Perkins, Somerton, AZ
506. Joe Barnes, Palm Springs, CA
507. Speck McMillen, Oklahoma City, OK
508. Allen Craine, Manvel, TX
509. Everet Vassar, Marland, OK
510. Clem Swarts, Tulsa, OK
511. Aubra Bowers, Allison, TX
512. Bill Hussmann, Lone Tree, WY
513. Ralph Jones, Claude, TX
514. Powder River Thompson, Lance Creek, WY
515. Urban Doan, Halkirk, AB. Can
516. George Yardley, Carlsbad, NM
517. Bob Morris, Tascosa, TX
518. Chas. Stickney, Sacramento, CA
519. Ike Chisum, San Francisco, CA
520. Dale Williams, Morrison, CO
521. Earvin Collins, N. Hollywood, CA
522. George Newsom, Cholame, CA
523. Frank Cornett,
524. Bub Fulkerson, Inglewood, CA
525. Jim Talbot, Huntington Park, CA
526. Manny Toskos, New York City, NY
527. Goldie Butner, Kent, CT
528. Sam Palhonus, Tulsa, OK
529. Frank Denham, Kellyville, OK
530. Russell Paulsen, Farmington, UT
531. Frank McDonald, Stavely, AB
532. Ernest Abold, Rushville, NE
533. Arthur Holder, Florey, TX
534. Harold Johnson, Hershey, NE
535. Virgil Stapp, Houston, TX
536. O. H. Noland, Houston, TX
537. Joe Kelsey, Tonasket, WA
538. Fred Baker, Lance Creek, WY
539. Robert Foehl, Chandler, AZ (Hon.)
540. Fritz Becker, Alamosa, CO
541. Frankie Burns, Alamosa, CO
542. Morris Cooper, Midland, TX
543. Fele Fernandez, Alamosa, CO
544. Clarence Ritter, Palm Springs, CA
545. John W. Taylor, Ramona, CA
546. Orville Shellenberger, Marietta, OK
547. Bernice Straughn, Marietta, OK (Hon)
548. George Tyler, Wilson, OK
549. Russell Wood, Ten Sleep, WY
550. Norman Person, Cresson, TX
551. Ed Bowman, Coolidge Dam, AZ
552. Darwin Parks, Casa Grande, AZ
553. Tex Doyle, Amarillo, TX
554. Cal Kennedy, Muskogee, OK
555. George Sands, Fairbanks, AZ (Hon.)
556. Geo. V. Cullington, Phoenix, AZ (Hon)
557. Hobart Flowers, Duncan, OK
558. Pauline Sawyers, Cheyenne, WY (Hon)
559. Bill Harmon, Cheyenne, WY (Hon)
560. Jack Van Ryder, Tucson, AZ
561. Arden McFadden, San Carlos, AZ
562. Bill Roer, Phoenix, AZ
563. Bill McMackin, Ellensburg, WA
564. Joe Bassett, Payson, AZ
565. G. B. Sandifer, Abilene, TX (Hon.)
566. Marion B. McClure, Abilene, TX (Hon.)
567. Sheriff Watson, Abilene, TX (Hon.)
568. Helen Lichtenstein, Reno, NV (Hon.)
569. Lile Karn, Reno, NV (Hon.)
570. K. W. Lewis, Tucson, AZ (Hon.)
571. Joe Coker, Wolf City, TX
572. Carl Dykes, Goldthwaite, TX
573. Dave Sanford, Midland, TX
574. Allen Cameron, Houston, TX
575. Salvesta Roan, Elk City, OK
576. W. B. Warren, Hockley, TX (Hon.)

577. Joe D. Hughes, Houston, TX (Hon.)
578. W. A. Lee, Houston, TX (Hon.)
579. Tom Booth, Booth TX (Hon.)
580. Frank Y. Dew, Dewalt, TX (Hon.)
581. Jack Wilson, Newark, TX
582. Alvin Jason, San Juan Bautista, CA
583. John Broderick, New York City, NY
584. Clay Haverty, Tucson, AZ (Hon.)
585. Johnny Williams, Ft Worth, TX
586. Mike Lewis, Pueblo, CO
587. Dale Stone, Beaumont, TX
588, Milton Mauboules, Nome, TX
589. Bruce Ross, Sayre, OK
590. Tommy Wilson, Belton, TX
591. Frank E. Newhagen, Denver, CO (Hon.)
592. Philip K. Wrigley, Chicago, IL (Hon.)
593. James V. Allred, Gov. of TX (Hon.)
594. Bud Spillsbury, Midland, TX
595. W. T. Woods, Ft Worth, TX
596. Teller Ammons, Gov., CO (Hon.)
597. Bobby Dickson,
598. Pauline Nesbitt, Nowata, OK (Hon.)
599. Gene Creed, Rye, CO (Hon.)
600. W. A. Tyler, (Hon.)
601. Tad Lucas, Ft Worth, TX (Hon.)
602. Lucyle Richards, Colorado City, TX (Hon.)
603. Peggy Long, Cresson, TX (Hon.)
604. Rose Breedon, Tucson, AZ (Hon.)
605. Vaughn Krieg, Rye, CO (Hon.)
606. Virginia Van Meter, Los Fresnos, TX (Hon.)
607. Mary Keen, Houston, TX (Hon.)
608. Gus Massey, N Ft Worth, TX (Hon.)
609. Bud Cook, Visalia, CA
610. Claire Thompson, Springtown, TX (Hon)
611. Cliff Majors, N. Ft Worth, TX (Hon.)
612. Dummy Hunter, Austin, TX
613. Kenneth Beach, Douglas, WY
614. Mervin L. Johnson, Pennsgrove, NJ
615. Harley Walsh, Kleinburg, Ont. Can
616. Grace White, Ringwood, OK (Hon.)
617. Vivian White, Ringold, Ok (Hon)
618. Vic Blackstone, Pensacola, FL
619. R. W. Leche, Gov. of LA (Hon.)
620. Frank Ryley, Phoenix, AZ (Hon.)
621. Sissy Minotto, Kirkland, AZ (Hon.)

The Cowboys' Turtle Association
Articles of Association
By-Laws and Rules
January 1, 1940

(This is the contents of the second book printed by the C.T.A.)

OFFICERS
Everett Bowman .... President
Hillside, Arizona
Rusty McGinty .... Vice President
Plains, Texas
Hugh Bennett .... Secretary-Treasurer
Ft. Thomas, Arizona

REPRESENTATIVES AND DIRECTORS
Saddle Bronc Riding .... Alvin Gordon
Newhall, California
Calf Roping .... Cecil Owsley
Tempe, Arizona
Steer Wrestling .... Tom Hogan
2719 E. 7th St., Tulsa, Oklahoma
Bareback Riding .... Chet McCarty
Rural Route 2, Hotchkiss, Colorado
Bull Riding .... Ken Roberts
Strong City, Kansas
Team Tying and Steer Roping .... Buck Sorrells
1602 E. 5th St., Tucson, Arizona

SPOKESMEN
Tom Taylor, for West Texas, Spofford, TX
George Wilderspin, for Central Texas, North Fort Worth, TX
Clinton Booth, for South Texas, Manvel, TX
Buck Eccles, for South Texas, Liberty, TX
Andy Curtis, for Oklahoma and Panhandle, El Reno, OK
Johnnie Schneider, for California, Livermore, CA
Joe Edwards, for Southern California, Irvine, CA
Stub Bartlemay, for the Northwest, Arlington, OR

ADVISORY BOARD
James Minotto	Francis J. Riley
Ethel M. Hopkins	Wanden M. La Farge

ARTICLES OF ASSOCIATION

The undersigned hereby certify that:

FIRST:

The name of this Association is and shall be;

THE COWBOYS' TURTLE ASSOCIATION

SECOND:

The Cowboys' Turtle Association (hereinafter sometimes referred to as the CTA) has been formed for the following purposes.

1. To organize the professional rodeo contestants of the U.S.A. for their mutual protection and benefit.
2. To raise the standards of cowboy contests, so they rank among the foremost American sports.
3. To co-operate, insofar as possible, with the management of all rodeos at which the members contest.
4. To protect members against unfairness on the part of any rodeo management.
5. To bring about honest advertising by the rodeo associations, so that the public may rely upon the truth of advertised events in which it is claimed that members of the CTA will participate.
6. To work for the betterment of conditions and of the rules governing rodeo events in which the members of the CTA take part.
7. To establish a central place for registration for the convenience of members.
8. To publish information concerning the dates of rodeos, the names of contestants, the prize money, and other particulars in which members are interested.
9. To create a fund to be used in case of death or accident for the benefit of members who have completed their payments to the CTA.

MEMBERSHIP

Third:

Members shall be such professional rodeo contestants as are provided in the by-laws.

MEETINGS

FOURTH:

1. A General Meeting shall be held once in each calendar year in Cheyenne, WY, to nominate three contestants from each of the six events specified in the by-laws to be voted upon by ballot for election to the Board of Directors.

2. Three contestants from each of the six events may be nominated at other meetings of the members, held at such places as may be designated by the Board, as provided in the by-laws.
3. An annual Meeting of the members of the CTA shall be held once in each calendar year at New York City for the announcement of the election of directors and the transaction of business. The Board of Directors shall make a full report of their activities during the preceding fiscal year, and recommend such measures for the future as they may think advisable; and they shall also report their election of officers.
4. A quorum at a general meeting shall be twenty-five members, and at an annual meeting shall be fifty.

FIFTH:
The President may call a meeting of the Board of Directors at any time, provided each member is given advance notice of the meeting.

SIXTH:
Any three Directors may also call a meeting, giving similar notice.

SEVENTH:
If the by-laws or rules are to be amended, a minimum of two days' notice must be given stating the purpose of the meeting.

EIGHTH:
Members shall present their cards of membership upon entering a CTA meeting upon request of a director or spokesman.

BOARD OF DIRECTORS

NINTH:
1. The Board of Directors shall consist of seven members – the President ex-officio and six members, one to represent each of six events.
2. The Board of Directors may appoint Spokesmen in different territories to aid the CTA in negotiations when the directors are not present. These spokesmen are to have jurisdiction over all events.
3. Both directors and spokesmen shall aid the Treasurer in the collection of dues and fines owed by the contestants.

TENTH:
At all meetings of the Board, four directors shall constitute a quorum.

ELEVENTH:
The legislative or rule-making power of the CTA shall be held by the Board of Directors. It shall have general supervision over the business and affairs of the Association; with the power to make, adopt, alter, or amend the by-laws as hereinafter specified. It may make all rules which

it considers necessary to carry out the purposes of this organization, and any contracts incidental thereto.

OFFICERS

TWELFTH:
1. The officers of the CTA shall be as follows:
   President, Vice-President, Secretary and Treasurer
   They shall be elected by the Board of Directors at the time of the annual meeting
   to serve for a period of one year or until their successors are elected.
2. The President shall preside at all meetings of the CTA and of the Board of Directors. He shall enforce the rules and regulations of the CTA and perform such other duties as shall be assigned to him by the Board of Directors. He shall, with the Secretary, sign all written contracts of the CTA.
3. In the absence or disability of the President, the **Vice-President** shall perform his duties.
4. The **Secretary** shall keep the minutes and other official reports of the CTA. He shall conduct its official correspondence and shall keep all records, books, documents, and papers relating to the CTA at such place as shall be designated by the Board of Directors. He shall also perform such other duties as shall be assigned to him by the Board.
5. The **Treasurer** shall keep account of all money received by him and shall deposit it in the name of the CTA in such depository as shall be designated by the Board of Directors. He shall not pay out or disburse any of the money of the CTA except by check, which must be signed by the President, or in case of his death, disability or absence, by the Vice-President, and countersigned by the Secretary of the CTA. At each annual meeting of the members he shall make a statement of the current financial condition of the CTA and a detailed report of its condition for the preceding fiscal year. The Treasurer shall be bonded.
6. The President shall be a member of the Board of Directors ex-officio but any of the above mentioned officers, other than the President, may also be elected members of the Board, and shall serve as Representatives of their events as well.
7. With the exception of the President and the Spokesmen, each director shall act as representative for members of the CTA contesting in the event for which he was elected as Director.
8. All officers and directors shall serve without salary or other compensation.
9. Officers, directors, and spokesmen may be removed at any time with or without (legal) cause by a majority vote of the Board of Directors.

10. Resignations of officers, directors, and spokesmen must be presented to the Board of Directors and be accepted by a majority vote of those present and voting before they become final.
11. The Board of Directors may fill any vacancy among the officers, directors, or spokesmen by vote of the majority of those present and voting at any meeting. Such election to be for the unexpired term.

AMENDMENTS

THIRTEENTH:

The Articles of Association may be amended at any time at any annual or general meeting of the members of the CTA by the vote of a majority of the members present, provided there is a quorum.

BY-LAWS
NOMINATION AND ELECTION TO THE BOARD OF DIRECTORS

1. Three contestants shall be nominated once in each calendar year chosen from the following six events; (1) Steer wrestling (2) Saddle Bronc Riding (3) Bareback horse Riding (4) Bull or Steer Riding (5) Team Tying and Steer Roping (6) Calf Roping, to be voted upon by ballot for the office of Directors.
    a. The Team Tying and Steer Roping Representative shall function as Calf Roping Representative if the latter is absent, and vice versa.
2. All three candidates may be nominated at the general meeting in Cheyenne (Wyo) or, an additional three, at the discretion of the Board of Directors, may be nominated at general meetings held at such places as may be designated by the Board. The three candidates from each event receiving the most votes shall be nominated for office.
3. The names of the contestants nominated at this meeting shall be published in the September and October issues of Hoofs and Horns magazine edited by Ma Hopkins of Tucson, Arizona, which is the official CTA publication. They shall be voted upon at the annual meeting held in New York City.
4. Each CTA member in good standing, will be entitled to cast one vote for a director chosen from the event or events in which he contests. The candidates receiving the highest number of votes shall constitute the Board of Directors for the ensuing year.
5. Members, who cannot be present at the meeting in New York, shall mail their votes before October first to the CTA care of W. M. La Farge, 1088 Park Avenue, New York City, N. Y. These ballots shall be counted and the results announced at the annual meeting.
6. Each member shall write his full name and address on his ballot; otherwise it will not be accepted or counted.

MEMBERSHIP AND DUES

1. Membership in the CTA is confined to professional rodeo contestants and rodeo contract performers. This is to include cowgirl bronc riders, trick riders, trick ropers, clowns, and announcers.
   a. Contract performers are not eligible to vote.
   b. Contract performers may be fined or suspended or both, at the discretion of the Board of Directors.
   c. If the CTA withdraws its members from contesting at a rodeo, it will not affect the previously made contracts of rodeo performers.
   d. Contract performers, however, may not accept contracts after the CTA serves notice that its members will be withdrawn from a given rodeo.
2. Eligibility for membership in the CTA shall be left to the discretion of the directors or spokesmen of said organization.
   a. Members of the CTA will refuse to contest at any rodeo with cowboys who, having qualified as professionals, have not joined the CTA.
   b. A non-professional may be defined as one who lives in the district in which the rodeo takes place, has never won first money at a major rodeo and has never contested outside of his district. Such an amateur may contest in either professional or amateur events, but not in both.
   c. Any director or spokesman shall have authority to inform rodeo managements as to which contestants have qualified as professionals but have not yet joined the CTA.
   d. If the rodeo management permits such a contestant to enter, the CTA reserves the right to withdraw its members from competition.
3. Annual dues of membership are hereby fixed at ten dollars a year, five dollars of which will be deposited in the Benefit fund.
4. Annual dues shall be payable before entering the first rodeo of the season at which a member contests.
5. Any member who does not pay his dues by July first of each year, whether he has contested or not, is liable to a fine, suspension or both. This rule will be strictly enforced.
6. Any member of the CTA who has not paid his dues for 1938, or any year previous to that, will be dropped from the list of CTA members and will not be permitted to contest at any rodeo. To be reinstated such a member must pay all back dues in full, plus five dollars for each year in which said dues have not been paid. This does not apply to members who have resigned from CTA.
7. Only members in good standing shall vote in the affairs of the CTA. No member who is in default as to payments for dues or fines, and no member who is at the time suspended, will be permitted to vote.
   a. The above rule does not apply to contract performers who are not eligible to vote at any time.

8. The CTA through its Board of Directors, shall adopt a card certifying the contestant's or contract performer's membership in the Association.
9. Election to honorary membership in the CTA shall be subject to the approval of a member of the Board of Directors or a Spokesman.
   Honorary members shall be given cards and insignia which differ from those of regular members. Annual dues for honorary members are hereby fixed at five dollars. Honorary members are not eligible to vote.
10. An advisory Committee may be appointed by the majority of the Board of Directors to serve the CTA in an advisory capacity for the period of one year, or until they are succeeded. Members of the Advisory Committee are not eligible to vote.
11. By-laws and rules may be amended by a majority vote of the Board of Directors.

RULES

1. **No CTA member shall contest, perform, or labor at any amateur rodeo.**
2. The CTA reserves the right to withdraw its members from rodeos where stock is furnished by a rodeo contractor who also furnishes stock to amateur shows.
   a. Notice is hereby given rodeo contractors that they must either furnish stock to professional or amateur shows, but not to both. This rule became effective January 1st, 1940.
   b. Stock furnished to professional rodeos may be used for amateur events but not for amateur days.
   c. If a rodeo contractor furnishes stock to amateur shows he shall never become eligible to furnish stock to professional rodeos.
3. No CTA member shall be allowed to contest at any rodeo unless the entry fees for each event are added to the guaranteed prize money of each event.
   a. No rodeo shall be responsible for returning a contestant's entry fees if he has contested in an event even once during the show. But if he is entered in other events in which he is unable to contest, the entry fees for those events must be returned.
4. No CTA member shall be allowed to contest at any rodeo unless competition is open to all members of the CTA in good standing.
   a. Therefore, no CTA member shall contest at any rodeo which places penalties or handicaps upon CTA members.
   b. No CTA member shall contest at any amateur rodeos or state championships or in special closed or amateur events. However, a rodeo having special events for local talent shall not be classified as an amateur rodeo by virtue of that fact alone.
   c. If a rodeo has a special day for amateur contests, no CTA member shall be permitted to contest, perform or labor.

5. No CTA member shall be allowed to ride for mount money unless a contest in the event is included in said rodeo's program.
   a. However, if five or less contestants are entered in an event, CTA members may ride, rope or wrestle for mount money.
6. No CTA member shall be allowed to contest at any rodeo unless the judges are experienced men and satisfactory to the Board of Directors of the CTA.
   a. The judges shall be passed upon by the three riding representatives of the CTA.
   b. If the judges are not satisfactory as flagmen, the ropers and bulldoggers reserve the right to select a flagman for whose services the judges shall pay.
7. If a rodeo hires its judges in advance, the names of the judges chosen must be submitted to the CTA for approval before they are printed on said rodeo's prize list.
   a. If a rodeo prints the names of judges on its prize list without having submitted them to the CTA for approval, the CTA reserves the right to withdraw its members from contesting under said judges.
   b. If a rodeo does not hire its judges in advance the rodeo committee may select competent men who shall be passed upon by the CTA members entered at said rodeo.
   c. Timers and flagmen must be men of experience. If the CTA does not consider the men chosen by a given rodeo to have adequate experience, they will expect cooperation from the management in replacing the unsatisfactory timers or flagmen.
   d. The decisions of all judges, flagmen, and timers who have been passed upon by the CTA shall be final, and no protest by the contestants will be permitted.
8. The CTA agrees to adopt the R.R.A. rules for rodeo contests and will insist that rodeo managements adhere to them.
9. Any member of the CTA who does not observe the above rules is liable to a fine, suspension, or both.
10. The CTA reserves the right to withdraw their members from competition in any rodeo which does not conform to the above rules or which refuses to cooperate with the Turtle Association in the arbitration of difficulties.

PENALTIES FOR INFRACTION OF RULES

1. **Any member of the CTA who contests, performs or works at a rodeo which has been boycotted by the CTA is liable to a fine, suspension, or both.**
2. Any member who shows himself financially irresponsible, that is, who passes bad checks or fails to pay his board or hotel bill during the

period of a given rodeo, shall be subject to a fine, suspension, or both. (Members must obtain and keep receipts when bills have been paid.)

a. If the Board sees fit, it may advance payment for outstanding bills incurred by members during a given rodeo.

b. The reinstatement of members whose obligations have been paid by the CTA shall be at the discretion of the Board of Directors.

3. Any member who does not pay his annual dues to the CTA before July first of each year shall be liable to a fine, suspension, or both.

4. Any member of the CTA who has not paid his dues for 1938, or any year previous to that, will be dropped from the list of CTA members and will not be permitted to contest at any rodeo. To be reinstated such a member must pay all back dues in full, plus five dollars for each year in which said dues have not been paid. This does not apply to members who have resigned from the CTA.

5. Any member who wishes to resign from the CTA must do so in writing. A member who withdraws in good faith shall be reinstated without fine or penalty, provided he has not contested, worked or performed at any rodeo during the time in which his resignation took effect.

a. In case a member has contested, worked or performed at a rodeo during the period of his resignation and wishes to be reinstated, he shall be fined, suspended, or both, according to the discretion of the Board of Directors before he shall be reinstated.

6. Any member who falsely represents himself as qualified to speak for the CTA shall be fined, suspended or both to the limit of the power of the Board of Directors.

a. The President, the representatives (Directors) or the spokesmen are the only members of the organization who have authority to make decisions for the CTA.

b. Certain members will carry letters from the Board of Directors authorizing them to collect dues, take in new members and collect bad bills.

7. Any member of the CTA who has a grievance against the organization shall present same to the representative of his event or to a spokesman. Any member who willfully causes trouble inside or outside the ranks of the CTA shall be liable to a fine, suspension or both.

8. Any member of the CTA who denies his membership and removes his CTA button on entering a rodeo, shall be fined to the fullest extent within the power of the Board of Directors.

9. Any member who makes himself liable to a fine must pay the same or post a bond of fifty dollars ($50.00) with the Secretary of the CTA until he has had a hearing before the Board of Directors.

10. If the Board of Directors finds him guilty, by the majority vote of all the Directors, he may be fined from $25.00 to $500.00 at their discretion, or

suspended, or both.

11. Any member of the CTA who has been fined and fails to pay one-quarter of his winnings at the time the prize money is won until the fine is paid, is liable to be expelled from the CTA and shall forfeit any part or portion of the fine he has already paid.

a. Any contract performer who has been fined and fails to pay one-quarter of each contract at the time said contract is paid, until the fine is paid in full, is liable to be expelled from the CTA and shall forfeit any part or portion of the fine he has already paid.

12. It is understood that no officer, director, member, or employee of the CTA shall be liable individually or otherwise for any breach of the above rules, or for any understanding or agreement between the CTA and the R.A.A. or with any other rodeo association.

POLICY

It is the policy of the CTA that each member present at a given rodeo shall attend all general meetings of the CTA.

It is the policy of the CTA to see that the prize money awarded in the four major events – saddle bronc riding, calf roping, steer wrestling, and bull (or Brahma steer) riding – shall be equal.

Therefore, the CTA reserves the right to withdraw its members from competition if the prize money is too unequally divided.

The CTA also reserves the right to withdraw its members if a rodeo does not include the above mentioned four major events in its program.

If a rodeo management wishes an absolute guarantee that members of the CTA will contest at a give rodeo after their arrival at said rodeo, they may submit their prize list in advance to any representative, or spokesman, or to the President of the CTA, who will return the prize list signed and OK'd.

The CTA shall be responsible for seeing that all approved prize lists shall be signed by at least three directors (representatives) or by the President.

Everett Bowman, President

Hugh Bennett, Secretary-Treasurer

Membership of the CTA
(Please note the list is not accurately alphabetized; however this is the exact way it was in the published book)

CTA#	NAME	C.T.A.#	NAME
29	Aber, Doff	144	Burk, Clyde
70	Arnold, Carl	187	Brown, Howard
227	Alvord, Fred	236	Bennett, Charlie
245	Allen, Red	273	Belden, Herb
286	Ambler, Jerry	287	Bedford, Cecil
298	Allen, Lonnie	306	Brady, Buff
329	Anderson, Gale	372	Ballard, Smokey
342	Adams, Dale	375	Brister, Jim
361	Askins, Bob	395	Bond, Paul
387	Avery, Emile	410	Buschbom, Ted
415	Aldridge, Charles	452	Bender, Bennie
432	Autry, Frank	499	Padgett, Berry
583	Allred, Judge James V. (Hon.)	540	Becker, Fritz
596	Ammons, Gov. Teller (Hon.)	551	Bowman, Ed
641	Adams, Mrs. Alice	564	Bassett, Joe
751	Armour, Bill	79	Booth, Tom (Hon.)
471	Altamarion	703	Burke, Dee
814	Albrecht, Chas.	725	Brannon, T. J.
779	Amburgee, J. D.	742	Breckenridge, Red
862	Armstrong, Bert	743	Burke, Jiggs
854	Adams, Francis	613	Beach, Kenneth
855	Arnold, Joe	618	Blackstone, Vick
861	Abercrombie, C. C.	355	Binns, H. D.
891	Arranto, Gene	631	Bassett, Lew
1019	Arnold, Edward	15	Blackfoot Elks Lodge (Hon.)
973	Andes, Chester	795	Beken, Henry
1142	Alsbaugh, Walter	797	Border, Alex
1150	Acton, Ernest	802	Barron, Curtis
8	Bennett, Hugh	806	Barnett, Keith
9	Bennett, Ralph	809	Bates, Chris S.
10	Bowman, John	819	Blackstone, Doc
15	Bowman, Everett	833	Booth, Leslie
59	Burrell, Joe	838	Burson, Wayne
69	Beloat, Arthur	766	Bass, Ray
83	Blevins, Earl	780	Bonner, A. Q.
89	Bartlemay, Stub	786	Beveridge, Ted M.
101	Booth, Clinton	789	Barnett, Ernie

CTA#	NAME	C.T.A.#	NAME
112	Bode, Andrew	850	Brodnax, Charles
129	Bascom, Weldon	867	Barnes, Charles
141	Barrett, Fred	868	Bell, Don
877	Burkitt, Buck	442	Cameron, Eddie
909	Bascom, Earl	503	Corbin, Goldie
966	Baker, Frank	542	Cooper, Morris
969	Black, Billy	556	Cullington, Geo. V.(Hon.)
975	Brooks, Louis	571	Coker, Joe
990	Ball, Hank	574	Cameron, Allen
1006	Butler, Archie	599	Creed, Gene
1008	Baxter, Larry	609	Cook, Bud
1012	Burroughs, Wayne	110	Carter, Barton
1036	Burnet, J. T.	676	Cook, Joe
1049	Burrows, Bob	718	Crisp, Bob
1051	Brown, Clyde	731	Clements, Violet
1058	Beals, Charley	8	Coze, Paul (Hon.)
1091	Barrett, Rip	746	Calen, Bobby
1097	Brannon, Leo	800	Campbell, Rex
1103	Bolton, Lorraine	816	Cox, Roy
1137	Bowman, Skeet	832	Coker, Johnny
1125	Baker, Bob	837	Cornish, Cecil
1140	Bolton, Tack	772	Crouch, Worth
1144	Barnett, Jane	762	Clute, Res.
64	Baird, Dr. Vernon (Hon.)	790	Chesson, Bo
56	Buchanan, R. B. (Hon.)	872	Cornett, Elmer
21	Carney, Paul	887	Colbert, Dude
44	Cox, Breezy	890	Coelho, Al
48	Cooper, Jackie	906	Cottrell, Diane
55	Carr, Clay	934	Christian, Lefty
72	Cropper, Melvin	941	Carroll, Roy
80	Campbell, Dave	943	Crawford, Lex
82	Crain, Paul	1001	Capps, Charlie
122	Curtis, Andy	1038	Cravens, Baldy
127	Creed, Shorty	1043	Chambers, Pinky
132	Curtis, Eddie	1046	Cox, Leo
150	Clay, Willie	1071	Churchill, Mont.
185	Crosby, Bob	1074	Colbert, Zeb
201	Cooper, Felix	1082	Clements, Pete
212	Curry, Roland	884	Coe, C.C.
247	Cash, Guy	28	Call, Grant (Hon.)
255	Cline, George	1116	Clarke, Estelle (Hon.)

CTA#	NAME	C.T.A.#	NAME
258	Cline, Doc	1119	Chitwood, Frank
270	Connley, Lawrence	1131	Cline, John
374	Cottrell, Lyle	1152	Cole, Chili
406	Colbert, Charlie	1156	Collier, Ralph
418	Clennon, Bart	1163	Cooper, Henry
1172	Campbell, Clay	956	Earp, Virgil
1170	Colcord, Frank	1035	Enos, Manuel
119	Dahl, Herb	1072	Ellison, Buddy
168	Del Re, M. W.	977	Elley, Morris
204	Dossey, Carl	1171	Evans, Buck
230	Davis, Buck	87	Fletcher, Kid
302	Daniels, Lary	149	Ferris, Gordon
341	Densmore, Speedy	210	Ferraro, Ned
515	Doan, Urban	242	Farris, Lee
553	Doyle, Tex	291	Fisher, Mike
580	Dew, Frank Y. (Hon.)	323	Fore, Oran
623	Dewey, Diamond D.	358	Forman, Tom
638	Downs, Jimmie	396	Finley, Luther
644	Doyle, Dusty	402	Finley, Frank
651	Davis, Gordon	543	Fernandez, Fele
670	Davis, Jack	557	Flowers, Hubert
717	Davis, Gordon	653	Fletcher, Al
828	Dowell, Buck	693	Fauts, John
840	Dudley, George	9	Fisher, Ham (Hon.)
785	Duncan, Keezie	813	Fancher, Sam
853	Dawson, Alvin	836	Finley, Larry
928	Dyer, Earl	606	Fletcher, Virginia
952	Davis, Roy	859	Francher, Virginia
930	Despain, Sidney	903	Fernandez, Ike
949	Dyer, Jack	921	Fancher, John
1010	Dwyer, Emmett	922	Fancher, Pete
1034	Dalton, Jack	945	Flowers, Marshall
1089	Dawson, Chet	946	Ferguson, Don
1153	Davis, Ben	964	Francis, Warren
63	Dudley, Dorris (Hon.)	1024	Feltman, Wallace
50	Dauckon, Fred (Hon.)	1027	Ferrante, Joe
54	Dillon, Roy M. (Hon.)	1028	Fuller, Wid
104	Eckols, Buck	1029	Fancher, Charlie
152	Edwards, Joe	1084	Forrester, Pete
169	Engelsman, Led	650	Flores, Jose
181	Eaton, Bill	1114	Fitzpatricks, Buddie

248	Evans, Bud	1122	Fredericks, Loren
321	Elfic, John	1146	Fletcher, Boyd
362	Estes, Bob	48	Faubion, W. L. (Hon.)
458	Elliott, Geo.	1122	Fowler, Don
596	Eskew, Jr.	3	Griffith, Dick
820	Evans, Eddie	13	Grace, Holloway
834	Ebner, Adolph	23	Greenough, Turk
45	Gordon, Alvin	183	Henley, Cecil
54	Getzwiller, Marion	226	Hastings, Mike
65	Gunter, Kenneth	246	Hart, Harry
68	Glenn, Rex	267	Helm, Cliff
91	Grubb, Pete	278	Hinton, Dee
190	Gill, Adolph	352	Hormer, Tommy
192	Gill, Emmett	376	Hudson, Jim
229	Gale, Floyd	377	Hancock, Bill
238	Gibson, Andy	385	Hovenkamp, Eddie
263	Goodspeed, Buck	392	Hatchel, Curley
265	Goodspeed, Jess	401	Henson, Heavy
290	Gaylor, Maynard	422	Hazen, Jimmie
350	Gamblin, Amye	465	Huskey, Lynn
412	Garrett, Raymond	484	Hanna, Bill
487	Gerig, John	501	Hines, Dan
492	Green, George	577	Hughes, Joe D. (Hon.)
637	Godshall, Jeanne (Hon.)	318	Haynes, Davis
639	Geiser, J. M.	705	Hopkins, Drew
645	Gould, Paul	715	Henderson, Swede
668	Greenough, Alice	724	Haverty, Bob
669	Greenough, Margie	728	Horner, Mildred Mix
745	Gordon, Jack	12	Hopp, Pete
827	Garner, Buck	753	Harris, Bayless
767	Glenn, Joe	721	Hepler, Elmer
863	Gould, Vernon	792	Hosley, Frank
870	Garcia, Vidal	826	Hoey, Jack
919	Gafford, Neal	22	Howe, J. C. (Hon.)
929	Gee, Carl	744	Hogue, Nip
960	Gentry, Guy	782	Hedges, Max
1042	Good, Jeff	783	Hobbs, Joker
1083	Greenough, Bill	881	Hussey, Shirley
1134	Graham, Nig	769	Holcomb, Homer
1159	Gordon, Jim	25	Hamburger, Phil (Hon.)
1141	Green, Carlos	876	Hightower, Clyde
65	Gelvin, Floyd (Hon.)	879	Henry, Carol

16	Harper, Melvin	882	House, George
28	Hancock, Sonny	894	Hunt, Ted
71	Heacock, Steve	896	Hess, Bob
75	Hogan, Tom	933	Herren, Dick
76	Hopkins, Ma (Hon.)	940	Huckfeldt, Carl
77	Hopkins, Pa (Hon.)	971	Holcomb, Millard
124	Hefner, Hoyt	987	Howell, Cecil
125	Hargis, Ken	996	Huff, Leo
997	Hensley, Gene	61	Jones, Gov. R. T. (Hon.)
998	Hood, Joe	57	Johnson, Everett (Hon.)
1005	Hamilton, Eugene	37	Knight, Harry
1014	Hitson, Jack	33	Kenney, James
1039	Henson, Ace	102	Knight, Nick
1075	Henderson, Carl	136	Kelley, Cleve
1086	Hadfield, Joe	195	Kell, Jess
1090	Hinkle, George	294	Knight, Tom
1100	Hope, G. W.	295	Kerscher, Pete
1105	Hood, Charley	366	Karstad, Leslie
1006	Hood, Marshall	489	Kohrs, Roy
1107	Hood, Lesley	605	Kreig, Vaughn
1108	Henry, Patrick	607	Keen, Mary
1117	Hickman, Chester	218	Kerscher, Jack
1157	Holland, Hank	569	Karn, Lile (Hon.)
1139	Hays, Edd	685	Kennedy, Dale
1154	Hassenpflug, Elmer	735	Keen, Bill
1165	Hines, Cherry Hale (Hon.)	559	Karmon, Bill
1166	Hanke, Eddie	825	Kerchgarber, Frank
43	Hanes, Willard (Hon.)	841	Kirkwood, Donald
58	Harris, Helen M. (Hon.)	843	Klebba, Joe
1177	Howard, Tex	775	Knight, L. R.
176	Irwin, Jim	878	Killough, Bill
322	Iron, Scrap	883	Kirkendall, Helen
851	Ingram, Bud	895	Kunz, Tommy
957	Iler, Bill	902	Kinner, J. R.
32	Jauregui, Andy	939	Kelley, Curley
86	Jacobs, Slats	979	Kelley, Fred
97	Jones, Charlie	989	Kemp, Carl
99	Jordan, John	1041	Kemm, Carl
235	Johnson, E. H. (Blacky)	1053	Kersh, Johnny
257	Jones, Eddie	1054	Kersh, Bubba
299	Jones, Cecil W.	1062	Keller, Art
407	Jones, Art	1085	Kane, Bill

CTA#	NAME	C.T.A.#	NAME
447	Jacobs, Len	1135	Kelley, Marion Ross
486	Jauregui, Ed	1161	Kersten, George
614	Johnson, Mervin L. (Hon.)	1173	Kutch, Hilton
704	Jones, Buck	14	Long, Hughie
771	Johnson, Merle	22	Linder, Herman
472	Jesperson, Allen	108	Lewis, Roy
953	Jarnigan, Logan	143	Lockett, Reese B.
938	Jackson, Jim	155	Logue, Harry
1015	Jernigan, Buck	232	Lowry, Fred
282	Lockyer, Terry	111	Merchant, Richard
349	Lindsey, John	120	Matthews, Roy
464	Lund, Ross	208	Mendes, John
473	Lyon, Bill	209	Mueller, H. H.
478	Littrell, Jerry	220	Mills, George
568	Lichtenstein, Helen (Hon.)	222	Mills, Hank
570	Lewis, K. W. (Hon.)	237	Mansfield, Toots
578	Lee, W. A. (Hon.)	239	Mundy, Irby
603	Long, Peggy	244	Miller, Richard
683	Like, James	271	Minotto, James (Hon.)
688	Laycock, Morris	347	Martin, Elmer
744	Louks, Wayne	364	Marion, Frank
1	LaFarge, W. M. (Hon.)	382	Matthews, Bob
799	Lewallen, G. K.	420	Martin, Prosser (Hon.)
807	Levins, Ross	423	Martinez, Pete
778	Lambert, Joe	502	Manning, Art
768	Lewis, Pat	608	Massey, Gus (Hon.)
770	Lefton, Abe	303	Maverty, Ray
857	Lando, Swede	611	Majors, Cliff (Hon.)
865	Louks, Dick	621	Minotto, Sissy (Hon.)
874	Lacy, C. D.	632	Marshall, Grant
888	Lewis, Russell	664	Mendes, Joe
889	Lee, Bob	666	Mounce, Ernest
924	Leonard, Jimmie	634	May, Buddy
944	Lockie, Bob	713	Montgomery, Arnold
978	Louis, Buster	722	Murray, Bob
1025	Lyan, Stan	793	Moody, W. C.
1052	Landers, Al	804	Martin, Roy
1069	Lamar, Curtis	824	Morris, Rufus
1070	Lamar, Carl	830	Milton, Lawrence
1088	Lamax, Joe	831	Marberger, M. E.
1094	Lindsey, Billy	825	Morris, Dale

CTA#	NAME	C.T.A.#	NAME
1121	Lingle, Floyd	842	Morris, PeeWee
1124	Lowery, Bill	781	Mitchell, Leonard
51	Lewis, H. G. (Hon.)	866	Mefford, Buddy
6	Murray, Leo	885	Miller, Inky
24	Martz, Frank	907	Markham, Jack
26	Moore, Earl	864	Morris, Al
62	Moe, Milt	826	Moore, Lee
93	Mulkey, Burel	954	Mitchell, Ralph
94	Mercer, Del	962	Montgomery, Lindsey
107	Merritt, King	970	Michel, Henry
109	Meyers, Herbert	984	Moore, Bullie
1002	Moran, Webb	988	McDonald, Red
1003	Marshall, Frank	991	McElvain, Lee
1017	Mark, John	1045	McPherson, Dick
1026	Meese, Ted	1081	McCrorey, Knotchie
1030	Mendes, Frank	1095	McSpott, Billy
1031	Mendes, Carl	916	McCrain, Archie
1044	Martin, Nub	1113	McCormick, J. D.
1055	Meeks, Bob	1160	McFall, Harry
1056	Meeks, Alford	1149	McFadden, Gordon
1087	Mitchell, Don	1145	McElroy, Curtis
1050	Mason, Rex	1147	McMackin, Bud
57	Matthews, E. R.	1	Nesbitt, Jimmie
1136	Maynard, Jack	31	Nesbitt, Donald
1115	Moore, Pete	419	Nuckols, Reno Texas Kidd
1128	Mehner, Vick Reno	591	Newhagen, Frank E. (Hon.)
1158	Matlock, Shorty	598	Nesbitt, Pauline
1162	Meyer, Leonard	1118	Martin, Vick Reno
29	Miller, Don (Hon.)	105	Nix, Bill
2	McGinty, Rusty	736	Nelson, Bud
20	McCrory, Howard	755	Nelson, Tim
67	McEuen, Albert	798	Nuckols, Grafton
39	McGee, Jimmie	869	Nissen, Bill
142	McClure, Jake	951	Newton, Slim
307	McFarland, Bill	47	O'Callahan, Fox
353	McCrory, Shorty	52	Owsley, Cecil
409	McCarty, Chet	280	Orr, Joe
507	McMillen, Speck	344	Olsen, Jimmie
563	McMacken, Bill	179	Owens, Mitchell
566	McClure, Marion (Hon,)	897	Owens, Herb
85	McCrory, Mickey	925	Olsen, Dutch

CTA#	NAME	C.T.A.#	NAME
311	McAdam, Hugh	910	Olsen, Bob
681	McEuen, Ed (Hon.)	1138	Oja, Andy
706	McWiggins, Zack	1127	Odle, John
811	McHolland, Jim	59	Oltrof, Jack G. (Hon.)
822	McDaniels, Bud	60	Oltrof, Mrs. Jack (Hon.)
776	McGuire, Bill	27	Pettigrew, Homer
846	McFarland, John	53	Parker, Bud
898	McNoulty, Pat	60	Pardee, E.
913	McBee, Blanche	114	Powers, Ted
914	McBee, Lloyd	154	Peters, Floyd
918	McCray, Wiley	283	Piper, Harold
959	McKenzie, Lester	324	Paul, Marvin
967	MacDonald, Dorothy	381	Plaskett, Pat
972	McCardwell, Mark	389	Parker, Rock
390	Parks, Bill	602	Lucyle Richards
505	Perkins, Len	106	Rooney, Lonnie
550	Person, Norman	620	Riley, Frank (Hon.)
552	Parks, Darwin	720	Roberts, Gerald
690	Pruett, Gene	2	Randolph, Floyd (Hon.)
727	Parks, Mary	749	Rand, Larry
821	Perkins, Jess	796	Reeves, Lem
18	Parker, Gus (Hon.)	803	Robinson, Andy
19	Paul, Clyde (Hon.)	810	Romans, Mason
788	Phillips, Dub	812	Rhea, Vance
844	Paxton, Trent	839	Ryder, Buster
852	Picture, Fred	784	Reavis, Jeff
858	Poston, James	661	Rivers, Bob
880	Pettcock, N. A.	651	Roberts, George
892	Peters, Ed	845	Rucker, Ed
904	Pepper, Rex	848	Randolph, Ray
908	Parker, Pat	871	Reagan, Bob
923	Posey, Hugh	875	Rogers, Nell
950	Padia, Walter	900	Ray, Russell
994	Parrish, Vester	912	Rogers, Eddie
1018	Patterson, George	915	Robison, John
1061	Pettigrew, A. J.	927	Red, Calgary
1129	Penick, John	968	Robellard, Jim
1151	Poage, Doug	981	Runyan, Vince
1143	Poage, Walton	999	Ross, Butch (Hon.)
42	Perkins, Arthur (Hon.)	1007	Roy, Guy
393	Quait, Jack	1020	Rochin, Butch

CTA#	NAME	C.T.A.#	NAME
441	Quirk, Frank	1023	Richardson, Bill
46	Rhodes, Tom	1032	Rambo, Gene
56	Rhodes, John	1037	Ross, Roy
57	Rude, Ike	1068	Raho, Frank
103	Roberts, Rube	1077	Rutledge, Shorty
117	Ross, Gene	1092	Rose, Parry
131	Ricker, Shorty	1098	Robertson, John
175	Robbins, Dick	1102	Roberts, Arnie
250	Ross, Hershel	1104	Robison, Tom
256	Ryan, Durard	1109	Roy, Mutt
259	Roberts, Ken	1175	Ramsey, V. H.
414	Riling, Raymond L. J. (Hon.)	52	Robertson, Jack (Hon.)
488	Rosenburg, B. B.	7	Shaw, Everett
544	Ritter, Clarence	30	Stillings, Floyd
575	Roan, Salvesta	38	Stout, David
589	Ross, Bruce	40	Snyder, Smokey
42	Schell, Asbury	740	Sultenfuss, Frank
61	Sorrells, Buck	754	Sloan, Jimmie
64	Shepard, Carl	791	Spence, Doc
73	Sellers, Jack	21	Story, Jack
81	Schwarz, Vic	760	Steelman, E. Hasea
95	Strickland, Hugh	764	Smith, Charley
100	Sellers, Earl	847	Sheilds, Chas.
147	Simon, Lee	23	Sartwells, J. W. (Hon.)
148	Simon, Doc	24	Strake, George W. (Hon.)
165	Skelton, Al	893	Seago, Roscoe
166	Schneider, Johnie	905	Stanger, Cecil
180	Sheppard, Chuck	911	Santos, Leonard
186	Schneider, Frankie	920	Simon, J. W.
193	Stewart, Roy	931	Scott, Paul
217	Shaw, Glen	932	Scott, Bob
234	Sewalt, Royce	935	Seay, Billy
249	Snively, Jay	936	Shellenberger, O. C.
260	Sievers, Bill	937	Strogn, B.
269	Starr, Dave	942	Smith, Jimmie
319	Sandall, Hubert	948	Schwarz, Tony A. H.
346	Soward, Ace	963	Sterling, Joe
348	Shellenberger, C. J.	986	Stober, Earl
356	Sanborn, Les	993	Strob, Roy
369	Strachan, John	995	Shaw, Jack
378	Stanton, Orville	1004	Soward, Glenn

CTA#	NAME	C.T.A.#	NAME
431	Stuart, Sam	1011	Saunders, Jim
439	Sherman, Jack	1021	Smith, Lee
449	Snively, Jim	1059	Sutton, Jim
466	Salinas, Tony	1064	Smith, Tommy
116	Salinas, Juan	1110	Sims, Blanket
409	Stanifer, Buck	1112	Shewly, Peck
565	Streeter, Jack	1120	Stuckey, Tom
518	Stickney, Chas.	1130	Sankey, Happy
555	Sands, Geo. (Hon.)	1132	Saylors, Leon C.
701	Skipworth, Jack	62	Sawyer, Ed (Hon.)
684	Staley, Jim	47	Schooley, Hershel (Hon.)
723	Sells, Albert	565	Sandefer, G. B. (Hon.)
1178	Seeley, George	594	Spillsbury, Bud
11	Stewart, Jacqueline A. Mrs. (Hon.)	19	Stanton, Ralph
747	Sisty, Alice	646	Shinn, Charles A.
737	Sultenfuss, Norman	671	Salisbury, Jack
738	Sultenfuss, Henry	674	Slocum, Tex
739	Sultenfuss, Leon	1065	Smith, Frank
4	Thompson, Red	961	Valdez, Shorty
5	Truitt, Dick	1040	Van Cator, Bill
49	Truan, Fritz	11	Whiteman, Hub
51	Turk, Charlie	12	Welch, Joe
115	Turk, Dad (Hon.)	35	Woods, Pat
308	Taylor, Bill	126	Watkins, Ward
313	Tiffin, Buck	128	Whiteman, Jim
343	Tompkins, Chas.	134	Wilderspin, Geo.
477	Taylor, Fritz	172	Wilder, D. R.
514	Thompson, Geo. D.	211	Wagner, Neil
545	Traylor, John W.	254	Walls, Elmo
600	Tyler, C. A. (Hon.)	333	Wills, Arnie
610	Thompson, Claire	340	Walden, Bob
36	Thode, Earl	345	Whaley, Slim
133	Thompson, Joe	365	Warren, Ralph
162	Taylor, Tom	394	Whitlow, Charlie
678	Travis, Pete	399	Ward, Geo.
829	Taylor, Pete	413	Wyatt, Buck
20	Tussing, L. Benton (Hon.)	450	Wilder, Dan
757	Thomas, Orville	463	Wilkinson, Bob
758	Thomas, John	498	Williams, Chuck
765	Taylor, Eddie	567	Watson, Bill (Hon.)
318	Todd, Brown	576	Warren, W. B.

CTA #	NAME	C.T.A. #	NAME
849	Tyler, Glenn	590	Wilson, Tommy
917	Taillon, Cy	592	Wrigley, Philip K.(Hon.)
982	Town, Bill	616	White, Grace
1016	Thorn, Leo	617	White, Vivian
1047	Tracy, Jack	549	Wood, Russell
1063	Tulley, Gerald	585	Williams, Johnnie
1073	Thompson, Ode	285	Wade, Jack
1080	Taylor, Karl	662	Winegar, Phil
1093	Taylor, Buck	677	Wood, Tom
1099	Thomas, Limey	748	Warren, Oscar
1148	Taylor, Babb	750	Warren, Jack
49	Talbot, Ray (Hon.)	752	Williams, Ken
425	Todd, Homer	801	Warren, J. O.
860	Upchurch, Robert	805	Webb, Pearson
206	Vincent, Merle	808	Webb, Byron
327	Van Meter, Frank	817	Wilcox, Don
497	Vance, Johnnie	787	Ward, Homer
606	Van Meter, Virginia	6	Whiteman, Paul (Hon.)
777	Vincent, Marion	873	Wood, Opal
763	Van Cleve, Paul	886	Wallesen, Whitey
965	Westinghouse, Buddy	53	Wheelis, Penn (Hon.)
974	Whitehorn, John	55	Wolf, Ralph R. (Hon.)
976	Willis, Arch L.	359	Yonnick, Buttons
983	Wyrick, Bennie	336	Young, I. W.
985	Ware, Slick	516	Yardley, George
1067	Wolf, Buster	815	Young, Mrs. I. W.
1076	Wofford, Earl	264	Youchum, Ted
1078	Wayne, Shorty	1133	Young, Tommy
1079	Whiteside, Bob	1155	York, A. C.
1096	Watson, Harold	58	Zumwalt, Oral
947	Wike, A. C.		
992	Whitaker, Lee		
1164	Whitten, David		
1174	Winnett, Horace		

Members Who Are Now Dropped, Dues Paid Up To 1939

NAME DUES PAID

Allen, Al, '37
Anderton, Dick, '37-'38
Alcorn, Cherokee, '37-'38
Anderson, A. J., '37
Amstrong, Phil, '37
Avery, Jack, '37-'38
Abold, Ernest, '37
Arano, Roy, '38
Barr, Endre, '37
Beache, John A., '37-'38
Batteate, Earl, '37
Bartram, John, '37-'38
Bartram, Dutch, '37-'38
Brunzell, Blondy, '37-'38
Borgess, Frank, '37
Boden, Bob, '37-'38
Bruce, Doug, '37-'38
Buckley, Buck, '37-'38
Bozen, Eddie, '37
Bell, Curley, '37-'38
Beasley, Carl, '37
Buschbom, Bill, '37
Clingman, Hugh, '37-'38
Cutler, Wayne, '37
Cheetham, Everett, '37-'38
Casteel, Art, '37
Cullen, Lary, '37
Collins, Earvie, '37-'38
Collins, Eddie, '37
Collins, Louie, '37
Cutler, Tex, '37
Conners, Beverley, '37-'38
Campadore, Frank, '37
Crainer, Allen, '37
Chissum, Ike, '37
Carey, Joe, '38
Chip, Yellow Stone, '38

NAME DUES PAID

Buschbom, Barney, '37
Beason, Fred, '37
Bailey, George, '37
Buffington, Owen, '37-'38
Buffington, E. E., '37
Biscaro, Bill, '37
Biscaro, Carl, '37
Bride, Tom, '37-'38
Barnhart, Albert, '37
Barnes, Joe, '37
Bowers, Aubrey, '37-'38
Butner, Goldie, '37-'38
Baker, Fred C., '37
Burns, Frankie, '38
Broderick, John, '38
Breedon, Rose, '38
Bays, Jimmie '38
Brock, Leonard, '38
Brady, Jack Brown, '38
Brown, Van, '38
Buckart, Chuck, '38
Bryant, Blackie, '38
Edmo, Lee '38
Emery, Ernest, '38
Fleming, Joel, '37-'38
Fernamburg, Dan, '37
Ferrario, Arnio, '37-'38
Fisher, Bob, '37
Foust, Doc, '37
Farrell, Joe, '37
French, Jimmie, '37
Ford, Clyde, Jr., '37
Felts, E., '37-'38
Folkerson, Bob, '37
Foehl, Robert, '38
Faulkner, Foreman, '38
Gardner, Ace, '37

NAME DUES PAID

Conwell, George, '38
Clark, Bill, '38
Cunningham, Bob, '38
Cook, Joe, '38
Crist, James, '38
Crain, Don, '38
Carey, Al, '38
Cor, Frank, '38
Dayton, Chick, '38
Deal, Martin, '37
Duckett, Charlie, '37
Dyer, H. L., '37
Drayer, John, '37-'38
Deck, Art, '37-'38
Davis, Casey, '37-'38
Daniels, George, '37
Dickson, Bobby, '38
Duarte, Hoot, '38
Duarte, Frank, '38
Doill, Bud, '38
Duby, Frenchie, '38
Davis, Harry, '38
Elliott, Sie, '37-'38
Emory, Harold, '37-'38
Edwards, Buck, '37
Elliott, Wiley, '37
Elliott, Bob, '37
Hannum, Walter, '37
Holder, Arthur, '37
Haverty, Clay, '38
Haverty, Pete, '38
Hatfield, George, '38
Hedge, Bill, '38
Holt, Jack, '38
Hagen, Johnny, '38
Hicks, Mickey, '38
Hollander, M. A., '38
Hulse, Ray, '38
Johnson, Dick, '37
Jones, Ralph, '37
Jones, Buff, '38

NAME DUES PAID

Gill, Adolph, '37-38
Glenn, O. C., '37-'38
Gafford, Roy, '37
Greenwood, Ross, '37
Goodson, Skip, '37
Geist, Johnnie, '37
Gardner, John, '37
Garbarino, George, '37
Gunyon, Sandy, '37
Galarno, Fred, '38
Grimes, Johnnie, '38
Henderson, Perry, '37
Horton, Bill, '37-'38
Horton, A. A., '37-'38
Hunter, Dick, '37
Hamilton, Wes, '37
Holder, A. J., '37-'38
Hayhurst, Alfred '37
Herrington, Ed,'37
Heacock, Walter, '37-'38
Houghton, Bob, '37
Hunsaker, Kenneth, '37-'38
Hannon, Chick, '37-'38
Haythorn, Walter, '37
Haythorn, Waldo, '37
Harp, Glenn, '37-'38
Hubbell, Rube, '37
Maxwell, Omer, '37-'38
Miller, H. T., '37
Martindale, Chick, '37-'38
Myers, Jack, '37-'38
Meeks, Verne, '38
Morrison, Bert F., '37
May, Earl, '37-'38
Morris, Johnnie, '38
Murray, Leonard, '37-'38
Noland, O. H., '37-'38
Mauboules, Milton, '38
Morris, Bob, '38
McCrory, Ted, '37-'38
McIntosh, George, '37-38

NAME DUES PAID	NAME DUES PAID
Johnson, Harold, '37	McIntosh, Archie, '37
Johnson, Bud, '38	McGinnis, Ray, '37-'38
Jason, Alvin, '38	McGinnis, Russell, '37
Jacobs, Iva Dell, '38	McIntyre, John, '37-'38
Jackson, Harold, '38	McCullough, Carl, '37
Kline, Clyde, '37	McGowan, James, '37
Koed, Whitey, '37	McDonald, Frank, '37
Kirk, Roy, '37	McFadden, Arden, '38
Kilfoyl, Cliff, '37-'38	Nelson, Rube, '37
Kay, Al, '37	Newsom, George, '37
Kelso, Joe, '37	Osborne, Ed, '37-'38
Kennedy, Cal, '38	Parrish, Dalton, '37
Kruger, Mose, '38	Peak, Justin, '37
Landon, Al, '38	Peterson, Buck, '37-'38
Lyne, Chas. '37-'38	Proctor, Sam '37
Lattemore, Chas. '37	Perkins, Tom, '37
Lockie, Bob, '37	Palhamus, Sam, '37-'38
Luffman, Paul, '37-'38	Paulson, Russell, '37-'38
Lee, Carl, '37-'38	Peelgren, Howard, '37-'38
Longricker, David, '37	Quigg, Raymond, '37-'38
Lowry, Glenn, '37-'38	Rogers, Vic, '37-'38
Lines, Milo, '37	Rucker, Hayden, '37-'38
Leuschner, C. O., '37-'38	Rielly, Maurice, '37
Lewis, Mike, '38	Ridley, Hugh, '37-'38
Lucas, Tad, '38	Rhodes, Jess, '37
Lyman, O. B., '38	Reiser, Fred, '38
Lucas, Jim, '37	Ranney, Austin, '37
Landers, Raymond, '38	Roer, Bill, '38
Robertson, Jim, '38	Smith, Dell, '38
Randolph, Florence, '38	Sutton, Tommy, '38
Slappert, Dick, '37-'38	Steams, Russell, '38
Saunders, Lloyd, '37	Scheffield, Clyde, '38
Shelton, Dick, '37	Stewart, Pat, '38
Stuart, Walt, '37-'38	Tivis, Melvin, '37
Shipp, Dave, '37	Tubbs, John, '37-'38
Stewart, Norman, '37-'38	Thompson, Don, '37-'38
Stewart, Whitey, '37-'38	Teague, Joe, '37
Shumaker, Floyd, '37	Teague, Dude, '37
Shipman, Tom, '37	Talbott, Jim, '37-'38
Stevenson, Walter, '37-'38	Taskos, Manny, '37
Scott, Deafie, '37	Tyler, George, '38

NAME DUES PAID	NAME DUES PAID
Smith, Eddie, '37	Tyler, C. A., '38
Stockwell, Ralph, '37	Tilenham, Frank, '37
Snively, Henry, '37-'38	Thomas, Keith, '38
Schell, Joe, '37-'38	Till, Bill, '38
Swarts, Clem, '37	*Vance, Lester,* '37
Stapp, Virgil, '37-'38	*Vassar, Everett,* '37
Shellenberger, Orville, '38	*Van Horn, Jim,* '38
Stranghn, Bernice, '38	Woods, Eddie, '38
Sands, Geo. '38	Wallace, Claude, '37
Sawyers, Pauline, '38	Ward, Leonard, '37
Sanford, Dave, '38	Wade, Joe H., '37
Stone, Dale, '38	Winegar, Ned, '37-'38
Stonehouse, Mel, '37-'38	Wilkinson, Billy, '37
Schrader, Johnnie, '38	Wilkinson, Al, '37
	Wallace, Jimmie, '37
	Williams, Harry, '37
	Webb, Lee, '37-'38
	Williams, Dale, '37
	Wilson, Jack, '38
	Woods, W. T. '38
	Walsh, Harley, '38
	Walls, Wesley, '37-'38
	Wilkinson, Jimmie, '37
	Whiting, Bob, '37-'38
	Wheeler, Buck, '38
	Whatley, Jack, '38
	Williams, John, '38
	Wilson, L. W. '38
	Walters, Pat, '38

MEMBERS WHO HAVE RESIGNED FROM C.T.A.

- 756. Callahan, Bill
- 773. Ellis, Mel
- 899. George, Bobby
- 901. George, Chris
- 268. Glenn, O. C.
- 50. Henderson, Perry
- 202. Maggini, Charlie
- 219. Massey, Gus
- 823. Meteer, Slim
- 1101. Payne, Junior
- 199. Sisco, Shorty
- 560. Van Ryder, Jack
- 650. Whiting, Bob

DECEASED MEMBER OF THE C.T.A.

- 43. Barkdoll, Lee
- 223. Breedon, Tom
- 130. Calwell, Junior
- 261. Cravens, Walter
- 184. Davis, Girard
- 572. Dykes, Carl
- 682. Gray, Reva
- 454. Henderson, Handy
- 41. Hill, Shorty
- 612. Hunter, Dummy
- 417. Keenan, Bud
- 66. Kennedy, Cecil
- 78. Knight, Pete
- 363. McMacken, Joe
- 41. Penrose, Spencer(Hon)
- 156. Truan, Bill
- 252. Wilkinson, Johnnie [#149]

The Cowboys' Turtle Association
Articles of Association, By-Laws and Rules
&
Members of the Association
1944

(This is the 3rd and last book printed by the C.T.A.)

OFFICERS

Everett Bowman..............................President
Rt. 1, Box 451A, Tempe, Arizona

Toots Mansfield......................Vice President
Box 546, Big Spring, Texas

Fannye Lovelady...................Secy-Treasurer
733 West McDowell Rd., Phoenix, Arizona

DIRECTORS

Louis Brooks..................Saddle Bronc Riding
Sweetwater, Texas

Clyde Burk..............................Calf Roping
Comanche, Oklahoma

Eddie Curtis........................Steer Wrestling
El Reno, Oklahoma

Dick Griffith...................Contract Performers
Scottsdale, Arizona

King Merritt.............Steer Roping-Team Tying
Federal, Wyoming

George Mills......................Bareback Riding
Montrose, Colorado

Smokey Snyder........................Bull Riding
Corona, California

SPOKESMEN

Jerry Ambler, St. Helens, Oregon
Stub Bartlemay, White Salmon, Washington
Joe Bassett, Payson, Arizona
Leonard Block, Livermore, California
W. W. Bomar, Clovis, New Mexico
Paul Carney, Kirkland, Arizona
Tom Coleman, Walsenburg, Colorado
Jackie Cooper, Newhall, California
Cecil Cornish, Waukomis, Oklahoma
Vern Goodrich, Newhall, California
J. K. Harris, Longview, Texas
Clyde Herbert, Beaumont, Texas
D. Hinton, Molalla, Washington
Shirley Hussey, Moses Lake, Washington
James Kinney, Marathon, Texas
Roy Lewis, House, New Mexico
Emmett Lynch, Walla Walla, Washington
Vic Montgomery, Ozona, Texas
Shorty McCrory, Waverley, New York
Fox O'Callahan, Newhall, California
Juan Salinas, Encinal, Texas
Paul Scott, Pocatello, Idaho
Glen Shaw, Eascalon, California
Charlie Smith, Rifle, Colorado
John Tubbs, Spokane, Washington
Frank Van Meter, Weiser, Idaho
Oral Zumwalt, Wolf Creek, Montana

ADVISORY COMMITTEE

Francis J. Riley, Ethel M. Hopkins
Jack Kriendler

ARTICLES OF ASSOCIATION

The Undersigned hereby certify that:

FIRST:
The name of this Association is and shall be;
THE COWBOYS' TURTLE ASSOCIATION

SECOND:
The Cowboys' Turtle Association (hereinafter sometimes referred to as the CTA) has been formed for the following purposes:

1. To organize the professional rodeo contestants of the U.S.A. for their mutual protection and benefit.
2. To raise the standards of cowboy contests, so they rank among the foremost American sports.
3. To co-operate, insofar as possible, with the management of all rodeos at which the members contest.
4. To protect members against unfairness on the part of any rodeo management.
5. To bring about honest advertising by the rodeo associations, so that the public may rely upon the truth of advertised events in which it is claimed that members of the CTA will participate.
6. To work for the betterment of conditions and of the rules governing rodeo events in which the members of the CTA take part.
7. To establish a central place for registration for the convenience of members.
8. To publish information concerning the dates of rodeos, the names of contestants, the prize money, and other particulars in which members are interested.
9. To create a fund to be used in case of death for the benefit of members who have completed their payments to CTA.

MEMBERSHIP

THIRD:
Members shall be such professional rodeo participants as are provided in the by-laws.

MEETINGS

FOURTH:
1. A General Meeting shall be held once in each calendar year in Cheyenne, Wyo., to nominate three contestants from each of the 7 events specified in the by-laws to be voted upon by ballot for election to the Board of Directors.
2. Three candidates from each of the 7 events may be nominated at other meetings of the members, held at such places as may be designated by the Board, as provided in the by-laws.
3. An Annual Meeting of the members of the CTA shall be held once in each calendar year at New York City for the announcement of the election of directors and the transaction of business. The Board of Directors shall make a full report of their activities during the preceding fiscal year, and recommend such measures for the future as they may think advisable; and the new board shall also report their election of officers.
4. A quorum at a general meeting shall be twenty-five members, and at an annual meeting shall be fifty.

FIFTH:
The President may call a meeting of the Board of Directors at any time, provided each member is given advance notice of the meeting.

SIXTH:
Any three directors may also call a meeting, giving similar notice.

SEVENTH:
If the by-laws or rules are to be amended, a minimum of two days' notice must be given, stating the purpose of the meeting.

EIGHTH:
Members shall present their cards of membership upon entering a CTA meeting upon request of a director or spokesman.

BOARD OF DIRECTORS

NINTH:

1. The Board of Directors shall consist of eight members – the President ex-officio and seven members, one to represent each of seven events.
2. The Board of Directors may appoint Spokesmen in different territories to aid the CTA in negotiations when the directors are not present. In case there is only the spokesman present he is to take the matter in question up with all of the boys present.

3. Both directors and spokesmen shall aid the Treasurer in the collection of dues and fines owed by the contestants where unable to send to main office.

TENTH:
At all meetings of the Board, four directors shall constitute a quorum.

ELEVENTH:
The legislative or rule-making power of the CTA shall be held by the Board of Directors. It shall have general supervision over the business and affairs of the Association; with the power to make, adopt, alter or amend the by-laws as hereinafter specified. It may make all rules which is considered necessary to carry out the purposes of this organization, and any contracts incidental thereto.

OFFICERS

TWELFTH:
1. The officers of the CTA shall be as follows:
   President, Vice President, Secretary and Treasurer.
   They shall be elected by the Board of Directors at the time of the annual meeting to serve for the period of one year or until their successors are elected.
2. The President shall preside at all meetings of the CTA and of the Board of Directors. He shall enforce all rules and regulations of the CTA and perform such other duties as shall be assigned to him by the Board of Directors.
3. In the absence or disability of the President, the Vice President shall perform his duties.
4. The Secretary shall keep the minutes and other official reports of the CTA. He shall conduct its official correspondence and shall keep all records, books, documents and papers relating to the CTA at such place as shall be designated by the Board of Directors.
5. The Treasurer shall keep account of all money received by him and shall deposit it in the name of the CTA in such depository as shall be designated by the Board of Directors. He shall not pay out or disburse any of the money of the CTA except by check, which must be signed by the President, or in case of his death, disability or absence, by the Vice President, and countersigned by the Secretary of the CTA. At each annual meeting of the members he shall make a statement of the current financial condition of the CTA and a detailed report of its condition for the preceding fiscal year. The Treasurer shall be bonded.
6. The President shall be a member of the Board of Directors ex-officio but any of the above mentioned officers, other than the President, may

also be elected members of the Board, and shall serve as Representatives of their events as well.
7. All officers and directors shall serve without salary or other compensation, except Secretary-Treasurer.
8. Officers, directors and spokesmen may be removed at any time with or without (legal) cause by a majority vote of the Board of Directors.
9. Resignations of officers, directors and spokesmen must be presented to the Board of Directors and be accepted by a majority vote of those present and voting before they become final.
10. The Board of Directors may fill any vacancy among the officers, directors or spokesmen by vote of the majority of those present and voting at any meeting. Such election to be for the unexpired term.
11. Any locality can petition for a spokesman if local conditions demand such action. In such a case the spokesman petitioned for must be passed on by the Board of Directors.

AMENDMENTS

THIRTEENTH:
The Articles of Association may be amended at any time at any annual or general meeting of the members of the CTA by the vote of a majority of the members present, provided there is a quorum.

BY-LAWS

NOMINATION AND ELECTION TO THE BOARD OF DIRECTORS
1. Three candidates shall be nominated once in each calendar year chosen from the following seven events: (1) Steer Wrestling, (2) Saddle Bronc Riding, (3) Bareback Horse Riding, (4) Bull or Steer Riding, (5) Team Tying and Steer Roping, (6) Calf Roping, and (7) Contract Performers, to be voted upon by ballot for the office of Directors.
    a. The Team Tying and Steer Roping Representative shall function as Calf Roping Representative if the latter is absent, and vice versa.
2. All three candidates may be nominated at the general meeting in Cheyenne (Wyo.) or, an additional three, at the discretion of the Board of Directors, may be nominated at general meetings held at such places as may be designated by the Board. The three candidates from each event receiving the most votes shall be nominated for office.
3. The names of the candidates nominated at this meeting shall be published in the September issue of Hoofs and Horns magazine, edited by Ma Hopkins of Tucson, Arizona, which is the official CTA publication. They shall be voted upon at the annual meeting held in New York City.

4. Each CTA member in good standing shall be entitled to cast one vote for a director chosen from the event or events in which he contests. The candidates receiving the highest number of votes shall constitute the Board of Directors for the ensuing year.
5. Members, who cannot be present at the meeting in New York, shall mail their votes before October first to the Secretary. These ballots shall be counted and the results announced at the annual meeting.
6. Each member shall write his full name and address on his ballot; otherwise it will not be accepted or counted.

MEMBERSHIP AND DUES

1. Membership in the CTA is confined to professional rodeo contestants and rodeo contract performers. This is to include cowgirl bronc riders, trick riders, trick ropers, clowns, announcers, and other contract performers that are considered a pertinent part of the rodeo.
    a. All above mentioned contract performers must be members of the CTA, and can not work any show where CTA members are barred.
    b. Contract performers may be fined or suspended or both, at the discretion of the Board of Directors.
    c. Contract performers, however, may not accept contracts after the CTA serves notice that its members will be withdrawn from a given rodeo.
2. Eligibility for membership in the CTA shall be left to the discretion of the directors, officers and spokesmen of said organization.
    a. Members of the CTA will refuse to contest at any rodeo with cowboys who, having qualified as professionals, have not joined the CTA.
    b. And director or spokesman or officers shall have authority to inform rodeo managements as to which contestants have qualified as professionals but have not yet joined the CTA.
    c. If the rodeo management permits such a contestant to enter, the CTA reserves the right to withdraw its members from competition.
3. Annual dues of membership are hereby fixed at ten dollars a year.
4. Annual dues shall be payable before entering the first rodeo of the season at which a member contests.
5. Any member who does not pay his dues by March 15th of each year whether he has contested or not is automatically suspended. To be reinstated, said member must have the approval of the Board of Directors.
6. Any member of the CTA who has not paid his dues for 1941, or any year previous to that, will be dropped from the list of CTA members

and will not be permitted to contest at any rodeo. To be reinstated such a member must pay all back dues in full, plus 10 dollars for each year in which said dues have not been paid.
7. Dues for cowgirl bronc riders who do nothing but ride broncs are five dollars per year.
8. Should any member of the CTA be taken into the Armed Forces soon after paying their dues shall have their dues refunded upon written request to the CTA office. CTA members in service shall be issued membership cards good for the duration without pay.
9. Only members in good standing shall vote in the affairs of the CTA. No member who is in default as to payments for dues or fines, and no member who is at the time suspended, will be permitted to vote.
10. The CTA, through its Board of Directors, shall adopt a card certifying the contestant's or contract performer's membership in the Association.
11. Election to honorary membership in the CTA shall be subject to the approval of a member of the Board of Directors, a Spokesman, or officers. Honorary members shall be given cards and insignia which differ from those of regular members. Annual dues for honorary members are hereby fixed at five dollars. Honorary members are not eligible to vote.
12. An Advisory Committee may be appointed by the majority of the Board of Directors to serve the CTA in an advisory capacity for the period of one year, or until they are succeeded. Members of the Advisory Committee are not eligible to vote.
13. By-laws and rules may be amended by a majority vote of the Board of Directors.

RULES

1. **No CTA member shall contest at any amateur rodeo.**
2. Rodeo stock contractors can not furnish stock to both professional and amateur shows. If a stock contractor furnished stock to an amateur show, they must stay amateur.
3. Stock Contractors are requested to make sure all prize lists have been approved by the CTA before signing a contract to furnish stock for a show.
4. No CTA member shall be allowed to contest at any rodeo unless the entry fees for each event are added to the guaranteed prize money of each event.
    a. No rodeo shall be responsible for returning a contestant's entry fee if he has contested in an event even once during the show. But if he is entered in other events in which he is unable to contest, the entry fees for those events must be returned.

5. No CTA member shall be allowed to contest at any rodeo unless competition is open to all members of the CTA in good standing.
> a. Therefore, no CTA member shall contest at any rodeo which places penalties or handicaps upon CTA members.
> b. No CTA member shall contest at any amateur rodeo or state championships or in special, closed, or amateur events. However, a rodeo having special events for local talent shall not be classified as an amateur rodeo by virtue of that fact alone.
> c. If a rodeo has a special day for amateur contests, no CTA member shall be permitted to contest.

6. If more than two events are held a show will not be considered a jack pot, and to qualify as a jack pot contest must be OK'd by CTA.

7. Open rodeo contests must be CTA and members cannot participate in contract or closed shows.

8. If an Amateur event is held in a professional show a like event must be held for the professionals.

9. No CTA member shall be allowed to ride for mount money unless a contest in the event is included in said rodeo's program.
> a. However, if five or less contestants are entered in the event, CTA members may ride, rope or wrestle for mount money.

10. No CTA member shall be allowed to contest at any rodeo unless the judges are experienced men, shall have been passed upon by the three riding representatives of the CTA, and are satisfactory to a majority of the Board of Directors of the CTA.
> a. If the judges are not satisfactory as flagmen, the ropers and bulldoggers reserve the right to select a flagman for whose services the judges shall pay.

11. If a rodeo hires its judges in advance, the names of the judges chosen must be submitted to the CTA for approval before they are printed on said rodeo's prize list.
> a. If a rodeo prints the names of the judges on its prize list without having submitted them to the CTA for approval, the CTA reserves the right to withdraw its members from contesting under said judges.
> b. If a rodeo does not hire its judges in advance the rodeo committee may select competent men who shall be passed upon by the CTA members entered at said rodeo.
> c. Timers and flagmen must be men of experience. If the CTA does not consider the men chosen by a given rodeo to have adequate experience, they will expect cooperation from the management in replacing the unsatisfactory timers or flagmen.

d. The decision of the judges, flagmen and timers who have been passed upon by the CTA shall be final, and no protest by the contestants will be permitted.

12. The CTA agrees to adopt the RAA rules for rodeo contests and will insist that rodeo managements adhere to them.

13. Any member of the CTA who does not observe the above rules is liable to a fine, suspension, or both.

14. The CTA reserves the right to withdraw their members from competition in any rodeo which does not conform to the above rules or which refuses to cooperate with the Turtle Association in the arbitration of difficulties.

PENALTIES FOR INFRACTION OF RULES

1. **Any member of the CTA who contests, performs or works at a rodeo which has been boycotted by the CTA is liable to a fine, suspension, or both.**

2. Any CTA member guilty of misconduct will be notified to appear before the Board of Directors for a meeting and if proven guilt of misconduct will be suspended – or fined – or both.
    a. If the Board sees fit, it may advance payment for outstanding bills incurred by members during a given rodeo.
    b. Members shall not be reinstated unless the CTA is repaid.

3. Any member who wishes to resign from the CTA must do so in writing. A member who withdraws in good faith shall be reinstated without fine or penalty, provided he has not contested, worked or performed at any rodeo during the time in which his resignation took effect.
    a. In case a member has contested, worked or performed at a rodeo during the period of his resignation and wishes to be reinstated, he shall be fined, suspended or both, according to the discretion of the Board of Directors before he shall be reinstated.

4. Any member who falsely represents himself as qualified to speak for the CTA shall be fined, suspended or both to the limit of the power of the Board of Directors.
    a. **The President, the representatives (Directors) or the spokesmen are the only members of the organization who have the authority to make decisions for the CTA.**
    b. Certain members will carry letters from the Board of Directors authorizing them to collect dues, take in new members and collect bad bills.

5. Any member of the CTA who has a grievance against the organization shall present same to the representative of his event or to a spokesman. Any member who willfully causes trouble inside or outside the ranks of the CTA shall be liable to a fine, suspension, or both.
6. Any member of the CTA who denies his membership and removes his CTA button on entering a rodeo, shall be fined to the fullest extent within the power of the Board of Directors.
7. Any member who makes himself liable to a fine must pay the same or post a bond of fifty dollars ($50.00) with the Secretary of the CTA until he has had a hearing before the Board of Directors.
8. If the Board of Directors finds him guilty, by the majority vote of all the Directors, he may be fined from $25.00 to $500.00 at their discretion, or suspended, or both.
9. Any member of the CTA who has been fined and fails to pay one-quarter of his winnings at the time the prize money is won until the fine is paid, is liable to be expelled from the CTA and shall forfeit any part or portion of the fine he has already paid.
    a. Any contract performer who has been fined and fails to pay one-quarter of each contract at the time said contract is paid, until the fine is paid in full, is liable to be expelled from the CTA and shall forfeit any part or portion of the fine he has already paid.
10. It is understood that no officer, director, member or employee of the CTA, shall be liable individually or otherwise for any breach of the above rules, or for any understanding or agreement between the CTA and the RAA or with any other rodeo association.
11. If the Rodeo Management furnishes feed for contestants' horses the CTA urges each member to ride in Grand Entries and Parades, and will sanction the fines placed by management for non-cooperation.

POLICY

It is the policy of the CTA that each member present at a given rodeo shall attend all general meetings of the CTA.

The CTA reserves the right to withdraw its members from competition if the prize money is too unequally divided.

If a rodeo management wishes absolute guarantee that members of the CTA will participate at a given rodeo after their arrival at said rodeo, they must submit their prize list for approval not later than thirty days prior to show dates to the main office of the Cowboys' Turtle Association, Phoenix, Arizona.

The CTA shall be responsible for seeing that all approved prize lists shall be signed by at least three directors (representatives) and the President or four Directors.

EVERETT BOWMAN, President

LIST OF TURTLES,
TURTLE # & ALPHABETICALLY

C.T.A. #	NAME	C.T.A. #	NAME
1388	Acay, Delmar	287	Bedford, Cecil
1631	Adair, Pud	273	Belden, Herb
342	Adams, Dale	H308	Bell, John H.
1206	Adams, Pete	452	Bender, Bennie
146	Ahern, Buck	8	Bennett, Hugh
309	Akers, Ves	338	Beren, John
1871	Allen, Del	499	Berry, Padgett
367	Allen, Frankie	207	Betts, Glenn M.
578	Allen, Hoss	1682	Billingsley, Red
2018	Allen, Jean	440	Bland, R. L., Jr.
245	Allen, Red	94	Blasingame, Jack
1850	Almond, John	1680	Blessing, Wag
496	Alrich, H. A.	1610	Block, Leonard
1445	Alrich, Hank	112	Bode, Andrew
1142	Alsbaugh, Walt	1620	Boen, Ken
471	Altamarino, Tony	63	Boen, Mrs. Ken
227	Alvord, Fred	1772	Bomar, W. W.
286	Ambler, Jerry	395	Bond, Paul
170	Anderson, Dick	101	Booth, Clinton
2008	Anderson, Dick	1028	Booth, Homer R.
379	Armstrong, Ted	797	Border, Alex
70	Arnold, Carl	766	Boss, Ray
891	Arrants, Gene	273	Bowen, Glenn W.
432	Autry, Frank	551	Bowman, Ed
1940	Axton, Bob	15	Bowman, Everett
1601	Bacon, Grant	10	Bowman, John
1691	Bacon, John	76	Bowyer, Chester
1405	Badsky, Fred	403	Boyd, Tom
1787	Bailey, Herb	1453	Brady, Buff, Jr.
404	Baker, J. Howard	312	Brady, Pat
24	Baker, Paddy	1348	Branch, Riley
372	Ballard, Smokey	485	Bride, Tom
1944	Barens, Roy	375	Brister, Jim
1566	Barmby, Bob	83	Broderick, John
789	Barnett, Ernie	850	Brodnax, Chas.
141	Barrett, Fred	975	Brooks, Louis
89	Bartlemay, Stub	178	Brown, Basil
564	Bassett, Joe	187	Brown, Howard
2022	Baughman, Wart	958	Brown, Jerry
540	Becker, Fritz	332	Brown, Pat

C.T.A. #	NAME	C.T.A. #	NAME
76	Brown, W. H. 'Tex'	252	Coelho, Al (Louis)
325	Browne, Robert	571	Coker, Joe
177	Brunton, Carol	1582	Colborn, Everett
388	Buetler, Lynn	200	Colborn, Rose Mary
515	Buffington, Ernest	1156	Collier, Ralph
1111	Bugg, Johnnie	521	Collins, Earvin
743	Burk, Jiggs	510	Connell, Junior
144	Burk, Clyde	609	Cook, Bud
1821	Burleson, W. E.	48	Cooper, Jackie
1882	Burns, Bobbie	837	Cornish, Cecil
1667	Burrough, George	374	Cotrell, Lyle
1409	Burrows, Bob	44	Cox, Breezy
498	Butts, Buster	696	Cox, Frank
1209	Byers, Chester	167	Cripe, A. J.
2004	Cabral, Louis	72	Cropper, Melvin
1629	Cahoe, Tommy	185	Crosby, Bob
191	Caldwell, Eddie	212	Curry, Roland
386	Campbell, Arlo	122	Curtis, Andy
308	Campbell, A. J. 'Jack'	132	Curtis, Eddie
1729	Capps, Kenneth	119	Dahl, Herb
331	Carey, Lawrence	324	Dahlberg, Shorty
21	Carney, Paul	302	Daniels, Lary
315	Carson, Ken	433	Daniels, Robert F.
373	Castanon, Frank	1374	Darnell, Fred
253	Casteel, Art	253	Davis, Harold
1684	Castro, Vern	1716	Davis, Merle
396	Cavanaugh, Tommy	1980	Deakins, Ab
1556	Cavender, Eugene	483	Dee, Clarence
360	Chaffie, Jim	168	Del Re, M. W.
1894	Chapman, John	1155	Demaree, George
461	Charles, Artie	556	Dikeman, Melvin
790	Chesson, Bo	1710	Dillon, Mutt
1119	Chitwood, Frank	1226	Dixon, Eddie
2016	Christensen, Bobbie	174	Dixon, Homer
1880	Christensen, Henry	1346	Dossey, Bernice
934	Christian, Lefty	204	Dossey, Carl
456	Clayton, Tommy	1204	Doucet, Poley
202	Clemans, W. J.	828	Dowell, Buck
258	Cline, Doc	1218	Dreyer, Polly
255	Cline, George	241	Drowne, Skip
1131	Cline, John	1736	Duarte, Ed
1989	Cline, Lawrence	1276	Dugger, Bufard
430	Cline, Leck	1048	Dunbar, Marvin
74	Clingman, Hugh	1734	Durfee. Tex
223	Coats, Bobby	949	Dyer, Jack

C.T.A. #	NAME	C.T.A. #	NAME
104	Echols, Buck	290	Gayler, Manerd
1833	Edmonson, Lince	487	Gerig. Kpjm
152	Edwards, Joe	54	Getzwiller, Marion
1568	Edwards, Sonny	192	Gill, Emmett
1938	Ellingwalt, P. W.	156	Glade, Pete
1997	Elliott, Cliff	1966	Glatfelder, Gene
1956	Elliott, Verne	1430	Glenn, Dick
1597	Emerson, Tex	1772	Glenn, Lester
481	Enders, Bob	2017	Golia, Philip
1035	Enos, Manuel	1537	Goodrich, Myrtle
1865	Espy, Jim	1538	Goodrich, Vern
362	Estes, Bob	263	Goodspeed, Buck
1828	Evans, Bert	645	Gould, Paul
219	Evans, Floyd James	13	Grace, Holloway
215	Facciola, Don B.	90	Graham, J. A.
415	Falk, Dr. Lane	123	Graham, Kenneth
813	Fancher, Sam	1236	Gray, Juanita
1847	Farnsworth, Dick	1237	Gray, Weaver
314	Farr, Carl	1141	Green, Carlos
316	Farr, Hugh	1539	Green, Ray
470	Farris, Zeano	668	Greenough, Alice
1223	Favors, Jack	669	Greenough, Marge
543	Fernandez, Fele	23	Greenough, Turk
903	Fernandez, Ike	289	Greenwood, Ross
414	Fidler, C. Lyall	3	Griffith, Dick
476	Finley, Evelyn	454	Gruwell, Gus
836	Finley, Larry	1830	Guidotti, Raymond L
1798	Fischer, Charles H.	65	Gunter, Kenneth
1735	Flagg, Slim	624	Guymon, Sandy
172	Flesher, Herbert	1937	Hale, Earl
459	Fletcher, Claude	1572	Hale, Mel
557	Flowers, Hubert	434	Hall, Clark
945	Flowers, Marshall	377	Hancock, Bill
1763	Folsom, Barney	1744	Hannan, Chick
480	Fonville, Paul	1960	Hansen, Curt
1774	Fort, Troy	1081	Hansen, Kenneth
1527	Fox, Dewey	1867	Hansen, Merrill
1541	Frazier, Larry	1954	Harper, Bert A.
444	Freeman, E. J.	1208	Harris, J. K.
1252	Fulkerson, Jasbo	246	Hart, Harry
173	Galbraith, Joe	226	Hastings, Mike
229	Gale, Floyd	724	Haverty, Bob
350	Gamblin, Amye	467	Haynes, I. D.
870	Garcia, Vidal	1139	Hays, Ed
391	Garner, Paul	422	Hazen, Jimmie

C.T.A. #	NAME	C.T.A. #	NAME
71	Heacock, Steve	1685	Jenkins, Jay
193	Hebert, Bubba	472	Jesperson, Allen
1727	Hebert, Clyde	424	Johnson, Dick
124	Hefner, Hoytt	1936	Johnson, Faye
879	Henry, Carol D.	704	Jones, Buck
1328	Henson, Claude	99	Jordon, John
401	Henson, Heavy	361	Jorgenson, Ivan
667	Hill, Clayton	1085	Kane, Bill
1832	Hill, Clinton	33	Kenney, James
856	Hill, Jess	1342	Knight, Faye
1708	Hill, Jim	37	Knight, Harry
184	Hill, Lawrence	102	Knight, Nick
501	Hines, Dan	1607	Knapp, Jack
1090	Hinkle, George	1069	Lamar, Curtis
278	Hinton, Dee	1848	LaRue, Walt
331	Hock, John	2051	Lawrence, Billy
1392	Hoffman, Don	1186	Laycock, Jim
75	Hogan, Tom	688	Laycock, Maurice
1390	Holcomb, Elmer	1947	Leach, Billy
233	Holder, A. J.	1873	Lee, Clarence
411	Homoki, Stephen Cook	453	Lee, Cotton
1105	Hood, Charley	770	Lefton, Abe
1107	Hood, Lesley	225	Leggett, Elton
728	Horner, Mildred Mix	799	Lewallen, G. K.
385	Hovencamp, Eddie	568	Lichtenstein, Helen
387	Howard, Bill	1756	Lilley, H. L.
1082	Howe, Don	22	Linder, Herman
188	Hubbard, Fay	349	Lindsey, John
443	Hubbell, Rube	288	Lindues, Louis
376	Hudson, Jim	1471	Lisenbee, Byron
416	Hull, Mark	155	Logue, Harry
1420	Hunter, Maynard	1579	Lohr, Art
881	Hussey, Shirley	1840	Lorimer, Chuck
171	Hutchinson, Lee	77	Lovelady, Fannye
417	Hydson, Shorty	1999	Lovelady, Sam
957	Iler, Bill	1124	Lowry, Bill
163	Iler, Mary	479	Lucas, Mitzi
176	Irwin, Jim	601	Lucas, Tad
160	Ivory, Perry	2010	Lufkin, Ned
1751	Ivory, Raymond 'Buster'	1532	Lynch, Emmet
86	Jacobs, Slats	1646	Maggini, Charlie
1466	Jamison, B. M. Jr.	1900	Malm, Ted
284	Jaques, Joseph	1953	Molone, Buddy
32	Jauregui, Andy	1927	Mann, Orval
486	Jauregui, Ed	1468	Mansfield, Bob

CTA #	NAME	C.T.A. #	NAME
237	Mansfield, Toots	20	McCrorey, Howard
445	Markcum, Wolf	353	McCrorey, Shorty
79	Marsh, Earl	822	McDaniel, Bud
632	Marshall, Grant	243	McEntire, John
1979	Marshall, Kermit	1149	McFadden, Gordon
189	Martin, Johnny	307	McFarland, Bill
1044	Martin, Nub	846	McFarland, John
423	Martinez, Pete	2	McGinty, Rusty
339	Mathews, Howard	776	McGuire, Bill
1778	Matlock, Harvey	1602	McKittrick, Walt
1158	Matlock, Shorty	268	McLaughlin, Donald
511	Meeks, Al	277	McLaughlin, Gene
1055	Meeks, Bob	1983	McLennon, Don
664	Mendes, Joe	1984	McLennon, Hope
208	Mendes, John	563	McMacken, Bill
111	Merchant, Richard	1936	McMahon, Ed
107	Merritt, King	706	McWiggins, Zack
109	Meyers, Herbert	282	Neal, Bill, Jr.
228	Miller, Bob	1875	Neal, Buddy
244	Miller, Richard	1678	Nelson, George W.
220	Mills, George	31	Nesbitt, Donald
222	Mills, Hank	158	Nichols, J. D.
354	Minor, Kenneth	105	Nix, Will
62	Moe, Milt	317	Nolan, Bob
1386	Montana, Louise	798	Nuckols, Grafton
1385	Montana, Montie	1306	Oakley, Russell Jack
1955	Montana's Troup	47	O'Callahan, Fox
1251	Montana, Montie Jr.	397	Ohrlin, Glenn
1601	Montgomery, Vic	1138	Oja, Andy
1888	Moore, Bob	484	O'Shea, Michael
26	Moore, Earl	297	Overson, Bob
1196	Moore, Ward	296	Overson, Don
1746	Morris, Claude	98	Owens, Del
842	Morris, Peewee	179	Owens, Mitchell
1649	Moss, Hoitt	60	Pardee, E
494	Mounce, Louis	53	Parker, Bud
209	Mueller, H. H.	390	Parks, Bill
93	Mulkey, Burel	552	Parks, Darwin
1934	Murphy, Hardy	994	Parrish, Vester
2024	Murray, Joe, Jr.	420	Paul, Chuck
6	Murray, Leo	2015	Payne, Gene H.
1612	McBride, Bill	473	Pearce, Joe
1737	McCarroll, Frank	460	Percifield, Jack
84	McCarty, Ed	505	Perkins, Len
1881	McCormick, Trixie	154	Peters, Floyd

C.T.A. #	NAME	C.T.A. #	NAME
320	Peterson, Buck	912	Rogers, Eddie
880	Pettcock, U. A.	1195	Rooke, Frank
27	Pettigrew, Homer	1092	Rose, Parry
1822	Pettit, Japson	474	Rothel, Bob
1084	Pettit, Wesley	1932	Rowe, Floyd
788	Phillips, Dub	462	Ruckdeschel, Hank
504	Pholson, Jim	57	Rude, Ike
161	Pickett, Joseph W.	1461	Rumsey, Jack
398	Piela, Jack	475	Russell, Phillip
92	Piela, Joe	436	Russell, S. G.
293	Pittman, Paul	256	Ryan, Duward
1151	Poage, Doug	407	Ryon, Don, Jr.
1143	Poage, Walton	116	Salinas, Juan
468	Pogue, John	466	Salinas, Tony
114	Powers, Ted	671	Salisbury, Jack
1286	Preston, C. P.	66	Saunders, Jack
300	Pretti, Bob	1011	Saunders, Jim R.
690	Pruett, Gene	42	Schell, Asbury
1806	Pruitt, I. V.	1783	Schmidt, Doc
1032	Rambo, Gene	186	Schneider, Frankie
221	Randall, Glenn H.	1993	Schrade, Jack
1818	Reeves, Jimmie	1491	Schumacher, Jim
796	Reeves, Lem	330	Schwartz, Jack
1637	Reger, Monty	81	Schwarz, Vic
1815	Reid, Nig	932	Scott, Bob
216	Reynolds, Brown Jug	931	Scott, Paul
196	Reynolds, Fess	1965	Searles, Kenney
56	Rhodes, John	1982	Selby, Bill
46	Rhodes, Tom	100	Sellers, Earl
598	Rider, Pauline (Nesbitt)	73	Sellers, Jack
1489	Ridley, Howard	723	Sells, Albert
305	Ridley, Hugh	234	Sewalt, Royce
1962	Rife, Syl	2020	Seward, Roy S.
1899	Riggs, Murray	7	Shaw, Everett
575	Roane, Sylvester	217	Shaw, Glen
175	Robbins, Dick	180	Sheppard, Chuck
1810	Roberson, A. A.	439	Sherman, Jack
651	Roberts, George (Kid)	1963	Shessler, Solly
720	Roberts, Gerald	847	Shields, Chas. A.
259	Roberts, Ken	1893	Shoulders, Marvin
491	Roberts, Marjorie	1182	Shultz, Chas.
103	Roberts, Rube	260	Sievers, Bill
714	Robertson, Jim	1203	Sikes, L. N.
1658	Robinson, Buck	426	Silvers, Joe S.
1437	Rogers, Bedell	1596	Siminoff, Yale

C.T.A. #	NAME	C.T.A. #	NAME
1692	Simms, Olan	51	Turk, Charlie
165	Skelton, Al	849	Tyler, Glenn
1643	Skinner, Ray	497	Vance, Johnnie
1935	Slim, Colorado	509	Vassar, Everett
754	Sloan, Jimmie	327	Van Meter, Frank
764	Smith, Charley	1797	Volz, John
1985	Smith, Jute	191	Wade, Joe H.
1641	Smith, M. L.	1905	Wadsworth, Glen
1855	Smith, Neal	1707	Walker, Ike
197	Smith, Roy	2002	Walker, George
40	Snyder, Smoky	135	Ward, Bill
1868	Sonnenberg, Virginia	464	Ward, Jack
61	Sorrels, Buckshot	400	Ward, James P.
249	Spealman, Bud	985	Ware, Slick
310	Spencer, Tim	1530	Watts, Bill
549	Spilsbury, Bud	1930	Webster, Shoat
369	Springer, Bennie	681	Wening, Richard
1961	Squires, Wally	139	Westfall, Howard
469	Standefer, Buck	345	Whaley, Slim
337	Starr, Hans	1977	Whatley, Todd
1343	St. Croy, Paul	1820	Whetsel, Joe
1225	Stensen, Joe	1123	White, Homer
351	Stewart, Whitey	1552	White, Jim
1477	Stroud, Francis	1269	White, Sam
193	Stuart, Roy	617	White, Vivian
1120	Stuckey, Tom	128	Whiteman, Jim
510	Swarts, Clem	214	Whorton, Al
579	Tacker, Ike	213	Whorton, Eddie
1299	Tacquard, Kidd	424	Wicker, Olds
1224	Talbot, Joe	363	Wier, Clyde
334	Targerson, Bill	817	Wilcox, Don
336	Targerson, Slim	134	Wilderspin, George
1823	Taylor, Dan	1812	Wilkens, Lefty
88	Teague, George	752	Williams, Ken
421	Teague, Joe	218	Williams, Pete
36	Thode, Earl	198	Williams, R. W.
757	Thomas, Orville	333	Wills, Arnie
1860	Thomas, Park	1726	Wofford, Earl
1842	Thomas, Ray	2013	Wood, Joe
1549	Thompson, Ralph	677	Wood, Tom
313	Tiffin, Buck	1877	Wright, Cecil
1235	Truan, Norma Holmes	1964	Wulfekuhler, L. W.
5	Truitt, Dick	516	Yardley, George
1903	Truman, Floyd (Sonny)	1100	Yates, Fayette
328	Tubbs, John	1013	York, S. A.

C.T.A. #	NAME
264	Youchum, Ted
1776	Young, Paul

C.T.A. #	NAME
451	Young, Weldon

WITHDRAWN FROM C.T.A.

C.T.A. #	NAME
806	Barnett, Keith
909	Bascom, Earl
640	Bays, Jimmie
1664	Bias, Charles
541	Burns, Frankie
1001	Capps, Charlie
628	Carey, Joe
519	Chisum, Ike
542	Cooper, Morris
699	Crain, Don
1912	Davis, Tea
515	Doan, Urban
698	Doiel, Bud
773	Ellis, Mel
1171	Evans, Buck
1251	Faircloth, Sig
921	Fancher, John
1463	Ferris, Hack
606	Fletcher, Virginia Van Meter
457	French, Jimmie
1028	Fuller, Wid
277	Gafford, Roy
960	Gentry, Guy
899	George, Bobby
268	Glenn, O. C.
221	Hamilton, Wes
445	Hannum, Walter
1009	Harmon, Del T.
782	Hedges, Max
50	Henderson, Perry
1307	Henry, Hugh
533	Holder, Arthur
998	Hood, Joe
151	Jenkins, Leslie
1286	Kalin, Ray
218	Kerscher, Jack

C.T.A. #	NAME
478	Litterell, Jerry
135	Leuschner, C. O.
865	Louks, Dick
397	Lowry, Glen
473	Lyon, Bill
146	Maxwell, Omer
1081	McCrorey, Knotchie
823	Meteer, Slim
344	Olsen, Pampa
528	Palhamus, Sam
1101	Payne, Junior
283	Piper, Harold
1197	Ragsdale, Fred
733	Randolph, Florence
1477	Reynolds, Jim
1319	Reynolds, Ray
602	Richards, Lucyle
622	Robertson, George
H52	Robertson, Jack
1109	Roy, Mutt
153	Saunders, Lloyd
479	Schell, Joe
199	Sisco, Shorty
1199	Stevens, Earl
740	Sultenfuss, Frank
738	Sultenfuss, Henry
739	Sultenfuss, Leon
737	Sultenfuss, Norman
1059	Sutton, Jim
1099	Thomas, Limey
1366	Thorn, Bob
1592	Tipton, H. T.
763	Van Cleve, Paul
560	Van Rider, Jack
140	Wallace, Claude
403	Wallice, Jimmie

C.T.A. #	NAME	C.T.A. #	NAME
730	Walters, Pat	79	Woods, Eddie
787	Ward, Homer	1155	York, A. C.
1212	Wheeler, Buck		

DECEASED MEMBERS OF C.T.A.

C.T.A. #	NAME	C.T.A. #	NAME
43	Barkdoll, Lee	1800	Jordan, Lon
1585	Bogan, Bill	1402	Knight, Jack
725	Brannon, Rose	78	Knight, Pete
877	Burkitt, Buck	1	Nesbitt, Jimmie
1012	Burroughs, Wayne	1805	Nunn, John
482	Conners, Beverly	142	McClure, Jake
1284	Couch, Worth N.	844	Paxton, Trent
453	Daniels, George	H30	Penrose, Spencer
H5	Dew, Frank Y.	319	Sandall, Hubert
1561	Dillon, Jack	986	Stober, Earl
553	Doyle, Tex	95	Strickland, Hugh
242	Ferris, Lee	1228	Welch, Slim
H65	Gelvin, Floyd	252	Wilkinson, Johnnie
682	Grey, Reva	873	Wood, Opal
41	Hill, Shorty		
612	Hunter, Dummy		

C.T.A. Members Serving In The Armed Forces of Our Country

C.T.A. #	NAME	C.T.A. #	NAME
1712	Albin, J. D.	1391	Becker, Johnny
298	Allen, Lonnie	795	Beken, Henry
1019	Arnold, Edward	1495	Bell, Melvin
1920	Arnold, Edward	236	Bennett, Charlie
1475	Atkinson, Almus	969	Black, Billy
1962	Autry, Gene	819	Blackstone, Doc
493	Barker, Dick	83	Blevins, Earl
1202	Barron, N. E.	1959	Bohlender, Ike
1758	Barton, Bill	833	Booth, Leslie
1932	Barton, Bill	1784	Boss, Ray

C.T.A. #	NAME	C.T.A. #	NAME
1353	Boyer, Bob	17	Fleming, Joel
1925	Boyhan, John H.	653	Fletcher, Al
1097	Brannon, Leo	87	Fletcher, Kid
703	Burk, Dee	1990	Forsyth, Rollin
1261	Burleigh, Bryan E.	1527	Fox, Dewey
59	Burrell, Joe	7	Goodspeed, Red
442	Cameron, Eddie	45	Gordon, Alvin
55	Carr, Clay	796	Gregory, Bern
261	Chambers, Bob	1483	Guy. Eddie
1732	Chapas, Max	1216	Haas, Chuck
1443	Chipman, John	1005	Hamilton, Eugene
1839	Coffey, Ed	28	Hancock, Sonny
406	Colbert, Charles	753	Harriss, Baylis
1152	Cole, Chili	1958	Haynes, Thos. D.
2014	Coe, H. A.	183	Henley, Cecil
887	Colbert, Dude (Chas.)	933	Herren, Dick
1719	Crawford, Bill	1117	Hickman, Chester
1576	Crossland, Leo	876	Hightower, William C.
1247	Darnel, Clarence	1650	Hillyer, Jack
1824	Davis, Arthur	1937	Hoggett, Chas.
230	Davis, Buck	1404	Holleyman, J. D.
2012	Dillon, Ben	1360	Howell, Chet
629	Duarte, Hoot	1958	Hurd, Lee R.
1959	Durham, John	1578	Jerrel, Jerry
1010	Dwyer, Emmett	299	Cecil Jones
1642	Dyer, Paul	1915	Kaaro, Jimmy
1721	Emery, Harold	1393	Kelley, Billy
296	Emory, Harold	1892	Kelley, Bob
169	Engelsman, Led	1308	Kelley, Jack
1525	Ensley, Allen	1394	Kelley, Truman
596	Eskew, Junior	295	Kerscher, Pete
1234	Eskew, Tom Mix	878	Killough, Buck
1616	Evans, Johnnie	294	Knight, Tom
859	Fancher, Ben	843	Klebba, Joe
1918	Felton, Boots	18	Koed, Whitely
1795	Fenack, Tony	489	Kohrs, Ray
203	Ferrario, Amil	670	Kudron, Joe
1869	Fetters, Bob	1608	Kumerle, Slim
1273	Fife, Harold	1221	Lane, Ralph
402	Finley, Frank	1569	Lasswell, Chuck
396	Finley, Luther	1414	Lawrence, Junior
1329	Fisher, Bud	683	Like, James
291	Fisher, Mike	1570	Linderman, Bud

C.T.A. #	NAME	C.T.A. #	NAME
857	Londos, Swede	2021	Roger, Buddy
1215	Lovelady, Shorty	1376	Ribelin, Tom
1906	Luer, Harvey	2014	Richardson, Lloyd
1025	Lyon, Stan	1890	Ritches, Bob
1900	Malm, Ted	1335	Robinson, Lucky
1426	Maddox, Everett	1341	Rooker, Bob
364	Marion, Frank	589	Ross, Bruce
382	Matthews, Bob	1874	Rogers, Pete
866	Mefford, Bud	1851	Sanders, George
697	Melville, Bob	1219	Servel, Pierre
1031	Mendes, Carl	1662	Shannon, L. V.
1030	Mendes, Frank	348	Shellenberger, C. J.
1749	Merritt, Dean	936	Shellenberger, D. C.
1896	Merritt, Hyde	2011	Sisco, Jack
1661	Miles, Dave	1694	Snure, Ben
1447	Miller, George	1831	Spruel, Johnny
1633	Mott, Eddie	1776	Stockdale, Champie
666	Mounce, Ernest	38	Stout, David
1829	Munson, Bryan	1946	Stoval, John
1289	Mutch, Ernest	1656	Swenson, Allen
1902	McBride, Dudley	19	Stanton, Ralph
1450	McCabe, Tommy	1496	Swartout, George
1113	McCormick, J. D.	1693	Taylor, Ed
67	McEuen, Albert	1401	Taylor, Hubert Jr.
1634	McEuen, Arthur	525	Talbot, Jim
1591	McDougle, Buck	1844	Teague, Earl
561	McFadden, Arden	1931	Thode, Henry
39	McGee, Jimmie	49	Truan, Fritz
1748	McLaughlin, James 'Spec'	961	Valdez, Shorty
755	Nelson, Tim	1580	Vinas, Joe
1444	Oldenberg, John	777	Vincent, Marion
1575	Oliver, Buck	211	Wagner, Neil
52	Owsley, Cecil	1397	Wallace, James A.
1916	Padgett, Ray	254	Walls, Elmo
1542	Palmer, Johnny	126	Watkins, Ward
389	Parker, Rock	965	Westinghouse, Buddy
322	Patch, Jim	1785	Whatley, Cliff
1387	Pattee, Alan	566	Whitaker, Vern
324	Paul, Marvin	794	White, Woodrow
1849	Pogue, John	11	Whiteman, Hub
1799	Porter, Jack C.	650	Whiting, Bob
235	Pribble, Mike O.	1248	Wilkins, Don
441	Quirk, Frank	1533	Witty, R. L.

C.T.A. #	NAME	C.T.A. #	NAME
55	Williams, Carl	1490	Woods, Charlie
1725	Williams, Jake	1645	Wright, Jim
1465	Williams, Lee Roy	359	Yonnick, Buttons

Honorary Members OF C.T.A.

C.T.A. #	NAME	C.T.A. #	NAME
123	Abbey, Chairman	63	Dudley, Dorris
107	Aber, Lynn	50	Dunckon, Fred
82	Addington, John E.	17	Dunn, P. C.
105	Agee, John	303	Echols, Ed
32	Allred, Gov. James	291	Elliott, Bill
33	Ammons, Teller	109	Evans, Bill
64	Baird, Dr. Vernon	280	Falk, Ace
307	Barnes, H. M.	48	Faubion, W. L.
308	Bell, John H.	79	Faulk, Hamilton
99	Bell, W. M.	9	Fisher, Ham
285	Ben, Rodeo Tailor	127	Forest, R. W.
15	Black Foot Elks Lodge	286	Francisco, Bill
128	Bonelli, William G.	292	Freyer, Dick
4	Booth, Tom	72	Frock, Eldon
129	Booth, W. H.	71	Fuentez, Juan
296	Brady, Kathleen	119	Fugitt, Jack
295	Brady, Dr. Leo	275	Gibson, John L.
305	Brink, M. E. 'Bob'	35	Godshall, Jeanne
81	Brown, Arthur	102	Goode, Jim
56	Buchanan, R. B.	100	Govier, H. R.
93	Butterfield, Chas.	43	Haines, Willard
28	Call, Grant	25	Hamberger, Phil
108	Carr, Bill	58	Harris, Helen M.
74	Conklin, Roy	289	Harris, Robert S.
300	Cooper, Tex	276	Hartman, Genl.
8	Coze, Paul	37	Hatfield, George
34	Cullington, George	38	Hines, Cherry Hale
114	Cummings, Harrie B.	294	Hofmann, R. J.
201	Davis, Lillian	76	Hopkins, Ma
66	Deglin, Ted	77	Hopkins, Pa
110	Dickson, Dick	12	Hopp, Pete
54	Dillon, Roy M.	22	Howe, J. C. 'Red
138	Doheny, Tim	307	Hughes, Chas. J.

C.T.A. #	NAME		C.T.A. #	NAME
36	Hughes, Joe D.	304	Newell, Pauline B	
272	Hutchins, Barbara K.	117	Newell, Walter L.	
14	Jernigan, Buck	83	Newhagen, Frank E.	
98	John, V. M.	300	O'Brien, Eddie	
39	Johnson, E. H.	59	Oltorf, Jack G.	
57	Johnson, Everett	60	Oltorf, Mrs. Jack G.	
40	Johnson, Mervin L.	18	Parker, Gus	
61	Jones, R. T. 'Bob'	19	Paul, Clyde	
73	Justin, H. J. & Sons	42	Perkins, Arthur	
137	Kellenberger, A. G.	13	Potter, Lyle Van	
10	Kilpatrick, Col. John Reed	139	Porter, Pat	
101	Kimmel, H. R.	2	Randolph, Floyd	
21	Kriendler, Jack	41	Rich, Cap	
299	Kriz, Joe	103	Riley, Frank	
1	La Farge, Wanden	7	Riling, Raymond	
69	Lahman, Jerry	290	Robison, Beanie	
96	Lane, Casper 'Cappy'	283	Rogers, Roy	
288	Lee, Albert	122	Root, Helene	
45	Lee, W. A.	120	Root, Lloyd L.	
293	Leonard, R. J.	121	Root, Louise	
51	Lewis, H. G.	999	Ross, Butch	
89	Lewis, K. W.	297	Rowett, Wm.	
104	Lockhart, Sonny	620	Ryley, Frank	
68	Lovejoy, Eiland	88	Sandefer, G. B.	
273	McDowell, Paul	86	Sands, George	
281	McCumber, W. R.	23	Sartwelle, J. W.	
46	McClure, Marion B.	67	Saunders, R. L.	
681	McEuen, Ed	62	Sawyers, Ed	
84	Majors, Cliff	87	Sawyers, Pauline	
502	Manning, Art	47	Schooley, Herschel	
116	Mansfield, Monte Jr.	130	Scoma, Joe	
80	Martens, Jack	131	Scully, J. M.	
3	Martin Prosser	271	Searls, R. D.	
85	Massey, Gus	135	Shepherd, V. H.	
125	Mason, Fred L.	111	Sherman, Harry	
27	Mathews, E. R.	646	Shinn, Chas. A.	
112	Meigs, Henry	278	Smith, Governor	
3	Michelson, Dr. Henry E.	302	Sommers, Gerald E.	
126	Miller, Arthur C.	16	Steelman, Hosea E.	
29	Miller, Dan	11	Stewart, Mrs. Jacqueline A.	
95	Moore, Frank	24	Strake, George W.	
134	Motschall, Katherine	49	Talbott, Ray H.	
136	Murrells, Dan T.	118	Templeton, M. L.	

C.T.A. #	NAME		C.T.A. #	NAME	
75	Thomas, Pat		31	Watson, Bill	
44	Traveller, Gil		277	Webb, Mg. J. R.	
292	Tunis, John W.		53	Wheelis, Penn	
115	Turk, Dad		106	White, Edwin R.	
306	Tyrell, Ace		6	Whiteman, Paul	
20	Tussing, L. Benton		274	Williams, Thomas O.	
281	Ungerer, Ray		78	Witham, Wayne	
284	Ward, Fay		55	Wolf, Ralph R.	
279	Warden, General		91	Wrigley, Phillip K.	
92	Warren, W. B.		90	Yoder, Phil	

DELINQUENT MEMBERS OF THE C.T.A.

C.T.A. #	NAME	YEAR	C.T.A. #	NAME	YEAR
1259	Abbott, G. S.	1944	613	Beach, Kenneth	1942,43,44
532	Abold, Ernest R.	1942,43,44	1318	Bearrow, Mark	1942,43,44
641	Adams, Mrs. Alice	1942,43,44	1731	Beeson, Dummy	1943.44
1992	Aepeehwish, Ellis	1944	1981	Bernard, Tim	1944
814	Albrecht, Chas.	1942,43,44	1524	Benedictis, Tony	1942.43.44
1858	Allen, James Robt.	1943,44	9	Bennett, Ralph	1944
1862	Allen, James Lee	1943,44	1677	Bentley, Bill	1942,43,44
1588	Alston, Tommie	1943,44	1564	Bentley, Bub	1944
2019	Anderson, Earl	1944	1534	Bentley, Don	1944
1666	Anderson, Elmond	1942,43,44	1540	Bergevin, Damase	1942,43,44
973	Andes, Chester	1942,43,44	1988	Bias, Chet	1944
1354	Andrews, Forrest	1944	365	Binns, H. D.	1943,44
855	Arnold, Joe	1943,44	1180	Bjornstod, Bill	1943,44
1262	Asbeck, Robert	1943,44	1636	Black, Alex	1942,43,44
361	Askins, Bob	1942,43,44	1356	Blackstone, Faye	1942,43,44
1699	Bandy, Don	1942,43,44	618	Blackstone, Vick	1943,44
138	Barnett, Johnny	1944	279	Boden, Bob	1944
802	Barron, Curtis	1942,43,44	1140	Bolton, Tack	1943,44
1945	Bartlett, Bill	1944	1942	Bond, Buck	1944
1921	Bartlett, Bronk	1943,44	1880	Booh, Al	1943.44
1994	Barton, Buzz	1944	1137	Bowman, Skeet	1944
205	Bartram, Dutch	1942.43.44	1586	Boyt, Cecil	1944
182	Bartrum, John	1942,43,44	1883	Bradford, Buck	1943.44
631	Bassett, Lew	1942,43,44	78	Bradley, Buzz	1944
809	Bates, Chris S.	1943,44	1914	Bragg, Nancy	1944
1253	Batey, Dub	1943,44	1168	Britt, Victor	1942,43,44
1767	Battistoni, Willie	1943,44	1517	Brock, James	1942,43,44

1944 CTA Rulebook & Membership

C.T.A. #	NAME	YEAR	C.T.A. #	NAME	YEAR
1418	Brooks, Bobby	1943,44	1272	Collier, A. J.	1942,43,44
1051	Brown, Clyde	1943,44	1522	Collier, Dick	1942,43,44
1777	Brown, Johnny	1943,44	435	Collins, Louie	1942,43,44
700	Brown, Van	1942,43,44	1935	Compton, Cy	1942,43,44
1913	Bryan, Russell	1942,43,44	270	Connley, Lawrence	1943,44
462	Buffington, E. E.	1942,43,44	1713	Cook, Homer	1943,44
1911	Burge, Emma	1943,44	201	Cooper, Felix	1943,44
1036	Burneet, JQ. T.	1942,43,44	503	Corbin, Goldie	1943,44
1593	Burns, Houston	1942,43,44	1370	Cosper, Geo.	1944
1006	Butler, Archie	1943,44	1615	Cotton, George	1942,43,44
527	Butner, Goldie	1942,43,44	1964	Couch, Jack	1944
1978	Byrd, Steve	1944	1375	Cox, G. W.	1943,44
1470	Calder, Jimmie	1942,43,44	1814	Cox, J. F.	1943,44
1837	Callahan, Bill	1943,44	1046	Cox, Leo	1942,43,44
574	Cameron, Allen	1943,44	1872	Cox, Lloyd	1943,44
1172	Campbell, Clay	1943,44	816	Cox, Roy	1942,43,44
80	Campbell, Dave	1943,44	1752	Cox, Victor	1943,44
1416	Caraway, R. B.	1943,44	508	Crainer, Allen	1943,44
1878	Carlin, Eugene V.	1943,44	1254	Crainer, Bill	1944
941	Carrell, Roy	1942,43,44	118	Cremer, Leo	1944
274	Cash, Guy	1942,43,44	1546	Crawley, Bill	1943,44
1683	Castro, Vic	1943,44	599	Creed, Gene	1942,43,44
1806	Cathemer, Tom	1943,44	127	Creed, Shorty	1942,43,44
1167	Chapman, Hugh	1943,44	159	Cutler, Wayne	1942,43,44
1505	Chism, Chas 'Smoky	1942,43,44	1034	Dalton, Jack	1942,43,44
1807	Christensen, Vic	1943,44	1689	Danley, Pete	1942,43,44
1991	Christensen, Whity	1944	1671	Darnell, Hank	1942,43,44
656	Clark, Bill	1942,43,44	1648	Eaade, Milton	1942,43,44
1987	Clark, Bobby	1944	1595	East, Tom Jr.	1943,44
2023	Clark, Gene	1944	181	Eaton, Bill	1943,44
1264	Clark, Lee	1944	834	Ebner, Adolph	1944
1241	Clary, Pat	1942,43,44	1773	Eddins, Add	1943.44
199	Clements, C. A.	1942,43,44	1672	Edmo, Hugh	1943,44
418	Clennon, Bart	1944	1809	Eilebrecht, Howard	1943,44
150	Clay, Willie	1943, 44	321	Elfic, John	1942,43,44
2006	Clinton, Bruce	1944	272	Elliot, Sie	1944
1331	Coats, Fred	1942,43,44	1686	Elmore, Ace	1942,43,44
1793	Cobb, Clarence	1943,44	1816	Ely, Marion	1943,44
1782	Cobb, Lee	1943,44	691	Emery, Ernest	1942,43,44
1207	Cochrane, Bill	1942,43,44	1950	Eskew, Jim	1944
1170	Colcord, Frank	1942,43,44	1864	Espy, H. C.	1943,44
1604	Coleman, Jimmy	1942,43,44	1320	Essap, Truman	1942,43,44
1367	Coleman, Tom	1944	248	Evans, Bud	1943,44

C.T.A. #	NAME	YEAR	C.T.A. #	NAME	YEAR
971	Holcomb, Millard	1942,43,44	366	Karstad, Leslie	1942,43,44
1567	Holmes, Joe	1942,43,44	1687	Keeline, Joe J. Jr.	1942,43,44
1696	Homan, Vance	1942,43,44	195	Kell, Jess	1942,43,44
147	Holton, Doc	1944	1062	Keller, Art	1942,43,44
1339	Hood, Lloyd	1942,43,44	136	Kelley, Cleve	1942,43,44
1100	Hope, G. W.	1943,44	1135	Kelley, Marvin Ross	1942,43,44
705	Holton, Doc	1944	1866	Kelley, Pat	1943,44
706	Hopkins, Drew	1942,43,44	1759	Kelly, Ross	1943,44
792	Hosley, Frank	1943,44	1293	Kelsey, Joe F.	1942,43,44
382	Horner, Tommy	1942,43,44	989	Kemp, Chuck	1943,44
96	Horton, Bill	1942,43,44	1720	Kendrick, E. M.	1942,43,44
882	House, George	1942,43,44	1188	Kenedy, Jack	1943,44
1688	Howard, V. L.	1942,43,44	1614	Kinnibrugh, Mack	1944
1361	Howell, Juanita	1944	1668	Kipp, Bill	1942,43,44
1177	Howard, Tex	1943,44	85	Kirchgraber, Frank	1942.43.44
940	Huckfeldt, Carl	1943,44	895	Kunz, Tommie	1942,43,44
1730	Hudgins, W. O.	1943,44	1173	Kutch, Hilton	1943,44
251	Hudson, Shorty	1944	1569	Ladman, Smoky	1943.44
1928	Hughes, Bill	1943,44	1876	Lane, H. L. Jr.	1944
996	Huff, Leo	1943,44	1846	Lane, Johnnie	1943,44
1562	Hunter, Roy	1942,43,44	1811	Larsen, Homer	1943,44
1624	Hutchinson, Geo. E	1942,43,44	980	Lawrence, W. B.	1942,43,44
164	Inks, Earl	1944	1665	Leavins, Ross	1943.44
1660	Irby, E. W. 'Lefty'	1942,43,44	1275	LeBleu, Dick	1944
1332	Irvine, Van	1944	336	Lee, Carl	1942.43.44
1870	Irwin, Slim	1943,44	1548	Lee, Joel	1942,43,44
1939	Jack, Cleo	1944	1613	Lemley, Lee	1942.43.44
709	Jackson, Harold	1944	768	Lewis, Pat	1942.43.44
1644	Jackson, Jack	1942,43,44	145	Lewis, Rose	1944
447	Jacobs, Len	1942,43,44	108	Lewis, Roy	1944
1854	Jaeneche, L. W.	1943,44	888	Lewis, Russell	1943,44
953	Jarnagin, Logan	1942,43,44	1700	Like, Jesse	1943,44
1781	Jeffrees, Weldon	1943,44	1757	Lilley, Bob J.	1944
1711	Jensen, Buck	1942,43,44	1913	Linderman, Bill	1944
1452	Johnson, Ben	1944	1121	Lingle, Floyd	1942.43.44
1934	Johnson, Buck	1944	1770	Livesay, L. W. Jr.	1943.44
407	Jones, Art	1944	1780	Livingston, Cal	1943,44
97	Jones, Charlie	1943,44	1755	Locke, Lloyd	1943,44
257	Jones, Eddie	1942,43,44	143	Lockett, Reese B.	1942,43,44
1705	Jones, Snooks	1943,44	194	Lohn, Sam	1944
1714	Jones, Tex	1943,44	1838	Lomax, Flavic	1943,44
1789	Kane, Joe	1943,44	14	Long, Hughie	1944
559	Karmon, W. (Blackie)	1943,44	744	Louks, Wayne	1942.43.44

C.T.A. #	NAMES	YEARS	C.T.A. #	NAME	YEARS
232	Lowry, Fred	1944	1594	Mullins, W. E.	1943,44
1948	Lucas, Billy	1944	239	Mundy, Irby	1943,44
719	Lyman, O. B.	1942,43,44	1718	Munroe, Butler	1943,44
184	Lyne, C. J.	1944	722	Murray, Bob	
1606	Mack, Gus	1942,43,44	1935	Myers, Virgil	1944
1478	Mahan, Abe	1943,44	311	McAdams, Hugh	1942,43,44
1193	Maher, Jim	1943,44	916	McCain, Archie	1942,43,44
1886	Markley, Bill	1944	1229	McCall, Curley	1942,43,44
1827	Marlow, Box	1943,44	1230	McCall, Thea	1942,43,44
1243	Marshall, Fouts	1943,44	1434	McCallum, Bryan	1944
1005	Marshall, Frank	1943,44	409	McCarty, Chet	1944
1118	Martin, Vic Reno	1943,44	1675	McConnell, Wally	1942,43,44
1724	Martin, Dutch	1943,44	1516	McCray, Mardell	1942,43,44
804	Martin, Roy	1942,43,44	918	McCray, Wiley	1944
151	Masterson, Harold	1944	85	McCrorey, Mickey	1944
2009	Mathis, Frank	1944	1760	McCuistion, Day	1943,44
120	Matthews, Roy	1944	148	McFall, Elmer	1944
1717	Mason, Buck	1943,44	1145	McElroy, Curtis	1942,43,44
303	Mavity, Ray	1942,43,44	1282	McElroy, Earl	1942,43,44
634	May, Buddy	1942,43,44	1611	McFarland, Otis	1942,43,44
360	May, Earl	1943.44	1600	McKinley, Jack	1942,43,44
1704	Mayfield, Buck	1942,43,44	1895	McLeran, Stub	1943,44
1026	Meese, Ted	1943.44	1740	McMahan, Jack	1943,44
1384	Merck, John	1943,44	1802	Newman, Pete	1943.44
1778	Meyer, John	1943,44	951	Newton, Slim	1942,43,44
1162	Meyer, Leonard	1942,43,44	1719	Nilsson, Gene	1943,44
1949	Miller, Wayne	1944	1344	Nimmo, Dave	1942,43,44
1841	Millet, G. A.	1943,44	1449	Nix, Buck	1942,43,44
621	Minotto, Sissy	1943,44	419	Nuckols, Reno Tx Kid	1944
1639	Minter, Cullen	1942,43,44	1884	Nunis, Sam	1943,44
1771	Mitcham, Brother	1943,44	1526	O'Conner, Chuck	1942,43,44
1657	Mitchell, Bill	1943,44	1754	Newt, O'Keefe	1943,44
781	Mitchell, Leonard	1942,43,44	910	Olsen, Bob	1944
1640	Moller, Wharton	1942,43,44	1305	Olsen, Fay	1942,43,44
1836	Monroe, Floyd	1944	925	Olsen, Dutch	1943,44
1625	Moran, Smokey	1942,43,44	1887	O'Neil, Jimmie	1942,44
1891	Moreaux, Shannon	1943,44	240	Osborne, Ed	1942,43,44
864	Morris, Al	1943,44	153	Ostrander, Dean	1944
1365	Morris, Logue	1942,43,44	897	Owens, Herb	1942,43,44
1231	Morris, Chip	1942.43.44	950	Padia, Walter	1942,43,44
1782	Morris, Rex	1943.44	1632	Parker, Luther (Tex)	1942,43,44
824	Morris, Rufus	1942,43,44	908	Parker, Pat	1944
1508	Moser, Roy	1944	1574	Parker, Tommy	1942,43,44

C.T.A. #	NAME	YEAR	C.T.A. #	NAME	YEAR
1623	Parshall, Alvin	1942,43,44	106	Rooney, Lonnie	1942,43,44
1741	Parsons, Jay	1843,44	117	Ross, Gene	1944
1018	Patterson, Geo.	1943,44	250	Ross, Herschel	1944
1788	Pattit, Wesley	1943,44	1037	Rose, Roy	1943,44
1389	Pearson, Frank	1944	1622	Rossi, Rex	1942,43,44
1676	Perry, Everett	1942,43,44	1461	Rumsey, Jack	1942,43,44
892	Peters, Ed	1942,43,44	1198	Russell, Blackie	1943,44
154	Peters, Floyd	1944	1715	Russell, Joe	1943,44
1129	Penick, John	1943,44	1077	Rutledge, Shorty	1943.44
550	Person, Norman	1943,44	1336	Ryan, Pat	1942,43,44
1061	Pettigrew, A. J.	1944	1409	Ryan, Windy	1942,43,44
1429	Pilchner, Bud	1942,43,44	356	Sanborn, Les	1944
923	Posey, Hugh	1943,44	911	Santos, Leonard	1942,43,44
1609	Poore, Dan	1944	1469	Saul, Jack	1942,43,44
858	Poston, James	1942,43,44	1583	Savage, Henry	1942.43.44
1579	Price, Robert	1942,43,44	1132	Saylors, Leon C.	1942,43,44
1573	Pruitt, Geter	1942,43,44	166	Schneider, Johnie	1942,43,44
1554	Pryor, Ray	1942,43,44	1654	Schultz, Ed	1942,43,44
393	Quait, Jack	1942,43,44	1908	Schutz, Larry	1944
1618	Quirk, Louis	1942,43,44	1924	Schwerd, Bill	1943,44
1619	Quick, Rabbit	1942,43,44	1769	Scott, J. R.	1943,44
1494	Ragan, Earl	1942,43,44	893	Seago, Roscoe	1942,43,44
1790	Ramsay, John	1944	1178	Seely, Geo.	1942,43,44
1175	Ramsay, V. H.	1942,43,44	1766	Sessions, Sam	1944
1427	Randall, Elmer	1942,43,44	1747	Shaffer, Jack	1943,44
1520	Ray, Al	1942,43,44	1922	Shanhan, Rocky	1943,44
1760	Ray, Durwood	1943,44	995	Shaw, Jack	1943,44
1358	Ray, Guy	1942,43,44	1563	Sharrah, Ira	1942,43,44
784	Reavis, Jeff	1943,44	64	Shepard, Carl	1942,43,44
1826	Regan, Johnny	1943,44	1885	Sherman, Joseph	1944
1697	Retzel, Frank	1942,43,44	1904	Shupp, Bob	1943,44
555	Rice, Ole	1942,43,44	1917	Simcox, S. W.	1943,44
1933	Rich, Marianne	1943,44	747	Sisty, Alice	1942,43,44
1804	Richardson, Bill	1943,44	701	Skipworth, Jack	1944
1515	Richardson, W. W.	1943,44	1503	Sky Eagle, George	1942,43,44
1489	Ridley, Harold	1942,43,44	1504	Sky Eagle, Sunbeam	1942,43,44
1382	Rigby, Jim E.	1942,43,44	1743	Slade, Don	1943,44
1852	Roberts, Dick	1942,43	137	Slappert, Dick	1943,44
803	Robinson, Andy	1942,43,44	647	Slosum, Rex	1942,43,44
1845	Robinson, Ralph	1943,44	1666	Smith, Dugin	1942,43,44
968	Robellard, Jim	1942,43,44	427	Smith, Eddie	1942,43,44
1232	Rogers, Brahma	1942,43,44	1021	Smith, Lee	1942,43,44
810	Romans, Mason	1942,43,44	1064	Smith, Tommy	1942,43,44

C.T.A. #	NAME	YEAR	C.T.A. #	NAME	YEAR
1295	Smith, Johnny	1943,44	2003	Van, Alice	1944
449	Snively, Jim	1944	206	Vincent, Merle	1942,43,44
140	Somerville, Stoney	1943	1647	Vines, Willard	1942,43,44
2000	Sorenson, Doc	1944	285	Wade, Jack	1944
345	Soward, Ace	1944	1726	Wafford, Earl	1944
1400	Spence, Bud	1943,44	340	Walden, Bob	1942,43,44
1742	Spurling, Jack	1943,44	1651	Wall, Barney	1942,43,44
684	Staley, Jim	1942,43,44	1998	Ward, Billy	1944
378	Stanton, Orville	1942,44	399	Ward, Geo.	1942,43,44
1559	Stetson, Marshall	1943,44	750	Warren, Jack	1942,43,44
1919	Stewart, Bandy	1943,44	748	Warren, Oscar	1943,44
30	Stillings, Floyd	1943,44	365	Warren, Ralph	1942,43,44
436	Stockwell, Ralph	1942,43,44	1705	Watson, Bill	1942,43,44
587	Stone, Dale	1944	1681	Weasa, Mel	1943,44
326	Stonehouse, Mel	1942,43,44	808	Webb, Byron	1942,43,44
995	Stroh, Ray	1942,43,44	805	Webb, Pearson	1942,43,44
1701	Stuart, Buck	1942,43,44	1555	Weinberg, Jules	1942,43,44
431	Stuart, Sam	1943,44	12	Welch, Joe	1944
194	Stuart, Walt	1942,43,44	1897	Wells, Jack	1943,44
1460	Swanson, Bud	1942,43,44	1368	Wells, Young	1943,44
1148	Taylor, Babb	1942,43,44	1925	West, Bob	1943,44
1093	Taylor, Buck	1942,43,44	1472	West, Earl	1942,43,44
477	Taylor, Fritz	1943,44	1123	White, Homer	1942,43,44
1448	Taylor, Harvey	1942,43,44	974	Whitehorn, John	1943,44
829	Taylor, Pete	1942,43,44	576	Whiteman, Joe	1942,43,44
162	Taylor, Tom	1942,43,44	394	Whitelow, Charlie	1944
1933	Te Poel, Lee E	1944	1758	Wharton, Ray	1944
1951	Thompson, J. T.	1944	1305	Wilcox, Virginia	1942,43,44
1016	Thorn, Leo	1942,43,44	450	Wilder, Don	1943,44
1557	Thorne, Joel	1942,43,44	463	Wilkinson, Bob	1943,44
1292	Thrasher, Matt	1942,43,44	262	Wilkinson, Billy	1944
1655	Tiger, Lucian	1942,43,44	224	Wilkinson, Jimmie	1944
425	Todd, Homer	1942,43,44	438	Williams, Harry	1943,44
982	Towns, Bill	1942,43,44	585	Williams, Johnny	1943,44
678	Travis, Pete	1942,43,44	1560	Williams, Robert	1942,43,44
1733	Travis, Tony	1943,44	1372	Williams, Tommy	1942,43,44
545	Traylor, John W.	1943,44	1709	Willis, Barney	1943,44
1063	Tully, Gerald	1942,43,44	1296	Wills, Russell	1942,43,44
1630	Twiford, Harold	1942,43,44	1589	Wilson, Mary	1942,43,44
1636	Umberger, Jim	1943,44	590	Wilson, Tommy	1943,44
1190	Utterback, Chick	1943,44	662	Winegar, Phil	1942,43,44
1433	Vail, Sidney H.	1942,43,44	1761	Wise, Delbert	1943,44
1745	Valania, Jo	1943,44	1067	Wolf, Buster	1942,43,44

C.T.A. #	NAME	YEAR
1765	Womack, Carl	1943,44
1856	Womack, Shorty	1943,44
1260	Wood, Ira	1942,43,44
1558	Wood, T. Brooks	1942,43,44
1316	Woodrow, Otho	1944
1861	Word, Bill	1943,44
1268	Wortman, Irvin	1944
680	Wortham, Tom	1944
413	Wyatt, Buck	1943,44
1926	Wyatt, Ray	1943,44
983	Wyrick, Bennie	1942,43,44
1138	Young, Tommy	1942,43,44
1621	Yturria, Frankie	1942,43,44
1545	Zufelt, Ralph	1942,43,44
58	Zumwalt, Oral	1942,43,44 #150

This completes the 1944 CTA Articles, By-Laws and Rules Book, plus Membership Lists.

It is known, some cowboys joined after this book was printed before it became the Rodeo Cowboys Association, March 15, 1945, that did not get printed in one of their three books.

Rodeo Association of America
Rules of Rodeo

The following rules governing the contests sanctioned and approved by the Rodeo Association of America are submitted for the information and guidance of the member organizations.

It is fully appreciated by the directors of the association that, owing to arena conditions and a variance in state laws and public sentiment relative to rodeo contests, the rules must be more or less flexible, and in drafting these rules the directors have attempted to regulate only such matters as are common to all contests regardless of where held or under what local restrictions.

The rules may be extended as the member organizations find necessary, but in no case should they be altered so as to make less difficult the successful participation in the various sanctioned contests. In this, the association must depend on the honor and good judgment of the local managers.

Whenever a member rodeo makes variations from the standard rules, then these variations must be printed in the prize list of that member rodeo.

JUDGES

Each member contest may name two or more persons to be known as RAA judges. They should be competent.

A list of all RAA judges will be printed from time to time in the RAA bulletin. Any member rodeo, any contestant or any person directly interested in rodeos may protest and ask that any RAA judge be disqualified by filing with the RAA secretary a written statement giving the reasons why said RAA judge should be disqualified. The protest will then be sent by the RAA secretary to the member rodeo of the RAA which appointed said judge, and then that member may immediately file an answer to the protest and the answer will then be mailed to each RAA director, and they will vote as to whether or not said person's name should be removed from said RAA judges list and the directors' vote will be final.

Each member rodeo must print on its prize list the names of the persons it expects to use as judges, taken from RAA list of judges. In case a judge listed in the prize list is not available for any cause whatsoever, then the member rodeo may select any other competent judge, either from the RAA list or not and said member to be the judge as to the person's competency.

PRIZE LIST

Prize lists of member contestants are to be printed, distributed and on file in the office of the RAA at least 60 days before the date of each contest, and amount of purses and entrance fee in each RAA event printed in the RAA bulletin at least 30 days prior to the contest.

ENTRY FEES

Entry fees are to be added to all purses in all RAA contests. (Note: In case any member desires to use any variation in the rules it must be plainly printed in the prize list.)

GENERAL REMARKS

The directors of the association particularly wish to impress on all member organizations the necessity for extreme care in the selection of judges, timers and all other officials called on to serve in contests recognized by the association and in which championships will be awarded by the association. These officials should be required to familiarize themselves with all rules governing the contests. The selection of competent officials will insure satisfaction to the contestants and save the local management and association annoyance and embarrassment.

The managers of member organizations should forward promptly to the secretary of the association the names and addresses of the successful contestants and the position awarded them, and also the time, if it is a contest in which time is the determining factor. Should disputes occur or protests be filed, written statements should be requested from judges and others interested, these to be submitted to the association for final decision.

The member organizations are urged to use the best quality livestock available for these contests and to conduct such contests with uniformity and fairness, and furthermore, they should attempt to keep the field or arena free at all times from spectators, non-participating contestants and livestock, to the end that there will be no dissatisfaction on the part of the contestants.

GENERAL RULES
of the
RODEO ASSOCIATION OF AMERICA

1. The management reserves the right to reject the entry of any contestant who has violated the general rules, who has been dishonest in the competitions, or who has proven to be undesirable in any recognized rodeo contest.
2. All contestants are required to read the rules carefully, particularly those relating to the contests or events in which they enter. Failure to understand rules will not be accepted as an excuse.
3. The managers assume no responsibility or liability for injury or damage to the person, property, or stock of any owner, contestant, or assistant. Each participant, by the act of his entry, waives all claims against the management for injuries he or his property, may sustain.
4. The timers, judges, and all other officials shall be appointed by the management and their decision will be final in all matters relating to the contest in which they are called to officiate.

RAA Rules of Rodeo   **Page 297**

5. Contestant should be at place indicated by management when drawing of places and horses are held. If they are not present, either in person or by representative, the management will name someone to draw for them and contestants must accept the selection. Numbers will be furnished by the management to all contestants and numbers must be displayed so as to be visible to spectators and judges.
6. Contestants must be on hand to answer call of arena director and must comply with all other rules of the management of each particular contest or exhibition held under the auspices of the Rodeo Association of America. When, in the opinion of the arena director, sufficient numbers of contestants are present for an event, there will be no delay because other contestants are not present.
7. Substitutes will not be permitted in any event or contest.
8. Requests for withdrawal from any event or contest and the return of entrance fee will be passed on by the management and such requests will not be considered (except in case of injury to contestant) unless made at least one day in advance.
9. The management may withdraw any contestant's name and entry, debar him from any or all events, and withhold any money due him, for violation of any of the governing rules or rules of the judges, or for any of the following offenses:

    Refusing to contest on animal drawn by or selected for him
    Being under the influence of liquor
    Rowdyism
    Mistreatment of stock
    Altercation with judges or officials
    Failure to give assistance when requested to do so by arena director, or for any other reason deemed sufficient by the management. (The management wishes especially to announce to all contestants that any attempt to "cheat" the judges, the rulers, or the stock may result in the contestant being disqualified and barred from further participation in any or all of the events held under the auspices of the Rodeo Association of America.)

10. All contestants must participate on call of the management.
11. All entry fees must be paid in advance. Contestants should ask for a receipt signed by the cashier, and should obtain their number when entry is made. Name must be signed in full and correct post office address given.
12. Should any contestant hereafter fail to immediately meet any financial obligation to a member, the fact shall at once be reported

to the secretary of this association, who shall immediately advise all members thereof, and the contestant shall be barred by said members from participating in any member rodeo until, after compliance with his obligation, the board of directors of this association shall have restored to him the right to contest.

13. The purpose of the Rodeo Association of America being to protect contestants equally with managements, from failure to pay prize money when won on conditions advertised, or to meet obligations to association judges, will cause the suspension of the member so offending; restoration to good standing shall lie in the discretion of the board of directors of the Rodeo Association of America after proof that the delinquent member has fully complied with its obligation. In case of dispute of fact in the above particulars, the matter will be referred to the board of directors, which will hear same on notice to parties interested.

Contestant is privileged, if he so desires, to see the records of all contestants in any event in which he takes part at the end of each day's contest, provided that said request be made at a time convenient to the clerk and when the records are available.

BRONC RIDING

Riders and horses for each day will be selected by management; horses to be furnished by management and riders will draw for mounts. If rider draws a horse he has once ridden during this contest, he must draw again. Contestant must ride as often, and on any horse, as judges deem necessary to determine winner. Riding to be done with plain halter, ONE rein and saddle, all of which will be furnished by the management. Saddles to be recognized and accepted association 14 ½ to 15 inch tree made and rigged on the Hamley design. When new saddles are bought they shall be 15 inch tree. Rein to be three or four-strand braided grass or cotton rope and not to exceed one inch in diameter, without tape and knots and must not be wrapped around hand. One arm free. Riders must not change hands on rein and rein hand must show daylight above horse's neck as rider leaves chute. Riding rein and hand must be on same side. Horses to be saddled in chute or arena as management may direct. Rider may cinch own saddle or examine same to determine if satisfactory. The matter of re-rides will be decided by the judges. After the horse leaves the starting place, everything the rider does will be counted for or against him.

be allowed each rider from time horse leaves the chute or snubbing post before signal is given by timer. Ride is completed when signal is given.

Any of the following offenses will disqualify a rider:
        Cheating in any manner
        Being bucked off

Changing hands on rein
Wrapping rein around hand
Pulling leather
Losing stirrup
Not being ready to ride when called
Use of any substance or preparation on any part of rider's clothing or on any part of his equipment; riding otherwise than with straight rein from halter ring to rider; riding with locked rowels, or rowels that will lock on spurs. (The judges will examine clothing, saddle, rein, and spurs and exception will be made if local rules make it necessary the covering of spur rowels.)

JUDGING BRONC RIDING

It is obvious that in awarding the world's championship in the bronc riding, the method of judging should be uniform, and while each member organization may prepare its own judge's sheet or chart, it is necessary that the following method be adopted:

Name and number of rider and name and number of horses;
Horse and rider rated separately on basis of 100 per cent;
Percentage of both horse and rider to be added, thus indicating final rating; Chart or sheet should also show position from which the judge observed the ride, to wit: right, left, front, or rear; Chart should also allow ample space for notation of judge concerning reasons for rating, disqualification, or other remarks giving all necessary information regarding the particular ride; Cards should be signed by judges, dated and should be retained by management for further reference.

STEER WRESTLING OR BULLDOGGING

Arena conditions will determine start and deadline rules; penalties for violations of these rules are matters for local determination.

There shall be three timers, a deadline referee, a field judge, and as many other officials as the local management find necessary.

Animals used for this contest should be closely inspected and objectionable ones eliminated.

Contestants will be disqualified if he attempts to, in any way, tamper with steers or chutes. Only one hazer allowed. Contestant must furnish own hazer and horses.

After steer crosses deadline he belongs to wrestler regardless of what happens. After catching steer, wrestler must bring it to a stop and twist it down. If steer is accidently knocked down or thrown down before being brought to a stop, or is thrown by wrestler putting animal's horns into ground, it must be let up on all four feet and then thrown. Steer will be considered down only when it is lying flat on its side, all four feet out and head straight. The fairness of catch and throw will be left to the judges and their decision will be final.

Hazer must retire from field as soon as wrestler catches his steer and must not render any assistance to contestant while contestant is working with steer. Failure to observe this rule will impose penalty on contestant.

There will be a time limit of two minutes on this contest. If wrestler has not caught and thrown his steer in two minutes he will be retire from arena on signal and be given no time.

STEER DECORATING

Arena conditions will determine start and deadline rules; penalties for violations of these rules are matters for local determination.

There shall be three timers, a deadline referee, a field judge, and as many other officials as the local management finds necessary. Animals used for this contest should be closely inspected and objectionable ones eliminated. Contestant will be disqualified if he attempts to, in any way, tamper with steers or chutes. Only one hazer allowed. Contestant must furnish own hazer and horses. After steer crosses deadline he belongs to decorator regardless of what happens. The decorator will leap from his horse to the head of the steer and then place a rubber band around nose of steer or band of ribbon on horn, according to the means of decorating adopted by the local management. If the decorator leaps and misses steer he will be allowed to use the hazer's horse to continue. Time limit one minute. Breaking of rubber bands or shortening of ribbons will disqualify contestant.

The steer must be on all four feet when decorated.

CALF ROPING

There shall be three timekeepers, a tie or field judge, a deadline referee and as many other officials as the local management finds necessary. Arena conditions will determine start and deadline rules should be imposed as local conditions warrant, but such penalties should be sufficiently drastic to prevent deliberate infractions that bring advantage to contestant. Animals used for this event should be inspected and objectionable ones eliminated. After calf crosses deadline he belongs to contestant (roper) regardless of what happens.

CATCH AS CATCH CAN

Two loops will be permitted and should he miss with both he must return and no time shall be allowed. Roping calf without releasing loop from hand is not permitted.

Rope must be on calf when roper gets hand on calf.

Contestant must adjust rope and reins in a manner that will prevent horse from dragging calf. Contestant must receive no assistance of any kind from the outside. If horse drags calf, field judge may stop horse and any penalty for such dragging will be a matter of local determination.

When a roper busts a calf intentionally in the opinion of the judges, the roper is disqualified.

Rope may be dallied or tied hard and fast — either is permissible. Contestant must dismount, go down rope and throw calf with hands and cross and tie any three feet. If calf is down when roper reaches it, the calf must be let up to his feet and thrown by hand. The tie must hold until passed on by the judge and roper must not touch calf after giving finish signal until after judge has completed his examination. If tie comes loose or calf gets to his feet before the tie has been ruled a fair one, the roper will be marked no time on calf. Judge should remove loop and turn calf over.

SINGLE STEER TYING

There shall be three timers, a deadline referee, and a tie or field judge, and as many other officials as the local management finds necessary. Animals for this contest should be carefully inspected and objectionable ones eliminated.

To be a qualified catch, rope must be on steer and tied to saddle, when roper starts to tie. Roping steer, without turning loose the loop, to be considered no catch. If foul catch is made, second rope may be used, but the rope must be released from either saddle or steer. (Note: Do not confuse this change and put it into the dally steer roping contest rules. It belongs to tying contests only - not dally roping.)

Steers to be given deadline start in accordance with arena conditions, the length of the start to be determined by local management. Contestants must furnish own horses and can receive no assistance of any character from the outside. Two ropes may be used. Steer must be roped around horns, over head or half head, or around neck, and loop may include one front foot. If steer is caught in a manner other than the one described above roper must not attempt to throw steer; if he does attempt to throw steer he will be signaled to withdraw. (The reason for this foul catch rule should be apparent to all ropers – it is to keep down criticism and opposition to this contest.) If foul catch is made, second rope may be used, but first rope must be released from saddle. Steer must be thrown and three feet crossed and tied. After roper signals a completed tie, he will bring his horse back toward steer so as to give ample slack to rope while judge is examining tie. Roper cannot touch steer after once giving finish signal. Judge will determine tie and his decision is final. If steer gets up after roper has signaled and before tie has been ruled a fair one, no time will be allowed on that steer. Penalties may be imposed as local management sees fit. It two or more ropers use same horse, contestants should make that fact known when entering so that management may arrange places that will give each roper a fair chance.

SINGLE DALLY STEER ROPING

There shall be three timekeepers, a tie or field judge, a deadline referee, and as many other officials as the local management finds necessary.

Arena conditions will determine start and deadline rules should be imposed as local conditions warrant, but such penalties should be sufficiently drastic to prevent deliberate infractions that might bring advantage to contestant. Animals used for this event should be inspected and objectionable ones eliminated.

Each contestant will be allowed one throw and on failure to catch must retire immediately from arena. Roper must dally to stop steer. No tied ropes allowed.

Steer belongs to roper after he crosses deadline regardless of what happens. Steer to be roped by head or horns or head and one horn. Five seconds fine for head or horns and one front foot. All other catches disqualify.

Time to be taken when horse has been brought to a stop facing steer with rope tight. If steer is handled roughly at any time, the contestant will be disqualified if in the opinion of the field judges he has intentionally done so. Any question as to catch in this contest will be decided by the judges.

DALLY TEAM ROPING

Arena conditions will determine start and deadline rules; penalties for violations of these rules are matter for local determination.

There shall be three timers, a deadline referee, a field judge, and as many other officials as the local management finds necessary.

Each contestant will be allowed to carry but one rope. Each team allowed four throws in all. Roper roping steer without turning loose the loop will be considered no catch.

Steer belongs to roper after he crosses deadline regardless of what happens. Ropers must dally to stop steer. No tied ropes allowed. Steer to be roped first by head or horns or head and one horn. Five seconds fine for head or horns and one front foot. All other catches disqualify. Steer to be roped by one or both hind feet. Allowing steer to back into loop not permitted. Straight time for two hind catches. Five seconds added to time for hind foot catch.

Steer to be stopped but not thrown. Time will be taken when steer is stopped, but horses facing steer in line with ropes tight. Steer must not be handled roughly at any time and ropers may be disqualified if in the opinion of the field judges they have intentionally done so. Any question as to catches in this contest will be decided by the judges.

TEAM TYING

Arena conditions will determine start and deadline rules; penalties for violations of these rules are matters for local management.

There are to be three timekeepers, a tie judge, a foul line judge and one starter. Steers will be given a deadline start in accordance with arena conditions, and when steer crosses deadline he is roper's steer regardless of what happens.

Team allowed only two loops at the lead and should they miss with both loops, team must retire from the arena and will receive no time; after steer is properly roped by the head, the other partner has two loops at steer's hind feet and should he miss with both loops, team will receive no time. If either roper ropes steer after judge's signal "No time", the team will be disqualified in all events for the rest of the contest.

One rope must first catch head, half head or horns of the animal and then the other roper must catch one or both hind feet. If the animal falls before the second rope is on the hind foot or feet, he must be permitted to regain his footing. Both ropes must be on steer when the tie is started. Steer must be tied by both hind legs below the hocks. Catch ropes will not be used in making the tie. Steer may be tripped, stretched, or tailed down. The roper will not be allowed to touch steer in any manner after signaling for time. Steer will be left tied down as long as deemed necessary by judges to ascertain if tie is complete. If steer gets loose before the judge passes on tie, team will be marked no time on that steer.

BULL AND STEER RIDING

Riders will be selected and stock for each day will be furnished by management. Riding may be done with loose rope and one hand, or rigging and one hand. Eight seconds will be allowed for ride before signal is given by timer.

Any of the following offenses will disqualify a rider:
- Cheating in any manner
- Being bucked off
- Not being ready to ride when called
- Touching animal with free hand
- Use of any substance or preparation on any part of rider's clothing or equipment

BAREBACK HORSE RIDING

Riders will be selected and stock for each day will be furnished by the management. One hand rigging to be used. Riders may use their own rigging if rigging is not over ten inches in width at hand hold and not over six-inch "D" ring, or not a freak – judges to decide on all rigging. Horses to be numbered and drawn for. Riders who are knocked off at chute or when a horse falls out of a chute, the rider to be entitled to a re-ride. Eight seconds will be allowed for ride before signal is given by timer. Time to start when horse leaves chute.

Any of the following offenses will disqualify a rider:

>Cheating in any manner
>Not being ready to ride when called
>Touching animal with free hand
>Use of any substance or preparation on any part of rider's clothing or equipment.

WILD COW MILKING

(No RAA Points Awarded for This Event)

Arena conditions will determine start and deadline rules; penalties for violations of these rules are matters for local determination.

There shall be three timers, a deadline referee, a field judge, and as many other officials as the local management finds necessary. Animals used for this contest should be closely inspected and objectionable ones eliminated.

Each contestant will be allowed to carry but one rope and can make two throws and on failure to catch must retire immediately from arena. Ropers must dally to stop cow. Tied ropes not allowed. If rope is caught or tied or not free on saddle horn before or after roper dismounts to milk cow, he will be disqualified and marked no time. Cow milk belongs to roper after she crosses deadline regardless of what happens. Catch as catch can. If cow is handled roughly at any time, the roper will be disqualified if in the opinion of the field judges he has intentionally done so. All muggers or helpers must stay out of arena until called.

Roper allowed one helper to hold cow. Roper must pick helper. No other mugger allowed in arena while roper is contesting. Roper must receive bottle from field judges, milk cow, run to flag judge and pour out milk. No milk, no time. Roper roping cow without turning loose the loop will be considered no catch. The judges decision will be final in this contest. #70

The above rules were posted in the April 1940 issue of the Hoofs & Horns magazine, pages 18 and 19. #59

The following month in the May issue of Hoofs & Horns, under the R.A.A. Bulletin page 21 the following was reported:

"A new rule in Bronc Riding makes it necessary for the contestant to spur first jump out of the starting place.

In all roping events, in Steer Wrestling and in Steer Decorating, the clause was struck out of the former rule – 'Calf or Steer belongs to roper, wrestler or decorator after he crosses dead line, regardless of what happens.' Also a ten second penalty for beating or breaking the barrier was added in these events. It also was decided not to penalize the contestant if the animal is accidentally injured or for broken horn in these events, as had previously been the rule.

In Calf Roping, a clause was added as follows – 'untie man must not touch calf other than take rope off, until judge has passed on tie.' Also in this event the requirement that the judge should take the loop off and turn the calf over was eliminated.

In Bull Riding, the contestants may use a hand rope and the rider must spur one jump out of first three. It is also required that the riders must not use sharp spurs or lock rowels; same to be passed on by the management.

In Bareback Horse Riding, among other offenses that disqualify rider, riding with locked spur rowels or rowels that will lock, was added." [71]

Rule Changes:
At the January 23, 24, 25, 1941 RAA Convention in Salinas, California, the following rule changes were made:

Bull or Steer Riding Rule Changes:

Riders, and bulls or steers will be selected by management for each performance. All bulls or steers to be numbered. Stock will be drawn for by the judges. If rider draws a bull or steer he has once ridden at this contest, he must draw again. Head fighting bulls or steers having bad horns must be de-horned or kept out of drawing.

Riding to be done with one hand and loose rope, with or without handhold, or rigging and one hand. No knots or hitches to prevent rope from falling off bull or steer when rider leaves him. Rope must have bell, no bell, no marking. *Eight seconds will be allowed for ride before signal is given by Timer. Time to start when bull or steer leaves chute. Riders who are knocked off at chute or, if bull or steer falls, to be entitled to a re-ride at discretion of judges. Rider not to use sharp spurs, or locked rowels, and not to spur bull in the chute before gate opens.

Any of the following offenses will disqualify a rider:
    Cheating in any manner
    Being bucked off
    Not being ready to ride when called
    Touching animal with free hand or hat
    Using sharp spurs or locked rowels
    Spurring bull or steer in chutes

Judging Bull or Steer Riding

Bull and rider rated separately on basis of one hundred percent. Percentage of both animal and rider to be added, thus indicating final rating.

*(Note: Rule of 8 seconds applies only to the United States. In Canada it is 10 seconds.)

Additions to Saddle Bronc Riding Rules
>Following "horse must be spurred first jump out of starting place" add – "and rider must continue to spur throughout ride to satisfaction of judges."
>>Add to "Offenses that disqualify" – "Failing to spur throughout ride to the satisfaction of judges." #82

The Rule Changes at the January 1942 RAA Convention in Colorado Springs are as follows:

Saddle Bronc Riding:
>Add to first paragraph the following:
>"Where three judges are used, one judge to mark horse and two judges to mark the ride, the three figures only to be added to determine the total points."

Steer Wrestling:
>Add to the first paragraph:
>"Wrestler must catch steer from horse."

Single Steer Roping:
>Add the following:
>"If roper throws steer twice and fails to complete the tie he must retire from the arena."

Bareback Riding:
>Add to reasons for granting re-ride:
>"If horse fails to buck, re-ride to be granted at the discretion of the judges.
>Horse must be spurred in shoulders first jump out of chute."

The convention approved two new RAA events and the Association now recognizes and will award points in Saddle Bronc Riding, Bull or Steer Riding, Bareback Riding, Calf Roping, Steer Wrestling, Steer Decorating, Dally Single Steer Roping, Single Steer Tying, Dally Team Roping, and Team Tying.

General Rules:
"Numbers must be worn on contestant's back or arm as the case may be." [89]

Cowboys' Turtle Association Members in Service World War II

A.
Pfc Robert Allen, Jr.
Pvt Almus 'Slim' Atkinson

B
Pvt W. C. 'Bill' Barton
John Becker
Melvin Bell
Charles M. Bennett, SM2/c
Pvt Chas. M. Berry
Billy Black
Pvt Lee R. 'Doc' Blackstone
Earl Blevins
Capt J. N. 'Ike' Bohlender
Cpl Roy O. Boss
Pvt Glenn Bowen
John Boyhan
Pvt Chas. Bob Boyer
Leo Brannon
Cpl Fred Bristow
Pvt Joe Burrell

C
Eddie Cameron
Pvt Clay Carr USMC
Pvt Victor R. Castro
Pvt Bob Chambers
Max Chapas
Pvt Bo Chesson
John Chipman
Ken Clark
Willie Clay
Pvt Ed Coffey
Lt C. A. 'Chili' Cole
Cpl Homer W. Cook

D
Clarence Darnell
Arthur Davis

Paul C. Densmore
Cpl Sid Despain
Hoot Duarte
Pvt John T. Durham
Emmett Dwyer
Pvt Paul B. Dyer

E
C. L. 'Buck' Echols
Hugh T. Edmo
S/Sgt Harold Emery
Allen Ensley
Pvt J. W 'Junior' Eskew
Johnnie Evans

F
Pvt Ben Fancher
Cpl Frederick Faulkner
Pfc Tony Fenack
Amil Ferrario
Pvt Robert G. Fetters
Pfc Chas. Frank Finley USMC
Sgt Luther E. Finley
Pvt Chas. H. Fisher
Garner B. 'Bud' Fisher
Mike Fisher
Al Fletcher
Pvt George L 'Kid' Fletcher
Pvt Roy Lawson Fore
Pfc Rollin Forsyth
Dewey Fox
Gerald 'Jerry' Fredericks
Pvt Loren Fredericks

G
Marion Getzwiller
Red Goodspeed
Turk Greenough
Pvt Bernard Gregory

Eddie Guy

H
Pfc Frank 'Chuck' Haas
Pvt Joe L. Hale
Sgt Woodrow 'Sonny' Hancock
Baylis Harriss
Eugene Hamilton
Cecil Henley
Major L. Gene Hensley
Chester Hickman
Pvt William C. Hightower
Jack Hillyer
T/Sgt J. D. Holleyman
Jimmie Hollihan
Pfc Joe Holmes
Chet Howell
T/Sgt Lee R. Hurd

I
Bill Iler

J
Pvt James Harold Jackson
Lt Weldon Jeffress
Pvt Jerry Jerrel
Cecil Jones

K
S/Sgt Jimmy Kaaro
Wm. Blackie Karman
Pvt T. J. 'Jack' Kennedy
Sgt Wm. 'Pete' Kerscher
Buck Killough
Sgt Joe H. Klebba
Cpl James Koed
Ray Kohrs
Pvt Ed Kummerle

L
Ralph Lane
Chuck Lasswell
Oscar 'Jr' Lawrence S1/s
S/Sgt James Like

Lt Morris Lindsey
Pvt Cal Livingston
Joe Lomax
Pvt B. J. 'Swede' Londo
Pvt 'Hughie' J. Long
Pvt Wayne Louks
Shorty Lovelady
Pvt Harvey Luer

M
Tommy McCabe
Pfc Wallace McConnell
Cpl J. D. McCormick, USMC
Howard McCrory
Buck McDougle
Albert McEuen
Arden McFadden
J. M. McLaughlin S1/e
S/Sgt Frank Mariam
Grant Marshall
Pvt Lyndon E. Marshall
Pvt Roy T. Martin
Cpl Robert Matthews
Robert F. 'Bob' Melville
Carl Mendes
Pfc Frank Mendes
Sgt J. Dean Merritt
Pvt James K. 'Hyde' Merritt
Pvt Herb Meyers
Henry A. Michel
Sgt Geo. Miller
Pvt G. A. 'Red' Millet
James Rufus Morris
Eddie Mott

N
Sgt Tim Nelson
Jimmie Nesbitt

O
John Oldenburg
Buck Oliver

P

Johnny Palmer
Pfc Thomas D. Parish, USMC
Rock Parker
Alan Pattee
Marvin Paul
John Pogue
Jack Porter
Mike Pribble

Q

Frank Quirk
Louis Quirk
Rabbit Quirk

R

Vernon H. Ramsey
Pfc Monte 'Buddy' Reger
Lloyd 'Spud' Richardson
Lucky Robinson
Sgt Robert E. Rooker

S

Pvt Bill Schwerd, USMC
Robert 'Rocky' Shanan
Cpl C. J. Shellenberger
Cpl David Shellenberger
Pvt Don Slade
Pvt James H. Sloan
Glenn I. Soward
Cpl B. M. Sprott
Pvt Orville Stanton
George Swarthouse

T

Pfc James A. Talbot
Ed Taylor
John Taylor
Sgt Earl Teague
Henry Thode
Sgt Fritz G. Truan, USMC
Pfc Sonny Tureman
Junior Turner

U

V

Shorty Valdez
T/Cpl Willard Vines

W

Pvt Neil Wagner
James A. Wallace
Cpl George W. Ward
Lt James 'Ward' Watkins
Buddy Westinghouse
Don Wilkins
R. J. Witt
Herbert 'Hub' Whiteman
Cpl Cliff Whatley
Sgt Vernon Whitaker
S/Sgt Charley F. Woods

Y

Buttons Yonnick (John Segleski)
#148

FOOTNOTES

1. Cowboys' Turtle Association Boston Petition
2. Book: "Horseman: Brand of A Legend", by Hugh L. Bennett, published 1992.
3. Conversations with Bart Clennon
4. Article: "Slow But Sure" by Willard Porter, Western Horseman, Sept. 1986
5. ProRodeo Sports News, End of Year Edition, 12-24-2010
6. Notes by author, Clay Reynolds, author of book: "Hundred Years of Heroes"
7. Article: "First Cowboy Union Ever Organized", Denver Post, 1-18-1932 and 1- 20-1932 entitled: "Cowpokes For Union to Improve Standards"
8. Book: "American Rodeo, From Buffalo Bill to Big Business", by Kristine Fredriksson, Texas A & M Press, 1985
9. Fort Worth Star Telegram, 3-12-1932
10. Conversation with Paul Bond, 2-2011
11. Corral Column, The Billboard, 3-30-1935
12. Book: "World's Oldest Rodeo" by Danny Freeman, published by Prescott Frontier Days, Inc., 1988
13. Book: 1938 CTA Articles of Association, By-Laws, Rules & Membership
14. Petition signed by competitors at Chicago Stadium rodeo, 4 pages
15. Minutes of November 6, 1936 Cowboys' Turtle Association Meeting
16. Hoofs & Horns, February 1941 issue
17. Letter from Tex Sherman dated 12-14-1936
18. Letter from Tex Sherman dated 12-19-1936
19. Hoofs & Horns, December 1937
20. Book: ProRodeo Cowboys Association Media Guide, 2010
21. Tentative Agenda of the Rodeo Association of America Convention, Reno, NV, 1-29-1937
22. Postal Telegram from Herman Linder to Hugh Bennett, 1-30-1937
23. Hoofs & Horns, May 1937 issue
24. Western Union Telegram from Maxwell McNutt to Hugh Bennett 2-13-1937
25. Letter from Southwest Exposition & Fat Stock Show Secretary-Manager, John B. Davis, to Hugh Bennett, 2-22-1937

26. Letter from Maxwell McNutt to Hugh Bennett, 2-24-37
27. Minutes of Cowboys' Turtle Association Meeting, 3-11-1937
28. First C.T.A. Articles of Association, By-Laws & Rules by Maxwell McNutt
29. Letter from Harry Montgomery, Chief of Bureau, Associated Press, to Hugh Bennett, 4-27-1937
30. Hoofs & Horns, June 1937 issue
31. Hoofs & Horns, July 1937 issue
32. Hoofs & Horns, October, 1937 issue
33. Minutes of C.T.A. Meeting, Cheyenne, Wyoming, July 27, 1937
34. Minutes of C.T.A. Meeting, July 30, 1937
35. Minutes of C.T.A. Meeting, October 8, 1937
36. Minutes of C.T.A. Special Meeting, New York City, NY, October 22, 1937
37. Cowboys' Turtle Association Rules for 1938
38. Minutes of first C.T.A. Convention, Fort Worth, TX, March 10, 1938
39. Statement signed by Peggy Long for CowGirl Bronk Riders dated 3-16-1938
40. Minutes of C.T.A. Meeting, Ogden, Utah, July 24, 1938
41. Hoofs & Horns, November 1937 issue
42. Hoofs & Horns, December 1937 issue
43. Hoofs & Horns, January 1938 issue
44. Hoofs & Horns, February. 1938 issue
45. Website: Ancestry.com
46. Website: Newspaper Archive.com
47. Conversation with D'Lyla Kerscher Longo, 2-2011
48. Hoofs & Horns, May, 1938 issue
49. Hoofs & Horns, June, 1938 issue
50. Hoofs & Horns, August 1938 issue
51. Hoofs & Horns, September 1938 issue
52. Hoofs & Horns, October 1938 issue
53. Hoofs & Horns, November 1938 issue
54. Hoofs & Horns, December 1938 issue
55. Hoofs & Horns, January 1939 issue
56. RAA Bulletin, January, 1939 issue
57. Hoofs & Horns, May 1939 issue
58. Hoofs & Horns, June 1939 issue
59. Conversation with G. K. Lewallen, 2-2011
60. Hoofs & Horns, July 1939 issue
61. Hoofs & Horns, August 1939 issue
62. Hoofs & Horns, September 1939 issue
63. Hoofs & Horns, October 1939 issue

Footnotes

64. Book: "Who's Who in Rodeo" by Willard Porter, published by Powder River Book Company, Oklahoma City, for Rodeo Historical Society
65. Book: "Bumfuzzled" by R. Lewis Bowman, published 1995
66. Hoofs & Horns, May, 1950 issue
67. Hoofs & Horns, January 1940 issue
68. Hoofs & Horns, February 1940 issue
69. Hoofs & Horns, March 1940 issue
70. Hoofs & Horns, April 1940 issue
71. Hoofs & Horns, May 1940 issue
72. Letter: Ellensburg Rodeo Committee Secretary to Everett Bowman, 5-9-1940
73. Hoofs & Horns, July 1940 issue
74. Conversation with Cecil Jones, 2-2011
75. Hoofs & Horns, June 1940 issue
76. Hoofs & Horns, August 1940 issue
77. Desert Magazine, article "Lady with Hoofs and Horns" August, 1947
78. Hoofs & Horns, article "Ma Hopkins, a Legend....", March-April, 1978
79. Tucson Citizen, article "First Lady of Rodeo Is Dead at Age 85", 11-4-1964
   And article "Ma Hopkins: Rodeo won't soon forget her" 2-20-1980
80. Hoofs & Horns, September 1940 issue
81. Hoofs & Horns, December 1940 issue
82. Hoofs & Horns, March 1941 issue
83. Hoofs & Horns, June 1941 issue
84. Hoofs & Horns, July 1941 issue
85. Hoofs & Horns, December 1941 issue
86. Hoofs & Horns, January 1942 issue
87. Hoofs & Horns, February 1942 issue
88. Hoofs & Horns, January 1941 issue
89. Hoofs & Horns, March 1942 issue
90. Hoofs & Horns, April 1942 issue
91. Hoofs & Horns, July 1942 issue
92. Hoofs & Horns, June 1942 issue
93. Hoofs & Horns, August 1942 issue
94. Hoofs & Horns, February 1943 issue
95. Hoofs & Horns, December 1942 issue
96. Hoofs & Horns, April 1943 issue
97. Hoofs & Horns, February 1944 issue
98. Hoofs & Horns, May 1943 issue
99. Hoofs & Horns, June 1943 issue
100. Conversation with Bern Gregory, 2-2011

101. Hoofs & Horns, July 1943 issue
102. Hoofs & Horns, August 1943 issue
103. Hoofs & Horns, March 1944 issue
104. Hoofs & Horns, April 1944 issue
105. Hoofs & Horns, May 1944 issue
106. Hoofs & Horns, January 1944 issue
107. Hoofs & Horns, January 1946 issue
108. Hoofs & Horns, January 1943 issue
109. Hoofs & Horns, June 1944 issue
110. Hoofs & Horns, July 1944 issue
111. Conversation with Imogene Veach Beals, 2-2011
112. Hoofs & Horns, December 1944 issue
113. Hoofs & Horns, August 1944 issue
114. Hoofs & Horns, September 1944 issue
115. Hoofs & Horns, March 1945 issue
116. Website: World War II Wikipedia
117. Notice of Special Meeting of Board of Directors of the CTA, 3-8-1945
118. Hoofs & Horns, June 1945 issue
119. Hoofs & Horns, May 1945 issue
120. Conversation with Sharon Shoulders, 2-2011
121. Hoofs & Horns, February 1945 issue
122. Hoofs & Horns, July 1945 issue
123. Hoofs & Horns, March 1946 issue
124. Hoofs & Horns, April 1946 issue
125. Conversation with Bill Fedderson, 2-2011
126. Conversation with Ray Wharton, 2-2011
127. Conversation with Gene McLaughlin, 2-2011
128. Conversation with D'Lynn Terry, 2-2011
129. Email from Tom Taylor, 2-2011
130. Conversation with Bob Chambers, 2-2011
131. Conversation with Louis Quirk, 2-2011
132. Conversation with Tater Decker, 2-2011
133. Conversation with Don "Jug" Reynolds, 2-2011
134. Book: Don "Brown Jug" Reynolds, The Last Little Beaver of the Movies, by Donn J. Moyer, published in 2006
135. Fort Worth Star Telegram, March 16, 1935
136. Interview with Holloway Grace, 10-2003
137. Conversation with Buff Douthitt, 3-2011
138. Conversation with Frank Quirk, 2-2011
139. Conversation with Faye Blackstone, 3-2011
140. Letter by Fannye Lovelady to Willard Porter, Rodeo Historical Society

Footnotes

141. Book: Cowboy Up! The History of Bull Riding, by Gail Hughbanks Woerner, Published by Eakin Press, 2001
142. Conversation with Bart Clennon, 3-2011
143. Conversation with Mitzi Riley, 3-2011
144. Conversation with Derek Clark, 3-2011
145. Letter: From Franklin Roosevelt to Mr. & Mrs. Thomas Quirk, 6-8-1944
146. Conversation with Kevin Fitzpatrick, 3-2011
147. Poem: The Turtles, by Dan Willis
148. Hoofs & Horns, CTA Members in Service, March & October, 1944
149. Book: 1940 Cowboys' Turtle Association Articles, etc., & Membership
150. Book: 1944 Cowboys' Turtle Association Articles, etc., & Membership
151. RAA Rules of Rodeo, Hoofs & Horns, April, 1940 Issue
152. Tucson Citizen, Article, "Ma Hopkins: Rodeo won't soon forget her" 2-20-1980
153. Conversation with John D. Holleyman, 3-2011
154. Book: 13 Flat, Tales of Thirty Famous Rodeo Ropers and Their Great Horses, by Willard Porter, published by A. S. Barnes & Co., 1967

Index

Symbols

129th Horse Cavalry 177
21 Club 151

A

Abbey, Chairman 286
Abbott, G.S. 288
Aber, Doff
    73, 80-81, 158-159, 169-172
    183, 196, 228, 247
Aber, Lynn 286
Abercrombie, C. C. 247
Abold, Ernest 234, 258, 288
Acay, Delmar 275
Acton, Ernest 247
Adair, Pud 275
Adams, Alice 25, 34, 288
Adams, Dale 232, 247, 275
Adams, Francis 247
Adams, Mrs. Alice 247
Adams, Pete 33, 275
Addington, John E. 286
Aepeehwish, Ellis 288
Agee, John 286
Ahern, Buck 275
Akers, Ves 275
Albin, J. D. 283
Albrecht, Chas 247, 288
Albuquerque, N. M 185
Alcorn, Cherokee 231, 258
Aldridge, Charles 247
Aledo, Texas 193
Allen, Al 229, 258
Allen, Del 275
Allen, Frankie 275
Allen, Hoss 275
Allen, James Lee 288
Allen, Jean 275

Allen, James Robert 307
Allen, Lonnie 231, 247, 283
Allen, Red 107, 231, 247, 275
Allen, Robert Jr. 307
Allred, Clyde 192
Allred, Judge James V. 247, 286
Almond, John 275
Alrich, H. A. 275
Alrich, Hank 275
Alsbaugh, Walt 247, 275
Alston, Tommie 288
Altamarino, Tony 275
Altamarion 247
Alvie, Mrs. Gordo 43
Alvord, Fred 230, 247, 275
Ambler, Jerry
    170, 231, 247, 264, 275
Amburgee, J. D. 247
Ammons, Gov. Teller 235, 247, 286
Amstrong, Phil 258
Anadarko, Okla. 185
Anderson, A. J 258
Anderson, Dick 229, 275
Anderson, Earl 288
Anderson, Elmond 288
Anderson, Gale 232, 247
Anderton, Dick 16, 258
Andes, Chester 247, 288
Andrews, Dick 169
Andrews, Forrest 288
Antone, Bud 180
Apple Valley, Calif. 192
Arano, Roy 258
Arizona State Industrial Commission
    201
Arlington, Ore 158
Armour, Bill 247
Armstrong, Bert 247
Armstrong, Carl 124

Armstrong, Phil 231, 258
Armstrong, Ted 275
Arnold, Carl
    26, 49, 113, 183, 207, 247, 275
Arnold, Carl, 228
Arnold, Edward 247, 283
Arnold, Joe 247, 288
Arranto, Gene 247
Arrants, Gene 275
Asbeck, Robert 288
Askins, Bob 33, 49, 232, 247, 288
Athena, Ore. 192
Atkinson, Almus 283
Auditorium Rodeo 162
Autry, Frank 247, 275
Autry, Gene 151, 155, 199, 283
Avery, Emile 232, 247
Avery, Jack 232, 258
Axton, Bob 275
Ayres, Toots 33

B

Bachman, Billy 212
Bacon, Grant 275
Bacon, John 275
Badsky, Fred 275
Bagdad, Ariz. 131
Bailey, George 258
Bailey, Herb 275
Baird, Dr. Vernon 248, 286
Baker, Bob 248
Baker, Frank 248
Baker, Fred 234
Baker, Fred C 258
Baker, J. Howard 275
Baker, Paddy 275
Ball, Hank 248
Ballard, Smokey 232, 247, 275
Bandera, Texas
    134, 152, 159, 169, 172, 193, 206

Bandy, Don 192, 288
Barens, Roy 275
Barkdoll, Lee 228, 262, 283
Barker, Dick 283
Barmby, Bob 275
Barnes, Charles 248
Barnes, H.M. 286
Barnes, Joe 234, 258
Barnes–Carruthers 32
Barnett, Ernie 247, 275
Barnett, Jane 248
Barnett, Johnny 288
Barnett, Keith 247, 282
Barnhart, Albert 234, 258
Barr, Endre 258
Barr, Endre, 229
Barrett, Fred 229, 248, 275
Barrett, Rip 248
Barron, Curtis 247, 288
Barron, N. E. 283
Bartlemay, Stub
    71, 158, 170, 229, 247, 264, 275
Bartlemay, Stub, 237
Bartlett, Bill 288
Bartlett, Bronk 288
Bartley, Gus 212
Barton, Bill 283
Barton, Buzz 288
Barton, John 230
Bartram, Dutch 258
Bartram, John 258
Bartrum, Dutch 230, 288
Bartrum, John 288
Bascom, Earl 248, 282
Bascom, Weldon 229, 248
Bass, Ray 247
Bassett, Joe
    158, 169, 170, 234, 247, 264, 275
Bassett, Lew 247, 288
Bates, Chris S. 247, 288
Batey, Dum 288
Baton Rouge, Louis 178

Index

Batteate, Earl 230, 258
Baughman, Wart 191, 275
Baxter, Larry 248
Bay City, Texas 178
Bays, Jimmie 258, 282
Beach, Kenneth 247, 288
Beache, John A 258
Beals, Charley 183, 190, 248
Beals, Imogene 183
Bearrow, Mark 288
Beasley, Carl 232, 258
Beasley, John 16
Beason, Fred 258
Becker, Fritz
    183, 191, 207, 234, 247, 275
Becker, Johnny 175, 283, 307
Bedford, Cecil
    184, 207, 231, 247, 275
Beeson, Dummy 288
Beeson, Fred 33, 107
Beeville, Texas 43
Beken, Henry 247, 283
Belden, Herb 247, 275
Bell, Curley 232, 258
Bell, Don 248
Bell, John H. 275, 286
Bell, Melvin 283, 307
Bell, W.M. 286
Bellflower, Calif. 43, 44
Beloat, Arthur 228, 247
Belvedere Hotel 31, 151
Benden, Herb 231
Benedictis, Tony 288
Bender, Ben 34
Bender, Bennie 233, 247, 275
Bennett, Charlie 247, 283
Bennett, Charlie, 230
Bennett, Hugh
    8, 16-17, 19, 28, 34-35, 37, 39-40,
    44-45, 47, 49, 66, 68, 72, 79, 93, 96,
    101, 117, 121, 139, 143, 162, 177,
    183, 188, 198, 228, 237, 247, 275

Bennett, Josie 42
Bennett, Ralph 16, 228, 247, 288
Bentley, Bill 288
Bentley, Bob 288
Bentley, Don 288
Beren, John 275
Berlin, Germany 90
Bernard, Tim 288
Berry, Padgett 188, 234, 275
Bessler, Joe 176
Bessler, Joseph 165
Bergevin, Damase 288
Bethel, Okla. 207
Betts, Glenn M. 275
Beutler Brothers 110
Beutler, Jake 124
Beutler, Lynn 124, 276
Beveridge, Ted M. 247
Bias, Charles 282, 288
Big Piney, Wyo 167-168
Big Spring, Texas 130, 175
Bill, Curly 33
Billboard 26, 148
Billboard Publishing Company 148
Billings, Mont. 176, 178, 185
Billingsley, Red 275
Binns, H. D. 247, 288
Biscaro, Bill 258
Biscaro, Carl, 258
Bjornstod, Bill 288
Black, Alex 288
Black, Billy 248, 283, 307
Blackfoot Elks Lodge 247, 286
Blackfoot, Idaho 158, 190
Blackstone, Doc 247, 283
Blackstone, Faye
    9, 116, 192, 212, 288
Blackstone Hotel 195
Blackstone, Vick 116, 247, 288
Bland, R. L., Jr. 275
Blasingame, Jack 275
Blessing, Faye 160

Blessing, Wag 275
Blevins, Earl 33, 229, 247, 283, 307
Block, Leonard 172, 264, 275
Bloomfield, Mont. 176
Bode, Andrew 229, 248, 275
Boden, Bob 231, 258, 288
Boeing Aircraft 183
Boen, Ken 275
Boen, Mrs. Ken 275
Bogan, Bill 283
Bohlender, Ike 283
Boise, Idaho 185
Bolton, Jack 33, 288
Bolton, Lorraine 248
Bolton, Tack 248
Bomar, W. W. 275
Bond, Buck 288
Bond, Paul
   9, 26, 75, 192, 232, 247, 275
Bonelli, William G. 286
Bonner, A. Q. 247
Booh, Al 288Boone, Ben 78
Booth, Clinton
   16, 158, 170, 207, 229, 237, 247, 275
Booth, Homer R. 275
Booth, Leslie 247, 283
Booth, Tom 235, 247, 286
Booth, W. H. 286
Border, Alex 247, 275
Borgess, Frank 230, 258
Boss, Ray 275, 283
Boston Garden 8, 15, 162
Boston, Mass.
   15, 17, 31, 68, 126, 167
Bowen, Glenn W. 275, 307
Bowers, Aubrey 234, 258
Bowie, Texas 193
Bowman, Ed 130, 234, 247, 275
Bowman, Everett
   16, 28, 34, 37, 43, 48, 49, 51-52, 54-55, 60, 65, 68, 70, 72, 75-76, 78, 82, 85-86, 89, 94, 96, 101, 103, 105-106, 108,-110, 114-115, 117-118, 120-121, 123-124, 126, 128-130, 133, 138, 140-141, 149-151, 158, 159, 166, 170, 183, 196, 198, 201, 203, 228, 237, 247, 263, 275
Bowman, Everett, 139
Bowman, John
   16, 43, 44, 66, 107, 108,-109, 207, 228, 247, 275
Bowman, Louis 89
Bowman, Skeet 248, 288
Bowman., Everett 69
Bowyer, Chester 275
Boyd, Cecil 288
Boyd, Tom 275
Boyer, Bob 284
Boyhan, John 284, 307
Boysen, Eddie 165, 232
Bozen, Eddie 258
Bradford, Buck 288
Bradley, Buzz 288
Brady, Buff 108, 160, 231, 247
Brady, Buff, Jr. 275
Brady, Jack Brown 258
Brady, Dr. Leo 286
Kathleen Brady 286
Brady, Pat 275
Bragg, Nancy Witmer 9, 192, 288
Branch, Riley 275
Brannon, Leo 248, 307
Brannon, Rose 283
Brannon, T. J. 247
Brazile, Sandy 9
Brazile, Trevor 9, 11, 20
Breckenridge, Red 247
Breedon, Rose 235, 258
Breedon, Tom 16, 72, 73, 230, 262
Bride, Tom 28, 207, 258, 275
Brink, M.E. Bob 286Brister, Jim
   232, 247, 275
Britt, Victor 288

Index

Brock, James 288Brock, Leonard 258
Broderick, John 235, 258, 275
Brodnax, Charles 248
Brodnax, Chas. 275
Bronte, Texas 191
Brooklyn, NY 119
Brooks, Louis
  169, 172, 177, 183, 187, 196,
  200, 206, 208, 248, 263, 275
Brown, Arthur 286
Brown, Basil 275
Brown, Buster 34
Brown, Clyde 248, 289
Brown, Freckles 175
Brown, Johnny 289
Brown, Howard 230, 247, 275
Brown, Jerry 275
Brown Jug 172
Brown, Pat 275
Brown, Van 258, 289
Brown, W. H. 'Tex 276
Brown, Walter 17
Browne, Robert 276
Bruce, Doug 231, 258
Brunton, Carol 276
Brunzell, Blondy 230, 258
Bryant, Blackie 258
Buchanan, R. B. 248, 286
Buckart, Chuck 258
Buckley, Buck 232, 258
Buena Park, Calif. 152
Buffalo, New York 162
Buffington, Ernest 258, 276, 289
Buffington, Owen 258
Bugg, Johnnie 276
Burge, Emma 289
Burge, "PeeWee" Ott 212
Burk, Clyde
  43, 117, 169, 177, 188, 229,
  247, 263, 276
Burk, Dee 181, 284
Burk, Jiggs 177, 206, 247, 276

Burkburnett, Texas 193
Burkitt, Buck 248, 283
Burleigh, Bryan E. 284Burleson, W.
  E. 276
Burma Road 178
Burnet, J. T. 248, 289
Burnett, Jane Smith 193
Burns, Bobbie 276
Burns, Frankie 234, 258, 282
Burns, Houston 289
Burns, Roy 16
Burrell, Cuff 120
Burrell, Joe 228, 247, 284, 307
Burrough, George 276
Burroughs, Wayne 248, 283
Burrows, Bob 248, 276
Burson, Polly 160, 212
Burson, Wayne 247
Burton, Pat 49
Buschbom, Barney 258
Buschbom, Bill 33, 233, 258
Buschbom, Jack 192
Buschbom, Ted 33, 247
Busick, Harold 171
Butcher's Union Hall 48
Butler, Archie 248, 289
Butner, Goldie 234, 258, 289
Butterfield, Chas. 286
Butts, Buster 276
Byers, Chester 276
Byrd, Steve 289

C

Cabral, Louis 276
Cahoe, Tommy 276
Calder, Limmie 289
Caldwell, Eddie 276
Caldwell, Idaho 178
Caldwell, Junior 229
Calen, Bob 20, 26
Calen, Bobby 248

Calgary, Alberta, Canada
    24, 62, 79, 108, 120, 167
Calgary Exposition and Stampede
    118, 126, 162
California Rodeo, (Salinas) 161-162
Call, Grant 248, 286
Callahan, Bill 262, 289
Calwell, Junior 262
Cameron, Allen 234, 248, 289
Cameron, Eddie 248, 284, 307
Camp Joseph H. Pendleton 179
Camp Swift, Texas 173
Camp Verde, Ariz. 76
Campadore, Frank 232, 258
Campbell, A. J. 'Jack' 276
Campbell, Arlo 276
Campbell, Clay 249, 289
Campbell, Dave
    33, 49, 94, 106, 158, 169, 170,
    183, 206, 207, 229, 248, 289
Campbell, Rex 248
Canada Kid 95
Capps, Charlie 248, 282
Capps, Kenneth 276
Caraway, R.B. 289
Cardston, Alberta 44, 96, 117
Cardston, Alberta, Canada
    44, 96, 117, 120
Carey, Al, 259
Carey, Joe 258, 282
Carey, Lawrence 276
Carlen, Eugene 289
Carlsbad, N.M. 133
Carney, Paul
    16, 20, 37, 75-76, 95, 109,
    117, 121, 134, 139, 228, 248,
    264, 276
Carr, Bill 286
Carr, Clay
    34, 121, 151, 158, 170,
    228, 248, 284, 307
Carroll, Roy 248, 289

Carson, Ken 276
Carter, Barton 33, 49, 138, 229, 248
Case, Jack 231
Cash, Guy 33, 231, 248, 289
Castanon, Frank 276
Casteel, Art 231, 258, 276
Castro, Vern 169, 276
Castro, Vic 169, 289
Cathemer, Tom 289
Cavanaugh, Tommy 276
Cavender, Eugene 276
Chaffie, Jim 276
Chambers, Bob
    9, 150, 177, 192, 284, 307
Chambers, Pinky 248
Chandler, Ariz. 134, 152, 206
Chaney, Murphy 188
Chaps, Max 284, 307
Chapman, Hugh 289
Chapman, John 276, 284, 307
Charles, Artie 276
Cheetham, Everett, 258
Chesson, Bo 207, 248, 276, 307
Chetham, Everett 49, 230
Cheyenne
    24, 55, 62, 66, 69, 79, 130, 138,
    150, 153, 167, 175, 185
Cheyenne Frontier Days
    126, 161-162, 207
Chicago, Ill. 32, 114, 138
Chicago Stadium Corporation 32
Chicago Stadium Rodeo 162
Chicago Tribune 160
Chicago World's Fair 91
Chip, Yellow Stone 258
Chism, Chas. "Smoky" 289
Chisum, Ike 234, 258, 282
Chitwood, Frank 249, 276
Cholame, Calif. 188
Christensen, Bobbie 276
Christensen, Henry 276
Christian, Lefty 248, 276

Index

Christensen, Vic 289
Christensen, Whity 289
Churchill, Mont. 248
Clancy, Foghorn 156
Claresholm, Alb., Canada 169
Clark, Bill 259, 289
Clark, Bobby 289
Clark, Derek 9, 71
Clark, Donna 9
Clark, Gene 289
Clark, Ken 307
Clark, Lee 289
Clarke, Estelle 248
Clarksville, Texas 158, 159
Clary, Pat 289
Clay, Willie 229, 248, 289, 307
Clayton, Okla. 192
Clayton, Tommy 276
Clemans, Bill
    151, 154, 156, 162, 170, 177
Clemans, W. J. 276
Clemens, Bill 155
Clements, C.A. 289
Clements, Pete 248
Clennon, Bart
    9, 16, 19, 70, 192, 249, 289
Cleveland Arena Rodeo 162
Cleveland, Ohio 101, 115, 167
Clifton, Ariz. 130
Cline, Doc 231, 249, 276
Cline, George 231, 248, 276
Cline, John 249, 276
Cline, Lawrence 276
Cline, Leck 276
Clingman, Hugh 228, 258, 276
Clinton, Bruce 289
Clute, Res. 248
Coats, Bobby 276
Coats, Fred 289
Cobb, Clarence 289
Cobb, Lee 289
Cochrane, Bill 289

Cody, Joe 33
Cody, Wyo. 152, 158
Coe, C.C. 248
Coe, H.A. 284
Coelho, Al 248, 276
Coffey, Ed 284, 307
Coker, Joe 234, 248, 276
Coker, Johnny 248
Colbert, Charles 232, 249, 284
Colbert, Dude 248, 284
Colbert, Zeb 248
Colborn, Everett
    117, 149, 170, 177, 190, 276
Colborn, Rose Mary 276
Colcord, Frank 249
Cole, Chili 173, 249, 284, 307
Coleman, Jimmy 289
Coleman, Tom 264, 289
Collell, Frenchie 192
Collier, A.J. 289
Collier, Dick 289
Collier, Ralph 183, 207, 249, 276
Collins, Earvie 258
Collins, Earvin 234, 276
Collins, Eddie 33, 258
Collins, Louie 258, 289
Colorado Springs, Colo. 164
Colorado State Cattle Board 148
Comanche, Okla.
    43, 117, 169, 188, 206
Compton, Cy 289
Compton, Myrtle Goodrich 25
Conklin, Roy 286
Conley, Lawrence 231, 289
Connell, Junior 276
Conners, Beverly 258, 283
Connley, Lawrence 249
Consolidated Vultee Aircraft 183
Conwell, George 16, 259
Cook, Bud 235, 248, 276
Cook, Homer 289
Cook, Joe 248, 259

Cooper, Felix 230, 248, 289
Cooper, Henry 249
Cooper, Jackie
    155, 183, 207, 228, 248, 264, 276
Cooper, Morris 234, 248, 282
Cooper, Tex 286
Cor, Frank 259
Corbin, Goldie 234, 248, 289
Cornett, Elmer 248
Cornett, Frank 234
Cornish, Cecil 248, 264, 276
Corona, N. M. 150, 193
Cosper, Geo. 289
Cotten, George 289
Cotrell, Lyle 276
Cottrell, Diane 248
Cottrell, Lyle 232, 249
Couch, Jack 289
Couch, Worth N. 283
Council Grove, Kans. 138
Cowboy Contestants Association 25
Cowboys' Amateur Association of
    America 156
Cox, Breezy
    49, 106-107 228, 248, 276
Cox, Frank 276
Cox, G.W. 289
Cox, J.F. 289
Cox, Leo 248, 289
Cox, Lloyd 289
Cox, Roy 248
Cox, Victor 289
Coze, Paul 248, 286
Crain, Don 259, 282
Crain, Paul 229, 248
Crainer, Allen 234, 258, 289
Cranier, Bill 289
Cravens, Baldy 248
Cravens, Walter 16, 78, 231, 262
Crawley, Bill 289
Crawford, Lex 248
Creed, Gene 33, 63, 235, 248, 289

Creed, Shorty
    33, 103, 159, 229, 248, 289
Cremer, Leo 126, 289
Cresson, Texas 159
Cripe, A. J. 276
Crisp, Bob 248
Crist, James 259
Crocker, Dave 212
Cropper, Melvin 228, 248, 276
Crosby, Bob 37, 49, 230, 248, 276
Crossfield, Alberta 43
Crossland, Leo 284
Crouch, Worth 248
Cullen, Larry 232
Cullen, Lary 258
Cullington, Geo. V. 248, 286
Cummings, Harry 286
Cunningham, Bob 259
Curry, Roland 230, 248, 276
Curtis, Andy 49, 229, 237, 248, 276
Curtis, Eddie
    16, 34, 37, 49, 67, 70, 73, 82, 85,
    86, 95, 96, 101, 105, 106, 109, 115,
    116, 120, 121, 124, 191, 208, 229,
    248, 263, 276
Cutler, Tex 258
Cutler, Wayne 230, 258, 289

D

Dahl, Herb 229, 249, 276
Dahlberg, Shorty 276
Dalhart, Texas 185
Dalton, Jack 249, 289
Daniels, George 233, 259, 283
Daniels, Larry 231
Daniels, Lary 249, 276
Daniels, Robert F. 276
Danley, Pete 289
Darnell, Clarence 284, 307
Darnell, Fred 276
Darnell, Hank 289

Index

Dauckon, Fred 249
Davis, Arthur 284, 307
Davis, Ben 249
Davis, Buck 230, 249, 284
Davis, Casey 232, 259
Davis, Ed 33
Davis, Girard 230, 262
Davis, Gordon 249
Davis, Harold 276
Davis, Harry 259
Davis, Jack 249
Davis, Lillian 286
Davis, Merle 276
Davis, Roy 249
Davis, Tea 282
Davis-Monthan Field 167
Dawson, Alvin 249
Dawson, Chet 249
Dayton, Chic 228
Dayton, Chick 259
Deadwood, S.D. 94
Deakins, Ab 276
Deal, Martin 230, 259
Dean, Dizzy 119
DeArman, Jonas 16
Deck, Art 232, 259
Decker, Tater 9, 171, 192, 212
Decker, Tom 9
Dee, Clarence 276
Deglin, Ted 286
Demaree, George 276
Denham, Frank 234
Dennis, Fay Knight 142
Dennis, Millie 9
Dennis, Walter 8
Densmore, Speedy 16, 232, 249
Denver Stock Show & Rodeo 63, 202
Despain, Sidney 249, 307
Dew, Frank Y. 249, 283
Dewey, Diamond D. 249
Dickinson Research Center
    39, 76, 90, 119, 149, 212

Dickson, Bobby 235, 259
Dickson, Dick 286
Dikeman, Melvin 276
Dillon, Ben 284
Dillon, Jack 283
Dillon, Mutt 276
Dillon, Roy M. 249, 286
DiMaggio, Joe 119
Dixon, Eddie 276
Dixon, Homer 276
Doan, Urban 234, 249, 282
Dodge City, Kans. 185, 168
Doheny, Tim 286
Doiel, Bud 282
Doill, Bud 259, 282
Donoghue, Tom 11
Dooley, Orie 212
Dorothy, Alb., Canada 172
Dos Cabezos, Ariz. 160
Dossey, Bernice 160, 276
Dossey, Carl
    151, 158, 170, 183, 196, 206, 230,
    249, 276
Doucet, Poley 276
Douglas Aircraft 183
Douthitt, Buff 9, 133, 192
Dowell, Buck 249, 276
Downs, Jimmie 249
Doyle, Dusty 249
Doyle, Tex 234, 249, 283
Drayer, John 232, 259
Dreyer, Polly 276
Drowne, Skip 276
Drumheller, Allen 78
Duarte, Ed 276
Duarte, Frank 259
Duarte, Hoot 259, 284, 307
Duby, Frenchie 259
Duckett, Charlie 230, 259
Dudley, Dorris 249, 286
Dudley, George 249
Dugger, Buford 192, 276

Dunbar, Marvin 276
Duncan, Keezie 249
Duncan, Okla. 208
Dunckon, Fred 286
Dunn, P.C. 286
Dupree, Jack 179
Durango, Colo. 149
Durfee, Tex 276
Durfey, Roy 9
Durham, John 284
Dwyer, Emmett 249, 284, 307
Dyer, Chock 49
Dyer, Earl 249
Dyer, H. L 259
Dyer, Jack 249, 276
Dyer, Paul 284
Dykes, Carl 234, 262

E

Eaade, Milton 289
Earp, Virgil 33, 249
Earp, Wyatt 168
East, Tom Jr. 289
Eaton, Bill 230, 249, 289
Eaton, Richard 9
Ebner, Adolph 212, 250, 289
Echols, Buck
    149, 158, 170, 237, 249, 277
Echols, Bucky 9
Echols, Ed 286
Eddins, Add 289
Edmo, Hugh 289
Edmo, Lee 258
Edmonson, Lince 277
Edwards, Buck 232, 259
Edwards, Joe 229, 237, 249, 277
Edwards, Ken 143
Edwards, Sonny 277
Eilebrecht, Howard 289
Elfie, John 289
Ekalaka, Mont. 178

El Paso, Texas 171
El Reno, Okla. 49, 120, 193, 208
El Segundo, Calif. 183
Elder, Ted 26
Elfic, John 231, 250
Elk City, Okla. 185
Elko, Nev. 179
Ellensburg, Wash.
    65, 72, 77, 85, 102, 108,
    114, 143, 154
Elley, Morris 249
Ellingwalt, P. W. 277
Elliott, Bill 286
Elliott, Bob 259
Elliott, Cliff 277
Elliott, Geo. 250
Elliott, Sie 231, 259, 289
Elliott, Verne 20, 26, 277
Elliott, Wiley 259
Ellis, Mel 262, 282
Ellison, Buddy 249
Elmore, Ace 289
Ely, Marion 289
Emerson, Tex 277
Emery, Ernest 258, 289
Emory, Harold 231, 259, 284, 307
Enders, Bob 277
Engelsman, Led 230, 249, 284
Enos, Manuel 249, 277
Ensley, Allen 284, 307
Erick, Okla. 150
Eskey, Jim 289
Eskew, Junior 250, 284
Eskew, Tom Mix 284
Esperson, Allen 252
Espy, H.C. 289
Espy, Jim 277
Essap, Truman 289
Estes, Bob 183, 207, 232, 250, 277
Evans, Bert 277
Evans, Bill 286
Evans, Buck 249, 282

Index

Evans, Bud 231, 250, 289
Evans, Eddie 250
Evans, Floyd James 277
Evans, John 33, 284

F

Facciola, Don B. 277
Faircloth, Sig 282
Falk, Ace 286
Falk, Dr. Lane 207, 277
Fancher, Ben 284, 307
Fancher, Charlie 249
Fancher, John 249, 282
Fancher, Pete 249
Fancher, Sam 249, 277
Farnsworth, Dick 277
Farr, Carl 277
Farr, Hugh 277
Farrell, Joe 33, 258
Farris, Lee 231, 249
Farris, Zeano 277
Faubion, W. L 250, 286
Faulk, Hamilton 286
Faulkner, Frederick 307
Faulkner, Foreman 258
Fauts, John 249
Favors, Jack 277
Fedderson, Bill 9, 191, 192, 193
Federal, Wyo. 158, 169, 175
Feltman, Wallace 249
Felton, Boots 284
Felts, E. 234, 258
Fenach, Tony 284, 307
Ferguson, Don 249
Fernamburg, Dan 229, 258
Fernandez, Fele 234, 249, 277
Fernandez, Ike 249, 277
Ferrante, Joe 249
Ferrario, Arnil 230, 284, 307
Ferrario, Arnio 258

Ferraro, Ned 230, 249
Ferris, Gordon 229, 249
Ferris, Hack 282
Ferris, Lee 283
Fetters, Bob 284
Fiddle Face 177
Fidler, C. Lyall 277
Fife, Harold 284
Fiesta de los Vaqueros 56, 161
Finch, Allyn 124
Finley, Evelyn 277
Finley, Frank
    16, 152, 173, 232, 249, 284, 307
Finley, Larry 249, 277
Finley, Luther
    174, 176, 232, 249, 284
First Frost 180
Fischer, Charles H. 277
Fisher, Bob 230, 258
Fisher, Bud 284
Fisher, Ham 249, 286
Fisher, Mike 231, 249, 284, 307
Fitzpatrick, Bud 171, 193
Fitzpatrick, Kevin 9
Fitzpatricks, Buddie 249
Five Minutes to Midnight 167
Flagg, Slim 277
Fleming, Joel 16, 228, 258, 284
Flesher, Herbert 277
Fletcher, Al 249, 284, 307
Fletcher, Boyd 250
Fletcher, Claude 277
Fletcher, Flaxie 103
Fletcher, Kid
    117, 152, 175, 208, 229, 249, 284
Fletcher, Virginia 249, 282
Florence, Ariz. 48, 151-152, 158, 162
Flores, Jose 249
Forest, R.W. 286
Florissant, Missouri 193

Flowers, Hubert 234, 249, 277
Flowers, Marshall 249, 277
Foehl, Robert 234, 258
Folkerson, Bob 258
Folsom, Barney 277
Fonville, Paul 277
Ford, Clyde, Jr. 258
Fore, Oran 231, 249
Foreman, Tom 232, 249
Forrester, Pete 249
Forsyth, Rollin 284, 307Fort Francis E. Warren 175
Fort Madison, Iowa 15
Fort Riley, Kans. 177, 180
Fort Smith, Ark. 178
Fort Thomas, Ariz. 47, 96, 117-118
Fort, Troy 277
Fort Worth
    25, 48, 55, 72, 79, 86, 93, 99, 101, 114, 121, 157, 167, 193, 196, 206, 207
Fort Worth Press 96
Fort Worth Star Telegram 26
Foust, Doc 232, 258
Fowler, Don 250
Fox, Dewey 277, 284, 307
Francher, Virginia 249
Francis, Warren 249
Fransicsco, Bill 286
Frazier, Larry 277
Fredericks, Loren 250, 307
Freeman, E. J. 277
French, Jimmie 258, 282
Fresno, Calif. 175
Freyer, Dick 286
Friend, Cecil 165
Frock, Eldon 286
Fuentez, Juan 286
Fugitt, Jack 286
Fulkerson, Bub 234
Fulkerson, Jasbo 142, 143, 277
Fuller, Wid 249, 282

Fullerton, Calif. 158
Furth, Germany, 181

G

Gafford, Brida 25
Gafford, Neal 250
Gafford, Roy 231, 259, 282
Galarno, Fred 259
Galbraith, Joe 277
Gale, Floyd
    49, 73, 110, 230, 250, 277
Galeton, Colo. 76, 134
Gamblin, Amye
    33, 207, 232, 250, 277
Gandolfi, Gail 9
Garbarino, George 234, 259
Garcia, Vidal 250, 277
Garden Valley, Calif. 193
Gardner, Ace 230, 258
Gardner, Cliff 110, 229
Gardner, John 259
Garner, Buck 250
Garner, Paul 277
Garrett, Raymond 250
Gaylor, Maynard 16, 231, 250, 277
Gee, Carl 250
Geibel, Marie 9
Geiser, J. M. 250
Geist, Johnnie 259
Gelvin, Floyd 250, 283
Gentry, Guy 250, 282
George, Bobby 262, 282
George, Chris 262
Gerig, John 250
Gerig. Kpjm 277
Getzwiller, Marion
    165, 212, 228, 250, 277, 307
Gibson, Andy 230, 250
Gibson, John L. 286
Gill, Adolph 230, 250, 259
Gill, Emmett 230, 250, 277

Index

Gill, Ernest 208
Gilliam, Arvil 33
Glade, Pete 277
Glatfelder, Gene 277
Glenn, Dick 277
Glenn, Joe 250
Glenn, Lester 277
Glenn, O. C. 259, 262, 282
Glenn, Rex 228, 250
Globe, Ariz. 172
Godshall, Jeanne 250, 286
Golia, Philip 277
Gonzales, Melissa 9
Good, Jeff 250
Goode, Jim 286
Goodrich, Myrtle 27, 160, 277
Goodrich, Vern 183, 207, 264, 277
Goodson, Skip 259
Goodspeed, Buck
    152, 231, 250, 277
Goodspeed, Jess 152, 231, 250
Goodspeed, Red 179, 284, 307
Goose Creek, Texas 184
Gordon, Alvin
    139, 151, 228, 250, 284
Gordon, Jack 250
Gordon, Jim 250
Gould, Paul 250, 277
Gould, Vernon 250
Govier, H.R. 286
Grace, Holloway
    33, 116, 183, 212, 228, 250, 277
Grady, N. M. 151, 159, 169
Graham, J. A. 277
Graham, Kenneth 277
Graham, Nig 250
Grand National Exposition 162
Gray, Juanita 277
Gray, Reva 262
Gray, Weaver 277
Great Falls, Mont 185
Green, Carlos 250, 277

Green Forest, Ark. 192
Green, George 250
Green, Ray 277
Greenough, Alice 25, 155, 250, 277
Greenough, Bill 250
Greenough, Margie 33, 250, 277
Greenough, Margie Henson 212
Greenough, Turk
    165, 228, 250, 277, 307
Greenwood, Ross 231, 259, 277
Gregory, Bern
    9, 175, 181, 193, 212, 284, 307
Grey, Reva 283
Griffith, Dick
    16, 20, 37, 63, 108, 134, 142, 152,
    155, 159, 160, 169, 170, 177, 183,
    195-196, 198, 200, 206, 228, 250,
    263, 277
Grimes, Johnnie 259
Grubb, Pete 95, 117, 151, 229, 250
Gruwell, Gus 193, 277
Guadalcanal 176
Guidotti, Raymond L 277
Gunn, Warren 212
Gunter, Kenneth 228, 250, 277
Gunyon, Sandy, 259
Guy, Eddie 284, 308
Guymon, Sandy 277

H

Haas, Chuck 284
Hadfield, Joe 251
Hagen, Johnny 259
Haines, Willard 286
Hale, Earl 277
Hale, Mel 277
Hall, Clark 277
Hamburger, Phil 250, 286
Hamilton, Eugene 251, 284, 308
Hamilton, Wes 230, 259, 282
Hamley Saddle Shop 70, 134

Hancock, Bill 188, 232, 250, 277
Hancock, Sonny 33, 228, 251, 284
Hanes, Willard 251
Hanesworth, Robert 126
Hanford, Calif 120
Hanke, Eddie 251
Hanna, Bill 250
Hannon, Chick 232, 259, 277
Hannum, Walter 259, 282
Hansen, Curt 277
Hansen, Kenneth 277
Hansen, Merrill 277
Hargis, Ken 229, 251
Harmon, Bill 234
Harmon, Del T. 282
Harold, James Jackson 308
Harp, Glenn 259
Harper, Bert A. 277
Harper, Melvin 16, 121, 251, 228
Harrington, Ed 231
Harris, Bayless 250, 284, 308
Harris, Helen M. 251, 286
Harris, Howard 44
Harris, J. K. 277
Harris, Robert S. 286
Hart, Bob 166
Hart, Harry
    106, 117, 134, 158, 170, 183, 207,
    231, 250, 277
Hartman, Genl. 286
Hassenpflug, Elmer 251
Hastings, Mike 230, 250, 277
Hatchel, Curley 232, 250
Hatfield, George 259, 286
Haverty, Bob 183, 250, 277
Haverty, Clay 235, 259
Haverty, Pete 259
Hayhurst, Alfred 231, 259
Haynes, Davis 250
Haynes, I. D. 277
Haynes, Thos. D. 284
Hays, Edd 251

Haythorn, Waldo 232, 259
Haythorn, Walter 232, 259
Hayward, Calif. 172, 180
Hazen, Jimmie 183, 250, 277
Heacock, Steve 103, 228, 251, 278
Heacock, Walter 231, 259
Hebbron, Elton 60
Hebert, Bubba 278
Hebert, Clyde 183, 278
Hedge, Bill 259
Hedges, Max 250, 282
Hefner, Hoytt
    16, 121, 158, 170, 229, 251,
    278
Helena, Mont. 134
Hell's Angel 168, 176
Helm, Cliff 107, 231, 250
Henderson, Carl 251
Henderson, Handy 233, 262
Henderson, Perry
    228, 259, 262, 282
Henderson, Swede 250
Henley, Cecil 230, 250, 284, 308
Henry, Carol 250, 278
Henry, Hugh 282
Henry, Patrick 251
Hensley, Gene 251
Henson, Ace 251
Henson, Bob 207
Henson, Claude 278
Henson, Heavy 33, 232, 250, 278
Hepler, Elmer 250
Herbert, Clyde 264
Herman, Ed 33
Herren, Dick 251. 284
Herrington, Ed 259
Hess, Bob 33, 251
Hickman, Chester 251, 284, 308
Hickman, Tom 26
Hicks, Mickey 167, 259
Hicks, Tillie Murphy 210
Hightower, Clyde 250

Index

Hightower, William C. 284
Hill, Clayton 278
Hill, Clinton 278
Hill, Jess 278
Hill, Jim 278
Hill, Lawrence 278
Hill, Shorty 228, 262, 283
Hillside, Ariz. 76, 96, 117, 120
Hillyer, Jack 284, 308
Hines, Cherry Hale 251, 286
Hines, Dan 234, 250, 278
Hinkle, George 251, 278
Hinton, Dee 233, 231, 250, 264, 278
Hinton, Okla. 65, 67, 72, 96
Hiram, Major E. Tuttle 63
Hitson, Jack 251
Hobbs, Joker 250
Hock, John 278
Hoey, Jack 250
Hoffman, Don 278
Hoffman, R.J. 286
Hogan, Tom
    33, 94, 139, 151, 184, 207, 228, 251, 278
Hoggett, Chas. 284
Hogue, Nip 250
Holcomb, Elmer 278
Holcomb, Homer 24, 26, 63, 250
Holcomb, Millard 251, 290
Holder, A. J. 259, 278
Holder, Arthur 234, 259, 282
Holland, Hank 251
Hollander, M. A 259
Holleyman, J.D. 284
Hollihan, Jimmie 308
Holt, Jack 259
Holmes, Joe 290, 308
Holton, Doc 290
Homan, Vance 290
Homer, Mrs. Holcomb 20
Homoki, Stephen Cook 278
Hood, Charley 251, 278

Hood, Joe 251, 282
Hood, Lesley 251, 278
Hood, Lloyd 290
Hood, Marshall 251
Hoofs & Horns
    42, 45, 51, 52, 57, 60, 65, 70, 77,
    79, 80, 82-83, 86, 96, 101-102,
    105, 107, 110, 113, 114, 118, 121,
    123, 124, 126, 131, 133, 138, 140,
    144, 146, 154, 156, 158, 160, 162,
    163, 164, 171, 173, 175, 179, 180,
    184, 197, 207
Hooper, Wash 120
Hope, G. W. 251, 290
Hope, N.M. 130
Hopkins, Drew 250, 290
Hopkins, Joseph 146
Hopkins, "Ma"
    57, 82, 96, 101, 118, 147, 164,
    173, 175, 228, 251, 286
Hopkins, "Pa" 228, 251, 286
Hopp, Pete 250, 286
Horner, Mildred Mix 250, 278
Horner, Tommy 16, 232, 250, 290
Horton, A. A. 259
Horton, Bill 229, 259, 290
Hosley, Frank 250, 290
Hotcher, Allan 33
Hotel Texas 121
Houghton, Bob 231, 259
House, George 251, 290
Houston Fat Stock Show Rodeo 162
Houston, Texas 139
Hovenkamp, Eddie 232, 250, 278
Howard, Bill 278
Howard Buick Automobile Co 134
Howard, Tex 251, 290
Howard, V.L. 290
Howe, Don 278
Howe, J. C. 250, 286
Howe, Jim 83
Howell, Cecil 251

Howell, Chet 284, 308
Howell, Juanita 290
Hubbard, Fay 278
Hubbell, Rube 259, 278
Huckaby, Billy 9
Huckfeldt, Carl 251, 290
Hudgins, W.O. 290
Hudson, Jim 160, 232, 250, 278
Hudson, Shorty 290
Huff, Leo 251, 290
Hughes, Bill 290
Hughes, Chas. J. 286
Hughes, Joe D. 250, 287
Hugo, Colo. 117, 152
Hull, Mark 172, 278
Hulse, Ray, 259
Hunsaker, Keith 232
Hunsaker, Kenneth 259
Hunt, Ted 251
Hunter, Dick 230, 259
Hunter, Dummy 235, 262, 283
Hunter, Maynard 278
Hunter, Roy 290
Hurd, Lee R. 284
Huskey, Lynn 20, 33, 250
Hussey, Shirley
  177, 183, 207, 250, 264, 278
Hussmann, Bill 234
Hutchins, Barbara K. 287
Hutchinson, Geo. E. 290
Hutchinson, Lee 278
Hybik, Carl 16
Hydson, Shorty 278

I

Iler, Bill 251, 278, 308
Iler, Mary 278
Ingersoll, Rufus 108
Ingram, Bud 251
Inks, Earl 290
Iowa's Championship Rodeo 161-162
Irby, E.W. "Lefty" 290
Irish, Ned 177
Irvine, Van 290
Irwin, Jim 230, 251, 278
Irwin, Sli 290
Ismay, Mont. 28
Ivory, Buster 212
Ivory, June 211
Ivory, Perry 49, 86, 230, 278
Ivory, Raymond 'Buster' 278
Iwo Jima 188

J

Jack, Cleo 290
Jackson, Clarence 144
Jackson, Harold 260, 290
Jackson, Jack 33, 290
Jackson, Jim 252
Jacobs, Iva Dell 260
Jacobs, Len 33, 252, 290
Jacobs, Slats
  105, 106, 229, 251, 278
Jaeneche, L. W. 290
Jamison, B. M. Jr. 278
Jaques, Joseph 278
Jarnigan, Logan 252, 290
Jason, Alvin 235, 260
Jauregui, Andy
  49, 86, 106, 108, 121, 228, 251, 278
Jauregui, Ed 252, 278
Jeffrees, Weldon 290, 308
Jenkins, Jay 278
Jenkins, Leslie 282
Jenson, Buck 290
Jernigan, Buck 252, 287
Jerrel, Jerry 284, 308
Jesperson, Allen 278
John B. Stetson Co. 134
Johnson, Ben 290
Johnson, Buck 290
Johnson, Bud 260

Index

Johnson, Buel 16
Johnson, Dick 278
Johnson, Dick, 259
Johnson, E. H. (Blacky) 251, 290
Johnson, Everett 251, 290
Johnson, Faye 278
Johnson, Harold 33, 234, 260
Johnson, Merle 252
Johnson, Mervin L. 252, 287
Johnson, Stub 212
Johnson, Col. W.T.
    19, 25, 31, 32, 40, 43, 101
Johns, V.M. 287
Jones, Art 232, 251, 290
Jones, Buck 252, 278
Jones, Buff 259
Jones, Cecil
    9, 143, 165, 173, 180, 193, 212, 251, 286, 308
Jones, Charles 229, 251, 290
Jones, Eddie 231, 251, 290
Jones, Fannye 162, 166, 171, 184
Jones, Gov. R. T. "Bob" 251, 287
Jones, Ralph 234, 259
Jones, Snooks 33, 290
Jones, Tex 290
Jordan, John
    26, 94, 109, 156, 229, 251, 278
Jordan, Lon 283
Jorgenson, Ivan 278

K

Kaaro, Jimmy 284, 308
Kaisers Vancouver Shipyard 183
Kalin, Ray 282
Kane, Bill 251, 278
Kane, Joe 290
Karman, Blackie 290, 308
Karmon, Bill 251
Karn, Lile 234, 251
Karstad, Les 34
Karstad, Leslie 232, 251, 290

Kay, Al, 260
Keas, Bill 179
Keeline, Joe J, Jr. 290
Keen, Bill 251
Keen, Mary Wilson 25, 27, 235, 251
Keenan, Bud 262
Kell, Jess 230, 251, 290
Kellenberger, A.G. 287
Keller, Art 251, 290
Kelley, Billy 284
Kelley, Bob 284
Kelley, Cleve 16, 229, 251, 290
Kelley, Curley 233, 251
Kelley, Fred 251
Kelley, Jack 284
Kelley, Marion Ross 252, 290
Kelley, Pat 290
Kelley, Truman 284
Kelly, Ross 290
Kelsey, Joe 234, 290
Kelso, Joe 260
Kemm, Carl 251
Kemp, Carl 251
Kemp, Chuck 290
Ken, Mrs. Boen 192
Kendrick, E.M. 290
Kennedy, Cal 234, 260
Kennedy, Cecil 113, 228, 262
Kennedy, Dale 212, 251
Kennedy, Jack 290
Kenney, James 228, 251, 278
Kerchgarber, Frank 251
Kerscher, D'Lyla Longo
    9, 78, 187, 190
Kerscher, Jack
    43, 49, 72, 86, 106, 230, 251, 282
Kerscher, Pete
    78, 95, 104, 107, 158, 170, 187, 190, 231, 251
Kersh, Bubba 251
Kersh, Johnny 251

Kersten, George 252
Kesler, Liz 9
Keyston Bros. Saddlery 134
Kid, Canada 16
Kilfoyl, Cliff 230, 260
Killough, Bill 251
Killough, Buck 284, 308
Kilpatrick, Col. John Reed 287
Kimmel, H. R. 287
Kinner, J. R. 251
Kinney, Jack 56
Kinney, James 264
Kinnibaugh, Mack 290
Kipp, Bill 290
Kirchgraber, Frank 290
Kirk, Roy 229, 260
Kirkendall, Helen 251
Kirkwood, Donald 251
Kirnan, Bea 20
Kirnan, Tommy 20
Kitchens, Frank, Jr. 165
Klamath Falls (Oregon) Rodeo 161
Klebba, Joe 251, 284
Kline, Clyde 260
Knapp, Jack 278
Knickerbocker Pictures 119
Knight, Babe" 228
Knight, Emily 162
Knight, Fay 183, 278
Knight, Harry
    26, 48, 49, 67, 68, 86, 117, 228, 251, 278
Knight, Jack 184, 283
Knight, L. R. 251
Knight, Nick
    152, 158, 183, 229, 251, 278
Knight, Pete 16, 43, 262, 283
Knight, Tom 231, 251, 284
Koed, James 308
Koed, Whitey 16, 228, 260, 284
Kohrs, Ray 251, 284, 308
Krashovitz, John 165

Kreig, Vaughn 251
Kremmling, Colo. 193
Krieg, Vaughn 20, 25, 33, 235
Kriendler, Jack 151, 264, 287
Kriz, Joe 287
Kruger, Mose 260
Kubitz, Louis 20, 26
Kudron, Joe 284
Kumerle, Slim 284
Kunz, Tommy 251, 290
Kutch, Hilton 252, 290

L

Lacy, C. D. 252
LaFarge, W. M. 252, 287
Ladman, Smoky 290
Lahman, Jerry 287
Lamar, Carl 252
Lamar, Curtis 252, 278
Lamax, Joe 252
Lambert, Joe 252
Lancaster, Calif. 134
Landers, Al 252
Landers, Raymond 260
Lando, Swede 252
Landon, Al 230, 260
Lane, Casper, "Cappy" 287
Lane, H.L. Jr. 290
Lane, Johnnie 290
Lane, Ralph 290
Larsen, Homer, 290
LaRue, Walt 212, 278
Lasswell, Chuck 284, 308
Las Vegas, N. M 185
Las Vegas, Nev. 169, 206
Lattemore, Charlie 230
Lattemore, Chas. 260
Lawrence, Billy 278
Lawrence, Junior 284
Lawrence, W.B. 290
Lawson, Roy Fore 307

Laycock, Jim 278
Laycock, Maurice 184, 207, 252, 278
Laycock, Morris
Leach, Billy 278
Leavins, Ross 290
KeBeau, Dick 290
Lee, Albert 287
Lee, Bob 252
Lee, Carl 260, 290
Lee, Carl, Beswick 232
Lee, Cherrie Osborne 155
Lee, Clarence 278
Lee, Cotton 278
Lee, Joel 290
Lee, W. A. 252, 287
Leesville, La. 193
Lefton, Abe 26, 252, 278
Leggett, Elton 278
Lemley, Lee 290
Lenepah, Okla. 193
Leonard, Jimmie 252
Leonard, R.J. 287
Lerosh, Bob 16
Leslie, . Jenkins 229
Leslie, F. Herrick 169
Leuschner, C. O 260
Leuschner, C. O. 282
Levi Strauss & Co. 134
Levi Strauss and Company 96
Levins, Ross 252
Lewallen, G. K. 252, 278
Lewis, H. G. 253, 287
Lewis, K. W. 252, 287
Lewis, Mike 235, 260
Lewis, Pat 252, 290
Lewis, Rose 290
Lewis, Roy
   184, 207, 229, 252, 264, 290
Lewis, Russell 252, 290
Lewiston RoundUp 133
Liberty, Texas 158
Liberty, Texas. 149

Lichtenstein, Helen 234, 252, 278
Lightning C Ranch 149
Like, James 252, 284, 308
Like, Jesse 290
Like, Jim 212
Lilley, Bob J. 290
Lilley, H. L. 278
Linder, Herman
   16, 44, 45, 48, 49, 70, 72, 85, 86,
   96, 109, 120, 212, 252, 278
Linder, Herman, 228
Linder, Warner 117
Linderman, Bill 172, 207, 208, 290
Linderman, Bud 170, 207, 208, 284
Lindsey, Billy 252
Lindsey, Earl
   196, 197, 198, 199, 204, 206
Lindsey, John 232, 252, 278
Lindsey, Morris 308
Lindues, Louis 278
Lines, Milo 260
Lingle, Floyd 253, 290
Lisenbee, Byron 278
Litterell, Jerry 282
Little Horse Creek, Wyo. 113
Littrell, Jerry 33, 252
Livermore, Calif. 169, 172
Livesay, L.W. Jr. 290
Livingston, Cal 290, 308
Livingston, Mont. 70, 113, 120
Locke, Lloyd 290
Lockett, Reese
   104, 105, 108, 252, 290
Lockie, Bob 231, 252, 260
Lockyer, Terry 231, 252
Lockhart, Sonny 287
Lodi, Calif.; 178
Logue, Harry 116, 230, 252, 278
Lohn, Sam 290
Lohr, Art 278
Lomax, Joe 308
Londos, Swede 285

Long, Hughie
 16, 48, 67, 68, 72, 73, 74, 82, 85,
 86, 95, 101, 106, 107, 121, 151,
 158, 159, 183, 228, 252, 290
Long, Jack
 20, 25, 34, 44, 52, 63, 100, 130,
 139, 155, 160, 177, 196
Long, Peggy 25, 99, 235, 252
Longricker, David 16, 232, 260
Longricker, David Hipe Wolrich
 Buel Johnson 16
Looney, Dorothy 143
Lorimer, Chuck 278
Los Angeles, (California) Coliseum
 Rodeo 161
Los Angeles, Calif. 96, 178
Los Angeles Coliseum 178
Louis, Buster 252
Louis, Joe 119, 165
Louks, Dick 252, 282
Louks, Wayne 252, 290, 308
Lovejoy, Eiland 287
Lovelady, Fannye
 183, 184, 192, 200, 205, 263, 278
Lovelady, Ralph 131
Lovelady, Sam 278
Lovelady, Shorty 285, 308
Lowry, Bill 253, 278
Lowry, Fred 252, 291
Lowry, Fred, 230
Lowry, Glen 232, 282
Lowry, Glenn 260
Lucas, Billy 291
Lucas, Buck 100
Lucas, Jim 230, 260
Lucas, Mitzi 278
Lucas, Mitzi (Riley) 193
Lucas, Mitzi Riley 9, 31, 100, 193
Lucas, Tad
 25, 27, 100, 143, 235, 260, 278
Luer, Harvey 285, 308
Luffman, Paul 231, 260

Lufkin, Ned 278
Lufkin, Ned 1751 Ivory, Raymond
 'Buster' 1532 Lynch
 278
Lund, Ross 252
Lyan, Stan 252
Lyman, O. B. 260, 291
Lynch, Emmet 278
Lynch, Emmett 264
Lyne, Chas 260
Lyne, C.J. 291
Lyon, Bill 252, 282
Lyon, Stan 285

M

MacDonald, Dorothy 254
Mack, Gus 291
Maddox, Everett 285
Madison Square Garden
 15, 17, 23, 25, 31, 32, 62, 71, 72,
 78, 101, 119, 120, 131, 155, 158,
 162, 177, 188, 190
Madison Square Garden Corp. 170
Madison Square Garden Rodeo
 118, 161
Mae, Ida Swift 90
Maggini, Charlie 230, 262, 278
Mahan, Abe 291
Maher, Jim 291
Majors, Cliff 235, 252, 287
Malm, Ted 278, 285
Mammoth, Ariz. 187
Mandan Rodeo Association 178
Mangum, Okla 160
Mann, Orval 278
Manning, Art 234, 252, 287
Mansfield, Bob 278
Mansfield, Mone Jr. 287
Mansfield, Toots
 134, 150, 152, 155, 157, 159, 169,
 172, 183, 196, 203, 204, 206, 208,
 230, 252, 263, 279

Index

Manvel, Texas 158
Marberger, M. E. 252
Mare Island 176
Mariam, Frank 308
Marion, Frank
    33, 115, 121, 232, 252, 285
Markley, Bill 291
Mark, John 253
Markcum, Wolf 279
Markham, Jack 253
Marlow, Box 291
Marsh, Earl 279
Marshall, Fouts 291
Marshall, Frank 212, 253, 291
Marshall, Grant 252, 279, 308
Marshall, Kermit 279
Martens, Jack 287
Martin, Chuck 163
Martin, Dutch 291
Martin, Elmer 33, 232, 252
Martin, Johnny 279
Martin, Nub 253, 279
Martin, Prosser 252, 287
Martin, Roy 252, 291
Martin, Vick Reno 253, 291
Martindale, Chick 231, 259
Martinez, Pete 252, 279
Martz, Frank 33, 228, 253
Mason, Buck 291
Mason, Fred L. 287
Mason, Rex 253
Massey, Gus 235, 252, 262, 287
Massey, Jim 33, 230
Masterson, Harold 291
Mateo County, Calif. 49
Mathews, E.R. 287
Mathews, Howard 279
Mathis, Frank 291
Matlock, Harvey 279
Matlock, Shorty 253, 279
Matthews, Bob 16, 232, 252, 285
Matthews, E. R. 253

Matthews, Roy
    16, 28, 229, 252, 291
Mauboules, Milton 235, 259
Mavity, Ray 134, 231, 252, 291
Maxwell, Omer 229, 282
Maxwell, Omer, 259
May, Buddy 252, 291
May, Earl 232, 259, 291
Mayeo, Roy 33
Mayfield, Buck 291
Maynard, Jack 253
McAdam, Hugh 231, 254, 291
McBee, Blanche 254
McBee, Lloyd 254
McBride, Bill 279
McCall, Curly 34, 291
McCall, Thea 291
McBride, Dudley 285
McCabe, Tommy 285, 308
McCain, Archie 291
McCallum, Bryan 291
McCardwell, Mark 254
McCarroll, Frank 279
McCarty, Chet
    139, 151, 232, 253, 291
McCarty, Ed 26, 279
McClure, Jake
    16, 28, 34, 115, 229, 253, 283
McClure, Marion 253, 287
McConnell, Wallace 291, 308
McCormick, J. D. 253, 285
McCormick, Red 33
McCormick, Trixie 143, 279
McCrain, Archie 253
McCray, Mardell 291
McCray, Wiley 254, 291
McCrorey, Howard 228, 279
McCrorey, Knotchie 253, 282
McCrorey, Shorty 279
McCrory, Howard
    16, 19, 94, 155, 253, 308
McCrory, Mickey 33, 229, 253, 291

McCrory, Shorty
    33, 184, 207, 232, 253, 264
McCrory, Ted 229, 259
McCuistion, Day 291
McCullough, Carl 231, 260
McCumber, W.R. 287
McDaniel, Bud 33, 254, 279
McDonald, Frank 159, 234, 260
McDonald, Grove 143
McDonald, Red 253
McDougal, Bucke 285, 308
McDowell, Paul 287
McElroy, Curtis 253, 291
McElroy, Earl 291
McElvain, Lee 253
McEntire, John 279
McEuen, Albert 228, 253, 285, 308
McEuen, Arthur 285
McEuen, Ed 254, 287
McFadden, Arden 234, 260, 285, 308
McFadden, Gordon 172, 253, 279
McFall, Elmer 291
McFall, Harry 253
McFarlan, Bill 231
McFarland, Bill 116, 253, 279
McFarland, John 254, 279
McFarland, Otis 291
McGee, Jimmie 16, 228, 253, 285
McGinnis, Billy 168
McGinnis, Ray 110, 230, 260
McGinnis, Russell 230, 260
McGinty, D'Lynn Terry 9
McGinty, Rusty
    16, 28, 34, 37, 43, 48, 50, 66, 70,
    72, 94, 96, 101, 121, 139, 151, 170,
    228, 237, 253, 279
McGowan, James 260
McGuire, Bill 254, 279
McHolland, Jim 254
McIntire, John 16
McIntosh, Archie 230, 260
McIntosh, George 27, 229, 259

McIntyre, John 231, 260
McKenzie, Lester 254
McKinley, Jack 291
McKittrick, Walt 279
McLaughlin, Donald 279
McLaughlin, Gene 9, 193, 279
McLaughlin, James 'Spec' 285
McLennon, Don 279
McLennon, Hope 279
McLeran, Stub 291
McMacken, Bill 253, 279
McMacken, Joe 262
McMackin, Bill 33, 81, 169, 234
McMackin, Bud 253
McMackin, Joe 33, 232
McMahan, Jack 291
McMahon, Ed 279
McMillen, Speck 234, 253
McNoulty, Pat 254
McNutt, Maxwell
    40, 44, 46, 48, 49, 54, 60, 62, 65-
    66, 84, 86, 101, 129, 138, 147, 148
McPherson, Dick 253
McSpott, Billy 253
McWiggins, Zack 254, 279
Meeks, Alford 253, 279
Meeks, Bob 253, 279
Meeks, Verne 231, 259
Meese, Ted 253, 291
Mefford, Buddy 33, 184, 207, 253, 285
Mehner, Vick Reno 253
Meigs, Henry 287
Meiji Stadium 180
Melville, Bob 285
Mendes, Carl 253, 285, 308
Mendes, Frank 212, 253, 285, 308
Mendes, Joe 252, 279
Mendes, John 212, 230, 252, 279
Mercer, Dell 229, 253
Merchant, Richard
    31, 43, 49, 86, 156, 229, 252, 279

Index

Merck, John 291
Merrill's Marauders 178
Merritt, Dean 285, 308
Merritt, Hyde 285
Merritt, King
  33, 49, 151, 158, 169, 170, 175,
  183, 198, 229, 253, 263, 279
Meteer, Slim 262, 282
Meyer, Betty 25
Meyer, John 291
Meyer, Leonard 253, 291
Meyers, Herbert
  121, 139, 229, 253, 279, 308
Meyers, Hub 16
Michel, Henry 253
Michelson, Dr. Henry E. 287
Midland Fair, Inc. 96
Miles City, Mont. 43
Miles, Dave 285
Miller, Arthur C. 287
Miller, Bob 279
Miller, Dan 287
Miller, Don 253
Miller, George 285, 308
Miller, H. T. 259
Miller, Inky 253
Miller, Richard 231, 252, 279
Miller, Wayne 291
Millet, G.A. 291
Mills, George
  159, 183, 195, 196, 230, 252, 263,
  279
Mills, George, 200
Mills, Hank
  121, 143, 155, 169, 230, 252, 279
Mills, N. M. 172, 187
Milton, Lawrence 252
Milwaukee, Wis. 185
Minneapolis Aquatennial Rodeo 162
Minnick, Lizzie 117
Minor, Kenneth 279
Minotto, DeMetrio 90

Minotto, James 90, 109, 237, 252
Minotto, Jimmie
  82, 85, 86, 89, 101, 102, 104,
  118, 127, 231
Minotto, Sissy 235, 252, 291
Minter, Cullen 291
Mithcham Brothers 291
Mitchell, Bill 291
Mitchell, Don 253
Mitchell, Leonard 253, 291
Mitchell, Ralph 253
Mix, Mildred Horner 25, 117
Modesto, Calif. 192
Moe, Milt 33, 49, 228, 253, 279
Moller, Wharton 291
Molone, Buddy 278
Moore, Frank 287
Monroe, Floyd 291
Montana, Louise 279
Montana, Montie 279
Montana, Montie Jr. 279
Montana, Montie, Jr. 193
Montana's Troup 279
Monte Vista, Colo. 24, 66, 148
Montgomery, Arnold 172, 252
Montgomery, Harry 50
Montgomery, Lindsey 253
Montgomery, Vic 184, 207, 264, 279
Montgomery Wards & Co. 134
Montrose, Colo. 159
Moody, W. C. 252
Moore, Bob 279
Moore, Bullie 253
Moore, Earl 33, 228, 253, 279
Moore, Frank 83, 120
Moore, Lee 253
Moore, Pete 253
Moore, Ward 279
Moorpark, Calif. 193
Moran, Smokey 291
Moran, Webb 253
Moreaux, Shannon 291

Morris, Al 253, 291
Morris, Bob 234, 259
Morris, Chip 291
Morris, Claude 279
Morris, Dale 252
Morris, Johnnie 259
Morris, Logue 291
Morris, PeeWee 253, 279
Morris, Rex 291
Morris, Rufus 252, 291
Morrison, Bert F 259
Morrison, Bill 179
Moser, Roy 291
Moss, Hoitt 279
Motschall, Katherine 287
Mott, Eddie 285, 308
Mounce, Ernest 252, 285
Mounce, Louis 279
Mueller, H. H. 252, 279
Mulkey, Burel
    16, 68, 69, 73, 75, 76, 82, 85, 86,
    95, 101, 108, 115, 117, 120, 121,
    128, 139, 229, 253, 279
Mullins, W.E. 291
Mundy, Irby 68, 108, 230, 252, 291
Munroe, Buter 291
Munson, Bryan 285
Murphy, Hardy 26, 279
Murray, Bob 252, 291
Murray, Joe, Jr. 193, 279
Murray, Leo 16, 49, 228, 253, 279
Murray, Leonard 259
Murrells, Dan. T. 287
Mutch, Ernest 285
Myers, Herb 73, 124
Myers, Hub 95
Myers, Jack 231, 259
Myers, Virgil 291

N

National Cowboy & Western
    Heritage Museum
    39, 76, 90, 119, 149, 212
National Cowboy Hall of Fame 200
National Rodeo Association
    172, 206, 208
National Western Stock Show &
    Rodeo 25, 154
Neal, Bill, Jr. 279
Neal, Buddy 279
Nelson, Bud 253
Nelson, George W. 279
Nelson, Rube 231, 260
Nelson, Tim 253, 285, 308
Nesbitt, Don 20, 49
Nesbitt, Donald 26, 228, 253, 279
Nesbitt, Jimmie
    28, 32, 86, 101, 228, 253, 283,
    308
Nesbitt, Pauline 25, 63, 235, 253,
New Caledonia 176
Newell, Pauline B. 287
Newell, Walter L. 287
New York City
    15-17, 31, 72, 76, 114, 120, 138,
    151
Newhagen, Frank E. 253, 287
Newhall, Calif. 158-159, 178
Newman, Pete 291 Newsom, George
    234, 260
Newt, O'Keefe 291
Newton, Slim 253, 291
Nichols, J. D. 279
Nilsson, Gene 291
Nimmo, Dave 291
Nissen, Bill 253
Nix, Bill 229, 253
Nix, Buck 291
Nix, Will 279
Nogales, Ariz. 75, 192

Index

Nolan, Bob 279
Noland, O. H 259
North American Cowboys Association 120
North Plymouth, Mass. 96
Northwest Cowboy Association 114
Nuckols, Grafton 253, 279
Nuckols, Reno Texas Kidd 253, 291
Nunnis, Sam 291
Nunn, John 283

O

Oakdale, Calif. 43, 44
O'Brien, Eddie 287
Oakley, Russell Jack 279
O'Callaha, Fox 264
O'Callahan, Fox 184, 207, 228, 253, 279
O'Conner, Chuck 291
Oceanside, Calif. 179
Odle, John 254
Ogden 102
Ogden, Utah 67, 79, 82, 85, 104, 129, 185
Ohrlin, Glenn 279
Oja, Andy 254, 279
Okemah, Okla. 152
Oklahoma City, Okla. 178, 185, 212
Oldenberg, John 285, 308
Oliver, Buck 285, 308
Olsen, Bob 254, 291
Olsen, Dutch 253, 291
Olsen, Fay 2 91
Olsen, Jimmie 232, 253
Olsen, Pampa 282
Oltrof, Jack G. 254, 287
Oltrof, Mrs. Jack 254, 287
O'Neill, Howard 177
O'Neill, Jimmie 291
Oracle, Ariz. 187
Orr, Joe 231, 253

Osborne, Ed 230, 260, 291
O'Shea, Michael 279
Ostrander, Dean 291
Overson, Bob 279
Overson, Don 279
Owens, Del 279
Owens, Herb 253, 291
Owens, Mitch 117
Owens, Mitchell 230, 253, 279
Owsley, Cecil 139, 228, 253, 285

P

Padgett, Berry 247
Padgett, Ray 285
Padia, Walter 254, 291
Palhamus, Sam 234, 260, 282
Palmer, Johnny 285, 309
Palmer, Lloyd 192, 193
Pardee, Doc 127
Pardee, E. 16, 28, 34, 228, 254, 279
Parker, Bud 228, 254, 279
Parker, Gus 254, 287
Parker, Luther 291
Parker, Pat 254, 291
Parker Ranch 178
Parker, Rock 121, 232, 254, 285, 309
Parker, Tommy 291
Parks, Bill 33, 232, 254, 279
Parks, Darwin 234, 254, 279
Parks, Mary 25, 33, 254
Parrish, Dalton 229, 260
Parrish, Fla. 192
Parrish, Vester 254, 279
Parshall, Alvin 292
Parsons, Jay 292
Patch, Jim 285
Patch, ScrapIron 111
Pattee, Alan 165, 285, 309
Patterson, George 254, 292
Pattit, Wesley 292
Paul Bond Boot Company 75

Paul, Chuck 279
Paul, Clyde 254, 287
Paul, Marvin 231, 254, 285, 309
Paulsen, Russell 234, 260
Pawhuska, Okla. 169
Paxton, Trent 254, 283
Payne, Gene H. 279
Payne, Junior 262, 282
Payson, Ariz. 158, 169
Peak, Justin 231, 260
Pearce, Joe 279
Pearson, Frank 292
Pearl Harbor, Hawaii, 163, 168
Pecos, Texas 150
Peelgren, Howard 231, 260
Pendleton, Ore.
   58, 62, 66, 70, 72, 102, 108, 160
Pendleton RoundUp
   77, 78, 79, 85,
   102, 113, 114, 143, 161
Penick, John 254, 292
Penrose, Spencer 262, 283
Pepper, Rex 254
Percifield, Jack 279
Perkins, Arthur 254, 287
Perkins, Jess 254
Perkins, Len 234, 254, 279
Perkins, Tom 232, 260
Perry, Everett 292
Person, Norman 234, 254, 292
Peters, Ed 254, 292
Peters, Floyd
   207, 229, 254, 279, 292
Peterson, Buck 231, 260, 280
Pettcock, N. A. 254
Pettcock, U. A. 280
Pettigrew, A. J. 254, 292
Pettigrew, Homer
   33, 151, 157, 159, 169, 170, 172,
   187, 196, 208, 212, 228, 254, 280
Pettit, Japson 280

Pettit, Wesley 280
Phillips, Dub
   184, 207, 208, 254, 280
Phoenix, Ariz.
   86, 94, 96, 101,
   151, 152, 158, 162, 178,
   184, 188, 195, 198, 201
Pholson, Jim 280
Pickett, Joseph W. 280
Picture, Fred 254
Piela, Jack 280
Piela, Joe 280
Pilcher, Bud 292
Piper, Harold 33, 231, 254, 282
Pitman, George 33
Pittman, Paul 280
Pittsburg, Okla 172
Plains, Texas 96, 101
Plaskett, Pat 232, 254
Plymouth Cordage Company 96
Poage, Doug 254, 280
Poage, Walton 184, 207, 254, 280
Pocatello, Idaho 134, 158
Pogue, John 280, 285, 309
Poore, Dan 292
Porter, Jack 285, 309
Porter, Pat 287
Porter Saddle and Harness Co.
   96, 135
Porter, Willard, 200
Portland, Ore 185
Posey, Hugh 254, 292
Poston, James 254, 292
Potter, Lyle Van 287
Powers, Ted 229, 254, 280
Prescott 62
Prescott's Frontier Days Rodeo 127
Preston, C. P. 280
Pretti, Bob 280
Pretty Prairie, Kans 185
Pribble, Mike 285, 309
Price, Robert 292

Index

Price, Utah 185
Pro Rodeo Hall of Fame 125
Proctor, Sam 260
Proctor, Sam, 232
Professional Rodeo Cowboys
 Association 11, 20, 203
ProRodeo Hall of Fame
 & Museum of the American Cow
 34-35, 40
Pruett, Gene 254, 280
Pruitt, Geter 292
Pruitt, I. V. 280
Pryor, Ray 292
Pueblo, Colo. 70, 72, 178
Puyallup, Wash 150

Q

Quait, Jack 34, 232, 254, 292
Quigg, Raymond 229, 260
Quirk, Frank
 9, 75, 111, 193, 255, 285, 309
Quirk, John 188
Quirk, Louis
 9, 111, 115, 188, 189, 193, 292
Quirk, Rabbit 292
Quirk, Richard 188
Quirk, Robert 188
Quirk, Thomas 188, 189
Quirk, Wilbert 188

R

RAA Bulletin 86, 120, 185
RAA News 153
Radio Corporation of America 203
Ragan, Earl 292
Ragsdale, Fred 282
Raho, Frank 255
Ralph, Dr. Lovelady 131
Rambo, Gene 184, 207, 255, 280
Ramsey, John 292
Ramsey, V. H. 255, 292

Ranch Romances 40
Rand, Larry 254
Randall, Glenn H. 280
Randolph, Florence
 25, 110, 260, 282
Randolph, Elmer 292
Randolph, Floyd 254, 287
Randolph, Ray 254
Ranney, Austin 260
Ray, Al 292
Ray, Durwood 292
Ray, Guy 292
Ray, Russell 254
Reagan, Bob 43, 254
Reagan, Johnny 292
Reagan, Rocky 43
Reale, Elio 165
Reavis, Jeff 254, 292
Red, Calgary 254
Red Lodge, Mont 172
Reed, John Fitzpatrick 170
Reeves, Jimmie 280
Reeves, Lem 254, 280
Reger, Monty 280
Reid, Nig 280
Reilly, Maurice 33
Reiser, Fred 260
Reno (Nevada) Rodeo 161
Reno, Nev 105
Reno, Nev. 24, 44, 65, 105, 158
Retzel, Frank 292
Reynolds, Brown Jug 280
Reynolds, Fess 150, 280
Reynolds, Jim 282
Reynolds, Ray 282
Rhea, Vance 254
Rhodes, Jess 260
Rhodes, John
 43, 117, 187, 228, 255, 280
Rhodes, Tom
 172, 207, 228, 255, 280

Rhodes, Tommy 187
Ribelin, Tom 285
Rice, Leland 156
Rice, Ole 33, 292
Rich, Cap 287
Rich, Marianne 292
Richards, Lou 141, 154
Richards, Lucyle 20, 235, 282
Richardson, Bill 255, 292
Richardson, Lloyd 285
Richardson, Spud 165, 309
Richardson, W.W. 292
Richmond, Calif. 169
Ricker, Shorty
    33, 103, 107, 229, 255
Rider, Pauline 280
Ridley, Harold 292
Ridley, Howard 280
Ridley, Hugh 33, 231, 260, 280
Rielly, Maurice 231, 260
Rife, Syl 280
Rigby, Jim E. 292
Riggs, Murray 183, 280
Riley, Frank 254, 287
Riling, Raymond L. J. 255, 287
Ritches, Bob 285
Ritner, Roy 79, 102
Ritter, Clarence 234, 255
Rivers, Bob 254
Riverside Hotel 44
Roan, Salvesta, 234
Roane, Sylvester 280
Robbins, Dick 230, 255, 280
Robellard, Jim 254, 292
Roberson, A. A. 280
Roberts, Arnie 255
Roberts, George 254, 280
Roberts, Gerald
    169, 183, 195, 198, 200, 206,
    254, 280

Roberts, Ken
    139, 170, 172, 184, 188, 191, 207,
    208, 231, 255, 280
Roberts, Kenn 33
Roberts, Marjorie 280
Roberts, Rube 20, 26, 229, 255
Robertson, George 282
Robertson, Jack 255, 282
Robertson, Jim 260, 280
Robertson, John 255
Robinson, Andy 254, 292
Robinson, Buck 280
Robinson, Lucky 285, 309
Ralph, Robinson 292
Robison, Beanie 287
Robison, John 254
Robison, Tom 255
Rochin, Butch 254
Rocky Ford, Colo. 113
Rodeo Association of America
    7, 23, 39, 46, 54, 58, 127,
    138, 139, 148
Rodeo Cowboys' Association
    162, 195, 197, 205
Rodeo Historical Society 200, 201
Rodeo Train 15, 31, 43
Roer, Bill 234, 260
Rogers, Bedell 280
Rogers, Buddy 285
Rogers, Brahma 292
Rogers, Eddie 254, 280
Rogers, Nell 254
Rogers, Pete 285
Rogers, Roy 177, 196, 287
Rogers, Vic 33, 230, 260
Rolling Hills, Wyo. 193
Romans, Mason 254, 292
Rooke, Frank 280
Rooker. Bob 285
Rooney, Lonnie
    33, 107, 229, 254, 292
Root, Helene 287

Index Page 345

Root, Louise 287
Rosaschi, Lester 193
Rose, Parry 255, 280
Rose, Roy 292
Rosenburg, B. B. 255
Ross, Bruce 235, 255, 285
Ross, Butch 254, 287
Ross, Gene
   76, 94, 152, 229, 255, 292
Ross, Herschell 33, 231, 255
Ross, Roy 255
Ross, Waldo 143, 152
Rossi, Rex 292
Roswell, N.M. 196, 206
Rothel, Bob 280
Rowe, Floyd 280
Rowell, Harry 104, 134, 171, 180
Rowett, Wm. 287
Roy, Guy 254
Roy, Mutt 255, 282
Royal Easter Show 143
Ruckdeschel, Hank 280
Rucker, Blacky 33
Rucker, Ed 212, 254
Rucker, Hayden 230, 260
Rude, Ike 228, 255, 280
Rugus, James Morris 308
Rumsey, Jack 280, 292
Runyan, Vince 254
Russell, Blackie 292
Russell, Joe 292
Russell, Phillip 280
Russell, S. G. 280
Rutledge, Shorty 255, 292
Ryan, Dick 180, 182
Ryan, Durant 231
Ryan, Durard 255
Ryan, Duward 280
Ryan, Pat 292
Ryan, Windy 292
Ryder, Buster 254
Ryley, Frank 235, 287

Ryon, Don, Jr. 280
Ryon, Druward 33
Ryser, Fred 233

S

Sacramento, Calif. 178
Salem, Oregon 192
Salinas 66, 79
Salinas, Calif.
   24, 39, 44, 54, 60, 79,
   84, 120, 151, 153, 162
Salinas, Juan 229, 256, 264, 280
Salinas, Tony 184, 207, 256, 280
Salisbury, Jack 256, 280
Salmon, Idaho 76, 117, 120
Salt Lake City, Utah 130, 185
San Angelo, Texas 208
San Antonio, Texas 181
San Bernadino, (California) National
   Rodeo 161
San Diego, Calif. 183
San Francisco, Calif. 96, 162, 178
San Juan Basin Rodeo Association
   133, 148
Sanborn, Lee 232, 292
Sanborn, Les 255
Sandall, Hubert 231, 255, 283
Sandefer, G. B. 256, 287
Sanders, George 285
Sands, George 234, 256, 261, 287
Sanford, Dave 234, 261
Sankey, Happy 256
Santa Fe, N. M. 192
Santos, Leonard 255, 292
Sartwells, J. W. 255, 287
Saul, Jack 292
Saunders, Jack 280
Saunders, Jim 256, 280
Saunders, Lloyd 49, 229, 260, 282
Saunders, R.L. 287
Savage, Henry 292

Sawyer, Ed 256, 287
Sawyers, Pauline 234, 261, 287
Saylors, Leon C. 256, 292
Sayre, Okla. 76, 152
Schaad, Gerrianne 9
Scheffield, Clyde 260
Schell, Asbury
    76, 135, 170, 228, 255, 280
Schell, Joe 261, 282
Schmidt, Doc 280
Schneider, Frankie 230, 255, 280
Schneider, Johnnie
    44, 230, 237, 250, 292
Schooley, Hershel 256, 287
Schrade, Jack 280
Schrader, Johnnie 261
Schultz, Ed 292
Schultz, Larry 292
Schumacher, Jimmy, 212, 280
Schwartz, Jack 280
Schwartz, Tony A. H. 255
Schwartz, Vic 229, 255, 280
Schwerd, Bill 292, 309
Scoma, Joe 287
Scott, Bob 255, 280
Scott, Deafie 260
Scott, J.R. 292
Scott, Paul 255, 264, 280
Scottsdale, Ariz.
    134, 152, 159, 169, 206
Scully, J.M. 287
Seago, Roscoe 255, 292
Searle, Stan
    24, 81, 83, 107, 147, 174
Searles, Kenney 280
Searls, R.D. 287
Sears Roebuck Co 151, 171
Seay, Billy 255

Seeley, George 256, 292
Segleski, John 165, 309
Selby, Bill 280
Sellars, Jack 228
Sellers, Earl 229, 255, 280
Sellers, Jack 255, 280
Sells, Albert 256, 280
Servel, Pierre 285
Sessions, Sam 292
Sewalt, Roy 230
Sewalt, Royce 255, 280
Seward, Roy S. 280
Shaffer, Jack 292
Shanhan, Rocky 292
Shanhan, L.V. 285
Sharp, Frank 49
Sharrah, Ira 292
Shaw, Everett
    16, 34, 48, 67, 68, 70, 73, 82, 85,
    86, 95, 108, 117, 121, 124, 128,
    158, 159, 170, 183, 188, 200, 207,
    208, 228, 255, 280
Shaw, Glen 230, 255, 264, 280
Shaw, Jack 177, 255, 292
Sheilds, Chas. 255
Shellenberger, C. J. 255, 285
Shellenberger, D. C. 255, 285
Shellenberger, David 309
Shellenberger, Orville 234, 261
Shelton, Dick 20, 230, 260
Shelton, Reine 20, 25, 27
Shepard, Carl 16, 228, 255, 292
Shepherd, V.H. 287
Sheppard, Carl 147
Sheppard, Chuck
    184, 207, 212, 230, 255, 280
Sheridan, Wyo 55
Sherman, Harry 287
Sherman, Jack 256, 280
Sherman, Joseph 292
Sherman, Tex 40, 41, 42
Shessler, Solly 280

Index

Shewly, Peck 256
Shields, Chas. A. 280
Shinn, Charles A. 256, 287
Shipman, Pete 33
Shipman, Tom 33, 232, 260
Shipp, Dave 231, 260
Shoulders, Jim 191, 192
Shoulders, Marvin
  184, 191, 207, 280
Shoulders, Sharon 9
Shreveport, La. 193
Shrine National Convention Rodeo
  96
Shultz, Chas. 280
Shumaker, Floyd 232, 260
Shupp, Bob 292
Sidney, Iowa
  24, 62, 79, 120, 162, 177
Sievers, Bill 231, 255, 280
Sikes, L. N. 280
Silacci, Ki 49
Silver Cloud 26
Silvers, Joe S. 280
Simcox, S.W. 292
Siminoff, Yale 280
Simms, Olan 281
Simon, Doc 229, 255
Simon, J. W. 255
Simon, Lee 229, 255
Sims, Blanket 256
Sisco, Jack 285
Sisco, Shorty 230, 262, 282
Sisty, Alice 256, 292
Skelton, Al 230, 255, 281
Skelton, Merle 179
Ski-Hi Stampede 148
Skinner, Ray 281
Skipworth, Jack 256, 292
Sky Eagle, George 292
Sky Eagle, Sunbeam 292
Slade, Don, 292, 309
Slappert, Dick 16, 229, 260, 292

Slim, Colorado 281
Slim, Dogtown 16
Sloan, Jimmie 255, 281
Slocum, Tex 33, 256
Slosum, Rex 292
Smith, Charley 255, 281
Smith, Charlie 184, 207, 264
Smith, Dell 260
Smith, Dude 192-193
Smith, Dugin 292
Smith, Eddie 261, 292
Smith, Frank 256
Smith, Governor 287
Smith, Jimmie 255
Smith, Johnny 293
Smith, Jute 281
Smith, Lee 256, 292
Smith, M. L. 281
Smith, Neal 281
Smith, Pat 173
Smith, Roy 281
Smith, Tex 212
Smith, Tommy 256, 292
Snively, Henry 261
Snively, Jay 33, 49, 231, 255
Snively, Jim 34, 256, 293
Snure, 285
Snyder, Smokey
  43-44, 73, 75, 86, 95, 121,
  152, 158, 170, 255, 263, 281
Sombrero Butte, Ariz. 43, 117, 172
Somerville, Stoney 293
Sommers, Gerald E. 287
Sonnenberg, Virginia 281
Sons of The Pioneers 196
Sorenson, Doc 293
Sorma, Agnes 90
Sorrells, Buck
  33, 158, 183, 198, 200, 228, 255
Sorrells, Buckshot
  121, 139, 151, 169, 170, 207
Sorrels, Buck 95

Sorrels, Buckshot 157, 196, 281
Southwest Aircraft, Inc. 190
Southwest Rodeo Association
    124, 156, 169, 172, 208
Southwestern Exposition and Fat
    Stock Show 26, 47, 96
Soward, Ace 232, 255, 293
Soward, Glenn 33, 255
Spanish Trails Fiesta 149
Spealman, Bud 281
Spence, Bud 293
Spence, Doc 255
Spencer, Tim 281
Spillsbury, Bud 235, 256
Spilsbury, Bud 281
Spokane, Wash. 183
Spratt, Bob 33
Springer, Bennie 281
Springerville, Ariz. 127
Springfield, Missouri 175
Springville, Calif. 193
Spruel, Johnny 285
Spurling, Jack 293
Squires, Wallis 207
Squires, Wally 184, 281
St Paul, Minn. 185
St. Croy, Paul 281
St., Marie Croy 142
St., Paul Croy 142
Stadtler, Phil 192, 212
Staley, Jim 256, 293
Standefer, Buck 281
Standifer, Buck 33
Stanger, Cecil 255
Stanifer, Buck 256
Stanton, Orville 232, 255, 293, 309
Stanton, Ralph 16, 228, 256, 283
Stapleton, Neb. 192
Stapp, Virgil 234, 261
Starr, Dave, 231
Starr, Hans 232, 281
Stavely, Alberta., Canada 159

Steams, Russell 260
Steelman, Hosea E. 255, 287
Stensen, Joe 281
Stephenville, Texas 193
Sterling, Joe 255
Stetson, Marshall 293
Stevens, Earl 282
Stevenson, Walter 232, 260
Stewart, Bandy 293
Stewart, Jacqueline A. Mrs 256, 287
Stewart, Norman 231, 260
Stewart, Pat 260
Stewart, Roy 230, 255
Stewart, Walt 230
Stewart, Whitey 232, 260, 281
Stickney, Chas. 234, 256
Stillings, Floyd
    49, 67, 68, 69, 73, 108, 158,
    228, 255, 293
Stober, Earl 255, 283
Stockdale, Champie 285
Stockwell, Ralph 261, 293
Stone, Dale 235, 261, 293
Stonehouse, Mel 232, 261, 293
Stonewall, Okla.
    48-49, 134, 158, 188, 208
Story, Jack 255
Stout, David 228, 255, 285
Stoval, John 285
Strachan, John 232, 255
Strake, George W. 255, 287
Straughn, Bernice 234, 261
Streeter, Jack 256
Strickland, Hugh 229, 255, 283
Strob, Roy 255
Strogn, B. 255
Stroh, Ray 293
Strong City, Kans. 169, 172, 188
Stroud, Francis 281
Stuart, Buck 33, 293
Stuart, Roy 281
Stuart, Sam 256, 293

Index

Stuart, Walt 260, 293
Stuckey, Tom 256, 281
Sultenfuss, Frank 255, 282
Sultenfuss, Henry 256, 282
Sultenfuss, Leon 256, 282
Sultenfuss, Norman 256, 282
Sutton, Jim 256, 282
Sutton, Tommy 260
Swanson, Bud 293
Swarthouse, George 285, 309
Swarts, Clem 234, 261, 281
Sweetwater, Texas 187, 206, 208
Swenson, Allen 285
Switzler, William 78

T

Tacker, Ike 281
Tacquard, Kidd 281
Taillon, Cy 126, 257
Talbot, Jim 234, 285
Talbot, Joe 281
Talbot, Ray 257, 287
Talbott, Jim 260
Targerson, Bill 281
Targerson, Slim 281
Taskos, Manny 260
Taylor, Babb 257, 293
Taylor, Bill 231, 256
Taylor, Buck 257, 293
Taylor, Dan 281
Taylor, Ed 285, 309
Taylor, Eddie 256
Taylor, Fritz 256, 293
Taylor, Harvey 293
Taylor, Hubert Jr. 285
Taylor, John 165, 309
Taylor, Karl 257
Taylor, Pete 256, 293
Taylor, Tom
    33, 121, 191, 230, 237, 256, 293

Te Poel, Lee E. 293
Teague, Dude 260
Teague, Earl 285, 309
Teague, George 281
Teague, Joe 260, 281
Tempe, Ariz. 170, 193
Templeton, M.L. 287
Terry, D'Lynn 50
Thatcher, Ariz. 192
Thode, Earl 49, 228, 256, 281
Thode, Henry 285, 309
Thomas, John 256
Thomas, Keith, 261
Thomas, Limey 257, 282
Thomas, Orville 256, 281
Thomas, Park 281
Thomas, Pat 148, 288
Thomas, Ray 281
Thompson, Claire 235, 256
Thompson, Don 232, 260
Thompson, Geo. D. 256
Thompson, Joe 33, 229, 256
Thompson, J.T. 293
Thompson, Ode 257
Thompson, Ralph 281
Thompson, Red
    16, 28, 68, 94, 96, 228, 256
Thorn, Bob 282
Thorn, Leo 257, 293
Thorne, Joel 293
Thrasher, Matt 293
Three Rivers, Texas 192
Tibbs, Casey 70
Tiffin, Buck 121, 231, 256, 281
Tiger, Lucian 293
Tilenham, Frank 261
Till, Bill 261
Timmons Aircraft 183
Tindall, Velda 25
Tipton, H. T. 282
Tivis, Melvin 16, 230, 260
Todd, Brown 256

Todd, Homer 257, 293
Tompkins, Charles 110, 256
Topeka, Kans. 185
Torrance, Pat Kilts 212
Toskos, Manny 234
Towns, Bill 257, 293
Tracy, Jack 257
Trail City, S. D 169
Traveller, Gil 288
Travis, Pete 256, 293
Travis, Tony 293
Traylor, John W. 256, 293
Truan, Bill 33, 230, 262
Truan, Fritz
   117, 128, 134, 139, 151, 157, 188,
   228, 256, 285
Truan, Norma Holmes 281
Truck, Bill 33
Truitt, Dick
   16, 34, 49, 67, 70, 73, 82, 85-86,
   94-95, 101, 105, 108-109, 115,
   134, 208, 228, 256, 281
Truman, Floyd 281
Truth or Consequences 190
Tubbs, John
   184, 207, 232, 260, 264, 281
Tucson, Ariz.
   24, 56, 120, 158, 167, 169, 183,
   192, 207
Tulley, Gerald 257, 293
Tunis, John W. 288
Tureman, Sonny 177, 309
Turk, Charley 228
Turk, Charlie 256, 281
Turk, Dad 229, 256, 288
Turner, Junior 309
Tussing, L. Benton 256, 288
Twain, Mark Clemens 117
Twilford, Harold 293
Twin Falls County Fair 96
Tyler, C. A. 256, 261
Tyler, George 234, 260
Tyler, Glenn 257, 281
Tyrell, Ace 288

U

Umberger, Jim 293
Ungerer, Ray 288
Utterback, Chick 293
United Cowboy's Turtle Association
   19, 37
United States Government War
   Bonds 198
Upchurch, Robert 257
Uvalde, Texas 137

V

V-J Day 188
Vail, Sydney H. 293
Valania, Jo 293
Valdez, Shorty 256, 285, 309
Van, Alice 293
Van Cator, Bill 256
Van Cleve, Paul 257, 282
Van, Jack Ryder 234
Van Meter, Frank
   107. 121, 232, 235, 257, 264, 281
Van Meter, Virginia 257
Van Nuys, Calif. 169, 183
Van Rider, Jack 282
Van Ryder, Jack 262
Vance, Johnnie 234, 257, 281
Vance, Lester 234
Vassar, Everet, 234
Vassar, Everett 281
Vaughn, Rusty 16
Veach, Imogene Beals
   9, 85, 166, 190, 212
Vinas, Joe 285
Vincent, Marion 257, 285
Vincent, Merle 230, 257, 293
Vines, Willard 293, 309

Index

Visalia, Calif. 151, 158
Volz, John 281

W

Waddy, Rowdy 26
Wade, Jack 152, 231, 257, 293
Wade, Joe H 261
Wade, Joe H. 281
Wadsworth, Glen 281
Wafford, Earl 293
Wagner, Neil 230, 256, 285, 309
Walden, Bob 232, 256, 293
Walker, George 281
Walker, Ike 281
Wall, Barney 293
Wallace, Claude 229, 261, 282
Wallace, James A. 285
Wallace, Jimmie 232, 261, 282
Wallesen, Whitey 257
Walls, Elmo 231, 256, 285
Walls, Wesley 229, 261
Walsh, Harley 143, 261
Walters, Pat 261, 283
Ward, Bill 281, 293
Ward, Fay 23, 288
Ward, George 232, 256, 293
Ward, Homer 257, 283
Ward, Jack 281
Ward, James P. 281
Ward, Leonard 86, 230, 261
Warden, General 288
Ware, Slick 257, 281
Warner, Alberta, Canada 152
Warner, Thelma 33
Warren, J. O. 257
Warren, Jack 257, 293
Warren, Oscar 257, 293
Warren, Ralph 232, 256, 293
Warren, W. B. 256, 288
Washington D.C. 167, 171

Watkins, Ward
   20, 175, 229, 256, 285
Watson, Bill 256
Watson, Harold 257
Watson, Sheriff 234
Watts, Bill 281
Wayne, Shorty 257
Weadick, Guy 118
Weasa, Mel 293
Webb, Byron 257, 293
Webb, J.R. 288
Webb, Lee 261
Webb, Pearson 257, 293
Webster, Shoat 9, 193, 208, 281
Weinberg, Jules 293
Welch, Joe
   16, 20, 28, 228, 256, 293
Welch, Slim 283
Wellington, Nev. 193
Wells, Jack 293
Wells, Young 293
Wening, Richard 281
West, Bob 293
West, Earl 293
Westfall, Howard 16, 229, 281
Westinghouse, Buddy 257, 285, 309
Whaley, Slim 208, 232, 256, 281
Wharton, Ray 9, 137, 193, 293
Whatley, Jack, 261
Whatley, Todd 191, 281
Wheeler, Buck 261, 283
Wheelis, Penn 257
Whetsel, Joe 281
Whitaker, Lee 257
Whitaker, Vernon 165
White, Grace 25, 27, 257
White, Homer 281
White, Jim 281
White, Sam 281
White, Vivian 25, 27, 115, 257, 281
Whitehorn, John 257

Whiteman, Hub
  16, 34, 37, 68, 69, 94, 121, 158, 159, 170, 196, 228, 256
Whiteman, Jim
  16, 94, 95, 229, 256, 281
Whiteman, Paul 257
Whiteside, Bob 257
Whiting, Bob 261, 262
Whitlow, Charles 152, 232, 256
Whitten, David 257
Whorton, Al 281
Whorton, Eddie 281
Wichita Falls, Texas 158
Wichita, Kans. 183
Wicker, Olds 281
Wier, Clyde 281
Wike, A. C. 257
Wilcox, Don 257, 281
Wild Bunch Contest Fair and Roundup Association 23
Wilder, D. R. 256
Wilder, Dan 256
Wilderspin, Geo. 256
Wilderspin, George 229, 237, 281
Wilkens, Lefty 281
Wilkins, Don 175
Wilkinson, Al 232, 261
Wilkinson, Billy 33, 231, 261
Wilkinson, Bob 256
Wilkinson, Bobby 75
Wilkinson, Jim 33
Wilkinson, Jimmie 230, 261
Wilkinson, John 113
Wilkinson, Johnnie 231, 262, 283
Willard H. Porter 201
Williams, Chuck 33, 234, 256
Williams, Dale 234, 261
Williams, Harry 261
Williams, John 261
Williams, Johnie 16
Williams, Johnnie 257
Williams, Johnny 235
Williams, Ken 257, 281
Williams, Pete 281
Williams, R. W. 281
Williamson, Shorty 49
Willis, Arch L. 257
Willis, Dan 211
Wills, Arnie 184, 207, 232, 256, 281
Wilson, Grady 33
Wilson, Jack 235, 261
Wilson, L. W. 261
Wilson, Tommy 235, 257
Winegar, Ned 261
Winegar, Ned, 230
Winegar, Phil 257
Winfield, Kans. 192
Winnemucca 80
Winnett, Horace 257
Wise, Delbert 193
Woerner, Cliff 9
Wofford, Earl 257, 281
Wolf, Buster 257
Wolf, Joe 16
Wolf, Ralph R. 257
Wolrich, Hipe 16
Wood, Joe 281
Wood, Opal 257, 283
Wood, Russell 234, 257
Wood, Tom 231, 257, 281
Woods, Eddie
  37, 68, 75, 229, 261, 283
Woods, Pat 228, 256
Woods, W. T. 261
Woodstown, N. J. 188
Woodstown, N.J. 44
Woodward, Okla. 175
World Champion Rodeo Corporation 117
Wort, Earl 33
Wright, Bob 133
Wright, Cecil 281
Wrigley, Philip K. 257
Wulfekuhler, L. W. 281

Index

Wyatt, Buck 233, 256
Wyrick, Bennie 257

X

XIT Rodeo 185

Y

Yale, Bugs 34
Yardley, George
 196, 198, 206, 234, 257, 281
Yates, Fayette 281
Yonnick, Buttons
 16, 111, 165, 166, 232, 257
York, A. C. 257, 283
York, S. A. 281
Youchum, Ted 231, 257, 282
Young, Ariz. 206
Young, I. W. 257
Young, Mrs. I. W. 257
Young, Paul 282
Young, Tommy 257
Young, Weldon 282

Z

Zaremba, Agnes 90
Zumwalt, Oral
 33, 207, 228, 257, 264

Additional Books Written By Gail Hughbanks Woerner

Cowboy Up
The History of Bull Riding
Paperback - 306 pages
$24.95

Fearless Funnymen
The History of the Rodeo Clown
Paperback - 223 pages
$18.95

Rope to Win
The History of Steer, Calf & Team Roping
Paperback - 277 pages
$26.95

Belly Full of Bedsprings
The History of Bronc Riding
Paperback - 260 pages
$24.95

Charley & Amanda
Meet Rusty the Rodeo Clown
Paperback - Children's Book
$10.95

All Available at www.CowboyBookworm.com

Author Bio

Gail Woerner was born and raised on a ranch in northeastern Colorado and worked with cattle and broke horses with her grandfather. She has written four books on the history of rodeo, a children's book on rodeo and numerous articles in various western-related magazines and periodicals including magazines in France, Canada and Australia. She presently writes a column on the website: rodeoattitude.com called 'Behind the Chutes & Elsewhere', which tells about rodeo cowboys and cowgirls of yesteryear. She also reviews other writer's books several times a year, and continually answers questions about rodeo from e-mail queries from around the globe.

Gail is the Chairman of the Oral History Project for the Rodeo Historical Society and interviews senior cowboys and cowgirls and those being inducted in to the Society's Hall of Fame. These videos and vocal recordings are housed in the archives of the National Cowboy & Western Heritage Museum in Oklahoma City.

Gail is the Chairman of the Rodeo Clown Reunion which is held at various rodeos across the nation and generally has forty retired laugh-getters, bullfighters and barrelmen attend. They don their familiar make-up and costumes and sign autographs and entertain the fans. She also writes a newsletter to numerous retired rodeo clowns and their widows monthly.

She received the Academy of Western Artists Will Rogers Medallion Award for Western Nonfiction for her book entitled, "Rope to Win, The History of Steer, Calf and Team Roping" in 2008. She received the American Cowboy Culture Award for Western Writing at the National Cowboy Symposium held in Lubbock, TX, in 2009. Gail lives near Austin, Texas, with her husband, Cliff.

Additional Titles From
Wild Horse Press

**Bob Crosby
World Champion Cowboy**
Paperback - 176 pages
$16.95

**Best Supporting Actors
Rodeo Clowns**
Paperback - 160 pages
$18.95

**Pete Knight
The Cowboy King**
Paperback - 208 pages
$18.95

All Available at www.CowboyBookworm.com

www.ingramcontent.com/pod-product-compliance
Lightning Source LLC
Chambersburg PA
CBHW022101150426
43195CB00008B/224